DOCUMENTS ON INTERNATIONAL LAW

DOCUMENTS
ON
INTERNATIONAL LAW

Handbook for Law Students
and Constitutional Lawyers

Edited by

PATRIC MZOLISI MTSHAULANA
Research Assistant to the President
of the Constitutional Court and
Lecturer in Law,
University of the North

JOHN DUGARD
Professor of Law,
University of the Witwatersrand

NEVILLE BOTHA
Professor of International Law,
University of South Africa

JUTA & CO, LTD
1996

First Published 1996

© Juta & Co, Ltd
PO Box 14373, Kenwyn 7790

ISBN 0 7021 3532 1

SET, PRINTED AND BOUND IN THE REPUBLIC OF SOUTH AFRICA
BY THE RUSTICA PRESS (PTY) LTD, NDABENI, CAPE
D4096

PREFACE

South Africa has played a substantial role in the development of international law. It was a founder member of the League of Nations and contributed positively to the maintenance of peace during the era of the League. South African forces fought side by side with the allied forces for the destruction of fascism and the South African Prime Minister, Jan Smuts, was one of the leading figures in the drafting of the United Nations Charter.

However, after the formation of the United Nations, South Africa's status as a member of the world community was greatly tarnished. South Africa's first international confrontation with the community came when it refused to hand over the control of South West Africa to the United Nations. This was followed by a dispute with India over South Africa's treatment of persons of Indian origin in violation of the United Nations Charter and an agreement of 1927 between India and South Africa. In 1952 the General Assembly of the United Nations first assumed jurisdiction over the policy of apartheid. Thereafter the General Assembly and later the Security Council repeatedly and regularly denounced South Africa for pursuing a policy of racial discrimination in violation of the United Nations Charter and other norms of international law.

South Africa's response to the United Nations was to argue that the question of the violation of fundamental rights in South Africa was a domestic affair and that the United Nations was barred by Article 2(7) of the Charter of the United Nations from interfering in the domestic affairs of South Africa.

This argument was convincingly rejected by the International Court of Justice in its advisory opinion on **Legal Consequences for States of the Continued Presence of South Africa in Namibia Notwithstanding Security Council Resolution 276 (1970)**, when it declared: 'It is undisputed, and is amply supported by documents annexed to South Africa's written statements in these proceedings, that the official government policy pursued by South Africa in Namibia is to achieve a complete physical separation of races and ethnic groups in separate areas within the Territory. . . . Under the Charter of the United Nations, [South Africa] had pledged itself to observe and respect, in a territory having an international status, human rights and fundamental freedoms for all without distinction as to race. To establish instead, and to enforce, distinctions, exclusions, restrictions and limitations exclusively based on grounds of race, colour, descent or national or ethnic origin which constitute a denial of fundamental human rights is a flagrant violation of the purposes and principles of the Charter' (1971 ICJ Reports 16 at 57).

The political isolation of the country was reflected in the attitude of the courts towards international law. Courts hesitated to apply norms of customary international law or to be guided by treaty obligations in the field of human rights.

Major changes have taken place since the adoption of the Constitution of the Republic of South Africa, Act 200 of 1993. Section 231 of the Constitution now regulates the relationship between South African law and international law. In terms of section 231(4) customary international law forms part of the law of the Republic unless it is inconsistent with the Constitution itself or an Act of Parliament. Treaties also form part of the law of the Republic if they have been approved in accordance with the procedures prescribed by section 231(2) and (3). The Constitution, and not the common law, is now the source for the applicability of international-law rules in South Africa. Human rights now enjoy a special place in our constitutional system as section 35(1) enjoins courts to 'have regard to public international law' in the interpretation of the Bill of Rights in Chapter 3 of the Constitution. Furthermore humanitarian law is given express recognition in section 227.

The inclusion of sections 35(1) and 231 in the Constitution has enhanced the status and role of international law within the legal system. No lawyer can now afford to practise law without some knowledge of international law. Inevitably this will have a major impact on legal education.

Most South African law libraries are unprepared for these changes in our law. Few libraries hold the basic international treaties that are now part of our constitutional legal order. Hence the present collection of materials which aims to provide students and practitioners with some of the treaties that comprise the foundation of contemporary international law.

PATRIC MTSHAULANA
JOHN DUGARD
NEVILLE BOTHA

ABBREVIATIONS

GA Res	General Assembly Resolution
ILM	International Legal Materials
UNTS	United Nations Treaty Series
European TS	European Treaty Series

CONTENTS

Page

G.   REGIONAL INSTRUMENTS

A. GENERAL

1. DECLARATION ON PRINCIPLES OF INTERNATIONAL LAW CONCERNING FRIENDLY RELATIONS AND CO-OPERATION AMONG STATES IN ACCORDANCE WITH THE CHARTER OF THE UNITED NATIONS
(GA RES 2625 (XXV) 1970)

PREAMBLE

The General Assembly,

Reaffirming in the terms of the Charter of the United Nations that the maintenance of international peace and security and the development of friendly relations and co-operation between nations are among the fundamental purposes of the United Nations,

Recalling that the peoples of the United Nations are determined to practise tolerance and live together in peace with one another as good neighbours,

Bearing in mind the importance of maintaining and strengthening international peace founded upon freedom, equality, justice and respect for fundamental human rights and of developing friendly relations among nations irrespective of their political, economic and social systems or the levels of their development,

Bearing in mind also the paramount importance of the Charter of the United Nations in the promotion of the rule of law among nations,

Considering that the faithful observance of the principles of international law concerning friendly relations and co-operation among States and the fulfilment in good faith of the obligations assumed by States, in accordance with the Charter, is of the greatest importance for the maintenance of international peace and security and for the implementation of the other purposes of the United Nations,

Noting that the great political, economic and social changes and scientific progress which have taken place in the world since the adoption of the Charter give increased importance to these principles and to the need for their more effective application in the conduct of States wherever carried on,

Recalling the established principle that outer space, including the Moon and other celestial bodies is not subject to national appropriation by claim of sovereignty, by means of use or occupation, or by any other means, and mindful of the fact that consideration is being given in the United Nations to the question of establishing other appropriate provisions similarly inspired,

Convinced that the strict observance by States of the obligation not to intervene in the affairs of any other State is an essential condition to ensure that nations live together in peace with one another, since the practice of any form of intervention not only violates the spirit and letter of the Charter, but also leads to the creation of situations which threaten international peace and security,

Recalling the duty of States to refrain in their international relations from military, political, economic or any other form of coercion aimed against the political independence or territorial integrity of any State,

Considering it essential that all States shall refrain in their international relations from the threat or use of force against the territorial integrity or political independence of any State, or in any other manner inconsistent with the purposes of the United Nations,

1

Considering it equally essential that all States shall settle their international disputes by peaceful means in accordance with the Charter.

Reaffirming, in accordance with the Charter, the basic importance of sovereign equality and stressing that the purposes of the United Nations can be implemented only if States enjoy sovereign equality and comply fully with the requirements of this principle in their international relations,

Convinced that the subjection of peoples to alien subjugation, domination and exploitation constitutes a major obstacle to the promotion of international peace and security,

Convinced that the principle of equal rights and self-determination of peoples constitutes a significant contribution to contemporary international law, and that its effective application is of paramount importance for the promotion of friendly relations among States, based on respect for the principle of sovereign equality,

Convinced in consequence that any attempt aimed at the partial or total disruption of the national unity and territorial integrity of a State or country or at its political independence is incompatible with the purposes and principles of the Charter,

Considering the provisions of the Charter as a whole and taking into account the role of relevant resolutions adopted by the competent organs of the United Nations relating to the content of the principles,

Considering that the progressive development and codification of the following principles:

(a) The principle that States shall refrain in their international relations from the threat or use of force against the territorial integrity or political independence of any State, or in any other manner inconsistent with the purposes of the United Nations,

(b) The principle that States shall settle their international disputes by peaceful means in such a manner that international peace and security and justice are not endangered,

(c) The duty not to intervene in matters within the domestic jurisdiction of any State, in accordance with the Charter,

(d) The duty of States to co-operate with one another in accordance with the Charter,

(e) The principle of equal rights and self-determination of peoples,

(f) The principle of sovereign equality of States,

(g) The principle that States shall fulfil in good faith the obligations assumed by them in accordance with the Charter,

so as to secure their more effective application within the international community, would promote the realization of the purposes of the United Nations,

Having considered the principles of international law relating to friendly relations and co-operation among States,

1. Solemnly proclaims the following principles:

The principle that States shall refrain in their international relations from the threat or use of force against the territorial integrity or political independence of any State, or in any other manner inconsistent with the purposes of the United Nations

Every State has the duty to refrain in its international relations from the threat or use of force against the territorial integrity or political independence of any State, or in any other manner inconsistent with the purposes of the United Nations. Such a threat or use of force constitutes a violation of international law and the Charter of the United Nations and shall never be employed as a means of settling international issues.

A war of aggression constitutes a crime against the peace, for which there is responsibility under international law.

In accordance with the purposes and principles of the United Nations, States have the duty to refrain from propaganda for wars of aggression.

Every State has the duty to refrain from the threat or use of force to violate the existing international boundaries of another State or as a means of solving international disputes, including territorial disputes and problems concerning frontiers of States.

Every State likewise has the duty to refrain from the threat or use of force to violate international lines of demarcation, such as armistice lines, established by or pursuant to an international agreement to which it is a party or which it is otherwise bound to respect. Nothing in the foregoing shall be construed as prejudicing the positions of the parties concerned with regard to the status and effects of such lines under their special regimes affecting their temporary character.

States have a duty to refrain from acts of riprisal involving the use of force.

Every State has the duty to refrain from any forcible action which deprives peoples referred to in the elaboration of the principle of equal rights and self-determination of their right to self-determination and freedom and independence.

Every State has the duty to refrain from organizing or encouraging the organization of irregular forces or armed bands, including mercenaries, for incursion into the territory of another State.

Every State has the duty to refrain from organizing, instigating, assisting or participating in acts of civil strife or terrorist acts in another State or acquiescing in organized activities within its territory directed towards the commission of such acts, when the acts referred to in the present paragraph involve a threat or use of force.

The territory of a State shall not be the object of military occupation resulting from the use of force in contravention of the provisions of the Charter. The territory of a State shall not be the object of acquisition by another State resulting from the threat or use of force. No territorial acquisition resulting from the threat or use of force shall be recognized as legal. Nothing in the foregoing shall be construed as affecting:

(a) Provisions of the Charter or any international agreement prior to the Charter régime and valid under international law; or

(b) The powers of the Security Council under the Charter.

All States shall pursue in good faith negotiations for the early conclusion of a universal treaty of general and complete disarmament under effective international control and strive to adopt appropriate measures to reduce international tensions and strengthen confidence among States.

All States shall comply in good faith with their obligations under the generally recognized principles and rules of international law with respect to the maintenance of international peace and security, and shall endeavour to make the United Nations security system based on the Charter more effective.

Nothing in the foregoing paragraphs shall be construed as enlarging or diminishing in any way the scope of the provisions of the Charter concerning cases in which the use of force is lawful.

The principle that States shall settle their international disputes by peaceful means in such a manner that international peace and security and justice are not endangered

Every State shall settle its international disputes with other States by peaceful means in such a manner that international peace and security and justice are not endangered.

States shall accordingly seek early and just settlement of their international disputes by negotiation, inquiry, mediation conciliation, arbitration, judicial settlement, resort to regional agencies or arrangements or other peaceful means of their choice. In seeking such a settlement the parties shall agree upon such peaceful means as may be appropriate to the circumstances and nature of the dispute.

The parties to a dispute have the duty, in the event of failure to reach a solution by any one of the above peaceful means, to continue to seek a settlement of the dispute by other peaceful means agreed upon by them.

States parties to an international dispute, as well as other States, shall refrain from any action which may aggravate the situation so as to endanger the maintenance of international peace and security, and shall act in accordance with the purposes and principles of the United Nations.

International disputes shall be settled on the basis of the sovereign equality of States and in accordance with the principle of free choice of means. Recourse to, or acceptance of, a settlement procedure freely agreed to by States with regard to existing or future disputes to which they are parties shall not be regarded as incompatible with sovereign equality.

Nothing in the foregoing paragraphs prejudices or derogates from the applicable provisions of the Charter, in particular those relating to the pacific settlement of international disputes.

The principle concerning the duty not to intervene in matters within the domestic jurisdiction of any State, in accordance with the Charter

No State or group of States has the right to intervene, directly or indirectly, for any reason whatever, in the internal or external affairs of any other State. Consequently, armed intervention and all other forms of interference or attempted threats against the personality of the State or against its political, economic and cultural elements, are in violation of international law.

No State may use or encourage the use of economic, political or any other type of measures to coerce another State in order to obtain from it the subordination of the exercise of its sovereign rights and to secure from it advantages of any kind. Also, no State shall organize, assist, foment, finance, incite or tolerate subversive, terrorist or armed activities directed towards the violent overthrow of the régime of another State, or interfere in civil strife in another State.

The use of force to deprive peoples of their national identity constitutes a violation of their inalienable rights and of the principle of non-intervention.

Every State has an inalienable right to choose its political, economic, social and cultural systems, without interference in any form by another State.

Nothing in the foregoing paragraphs shall be construed as affecting the relevant provisions of the Charter relating to the maintenance of international peace and security.

The duty of States to co-operate with one another in accordance with the Charter

States have the duty to co-operate with one another, irrespective of the differences in their political, economic and social systems, in the various spheres of international relations, in order to maintain international peace and security and to promote international economic stability and progress, the general welfare of nations and international co-operation free from discrimination based on such differences.

To this end:

(a) States shall co-operate with other States in the maintenance of international peace and security;

(b) States shall co-operate in the promotion of universal respect for, and observance of, human rights and fundamental freedoms for all, and in the elimination of all forms of racial discrimination and all forms of religious intolerance;

(c) States shall conduct their international relations in the economic, social, cultural, technical and trade fields in accordance with the principles of sovereign equality and non-intervention;

(d) States Members of the United Nations have the duty to take joint and separate action in co-operation with the United Nations in accordance with the relevant provisions of the Charter.

States should co-operate in the economic, social and cultural fields as well as in the field of science and technology and for the promotion of international cultural and educational progress. States should co-operate in the promotion of economic growth throughout the world, especially that of the developing countries.

The principle of equal rights and self-determination of peoples

By virtue of the principle of equal rights and self-determination of peoples enshrined in the Charter of the United Nations, all peoples have the right freely to determine, without external interference, their political status and to pursue their economic, social and cultural development, and every State has the duty to respect this right in accordance with the provisions of the Charter.

Every State has the duty to promote, through joint and separate action, realization of the principle of equal rights and self-determination of peoples, in accordance with the provisions of the Charter, and to render assistance to the United Nations in carrying out the responsibilities entrusted to it by the Charter regarding the implementation of the principle, in order:

(a) To promote friendly relations and co-operation among States; and

(b) To bring a speedy end to colonialism, having due regard to the freely expressed will of the peoples concerned;

and bearing in mind that subjection of peoples to alien subjugation, domination and exploitation constitutes a violation of the principle, as well as a denial of fundamental human rights, and is contrary to the Charter.

Every State has the duty to promote through joint and separate action universal respect for and observance of human rights and fundamental freedoms in accordance with the Charter.

The establishment of a sovereign and independent State, the free association or integration with an independent State or the emergence into any other political status freely determined by a people constitute modes of implementing the right of self-determination by that people.

Every State has the duty to refrain from any forcible action which deprives peoples referred to above in the elaboration of the present principle of their right to self-determination and freedom and independence. In their actions against, and resistance to, such forcible action in pursuit of the exercise of their right to self-determination, such peoples are entitled to seek and to receive support in accordance with the purposes and principles of the Charter.

The territory of a colony or other Non-Self-Governing Territory has, under the Charter, a status separate and distinct from the territory of the State administering it; and such separate and distinct status under the Charter shall exist until the people of the colony or Non-Self-Governing Territory have exercised their right of self-determination in accordance with the Charter, and particularly its purposes and principles.

Nothing in the foregoing paragraphs shall be construed as authorizing or encouraging any action which would dismember or impair, totally or in part, the territorial integrity or political unity of sovereign and independent States conducting themselves in compliance with the principle of equal rights and self-determination of peoples as described above and thus possessed of a government representing the whole people belonging to the territory without distinction as to race, creed or colour.

Every State shall refrain from any action aimed at the partial or total disruption of the national unity and territorial integrity of any other State or country.

The principle of sovereign equality of States

All States enjoy sovereign equality. They have equal rights and duties and are equal members of the international community, notwithstanding differences of an economic, social, political or other nature.

In particular, sovereign equality includes the following elements:

(a) States are juridically equal;

(b) Each State enjoys the rights inherent in full sovereignty;

(c) Each State has the duty to respect the personality of other States;

(d) The territorial integrity and political independence of the State are inviolable;

(e) Each State has the right freely to choose and develop its political, social, economic and cultural systems;

(f) Each State has the duty to comply fully and in good faith with its international obligations and to live in peace with other States.

The principle that States shall fulfil in good faith the obligations assumed by them in accordance with the Charter

Every State has the duty to fulfil in good faith the obligations assumed by it in accordance with the Charter of the United Nations.

Every State has the duty to fulfil in good faith its obligations under the generally recognized principles and rules of international law.

Every State has the duty to fulfil in good faith its obligations under international agreements valid under the generally recognized principles and rules of international law.

Where obligations arising under international agreements are in conflict with the obligations of Members of the United Nations under the Charter of the United Nations, the obligations under the Charter shall prevail.

GENERAL PART

2. Declares that:

In their interpretation and application the above principles are interrelated and each principle should be construed in the context of the other principles.

Nothing in this Declaration shall be construed as prejudicing in any manner the provisions of the Charter or the rights and duties of Member States under the Charter or the rights of peoples under the Charter, taking into account the elaboration of these rights in this Declaration

3. Declares further that:

The principles of the Charter which are embodied in this Declaration constitute basic principles of international law, and consequently appeals to all States to be guided by these principles in their international conduct and to develop their mutual relations on the basis of the strict observance of these principles.

2.   RESOLUTION ON THE DEFINITION OF AGGRESSION

(GA RES 3314 (XXIX) 1974)

The General Assembly,

Basing itself on the fact that one of the fundamental purposes of the United Nations is to maintain international peace and security and to take effective collective measures for the protection and removal of threats to the peace, and for the suppression of acts of aggression or other breaches of the peace,

Recalling that the Security Council, in accordance with Article 39 of the Charter of the United Nations, shall determine the existence of any threat to the peace, breach of the peace or act of aggression and shall make recommendations, or decide what measures shall be taken in accordance with Articles 41 and 42, to maintain or restore international peace and security,

Recalling also the duty of States under the Charter to settle their international disputes by peaceful means in order not to endanger international peace, security and justice,

Bearing in mind that nothing in this Definition shall be interpreted as in any way affecting the scope of the provisions of the Charter with respect to the functions and powers of the organs of the United Nations,

Considering also that, since aggression is the most serious and dangerous form of the illegal use of force, being fraught, in the conditions created by the existence of all types of weapons of mass destruction, with the possible threat of a world conflict and all its catastrophic consequences, aggression should be defined at the present stage,

Reaffirming the duty of States not to use armed force to deprive peoples of their right to self-determination, freedom and independence, or to disrupt territorial integrity,

Reaffirming also that the territory of a State shall not be violated by being the object, even temporarily, of military occupation or of other measures of force taken by another State in contravention of the Charter, and that it shall not be the object of acquisition by another State resulting from such measures or the threat thereof,

Reaffirming also the provisions of the Declaration on Principles of International Law concerning Friendly Relations and Co-operation among States in accordance with the Charter of the United Nations,

Convinced that the adoption of a definition of aggression ought to have the effect of deterring a potential aggressor, would simplify the determination of acts of aggression and the implementation of measures to suppress them and would also facilitate the protection of the rights and lawful interests of, and the rendering of assistance to, the victim,

Believing that, although the question whether an act of aggression has been committed must be considered in the light of all the circumstances of each particular case, it is nevertheless desirable to formulate basic principles as guidance for such determination,

Adopts the following Definition of Aggression:

Article 1

Aggression is the use of armed force by a State against the sovereignty, territorial integrity or political independence of another State, or in any other manner inconsistent with the Charter of the United Nations, as set out in this Definition.

Explanatory note: In this Definition the term "State":

(a) Is used without prejudice to questions of recognition or to whether a State is a member of the United Nations;

(b) Includes the concept of a "group of States" where appropriate.

Article 2

The first use of armed force by a State in contravention of the Charter shall constitute *prima facie* evidence of an act of aggression although the Security Council may, in conformity with the Charter, conclude that a determination that an act of aggression has been committed would not be justified in the light of other relevant circumstances, including the fact that the acts concerned or their consequences are not of sufficient gravity.

Article 3

Any of the following acts, regardless of a declaration of war, shall, subject to and in accordance with the provisions of article 2, qualify as an act of aggression:

(a) The invasion or attack by the armed forces of a State of the territory of another State, or any military occupation, however temporary, resulting from such invasion or attack, or any annexation by the use of force of the territory of another State or part thereof;

(b) Bombardment by the armed forces of a State against the territory of another State or the use of any weapons by a State against the territory of another State;

(c) The blockade of the ports or coasts of a State by the armed forces of another State;

(d) An attack by the armed forces of a State on the land, sea or air forces, or marine and air fleets of another State;

(e) The use of armed forces of one State which are within the territory of another State with the agreement of the receiving State, in contravention of the conditions provided for in the agreement or any extension of their presence in such territory beyond the termination of the agreement;

(f) The action of a State in allowing its territory, which it has placed at the disposal of another State, to be used by that other State for perpetrating an act of aggression against a third State;

(g) The sending by or on behalf of a State of armed bands, groups, irregulars or mercenaries, which carry out acts of armed force against another State of such gravity as to amount to the acts listed above, or its substantial involvement therein.

Article 4

The acts enumerated above are not exhaustive and the Security Council may determine that other acts constitute aggression under the provisions of the Charter.

Article 5

1. No consideration of whatever nature, whether political, economic, military or otherwise, may serve as a justification for aggression.

2. A war of aggression is a crime against international peace. Aggression gives rise to international responsibility.

3. No territorial acquisition or special advantage resulting from aggression is or shall be recognized as lawful.

Article 6

Nothing in this Definition shall be construed as in any way enlarging or diminishing the scope of the Charter, including its provisions concerning cases in which the use of force is lawful.

Article 7

Nothing in this Definition, and in particular article 3, could in any way prejudice the right to self-determination, freedom and independence, as derived from the Charter, of peoples forcibly deprived of that right and referred to in the Declaration on Principles of International Law concerning Friendly Relations and Co-operation among States in accordance with the Charter of the United Nations, particularly peoples under colonial and racist régimes or other forms of alien domination; nor the right of these peoples to struggle to that end and to seek and receive support, in accordance with the principles of the Charter and in conformity with the above-mentioned Declaration.

Article 8

In their interpretation and application the above provisions are interrelated and each provision should be construed in the context of the other provisions.

3. UNITED NATIONS MODEL TREATY ON EXTRADITION
(GA Res 45/116 (1990) 30 ILM 1407 (1991))

The ....and the ....
Desirous of making more effective the co-operation of the two countries in the control of crime by concluding a treaty on extradition,
Have agreed as follows:

Article 1 *Obligation to extradite*

Each Party agrees to extradite to the other, upon request and subject to the provisions of the present Treaty, any person who is wanted in the requesting State for prosecution for an extraditable offence or for the imposition or enforcement of a sentence in respect of such an offence.

Article 2 *Extraditable offences*

1. For the purposes of the present Treaty, extraditable offences are offences that are punishable under the laws of both Parties by imprisonment or other deprivation of liberty for a maximum period of at least [one/two] year(s), or by a more severe penalty. Where the request for extradition relates to a person who is wanted for the enforcement of a sentence of imprisonment or other deprivation of liberty imposed for such an

offence, extradition shall be granted only if a period of at least [four/six] months of such sentence remains to be served.

2. In determining whether an offence is an offence punishable under the laws of both Parties, it shall not matter whether:

(a) The laws of the Parties place the acts or omissions constituting the offence within the same category of offence or denominate the offence by the same terminology;

(b) Under the laws of the Parties the constituent elements of the offence differ, it being understood that the totality of the acts or omissions as presented by the requesting State shall be taken into account.

3. Where extradition of a person is sought for an offence against a law relating to taxation, customs duties, exchange control or other revenue matters, extradition may not be refused on the ground that the law of the requested State does not impose the same kind of tax or duty or does not contain a tax, customs duty or exchange regulation of the same kind as the law of the requesting State.

4. If the request for extradition includes several separate offences each of which is punishable under the laws of both Parties, but some of which do not fulfil the other conditions set out in paragraph 1 of the present article, the requested Party may grant extradition for the latter offences provided that the person is to be extradited for at least one extraditable offence.

Article 3 *Mandatory grounds for refusal*

Extradition shall not be granted in any of the following circumstances:

(a) If the offence for which extradition is requested is regarded by the requested State as an offence of a political nature;

(b) If the requested State has substantial grounds for believing that the request for extradition has been made for the purpose of prosecuting or punishing a person on account of that person's race, religion, nationality, ethnic origin, political opinions, sex or status, or that that person's position may be prejudiced for any of those reasons;

(c) If the offence for which extradition is requested is an offence under military law, which is not also an offence under ordinary criminal law;

(d) If there has been a final judgment rendered against the person in the requested State in respect of the offence for which the person's extradition is requested;

(e) If the person whose extradition is requested has, under the law of either Party, become immune from prosecution or punishment for any reason, including lapse of time or amnesty;

(f) If the person whose extradition is requested has been or would be subjected in the requesting State to torture or cruel, inhuman or degrading treatment or punishment or if that person has not received or would not receive the minimum guarantees in criminal proceedings, as contained in the International Covenant on Civil and Political Rights, article 14;

(g) If the judgment of the requesting State has been rendered in absentia, the convicted person has not had sufficient notice of the trial or the opportunity to arrange for his or her defence and has not had or will not have the opportunity to have the case retried in his or her presence.

Article 4 *Optional grounds for refusal*

Extradition may be refused in any of the following circumstances:

(*a*) If the person whose extradition is requested is a national of the requested State. Where extradition is refused on this ground, the requested State shall, if the other State so requests, submit the case to its competent authorities with a view to taking appropriate action against the person in respect of the offence for which extradition had been requested;

(*b*) If the competent authorities of the requested State have decided either not to institute or to terminate proceedings against the person for the offence in respect of which extradition is requested;

(*c*) If a prosecution in respect of the offence for which extradition is requested is pending in the requested State against the person whose extradition is requested;

(*d*) If the offence for which extradition is requested carries the death penalty under the law of the requesting State, unless that State gives such assurance as the requested State considers sufficient that the death penalty will not be imposed or, if imposed, will not be carried out;

(*e*) If the offence for which extradition is requested has been committed outside the territory of either Party and the law of the requested State does not provide for jurisdiction over such an offence committed outside its territory in comparable circumstances;

(*f*) If the offence for which extradition is requested is regarded under the law of the requested State as having been committed in whole or in part within that State. Where extradition is refused on this ground, the requested State shall, if the other State so requests, submit the case to its competent authorities with a view to taking appropriate action against the person for the offence for which extradition had been requested;

(*g*) If the person whose extradition is requested has been sentenced or would be liable to be tried or sentenced in the requesting State by an extraordinary or *ad hoc* court or tribunal;

(*h*) If the requested State, while also taking into account the nature of the offence and the interests of the requesting State, considers that, in the circumstances of the case, the extradition of that person would be incompatible with humanitarian considerations in view of age, health or other personal circumstances of that person.

Article 5 *Channels of communication and required documents*

1. A request for extradition shall be made in writing. The request, supporting documents and subsequent communications shall be transmitted through the diplomatic channel, directly between the ministries of justice or any other authorities designated by the Parties.

2. A request for extradition shall be accompanied by the following:

(*a*) In all cases,

  (i) As accurate a description as possible of the person sought, together with any other information that may help to establish that person's identity, nationality and location;

  (ii) The text of the relevant provision of the law creating the offence or, where necessary, a statement of the law relevant to the offence and a statement of the penalty that can be imposed for the offence;

(*b*) If the person is accused of an offence, by a warrant issued by a court of other competent judicial authority for the arrest of the person or a certified copy of that warrant, a statement of the offence for which extradition is requested and a description of the acts or omissions constituting the alleged offence, including an indication of the time and place of its commission;

(c) If the person has been convicted of an offence, by a statement of the offence for which extradition is requested and a description of the acts or omissions constituting the offence and by the original or certified copy of the judgment or any other document setting out the conviction and the sentence imposed, the fact that the sentence is enforceable, and the extent to which the sentence remains to be served;

(d) If the person has been convicted of an offence in his or her absence, in addition to the documents set out in paragraph 2*(c)* of the present article, by a statement as to the legal means available to the person to prepare his or her defence or to have the case retried in his or her presence;

(e) If the person has been convicted of an offence but no sentence has been imposed, by a statement of the offence for which extradition is requested and a description of the acts or omissions constituting the offence and by a document setting out the conviction and a statement affirming that there is an intention to impose a sentence.

3. The documents submitted in support of a request for extradition shall be accompanied by a translation into the language of the requested State or in another language acceptable to that State.

Article 6 *Simplified extradition procedure*

The requested State, if not precluded by its law, may grant extradition after receipt of a request for provisional arrest, provided that the person sought explicitly consents before a competent authority.

Article 7 *Certification and authentication*

Except as provided by the present Treaty, a request for extradition and the documents in support thereof, as well as documents or other material supplied in response to such a request, shall not require certification or authentication.

Article 8 *Additional information*

If the requested State considers that the information provided in support of a request for extradition is not sufficient, it may request that additional information be furnished within such reasonable time as it specifies.

Article 9 *Provisional arrest*

1. In case of urgency the requesting State may apply for the provisional arrest of the person sought pending the presentation of the request for extradition. The application shall be transmitted by means of the facilities of the International Criminal Police Organization, by post or telegraph or by any other means affording a record in writing.

2. The application shall contain a description of the person sought, a statement that extradition is to be requested, a statement of the existence of one of the documents mentioned in paragraph 2 of article 5 of the present Treaty, authorizing the apprehension of the person, a statement of the punishment that can be or has been imposed for the offence, including the time left to be served and a concise statement of the facts of the case, and a statement of the location, where known, of the person.

3. The requested State shall decide on the application in accordance with its law and communicate its decision to the requesting State without delay.

4. The person arrested upon such an application shall be set at liberty upon the expiration of [40] days from the date of arrest if a request for extradition, supported by the relevant documents specified in paragraph 2 of article 5 of the present Treaty, has not been received. The present paragraph does not preclude the possibility of conditional release of the person prior to the expiration of the [40] days.

5. The release of the person pursuant to paragraph 4 of the present article shall not prevent rearrest and institution of proceedings with a view to extraditing the person sought if the request and supporting documents are subsequently received.

Article 10 *Decision on the request*

1. The requested State shall deal with the request for extradition pursuant to procedures provided by its own law, and shall promptly communicate its decision to the requesting State.

2. Reasons shall be given for any complete or partial refusal of the request.

Article 11 *Surrender of the person*

1. Upon being informed that extradition has been granted, the Parties shall, without undue delay, arrange for the surrender of the person sought and the requested State shall inform the requesting State of the length of time for which the person sought was detained with a view to surrender.

2. The person shall be removed from the territory of the requested State within such reasonable period as the requested State specifies and, if the person is not removed within that period, the requested State may release the person and may refuse to extradite that person for the same offence.

3. If circumstances beyond its control prevent a Party from surrendering or removing the person to be extradited, it shall notify the other Party. The two Parties shall mutually decide upon a new date of surrender, and the provisions of paragraph 2 of the present article shall apply.

Article 12 *Postponed or conditional surrender*

1. The requested State may, after making its decision on the request for extradition, postpone the surrender of a person sought, in order to proceed against that person, or, if that person has already been convicted, in order to enforce a sentence imposed for an offence other than that for which extradition is sought. In such a case the requested State shall advise the requesting State accordingly.

2. The requested State may, instead of postponing surrender, temporarily surrender the person sought to the requesting State in accordance with conditions to be determined between the Parties.

Article 13 *Surrender of property*

1. To the extent permitted under the law of the requested State and subject to the rights of third parties, which shall be duly respected, all property found in the requested State that has been acquired as a result of the offence or that may be required as evidence shall, if the requesting State so requests, be surrendered if extradition is granted.

2. The said property may, if the requesting State so requests, be surrendered to the requesting State even if the extradition agreed to cannot be carried out.

3. When the said property is liable to seizure or confiscation in the requested State, it may retain it or temporarily hand it over.

4. Where the law of the requested State or the protection of the rights of third parties so require, any property so surrendered shall be returned to the requested State free of charge after the completion of the proceedings, if that State so requests.

Article 14 *Rule of speciality*

1. A person extradited under the present Treaty shall not be proceeded against, sentenced, detained, re-extradited to a third State, or subjected to any other restriction of personal liberty in the territory of the requesting State for any offence committed before surrender other than:

(a) An offence for which extradition was granted;

(b) Any other offence in respect of which the requested State consents. Consent shall be given if the offence for which it is requested is itself subject to extradition in accordance with the present Treaty.

2. A request for the consent of the requested State under the present article shall be accompanied by the documents mentioned in paragraph 2 of article 5 of the present Treaty and a legal record of any statement made by the extradited person with respect to the offence.

3. Paragraph 1 of the present article shall not apply if the person has had an opportunity to leave the requesting State and has not done so within [30/45] days of final discharge in respect of the offence for which that person was extradited or if the person has voluntarily returned to the territory of the requesting State after leaving it.

Article 15 *Transit*

1. Where a person is to be extradited to a Party from a third State through the territory of the other Party, the Party to which the person is to be extradited shall request the other Party to permit the transit of that person through its territory. This does not apply where air transport is used and no landing in the territory of the other Party is scheduled.

2. Upon receipt of such a request, which shall contain relevant information, the requested State shall deal with this request pursuant to procedures provided by its own law. The requested State shall grant the request expeditiously unless its essential interests would be prejudiced thereby.

3. The State of transit shall ensure that legal provisions exist that would enable detaining the person in custody during transit.

4. In the event of an unscheduled landing, the Party to be requested to permit transit may, at the request of the escorting officer, hold the person in custody for [48] hours, pending receipt of the transit request to be made in accordance with paragraph 1 of the present article.

Article 16 *Concurrent requests*

If a Party receives requests for extradition for the same person from both the other Party and a third State it shall, at its discretion, determine to which of those States the person is to be extradited.

Article 17 *Costs*

1. The requested State shall meet the cost of any proceedings in its jurisdiction arising out of a request for extradition.

2. The requested State shall also bear the costs incurred in its territory in connection with the seizure and handing over of property, or the arrest and detention of the person which extradition is sought.

3. The requesting State shall bear the costs incurred in conveying the person from the territory of the requested State, including transit costs.

Article 18 *Final provisions*

1. The present Treaty is subject to [ratification, acceptance or approval]. The instruments of [ratification, acceptance or approval] shall be exchanged as soon as possible.

2. The present Treaty shall enter into force on the thirtieth day after the day on which the instruments of [ratification, acceptance or approval] are exchanged.

3. The present Treaty shall apply to requests made after its entry into force, even if the relevant acts or omissions occurred prior to that date.

4. Either Contracting Party may denounce the present Treaty by giving notice in writing to the other Party. Such denunciation shall take effect six months following the date on which such notice is received by the other Party.

IN WITNESS WHEREOF the undersigned, being duly authorized thereto by their respective Governments, have signed the present Treaty.

DONE at .... on .... in the ....

and .... languages, [both/all] texts being equally authentic.

B. INTERNATIONAL ORGANISATIONS

4. THE UNITED NATIONS CHARTER

We the Peoples of the United Nations

Determined to save succeeding generations from the scourge of war, which twice in our lifetime has brought untold sorrow to mankind, and

to reaffirm faith in fundamental human rights, in the dignity and worth of the human person, in the equal rights of men and women and of nations large and small, and

to establish conditions under which justice and respect for the obligations arising from treaties and other sources of international law can be maintained, and

to promote social progress and better standards of life in large freedom,

And for these ends to practice tolerance and live together in peace with one another as good neighbours, and

to unite our strength to maintain international peace and security, and

to ensure by the acceptance of principles and the institution of methods, that armed force shall not be used, save in the common interest, and

to employ international machinery for the promotion of the economic and social advancement of all peoples.

Have resolved to combine our efforts to accomplish these aims. Accordingly, our respective Governments, through representatives assembled in the city of San Francisco, who have exhibited their full powers found to be in good and due form, have agreed to the present Charter of the United Nations and do hereby establish an international organization to be known as the United Nations.

CHAPTER I Purposes and Principles

Art. 1. The Purposes of the United Nations are:

1. To maintain international peace and security, and to that end: to take effective collective measures for the prevention and removal of threats to the peace, and for the suppression of acts of aggression or other breaches of the peace, and to bring about by peaceful means, and in conformity with the principles of justice and international law, adjustment or settlement of international disputes or situations which might lead to a breach of the peace;

2. To develop friendly relations among nations based on respect for the principle of equal rights and self-determination of peoples, and to take other appropriate measures to strengthen universal peace;

3. To achieve international co-operation in solving international problems of an economic, social, cultural, or humanitarian character, and in promoting and encouraging respect for human rights and for fundamental freedoms for all without distinction as to race, sex, language, or religion; and

4. To be a center for harmonizing the actions of nations in the attainment of these common ends.

Art. 2. The Organization and its Members, in pursuit of the Purposes stated in Article 1, shall act in accordance with the following Principles.

1. The Organization is based on the principle of the sovereign equality of all its Members.

2. All Members, in order to ensure to all of them the rights and benefits resulting from membership, shall fulfil in good faith the obligations assumed by them in accordance with the present Charter.

3. All Members shall settle their international disputes by peaceful means in such a manner that international peace and security, and justice, are not endangered.

4. All Members shall refrain in their international relations from the threat or use of force against the territorial integrity or political independence of any state, or in any other manner inconsistent with the Purposes of the United Nations.

5. All Members shall give the United Nations every assistance in any action it takes in accordance with the present Charter, and shall refrain from giving assistance to any state against which the United Nations is taking preventive or enforcement action.

6. The Organization shall ensure that states which are not Members of the United Nations act in accordance with these Principles so far as may be necessary for the maintenance of international peace and security.

7. Nothing contained in the present Charter shall authorize the United Nations to intervene in matters which are essentially within the domestic jurisdiction of any state or shall require the Members to submit such matters to settlement under the present Charter, but this principle shall not prejudice the application of enforcement measures under Chapter VII.

CHAPTER II Membership

Art. 3. The original Members of the United Nations shall be the states which, having participated in the United Nations Conference on International Organization at San Francisco, or having previously signed the Declaration by United Nations of 1 January 1942, signed the present Charter and ratify it in accordance with Article 110.

Art. 4. 1. Membership in the United Nations is open to all other peace-loving states which accept the obligations contained in the present Charter and, in the judgment of the Organization, are able and willing to carry out these obligations.

2. The admission of any such state to membership in the United Nations will be effected by a decision of the General Assembly upon the recommendation of the Security Council.

Art. 5. A Member of the United Nations against which preventive or enforcement action has been taken by the Security Council may be suspended from the exercise of the rights and privileges of membership by the General Assembly upon the recommendation of the Security Council. The exercise of these rights and privileges may be restored by the Security Council.

Art. 6. A Member of the United Nations which has persistently violated the Principles contained in the present Charter may be expelled from the Organization by the General Assembly upon the recommendation of the Security Council.

CHAPTER III Organs

Art. 7. 1. There are established as the principal organs of the United Nations: a General Assembly, a Security Council, an Economic and Social Council, a Trusteeship Council, an International Court of Justice, and a Secretariat.

2. Such subsidiary organs as may be found necessary may be established in accordance with the present Charter.

Art. 8. The United Nations shall place no restrictions on the eligibility of men and women to participate in any capacity and under conditions of equality in its principal and subsidiary organs.

CHAPTER IV **The General Assembly**

Art. 9. 1. The General Assembly shall consist of all the Members of the United Nations.

2. Each Member shall have not more than five representatives in the General Assembly.

Art. 10. The General Assembly may discuss any questions or any matters within the scope of the present Charter or relating to the powers and functions of any organs provided for in the present Charter, and, except as provided in Article 12, may make recommendations to the Members of the United Nations or to the Security Council or to both on any such questions or matters.

Art. 11. 1. The General Assembly may consider the general principles of co-operation in the maintenance of international peace and security, including the principles governing disarmament and the regulation of armaments, and may make recommendations with regard to such principles to the Members or to the Security Council or to both.

2. The General Assembly may discuss any questions relating to the maintenance of international peace and security brought before it by any Member of the United Nations, or by the Security Council, or by a state which is not a Member of the United Nations in accordance with Article 35, paragraph 2, and, except as provided in Article 12, may make recommendations with regard to any such question to the state or states concerned or to the Security Council or to both. Any such question on which action is necessary shall be referred to the Security Council by the General Assembly either before or after discussion.

3. The General Assembly may call the attention of the Security Council to situations which are likely to endanger international peace and security.

4. The powers of the General Assembly set forth in this Article shall not limit the general scope of Article 10.

Art. 12. 1. While the Security Council is exercising in respect of any dispute or situation the function assigned to it in the present Charter, the General Assembly shall not make any recommendation with regard to that dispute or situation unless the Security Council so requests.

2. The Secretary-General, with the consent of the Security Council, shall notify the General Assembly at each session of any matters relative to the maintenance of international peace and security which are being dealt with by the Security Council and shall similarly notify the General Assembly, or the Members of the United Nations if the General Assembly is not in session, immediately the Security Council ceases to deal with such matters.

Art. 13. 1. The General Assembly shall initiate studies and make recommendations for the purpose of:

(a) promoting international co-operation in the political field and encouraging the progressive development of international law and its codification;

(b) promoting international co-operation in the economic, social, cultural, educational, and health fields, and assisting in the realization of human rights and fundamental freedoms for all without distinction as to race, sex, language, or religion.

2. The further responsibilities, functions and powers of the General Assembly with respect to matters mentioned in paragraph 1*(b)* above are set forth in Chapters IX and X.

Art. 14. Subject to the provisions of Article 12, the General Assembly may recommend measures for the peaceful adjustment of any situation, regardless of origin, which it deems likely to impair the general welfare or friendly relations among nations, including situations resulting from a violation of the provisions of the present Charter setting forth the Purposes and Principles of the United Nations.

Art. 15. 1. The General Assembly shall receive and consider annual and special reports from the Security Council: these reports shall include an account of the measures that the Security Council has decided upon or taken to maintain international peace and security.

2. The General Assembly shall receive and consider reports from the other organs of the United Nations.

Art. 16. The General Assembly shall perform such functions with respect to the international trusteeship system as are assigned to it under Chapters XII and XIII, including the approval of the trusteeship agreements for areas not designated as strategic.

Art. 17. 1. The General Assembly shall consider and approve the budget of the Organization.

2. The expenses of the Organization shall be borne by the Members as apportioned by the General Assembly.

3. The General Assembly shall consider and approve any financial and budgetary arrangements with specialized agencies referred to in Article 57 and shall examine the administrative budgets of such specialized agencies with a view to making recommendations to the agencies concerned.

Art. 18. 1. Each member of the General Assembly shall have one vote.

2. Decisions of the General Assembly on important questions shall be made by a two-thirds majority of the members present and voting. These questions shall include: recommendations with respect to the maintenance of international peace and security, the election of the non-permanent members of the Security Council, the election of the members of the Economic and Social Council, the election of members of the Trusteeship Council in accordance with paragraph 1*(c)* of Article 86, the admission of new Members to the United Nations, the suspension of the rights and privileges of membership, the expulsion of Members, questions relating to the operation of the trusteeship system, and budgetary questions.

3. Decisions on other questions, including the determination of additional categories of questions to be decided by a two-thirds majority, shall be made by a majority of the members present and voting.

Art. 19. A Member of the United Nations which is in arrears in the payment of its financial contributions to the Organization shall have no vote in the General Assembly if the amount of its arrears equals or exceeds the amount of the contributions due from it for the preceding two full years. The General Assembly may, nevertheless, permit such a Member to vote if it is satisfied that the failure to pay is due to conditions beyond the control of the Member.

Art. 20. The General Assembly shall meet in regular annual sessions and in such special session as occasion may require. Special sessions shall be convoked by the Secretary-General at the request of the Security Council or of a majority of the Members of the United Nations.

Art. 21. The General Assembly shall adopt its own rules of procedure. It shall elect its President for each session.

Art. 22. The General Assembly may establish such subsidiary organs as it deems necessary for the performance of its functions.

CHAPTER V **The Security Council**

Art. 23. 1. The Security Council shall consist of fifteen Members of the United Nations. The Republic of China, France, the Union of Soviet Socialist Republics, the United Kingdom of Great Britain and Northern Ireland, and the United States of America shall be permanent members of the Security Council. The General Assembly shall elect ten other Members of the United Nations to be non-permanent members of the Security Council, due regard being specially paid, in the first instance to the contribution of Members of the United Nations to the maintenance of international peace and security and to the other purposes of the Organization, and also to equitable geographical distribution.

2. The non-permanent members of the Security Council shall be elected for a term of two years. In the first election of the non-permanent members after the increase of the membership of the Security Council from eleven to fifteen, two of the four additional members shall be chosen for a term of one year. A retiring member shall not be eligible for immediate re-election.

3. Each member of the Security Council shall have one representative.

Art. 24. 1. In order to ensure prompt and effective action by the United Nations, its Members confer on the Security Council primary responsibility for the maintenance of international peace and security, and agree that in carrying out its duties under this responsibility the Security Council acts on their behalf.

2. In discharging these duties the Security Council shall act in accordance with the Purposes and Principles of the United Nations. The specific powers granted to the Security Council for the discharge of these duties are laid down in Chapters VI, VII, VIII, and XII.

3. The Security Council shall submit annual and, when necessary, special reports to the General Assembly for its consideration.

Art. 25. The Members of the United Nations agree to accept and carry out the decisions of the Security Council in accordance with the present Charter.

Art. 26. In order to promote the establishment and maintenance of international peace and security with the least diversion for armaments of the world's human and economic resources, the Security Council shall be responsible for formulating, with the assistance of the Military Staff Committee referred to in Article 47, plans to be submitted to the Members of the United Nations for the establishment of a system for the regulation of armaments.

Art. 27. 1. Each member of the Security Council shall have one vote.

2. Decisions of the Security Council on procedural matters shall be made by an affirmative vote of nine members.

3. Decisions of the Security Council on all other matters shall be made by an affirmative vote of nine members including the concurring votes of the permanent members; provided that, in decisions under Chapter VI, and under paragraph 3 of Article 52, a party to a dispute shall abstain from voting.

Art. 28. 1. The Security Council shall be so organized as to be able to function continuously. Each member of the Security Council shall for this purpose be represented at all times at the seat of the Organization.

2. The Security Council shall hold periodic meetings at which each of its members may, if it so desires, be represented by a member of the government or by some other specially designated representative.

3. The Security Council may hold meetings at such places other than the seat of the Organization as in its judgment will best facilitate its work.

Art. 29. The Security Council may establish such subsidiary organs as it deems necessary for the performance of its functions.

Art. 30. The Security Council shall adopt its own rules of procedure, including the method of selecting its President.

Art. 31. Any Member of the United Nations which is not a member of the Security Council may participate, without vote, in the discussion of any question brought before the Security Council whenever the latter considers that the interests of the Member are specially affected.

Art. 32. Any Member of the United Nations which is not a member of the Security Council or any state which is not a Member of the United Nations, if it is a party to a dispute under consideration by the Security Council, shall be invited to participate, without vote, in the discussion relating to the dispute. The Security Council shall lay down such conditions as it deems just for the participation of a state which is not a Member of the United Nations.

CHAPTER VI Pacific Settlement of Disputes

Art. 33. 1. The parties to any dispute, the continuance of which is likely to endanger the maintenance of international peace and security, shall, first of all, seek a solution by negotiation, enquiry, mediation, conciliation, arbitration, judicial settlement, resort to regional agencies or arrangements, or other peaceful means of their own choice.

2. The Security Council shall, when it deems necessary, call upon the parties to settle their dispute by such means.

Art. 34. The Security Council may investigate any dispute, or any situation which might lead to international friction or give rise to a dispute, in order to determine whether the continuance of the dispute or situation is likely to endanger the maintenance of international peace and security.

Art. 35. 1. Any Member of the United Nations may bring any dispute, or any situation of the nature referred to in Article 34, to the attention of the Security Council or of the General Assembly.

2. A state which is not a Member of the United Nations may bring to the attention of the Security Council or of the General Assembly any dispute to which it is a party if it accepts in advance, for the purposes of the dispute, the obligations of pacific settlement provided in the present Charter.

3. The proceedings of the General Assembly in respect of matters brought to its attention under this Article will be subject to the provisions of Articles 11 and 12.

Art. 36. 1. The Security Council may, at any stage of a dispute of the nature referred to in Article 33 or of a situation of like nature, recommend appropriate procedures or methods of adjustment.

2. The Security Council should take into consideration any procedures for the settlement of the dispute which have already been adopted by the parties.

3. In making recommendations under this Article the Security Council should also take into consideration that legal disputes should as a general rule be referred by the parties to the International Court of Justice in accordance with the provisions of the Statute of the Court.

Art. 37. 1. Should the parties to a dispute of the nature referred to in Article 33 fail to settle it by the means indicated in that Article, they shall refer it to the Security Council.

2. If the Security Council deems that the continuance of the dispute is in fact likely to endanger the maintenance of international peace and security, it shall decide whether to take action under Article 36 or to recommend such terms of settlement as it may consider appropriate.

Art. 38. Without prejudice to the provisions of Articles 33 to 37, the Security Council may, if all the parties to any dispute so request, make recommendations to the parties with a view to a pacific settlement of the dispute.

CHAPTER VII **Action with Respect to Threats to the Peace, Breaches of the Peace, and Acts of Aggression**

Art. 39. The Security Council shall determine the existence of any threat to the peace, breach of the peace, or act of aggression and shall make recommendations, or decide what measures shall be taken in accordance with Articles 41 and 42, to maintain or restore international peace and security.

Art. 40. In order to prevent an aggravation of the situation, the Security Council may, before making the recommendation or deciding upon the measures provided for in Article 39, call upon the parties concerned to comply with such provisional measures as it deems necessary or desirable. Such provisional measures shall be without prejudice to the rights, claims, or position of the parties concerned. The Security Council shall duly take account of failure to comply with such provisional measures.

Art. 41. The Security Council may decide what measures not involving the use of armed forces are to be employed to give effect to its decisions, and it may call upon the Members of the United Nations to apply such measures. These may include complete or partial interruption of economic relations and of rail, sea, air, postal, telegraphic, radio, and other means of communication, and the severance of diplomatic relations.

Art. 42. Should the Security Council consider the measures provided for in Article 41 would be inadequate or have proved to be inadequate, it may take such action by air, sea, or land forces as may be necessary to maintain or restore international peace and security. Such action may include demonstrations, blockade, and other operations by air, sea or land forces of Members of the United Nations.

Art. 43. 1. All Members of the United Nations, in order to contribute to the maintenance of international peace and security, undertake to make available to the Security Council, on its call and in accordance with a special agreement or agreements, armed forces, assistance, and facilities, including the rights of passage, necessary for the purpose of maintaining international peace and security.

2. Such agreement or agreements shall govern the numbers and types of forces, their degree of readiness and general location, and the nature of the facilities and assistance to be provided.

3. The agreement or agreements shall be negotiated as soon as possible on the initiative of the Security Council. They shall be concluded between the Security Council and Members or between the Security Council and groups of Members and shall be subject to ratification by the signatory states in accordance with their respective constitutional processes.

Art. 44. When the Security Council has decided to use force it shall, before calling upon a Member not represented on it to provide armed forces in fulfilment of the obligations assumed under Article 43, invite that Member, if the Member so desires, to participate in the decisions of the Security Council concerning the employment of contingents of that Member's armed forces.

Art. 45. In order to enable the United Nations to take urgent military measures, Members shall hold immediately available national air-force contingents for combined international enforcement action. The strength and degree of readiness of these contingents and plans for their combined action shall be determined, within the limits laid down in the special agreement or agreements referred to in Article 43, by the Security Council with the assistance of the Military Staff Committee.

Art. 46. Plans for the application of armed forces shall be made by the Security Council with the assistance of the Military Staff Committee.

Art. 47. 1. There shall be established a Military Staff Committee to advise and assist the Security Council on all questions relating to the Security Council's military requirements for the maintenance of international peace and security, the employment and command of forces placed at its disposal, the regulation of armaments, and possible disarmament.

2. The Military Staff Committee shall consist of the Chiefs of Staff of the permanent members of the Security Council or their representatives. Any Member of the United Nations not permanently represented on the Committee shall be invited by the Committee to be associated with it when the efficient discharge of the Committee's responsibilities requires the participation of that Member in its work.

3. The Military Staff Committee shall be responsible under the Security Council for the strategic direction of any armed forces placed at the disposal of the Security Council. Questions relating to the command of such forces shall be worked out subsequently.

4. The Military Staff Committee, with the authorization of the Security Council and after consultation with appropriate regional agencies, may establish regional subcommittees.

Art. 48. 1. The action required to carry out the decisions of the Security Council for the maintenance of international peace and security shall be taken by all the Members of the United Nations or by some of them, as the Security Council may determine.

2. Such decisions shall be carried out by the Members of the United Nations directly and through their action in the appropriate international agencies of which they are members.

Art. 49. The Members of the United Nations shall join in affording mutual assistance in carrying out the measures decided upon by the Security Council.

Art. 50. If preventive or enforcement measures against any state are taken by the Security Council, any other state, whether a Member of the United Nations or not, which finds itself confronted with special economic problems arising from the carrying out of those measures shall have the right to consult the Security Council with regard to a solution of those problems.

Art. 51. Nothing in the present Charter shall impair the inherent right of individual or collective self-defence if an armed attack occurs against a Member of the United Nations, until the Security Council has taken measures necessary to maintain international peace and security. Measures taken by Members in the exercise of this right of self-defense shall be immediately reported to the Security Council and shall not in any way affect the authority and responsibility of the Security Council under the present Charter to take at any time such action as it deems necessary in order to maintain or restore international peace and security.

CHAPTER VIII Regional Arrangements

Art. 52. 1. Nothing in the present Charter precludes the existence of regional arrangements or agencies for dealing with such matters relating to the maintenance of international peace and security as are appropriate for regional action, provided that such arrangements or agencies and their activities are consistent with the Purposes and Principles of the United Nations.

2. The Members of the United Nations entering into such arrangements or constituting such agencies shall make every effort to achieve pacific settlement of local disputes through such regional arrangements or by such regional agencies before referring them to the Security Council.

3. The Security Council shall encourage the development of pacific settlement of local disputes through such regional arrangements or by such regional agencies either on the initiative of the states concerned or by reference from the Security Council.

4. This Article in no way impairs the application of Articles 34 and 35.

Art. 53. 1. The Security Council shall, where appropriate, utilize such regional arrangements of agencies for enforcement action under its authority. But no enforcement action shall be taken under regional arrangements or by regional agencies without the authorization of the Security Council, with the exception of measures against any enemy state, as defined in paragraph 2 of this Article, provided for pursuant to Article 107 or in regional arrangements directed against renewal of aggressive policy on the part of any such state, until such time as the Organization may, on request of the Governments concerned, be charged with the responsibility for preventing further aggression by such a state.

2. The term enemy state as used in paragraph 1 of this Article applies to any state which during the Second World War has been an enemy of any signatory of the present Charter.

Art. 54. The Security Council shall at all times be kept fully informed of activities undertaken or in contemplation under regional arrangements or by regional agencies for the maintenance of international peace and security.

CHAPTER IX   International Economic and Social Co-operation

Art. 55. With a view to the creation of conditions of stability and well-being which are necessary for peaceful and friendly relations among nations based on respect for the principle of equal rights and self-determination of peoples, the United Nations shall promote:

(a) higher standards of living, full employment, and conditions of economic and social progress and development;

(b) solutions of international economic, social, health, and related problems; and international cultural and educational co-operation; and

(c) universal respect for, and observance of, human rights and fundamental freedoms for all without distinction as to race, sex, language, or religion.

Art. 56. All Members pledge themselves to take joint and separate action in co-operation with the Organization for the achievements of the purposes set forth in Article 55.

Art. 57. 1. The various specialized agencies, established by inter-governmental agreement and having wide international responsibilities, as defined in their basic instruments, in economic, social, cultural, educational, health, and related fields, shall be brought into relationship with the United Nations in accordance with the provisions of Article 63.

2. Such agencies thus brought into relationship with the United Nations are hereinafter referred to as specialized agencies.

Art. 58. The Organization shall make recommendations for the co-ordination of the policies and activities of the specialized agencies.

Art. 59. The Organization shall, where appropriate, initiate negotiations among the states concerned for the creation of any new specialized agencies required for the accomplishment of the purposes set forth in Article 55.

Art. 60. Responsibility for the discharge of the functions of the Organization set forth in this Chapter shall be vested in the General Assembly and, under the authority of the General Assembly, in the Economic and Social Council, which shall have for this purpose the powers set forth in Chapter X.

CHAPTER X The Economic and Social Council

Art. 61. 1. The Economic and Social Council shall consist of fifty-four Members of the United Nations elected by the General Assembly.

2. Subject to the provisions of paragraph 3, eighteen members of the Economic and Social Council shall be elected each year for a term of three years. A retiring member shall be eligible for immediate re-election.

3. At the first election after the increase in the membership of the Economic and Social Council from twenty-seven to fifty-four members, in addition to the members elected in place of the nine members whose term of office expires at the end of that year, twenty-seven additional members shall be elected. Of these twenty-seven additional members, the term of office of nine members so elected shall expire at the end of one year, and of nine other members at the end of two years, in accordance with arrangements made by the General Assembly.

4. Each member of the Economic and Social Council shall have one representative.

Art. 62. 1. The Economic and Social Council may make or initiate studies and reports with respect to international economic, social, cultural, educational, health, and related matters and may make recommendations with respect to any such matters to the General Assembly, to the Members of the United Nations and to the specialized agencies concerned.

2. It may make recommendations for the purpose of promoting respect for, and observance of, human rights and fundamental freedoms for all.

3. It may prepare draft conventions for submission to the General Assembly, with respect to matters falling within its competence.

4. It may call, in accordance with the rules prescribed by the United Nations, international conferences on matters falling within its competence.

Art. 63. 1. The Economic and Social Council may enter into agreements with any of the agencies referred to in Article 57, defining the terms on which the agency concerned shall be brought into relationship with the United Nations. Such agreements shall be subjected to approval by the General Assembly.

2. It may co-ordinate the activities of the specialized agencies through consultation with and recommendations to such agencies and through recommendations to the General Assembly and to the Members of the United Nations.

Art. 64. 1. The Economic and Social Council may take appropriate steps to obtain regular reports from the specialized agencies. It may make arrangements with the Members of the United Nations and with the specialized agencies to obtain reports on the steps taken to give effect to its own recommendations and to recommendations on matters falling within its competence made by the General Assembly.

2. It may communicate its observation on these reports to the General Assembly.

Art. 65. The Economic and Social Council may furnish information to the Security Council and shall assist the Security Council upon its request.

Art. 66. 1. The Economic and Social Council shall perform such functions as fall within its competence in connection with the carrying out of the recommendations of the General Assembly.

2. It may, with the approval of the General Assembly, perform services at the request of the Members of the United Nations and at the request of specialized agencies.

3. It shall perform such other functions as are specified elsewhere in the present Charter or as may be assigned to it by the General Assembly.

Art. 67. 1. Each member of the Economic and Social Council shall have one vote.

2. Decisions of the Economic and Social Council shall be made by a majority of the members present and voting.

Art. 68. The Economic and Social Council shall set up commissions in economic and social fields for the promotion of human rights, and such other commissions as may be required for the performance of its functions.

Art. 69. The Economic and Social Council shall invite a member of the United Nations to participate, without vote, in its deliberations or any matter of particular concern to that Member.

Art. 70. The Economic and Social Council may make arrangements for representatives of the specialized agencies to participate, without vote, in its deliberations and in those of the commissions established by it, and for its representatives to participate in the deliberations of the specialized agencies.

Art. 71. The Economic and Social Council may make suitable arrangements for consultation with non-governmental organizations which are concerned with matters within its competence. Such arrangements may be made with international organizations and, where appropriate with national organizations after consultation with the Member of the United Nations concerned.

Art. 72. 1. The Economic and Social Council shall adopt its own rules of procedure, including the method of selecting its President.

2. The Economic and Social Council shall meet as required in accordance with its rules, which shall include provision for the convening of meetings on the request of a majority of its members.

CHAPTER XI Declaration regarding Non-self-governing Territories

Art. 73. Members of the United Nations which have or assume responsibilities for the administration of territories whose peoples have not yet attained a full measure of self-government recognize the principle that the interests of the inhabitants of these territories are paramount, and accept as a sacred trust the obligation to promote to the utmost, within the system of international peace and security established by the present Charter, the well-being of the inhabitants of these territories, and, to this end:

(a) to ensure, with due respect for the culture of the peoples concerned, their political, economic, social, and educational advancement, their just treatment, and their protection against abuses;

(b) to develop self-government, to take due account of the political aspirations of the peoples, and to assist them in the progressive development of their free political institutions, according to the particular circumstances of each territory and its peoples and their varying stages of advancement;

(c) to further international peace and security;

(d) to promote constructive measures of development, to encourage research, and to co-operate with one another and, when and where appropriate, with specialized international bodies with a view to the practical achievement of the social, economic, and scientific purposes set forth in this Article; and

(e) to transmit regularly to the Secretary-General for information purposes, subject to such limitation as security and constitutional considerations may require, statistical and other information of a technical nature relating to economic, social, and educational conditions in the territories for which they are respectively responsible other than those territories to which Chapters XII and XIII apply.

Art. 74. Members of the United Nations also agree that their policy in respect of the territories to which this Chapter applies, no less than in respect of their metropolitan areas, must be based on the general principle of goodneighbourliness, due account being taken of the interests and well-being of the rest of the world, in social, economic, and commercial matters.

CHAPTER XII International Trusteeship System

Art. 75. The United Nations shall establish under its authority an international trusteeship system for the administration and supervision of such territories as may be placed thereunder by subsequent individual agreements. These territories are hereinafter referred to as trust territories.

Art. 76. The basic objectives of the trusteeship system, in accordance with the Purposes of the United Nations laid down in Article 1 of the present Charter, shall be:

(a) to further international peace and security;

(b) to promote the political, economic, social, and educational advancement of the inhabitants of the trust territories, and their progressive development towards self-government or independence as may be appropriate to the particular circumstances of each territory and its peoples and the freely expressed wishes of the peoples concerned, and as may be provided by the terms of each trusteeship agreement.

(c) to encourage respect for human rights and for fundamental freedoms for all without distinction as to race, sex, language, or religion, and to encourage recognition of the interdependence of the peoples of the world; and

(d) to ensure equal treatment in social, economic, and commercial matters for all Members of the United Nations and their nationals, and also equal treatment for the latter in the administration of justice, without prejudice to the attainment of the foregoing objectives and subject to the provisions of Article 80.

Art. 77. 1. The trusteeship system shall apply to such territories in the following categories as may be placed thereunder by means of trusteeship agreements:

(a) territories now held under mandate;

(b) territories which may be detached from enemy states as a result of the Second World War; and

(c) territories voluntarily placed under the system by states responsible for their administration.

2. It will be a matter for subsequent agreement as to which territories in the foregoing categories will be brought under the trusteeship system and upon what terms.

Art. 78. The trusteeship system shall not apply to territories which have become Members of the United Nations, relationship among which shall be based on respect for the principle of sovereign equality.

Art. 79. The terms of trusteeship for each territory to be placed under the trusteeship system, including any alteration or amendment, shall be agreed upon by the states directly concerned, including the mandatory power in the case of territories held under mandate by a Member of the United Nations, and shall be approved as provided for in Articles 83 and 85.

Art. 80. 1. Except as may be agreed upon in individual trusteeship agreements, made under Articles 77, 79, and 81, placing each territory under the trusteeship system, and until such agreements have been concluded, nothing in this Chapter shall be construed in or of itself to alter in any manner the rights whatsoever of any states or any peoples or the terms of existing international instruments to which Members of the United Nations may respectively be parties.

2. Paragraph 1 of this Article shall not be interpreted as giving grounds for delay or postponement of the negotiation and conclusion of agreements for placing mandated and other territories under the trusteeship system as provided for in Article 77.

Art. 81. The trusteeship agreement shall in each case include the terms under which the trust territory will be administered and designate the authority which will exercise the administration of the trust territory. Such authority, hereinafter called the administering authority, may be one or more states or the Organization itself.

Art. 82. There may be designated, in any trusteeship agreement, a strategic area or areas which may include part or all of the trust territory to which the agreement applies, without prejudice to any special agreement or agreements made under Article 43.

Art. 83. 1. All functions of the United Nations relating to strategic areas, including the approval of the terms of the trusteeship agreements, and of their alteration or amendment, shall be exercised by the Security Council.

2. The basic objectives set forth in Article 76 shall be applicable to the people of each strategic area.

3. The Security Council shall, subject to the provisions of the trusteeship agreements and without prejudice to security considerations, avail itself of the assistance of the Trusteeship Council to perform those functions of the United Nations under the trusteeship system relating to political, economic, social, and educational matters in the strategic areas.

Art. 84. It shall be the duty of the administering authority to ensure that the trust territory shall play its part in the maintenance of international peace and security. To this end the administering authority may make use of volunteer forces, facilities, and assistance from the trust territory in carrying out the obligations towards the Security Council undertaken in this regard by the administering authority, as well as for local defense and the maintenance of law and order within the trust territory.

Art. 85. 1. The functions of the United Nations with regard to trusteeship agreements for all areas not designated as strategic, including the approval of the terms of the trusteeship agreements and of their alteration or amendment, shall be exercised by the General Assembly.

2. The Trusteeship Council, operating under the authority of the General Assembly, shall assist the General Assembly in carrying out these functions.

CHAPTER XIII The Trusteeship Council

Art. 86. 1. The Trusteeship Council shall consist of the following Members of the United Nations:

(a) those Members administering trust territories;

(b) such of those Members mentioned by name in Article 23 as are not administering trust territories; and

(c) as many other Members elected for three-year terms by the General Assembly as may be necessary to ensure that the total number of members of the Trusteeship Council is equally divided between those Members of the United Nations which administer trust territories and those which do not.

2. Each member of the Trusteeship Council shall designate one specially qualified person to represent it therein.

Art. 87. The General Assembly and, under its authority, the Trusteeship Council, in carrying out their functions, may:

(a) consider reports submitted by the administering authority;

(b) accept petitions and examine them in consultation with the administering authority;

(c) provide for periodic visits to the respective trust territories at times agreed upon with the administering authority; and

(d) take these and other actions in conformity with the terms of the trusteeship agreements.

Art. 88. The Trusteeship Council shall formulate a questionnaire on the political, economic, social, and educational advancement of the inhabitants of each trust territory, and the administering authority for each trust territory within the competence of the General Assembly shall make an annual report to the General Assembly upon the basis of such questionnaire.

Art. 89. 1. Each member of the Trusteeship Council shall have one vote.

2. Decisions of the Trusteeship Council shall be made by a majority of the members present and voting.

Art. 90. 1. The Trusteeship Council shall adopt its own rules of procedure, including the method of selecting its President.

2. The Trusteeship Council shall meet as required in accordance with its rules, which shall include provision for the convening of meetings on the request of a majority of its members.

Art. 91. The Trusteeship Council shall, when appropriate, avail itself of the assistance of the Economic and Social Council and of the specialized agencies in regard to matters with which they are respectively concerned.

CHAPTER XIV **The International Court of Justice**

Art. 92. The International Court of Justice shall be the principal judicial organ of the United Nations. It shall function in accordance with the annexed Statute, which is based upon the Statute of the Permanent Court of International Justice and forms an integral part of the present Charter.

Art. 93. 1. All Members of the United Nations are *ipso facto* parties to the Statute of the International Court of Justice.

2. A state which is not a Member of the United Nations may become a party to the Statute of the International Court of Justice on conditions to be determined in each case by the General Assembly upon the recommendation of the Security Council.

Art. 94. 1. Each Member of the United Nations undertakes to comply with the decision of the International Court of Justice in any case to which it is a party.

2. If any party to a case fails to perform the obligations incumbent upon it under a judgment rendered by the Court, the other party may have recourse to the Security Council, which may, if it deems necessary, make recommendations or decide upon measures to be taken to give effect to the judgment.

Art. 95. Nothing in the present Charter shall prevent members of the United Nations from entrusting the solution of their differences to other tribunals by virtue of the agreements already in existence or which may be concluded in the future.

Art. 96. 1. The General Assembly or the Security Council may request the International Court of Justice to give an advisory opinion on any legal question.

2. Other organs of the United Nations and specialized agencies, which may at any time be so authorized by the General Assembly, may also request advisory opinions of the Court on legal questions arising within the scope of their activities.

CHAPTER XV **The Secretariat**

Art. 97. The Secretariat shall comprise a Secretary-General and such staff as the Organization may require. The Secretary-General shall be appointed by the General Assembly upon the recommendation of the Security Council. He shall be the chief administrative officer of the Organization.

Art. 98. The Secretary-General shall act in that capacity in all meetings of the General Assembly of the Security Council of the Economic and Social Council, and of the Trusteeship Council, and shall perform such other functions as are entrusted to him by these organs. The Secretary-General shall make an annual report to the General Assembly on the work of the Organization.

Art. 99. The Secretary-General may bring to the attention of the Security Council any matter which in his opinion may threaten the maintenance of international peace and security.

Art. 100. 1. In the performance of their duties the Secretary-General and the staff shall not seek or receive instructions from any government or from any other authority external to the Organization. They shall refrain from any action which might reflect on their position as international officials responsible only to the Organization.

2. Each Member of the United Nations undertakes to respect the exclusively international character of the responsibilities of the Secretary-General and the staff and not to seek to influence them in the discharge of their responsibilities.

Art. 101. 1. The staff shall be appointed by the Secretary-General under regulations established by the General Assembly.

2. Appropriate staffs shall be permanently assigned to the Economic and Social Council, the Trusteeship Council, and, as required, to other organs of the United Nations. These staffs shall form a part of the Secretariat.

3. The paramount consideration in the employment of the staff and in the determination of the conditions of service shall be the necessity of securing the highest standards of efficiency, competence, and integrity. Due regard shall be paid to the importance of recruiting the staff on as wide a geographical basis as possible.

CHAPTER XVI **Miscellaneous Provisions**

Art. 102. 1. Every treaty and every international agreement entered into by any Member of the United Nations after the present Charter comes into force shall as soon as possible be registered with the Secretariat and published by it.

2. No party to any such treaty or international agreement which has not been registered in accordance with the provisions of paragraph 1 of this Article may invoke that treaty or agreement before any organ of the United Nations.

Art. 103. In any event of a conflict between the obligations of the Members of the United Nations under the present Charter and their obligations under any other international agreement, their obligations under the present Charter shall prevail.

Art. 104. The Organization shall enjoy in the territory of each of its Members such legal capacity as may be necessary for the exercise of its functions and the fulfilment of its purposes.

Art. 105. 1. The Organization shall enjoy in the territory of each of its Members such privileges and immunities as are necessary for the fulfilment of its purposes.

2. Representatives of the Members of the United Nations and officials of the Organization shall similarly enjoy such privileges and immunities as are necessary for the independent exercise of their function in connexion with the Organization.

3. The General Assembly may make recommendations with a view to determining the details of the application of paragraphs 1 and 2 of this Article or may propose conventions to the Members of the United Nations for this purpose.

CHAPTER XVII **Transitional Security Arrangements**

Art. 106. Pending the coming into force of such special agreements referred to in Article 43 as in the opinion of the Security Council enable it to begin the exercise of its responsibilities under Article 42, the parties to the Four-Nations Declaration, signed at Moscow, October 30, 1943, and France, shall, in accordance with the provisions of paragraph 5 of that Declaration, consult with one another and as occasion requires with other Members of the United Nations with a view to such joint action on behalf of the Organization as may be necessary for the purpose of maintaining international peace and security.

Art. 107. Nothing in the present Charter shall invalidate or preclude action, in relation to any state which during the Second World War has been an enemy of any signatory to the present Charter, taken or authorized as a result of that war by the Governments having responsibility for such action.

CHAPTER XVIII **Amendments**

Art. 108. Amendments to the present Charter shall come into force for all Members of the United Nations when they have been adopted by a vote of two thirds of the members of the General Assembly and ratified in accordance with their respective constitutional processes by two thirds of the Members of the United Nations, including all the permanent members of the Security Council.

Art. 109. 1. A General Conference of the Members of the United Nations for the purpose of reviewing the present Charter may be held at a date and place to be fixed by a two thirds vote of the members of the General Assembly and by a vote of any seven members of the Security Council. Each Member of the United Nations shall have one vote in the conference.

2. Any alteration of the present Charter recommended by a two thirds vote of the conference shall take effect when ratified in accordance with their respective constitutional processes by two thirds of the Members of the United Nations including all the permanent members of the Security Council.

3. If such a conference has not been held before the tenth annual session of the General Assembly following the coming into force of the present Charter, the proposal to call such a conference shall be placed on the agenda of that session of the General Assembly, and the conference shall be held if so decided by a majority vote of the members of the General Assembly and by a vote of any seven members of the Security Council.

CHAPTER XIX Ratification and Signature

Art. 110. 1. The present Charter shall be ratified by the signatory states in accordance with their respective constitutional processes.

2. The ratifications shall be deposited with the Government of the United States of America, which shall notify all the signatory states of each deposit as well as the Secretary-General of the Organization when he has been appointed.

3. The present Charter shall come into force upon the deposit of ratification by the Republic of China, France, the Union of Soviet Socialist Republics, the United Kingdom of Great Britain and Northern Ireland, and the United States of America, and by a majority of the other signatory states. A protocol of the ratifications deposited shall thereupon be drawn up by the Government of the United States of America which shall communicate copies thereof to all the signatory states.

4. The states signatory to the present Charter which ratify it after it has come into force will become original members of the United Nations on the date of the deposit of their respective ratifications.

Art. 111. The present Charter, of which the Chinese, French, Russian, English, and Spanish texts are equally authentic, shall remain deposited in the archives of the Government of the United States of America. Duly certified copies thereof shall be transmitted by that Government to the Governments of the other signatory states.

5. THE STATUTE OF THE INTERNATIONAL COURT OF JUSTICE

Art. 1. *The International Court of Justice* established by the Charter of the United Nations as the principal judicial organ of the United Nations as the principal organ of the United Nations shall be constituted and shall function in accordance with the provisions of the present Statute.

CHAPTER I Organization of the Court

Art. 2. The Court shall be composed of a body of independent judges, elected regardless of their nationality from among persons of high moral character, who possess the qualifications required in their respective countries for appointment to the highest judicial offices, or are jurisconsults of recognized competence in international law.

Art. 3. 1. The Court shall consist of fifteen members, no two of whom may be nationals of the same state.

2. A person who for the purposes of membership in the Court could be regarded as a national of more than one state shall be deemed to be a national of the one in which he ordinarily exercises civil and political rights.

Art. 4. 1. The members of the Court shall be elected by the General Assembly and by the Security Council from a list of persons nominated by the national groups in the Permanent Court of Arbitration, in accordance with the following provisions.

2. In the case of Members of the United Nations not represented in the Permanent Court of Arbitration, candidates shall be nominated by national groups appointed for this purpose by their governments under the same conditions as those prescribed for

members of the Permanent Court of Arbitration by Article 44 of the Convention of The Hague of 1907 for the pacific settlement of international disputes.

3. The conditions under which a state which is a party to the present Statute but is not a member of the United Nations may participate in electing the members of the Court shall, in the absence of a special agreement, be laid down by the General Assembly upon recommendation of the Security Council.

Art. 5. 1. At least three months before the date of the election, the Secretary-General of the United Nations shall address a written request to the members of the Permanent Court of Arbitration belonging to the states which are parties to the present Statute, and to the members of the national groups appointed under Article 4, paragraph 2, inviting them to undertake, within a given time, by national groups, the nomination of persons in a position to accept the duties of the member of the Court.

2. No group may nominate more than four persons, not more than two of whom shall be of their own nationality. In no case may the number of candidates nominated by a group be more than double the number of seats to be filled.

Art. 6. Before making these nominations, each national group is recommended to consult its highest court of justice, its legal facilities and schools of law, and its national academies and national sections of international academies devoted to the study of law.

Art. 7. 1. The Secretary-General shall prepare a list in alphabetical order of all the persons thus nominated. Save as provided in Article 12, paragraph 2, these shall be the only persons eligible.

Art. 8. The General Assembly and the Security Council shall proceed independently of one another to elect the members of the Court.

Art. 9. At every election, the electors shall bear in mind not only that the persons to be elected should individually possess the qualifications required, but also that in the body as a whole the representation of the main forms of civilization and of the principal legal system of the world should be assured.

Art. 10. 1. Those candidates who obtain an absolute majority of votes in the General Assembly and in the Security Council shall be considered as elected.

2. Any vote of the Security Council, whether for the election of judges or for the appointment of members of the conference envisaged in Article 12, shall be taken without any distinction between permanent and non-permanent members of the Security Council.

3. In the event of more than one national of the same State obtaining an absolute majority of the votes both of the General Assembly and of the Security Council, the eldest of these only shall be considered as elected.

Art. 11. If, after the first meeting held for the purpose of the election, one or more seats remain to be filled, a second and, if necessary, a third meeting shall take place.

Art. 12. 1. If, after the third meeting, one or more seats still remain unfilled, a joint conference consisting of six members, three appointed by the General Assembly and three by the Security Council, may be formed at any time at the request of either the General Assembly or the Security Council, for the purpose of choosing by the vote of an absolute majority one name for each seat still vacant, to submit to the General Assembly and the Security Council for their respective acceptance.

2. If the joint conference is unanimously agreed upon any person who fulfils the required conditions, he may be included in its list, even though he was not included in the list of nominations referred to in Article 7.

3. If the joint conference is satisfied that it will not be successful in procuring an election, those members of the Court who have already been elected shall, within a period to be fixed by the Security Council, proceed to fill the vacant seats by selection from among the candidates who have obtained votes either in the General Assembly or in the Security Council.

4. In the event of an equality of votes among the judges, the eldest judge shall have a casting vote.

Art. 13. 1. The members of the Court shall be elected for nine years and may be re-elected, provided, however, that of the judges elected at the first election, the terms of five judges shall expire at the end of three years and the terms of five more judges shall expire at the end of six years.

2. The judges whose terms are to expire at the end of the above-mentioned initial periods of three and six years shall be chosen by lot to be drawn by the Secretary-General immediately after the first election has been completed.

3. The members of the Court shall continue to discharge their duties until their places have been filled. Though replaced, they shall finish any cases which they may have begun.

4. In the case of the resignation of a member of the Court, the resignation shall be addressed to the President of the Court for transmission to the Secretary-General. This last notification makes the place vacant.

Art. 14. Vacancies shall be filled by the same method as that laid down for the first election, subject to the following provision: the Secretary-General shall, within one month of the occurrence of the vacancy, proceed to issue the invitations provided for in Article 5, and the date of the election shall be fixed by the Security Council.

Art. 15. A member of the Court elected to replace a member whose term of office has not expired shall hold office for the remainder of his predecessor's term.

Art. 16. 1. No member of the Court may exercise any political or administrative function, or engage in any other occupation of a professional nature.

2. Any doubt on this point shall be settled by the decision of the Court.

Art. 17. 1. No member of the Court may act as agent, counsel or advocate in any case.

2. No member may participate in the decision of any case in which he has previously taken part as agent, counsel or advocate for one of the parties, or as a member of a national or international court, or of a commission of enquiry, or in any other capacity.

3. Any doubt on this point shall be settled by the decision of the Court.

Art. 18. 1. No member of the Court can be dismissed unless, in the unanimous opinion of the other members, he has ceased to fulfil the required conditions.

2. Formal notification thereof shall be made to the Secretary-General by the Registrar.

3. This notification makes the place vacant.

Art. 19. The members of the Court, when engaged on the business of the Court, shall enjoy diplomatic privileges and immunities.

Art. 20. Every member of the Court shall, before taking up his duties, make a solemn declaration in open Court that he will exercise his powers impartially and conscientiously.

Art. 21. 1. The Court shall elect its President and Vice-President for three years: they may be re-elected.

2. The Court shall appoint its Registrar and may provide for the appointment of such other officers as may be necessary.

Art. 22. 1. The seat of the Court shall be established at The Hague. This, however, shall not prevent the Court from sitting and exercising its functions elsewhere whenever the Court considers it desirable.

2. The President and the Registrar shall reside at the seat of the Court.

Art. 23. 1. The Court shall remain permanently in session, except during the judicial vacations, the dates and duration of which shall be fixed by the Court.

2. Members of the Court are entitled to periodic leave, the dates and duration of which shall be fixed by the Court, having in mind the distance between The Hague and the home of each judge.

3. Members of the Court shall be bound, unless they are on leave or prevented from attending by illness or other serious reasons duly explained to the President, to hold themselves permanently at the disposal of the Court.

Art. 24. 1. If, for some special reason, a member of the Court considers that he should not take part in the decision of a particular case, he shall so inform the President.

2. If the President considers that for some special reason one of the members of the Court should not sit in a particular case, he shall give him notice accordingly.

3. If in any such case the member of the Court and the President disagree, the matter shall be settled by the decision of the Court.

Art. 25. 1. The full Court shall sit except when it is expressly provided otherwise in the present Statute.

2. Subject to the condition that the number of judges available to constitute the Court is not thereby reduced below eleven, the Rules of Court may provide for allowing one or more judges, according to circumstances and in rotation, to be dispensed from sitting.

3. A quorum of nine judges shall suffice to constitute the Court.

Art. 26. 1. The Court may from time to time form one or more Chambers, composed of three or more judges as the Court may determine, for dealing with particular categories of cases; for example, labour cases and cases relating to transit and communications.

2. The Court may at any time form a Chamber for dealing with a particular case. The number of judges to constitute such a Chamber shall be determined by the Court with the approval of the parties.

3. Cases shall be heard and determined by the Chambers provided for in this Article if the parties so request.

Art. 27. A judgment given by any of the Chambers provided for in Articles 26 and 29 shall be considered as rendered by the Court.

Art. 28. The Chambers provided for in Articles 26 and 29 may, with the consent of the parties, sit and exercise their functions elsewhere than at The Hague.

Art. 29. With a view to the speedy despatch of business, the Court shall form annually a Chamber composed of five judges which, at the request of the parties, may hear and determine cases by summary procedure. In addition, two judges shall be selected for the purpose of replacing judges who find it impossible to sit.

Art. 30. 1. The Court shall frame rules for carrying out its functions. In particular, it shall lay down rules of procedure.

2. The Rules of the Court may provide for accessors to sit with the Court or with any of its Chambers, without the right to vote.

Art. 31. 1. Judges of the nationality of each of the parties shall retain their right to sit in the case before the Court.

2. If the Court includes upon the Bench a judge of the nationality of one of the parties, any other party may choose a person to sit as judge. Such person shall be chosen preferably from among those persons who have been nominated as candidates as provided in Articles 4 and 5.

3. If the Court includes upon the Bench no judge of the nationality of the parties, each of these parties may proceed to choose a judge as provided in paragraph 2 of this Article.

4. The provisions of this Article shall apply to the case of Articles 26 and 29. In such cases, the President shall request one or, if necessary, two of the members of the Court forming the Chamber to give place to the members of the Court of the nationality of the parties concerned, and, failing such, or if they are unable to be present, to the judges specially chosen by the parties.

5. Should there be several parties in the same interest, they shall, for the purpose of the preceding provisions, be reckoned as one party only. Any doubt upon this point shall be settled by the decision of the Court.

6. Judges chosen as laid down in paragraphs 2, 3 and 4 of this Article shall fulfil the conditions required by Articles 2, 17 (paragraph 2), 20 and 24 of the present Statute. They shall take part in the decision on terms of complete equality with their colleagues.

Art. 32. 1. Each member of the Court shall receive an annual salary.

2. The President shall receive a special annual allowance.

3. The Vice-President shall receive a special allowance for every day on which he acts as President.

4. The judges chosen under Article 31, other than members of the Court, shall receive compensation for each day on which they exercise their functions.

5. These salaries, allowances and compensation shall be fixed by the General Assembly. They may not be decreased during the term of office.

6. The salary of the Registrar shall be fixed by the General Assembly on the proposal of the Court.

7. Regulations made by the General Assembly shall fix the conditions under which retirement pensions may be given to members of the Court, and to the Registrar, and the conditions under which members of the Court and the Registrar shall have their travelling expenses refunded.

8. The above salaries, allowances and compensation shall be free of all taxation.

Art. 33. The expenses of the Court shall be borne by the United Nations in such a manner as shall be decided by the General Assembly.

CHAPTER II **Competence of the court**

Art. 34. 1. Only States may be parties in cases before the Court.

2. The Court, subject to and in conformity with its Rules, may request of public international organizations information relevant to cases before it, and shall receive such information presented by such organizations on their own initiative.

3. Whenever the construction of the constituent instrument of a public international organization or of an international convention adopted thereunder is in question in a case before the Court, the Registrar shall so notify the public international organization concerned and shall communicate to it copies of all the written proceedings.

Art. 35. 1. The Court shall be open to the States parties to the present Statute.

2. The conditions under which the Court shall be open to other States shall, subject to the special provisions contained in treaties in force, be laid down by the Security Council, but in no case shall such conditions place the parties in a position of inequality before the Court.

3. When a State which is not a Member of the United Nations is a party to a case, the Court shall fix the amount which that party is to contribute towards the expenses of the Court. This provision shall not apply if such State is bearing a share of the expenses of the Court.

Art. 36. 1. The jurisdiction of the Court comprises all cases which the parties refer to it and all matters specially provided for in the Charter of the United Nations or in treaties and conventions in force.

2. The States parties to the present Statute may at any time declare that they recognize as compulsory *ipso facto* and without special agreement, in relation to any other State accepting the same obligation, the jurisdiction of the Court in all legal disputes concerning:

(a) the interpretation of a treaty;

(b) any question of international law;

(c) the existence of any fact which, if established, would constitute a breach of an international obligation;

(d) the nature or extent of the reparation to be made for the breach of an international obligation.

3. The declaration referred to above may be made unconditionally or on condition of reciprocity on the part of several or certain States, or for a certain time.

4. Such declarations shall be deposited with the Secretary-General of the United Nations, who shall transmit copies thereof to the parties to the Statute and to the Registrar of the Court.

5. Declarations made under Article 26 of the Statute of the Permanent Court of International Justice and which are still in force shall be deemed, as between the parties to the present Statute, to be acceptances of the compulsory jurisdiction of the International Court of Justice for the period which they still have to run and in accordance with their terms.

6. In the event of a dispute as to whether the Court has jurisdiction, the matter shall be settled by the decision of the Court.

Art. 37. Whenever a treaty or convention in force provides for reference of a matter to a tribunal to have been instituted by the League of Nations, or to the Permanent Court of International Justice, the matter shall, as between the parties to the present Statute, be referred to the International Court of Justice.

Art. 38. 1. The Court, whose function is to decide in accordance with international law such disputes as are submitted to it, shall apply:

(a) international conventions, whether general or particular, establishing rules expressly recognized by the contesting States;

(b) international custom, as evidence of a general practice accepted as law;

(c) the general principles of law recognized by civilized nations;

(d) subject to the provisions of Article 59, judicial decisions and the teachings of the most highly qualified publicists of the various nations, as subsidiary means for the determination of the rules of law.

2. This provision shall not prejudice the power of the Court to decide a case *ex aequo et bono*, if the parties agree thereto.

CHAPTER III Procedure

Art. 39. 1. The official languages of the Court shall be French and English. If the parties agree that the case shall be conducted in French, the judgment shall be delivered in French. If the parties agree that the case shall be conducted in English, the judgment shall be delivered in English.

2. In the absence of an agreement as to which language shall be employed, each party may, in the pleadings, use the language which it prefers; the decision of the Court shall be given in French and English. In this case the Court shall at the same time determine which of the two texts shall be considered as authoritative.

3. The Court shall, at the request of any party, authorize a language other than French and English to be used by that party.

Art. 40. 1. Cases are brought before the Court, as the case may be, either by the notification of the special agreement or by a written application addressed to the Registrar. In either case the subject of the dispute and the parties shall be indicated.

2. The Registrar shall forthwith communicate the application to all concerned.

3. He shall also notify the Members of the United Nations through the Secretary-General, and also any other States entitled to appear before the Court.

Art. 41. 1. The Court shall have the power to indicate, if it considers that circumstances so require, any provisional measures which ought to be taken to preserve the respective rights of either party.

2. Pending the final decision, notice of the measures suggested shall forthwith be given to the parties and to the Security Council.

Art. 42. 1. The parties shall be represented by agents.

2. They may have the assistance of counsel or advocates before the Court.

3. The agents, counsel and advocates of parties before the Court shall enjoy the privileges and immunities necessary to the independent exercise of their duties.

Art. 43. 1. The procedure shall consist of two parts: written and oral.

2. The written proceedings shall consist of the communication to the Court and to the parties of Memorials, Counter-Memorials and, if necessary, Replies; also all papers and documents in support.

3. These communications shall be made through the Registrar, in the order and within the time fixed by the Court.

4. A certified copy of every document produced by one party shall be communicated to the other party.

5. The oral proceedings shall consist of the hearing by the Court of witnesses, experts, agents, counsel and advocates.

Art. 44. 1. For the services of all notices upon persons other than the agents, counsel and advocates, the Court shall apply direct to the government of the State upon whose territory the notice has to be served.

2. The same provision shall apply whenever steps are to be taken to procure evidence on the spot.

Art. 45. The hearing shall be under the control of the President or, if he is unable to preside, of the Vice-President; if neither is able to preside, the senior judge present shall preside.

Art. 46. The hearing in Court shall be public, unless the Court shall decide otherwise, or unless the parties demand that the public be not admitted.

Art. 47. 1. Minutes shall be made at each hearing and signed by the Registrar and the President.

2. The minutes alone shall be authentic.

Art. 48. The Court shall make orders for the conduct of the case, shall decide the form and time in which each party must conclude its arguments, and make all arrangements connected with the taking of evidence.

Art. 49. The Court may, even before the hearing begins, call upon the agents to produce any document or to supply any explanations. Formal note shall be taken of any refusal.

Art. 50. The Court may, at any time, entrust any individual, body, bureau, commission or other organization that it may select, with the task of carrying out an enquiry or giving an expert opinion.

Art. 51. During the hearing any relevant questions are to be put to the witnesses and experts under the conditions laid down by the Court in the rules of procedure referred to in Article 30.

Art. 52. After the Court has received the proofs and evidence within the time specified for the purpose, it may refuse to accept any further oral or written evidence that one party may desire to present unless the other side consents.

Art. 53. 1. Whenever one of the parties does not appear before the Court, or fails to defend its case, the other party may call upon the Court to decide in favour of its claim.

2. The Court must, before doing so, satisfy itself, not only that it has jurisdiction in accordance with Articles 36 and 37, but also that the claim is well founded in fact and law.

Art. 54. 1. When, subject to the control of the Court, the agents, counsel and advocates have completed their presentations of the case, the President shall declare the hearing closed.

2. The Court shall withdraw to consider the judgment.

3. The deliberations of the Court shall take place in private and remain secret.

Art. 55. 1. All questions shall be decided by a majority of the judges present.

2. In the event of an equality of votes, the President or the judge who acts in his place shall have a casting vote.

Art. 56. 1. The judgment shall state the reasons on which it is based.

2. It shall contain the names of the judges who have taken part in the decision.

Art. 57. If the judgment does not represent in whole or in part the unanimous opinion of the judges, any judge shall be entitled to deliver a separate opinion.

Art. 58. The judgment shall be signed by the President and by the Registrar. It shall be read in open Court, due notice having been given to the agents.

Art. 59. The decision of the Court has no binding force except between the parties and in respect of that particular case.

Art. 60. The judgment is final and without appeal. In the event of dispute as to the meaning or scope of the judgment, the Court shall construe it upon the request of any party.

Art. 61. 1. An application for revision of a judgment may be made only when it is based upon the discovery of some fact of such a nature as to be a decisive factor, which fact was, when the judgment was given, unknown to the Court and also to the party claiming revision, always provided that such ignorance was not due to negligence.

2. The proceedings for revision shall be opened by a judgment of the Court expressly recording the existence of the new fact, recognizing that it has such a character as to lay the case open to revision, and declaring the application admissible on this ground.

3. The Court may require previous compliance with the terms of the judgment before it admits proceedings in revision.

4. The application for revision must be made at latest within six months of the discovery of the new fact.

5. No application for revision may be made after the lapse of ten years from the date of the judgment.

Art. 62. 1. Should a State consider that it has an interest of a legal nature which may be affected by the decision in the case, it may submit a request to the Court to be permitted to intervene.

2. It shall be for the Court to decide upon this request.

Art. 63. 1. Whenever the construction of a convention to which States other than those concerned in the case are parties is in question, the Registrar shall notify all such States forthwith.

2. Every State so notified has the right to intervene in the proceedings, but if it uses this right, the construction given by the judgment will be equally binding upon it.

Art. 64. Unless otherwise decided by the Court, each party shall bear its own costs.

CHAPTER IV Advisory opinions

Art. 65. 1. The Court may give an advisory opinion on any legal question at the request of whatever body may be authorized by or in accordance with the Charter of the United Nations to make such a request.

2. Questions upon which the advisory opinion of the Court is asked shall be laid before the Court by means of a written request containing an exact statement of the question upon which an opinion is required, and accompanied by all documents likely to throw light upon the question.

Art. 66. 1. The Registrar shall forthwith give notice of the request for an advisory opinion to all States entitled to appear before the Court.

2. The Registrar shall also, by means of a special and direct communication, notify any State entitled to appear before the Court or international organization considered by the Court, or, should it not be sitting, by the President, as likely to be able to furnish information on the question, that the Court will be prepared to receive, within a time-limit to be fixed by the President, written statements, or to hear, at a public sitting to be held for the purpose, oral statements relating to the question.

3. Should any such State entitled to appear before the court have failed to receive the special communication referred to in paragraph 2 of this Article, such State may express a desire to submit a written statement or to be heard; and the Court will decide.

4. States and organizations having presented written or oral statements or both shall be permitted to comment on the statements made by other States or organizations in the form, to the extent and within the time-limits which the Court, or, should it not be sitting, the President, shall decide in each particular case. Accordingly, the Registrar shall in due time communicate any such written statements to States and organizations having submitted similar statements.

Art. 67. The Court shall deliver its advisory opinions in open Court, notice having been given to the Secretary-General and to the representatives of Members of the United Nations, of other States and of international organizations immediately concerned.

Art. 68. In the exercise of its advisory functions, the Court shall further be guided by the provisions of the present Statute which apply in contentious cases to the extent to which it recognizes them to be applicable.

CHAPTER V Amendment

Art. 69. Amendments to the present Statute shall be affected by the same procedure as is provided by the Charter of the United Nations for amendments to that Charter, subject however to any provisions which the General Assembly upon recommendation of the Security Council may adopt concerning the participation of States which are parties to the present Statute but are not Members of the United Nations.

Art. 70. The Court shall have power to propose such amendments to the present Statute as it may deem necessary, through written communications to the Secretary-General, for consideration in conformity with the provisions of Article 69.

6. THE CHARTER OF THE ORGANIZATION OF AFRICAN UNITY
(2 ILM 766 (1963))

We, the Heads of African States and Governments assembled in the City of Addis Ababa, Ethiopia;

CONVINCED that it is the inalienable right of all people to control their own destiny;

CONSCIOUS of the fact that freedom, equality, justice and dignity are essential objectives for the achievement of the legitimate aspirations of the African peoples;

CONSCIOUS of our responsibility to harness the natural and human resources of our continent for the total advancement of our peoples in spheres of human endeavour;

INSPIRED by a common determination to promote understanding among our peoples and co-operation among our States in response to the aspirations of our peoples for brotherhood and solidarity, in a larger unity transcending ethnic and national differences;

CONVINCED that, in order to translate this determination into a dynamic force in the cause of human progress, conditions for peace and security must be established and maintained;

DETERMINED to safeguard and consolidate the hard-won independence as well as the sovereignty and territorial integrity of our States, and to fight against neo-colonialism in all its forms;

DEDICATED to the general progress of Africa;

PERSUADED that the Charter of the United Nations and the Universal Declaration of Human Rights, to the principles of which we reaffirm our adherence, provide a solid foundation for peaceful and positive co-operation among states;

DESIROUS that all African States should henceforth unite so that the welfare and well-being of their peoples can be assured;

RESOLVED to reinforce the links between our states by establishing and strengthening common institutions;

HAVE agreed to the present Charter.

Article I ESTABLISHMENT

1. The High Contracting Parties do by the present Charter establish an Organization to be known as the ORGANIZATION OF AFRICAN UNITY.

2. The Organization shall include the Continental African States, Madagascar and other Islands surrounding Africa.

Article II PURPOSES

1. The Organization shall have the following purposes:

(a) to promote the unity and solidarity of the African States;

(b) to co-ordinate and intensify their co-operation and efforts to achieve a better life for the peoples of Africa;

(c) to defend their sovereignty, their territorial integrity and independence;

(d) to eradicate all forms of colonialism from Africa; and

(e) to promote international co-operation, having due regard to the Charter of the United Nations and the Universal Declaration of Human Rights.

2. To these ends, the Member States shall co-ordinate and harmonize their general policies, especially in the following fields:

(a) political and diplomatic co-operation;

(b) economic co-operation, including transport and communications;

(c) educational and cultural co-operation;

(d) health, sanitation, and nutritional co-operation;

(e) scientific and technical co-operation; and

(f) co-operation for defence and security.

Article III PRINCIPLES

The Member States, in pursuit of the purposes stated in Article II, solemnly affirm and declare their adherence to the following principles:

1. the sovereign equality of all Member States;

2. non-interference in the internal affairs of States;

3. respect for the sovereignty and territorial integrity of each State and for its inalienable right to independent existence;

4. peaceful settlement of disputes by negotiation, mediation, conciliation or arbitration;

5. unreserved condemnation, in all its forms, of political assassination as well as of subversive activities on the part of neighbouring States or any other State;

6. absolute dedication to the total emancipation of the African territories which are still dependent;

7. affirmation of a policy of non-alignment with regard to all blocs.

Article IV MEMBERSHIP

Each independent sovereign African State shall be entitled to become a Member of the Organization.

Article V RIGHTS AND DUTIES OF MEMBER STATES

All Member States shall enjoy equal rights and have equal duties.

Article VI

The Member States pledge themselves to observe scrupulously the principles enumerated in Article III of the present Charter.

Article VII INSTITUTIONS

The Organization shall accomplish its purposes through the following principal institutions:

1. the Assembly of Heads of State and Government;
2. the Council of Ministers;
3. the General Secretariat;
4. the Commission of Mediation, Conciliation and Arbitration.

Article VIII THE ASSEMBLY OF HEADS OF STATE AND GOVERNMENT

The Assembly of Heads of State and Government shall be the supreme organ of the Organization. It shall, subject to the provisions of this Charter, discuss matters of common concern to Africa with a view to co-ordinating and harmonizing the general policy of the Organization. It may in addition review the structure, functions and acts of all the organs and any specialized agencies which may be created in accordance with the present Charter.

Article IX

The Assembly shall be composed of the Heads of State and Government or their duly accredited representatives and it shall meet at least once a year. At the request of any Member State and on approval by a two-thirds majority of the Member States, the Assembly shall meet in extraordinary session.

Article X

1. Each Member State shall have one vote.

2. All resolutions shall be determined by a two-thirds majority of the Members of the Organization.

3. Questions of procedure shall require a simple majority. Whether or not a question is one of procedure shall be determined by a simple majority of all Member States of the Organization.

4. Two-thirds of the total membership of the Organization shall form a quorum at any meeting of the Assembly.

Article XI

The Assembly shall have the power to determine its own rules of procedure.

Article XII THE COUNCIL OF MINISTERS

1. The Council of Ministers shall consist of Foreign Ministers or such other Ministers as are designated by the Governments of Member States.

2. The Council of Ministers shall meet at least twice a year. When requested by any Member State and approved by two-thirds of all Member States, it shall meet in extraordinary session.

Article XIII

1. The Council of Ministers shall be responsible to the Assembly of Heads of State and Government. It shall be entrusted with the responsibility of preparing conferences of the Assembly.

2. It shall take cognizance of any matter referred to it by the Assembly. It shall be entrusted with the implementation of the decision of the Assembly of Heads of State and Government. It shall co-ordinate inter-African co-operation in accordance with the instructions of the Assembly and in conformity with Article II(2) of the present Charter.

Article XIV

1. Each Member State shall have one vote.

2. All resolutions shall be determined by a simple majority of the members of the Council of Ministers.

3. Two-thirds of the total membership of the Council of Ministers shall form a quorum for any meeting of the Council.

Article XV

The Council shall have the power to determine its own rules of procedure.

Article XVI GENERAL SECRETARIAT

There shall be an Administrative Secretary-General of the Organization, who shall be appointed by the Assembly of Heads of State and Government. The Administrative Secretary-General shall direct the affairs of the Secretariat.

Article XVII

There shall be one or more Assistant Secretaries-General of the Organization, who shall be appointed by the Assembly of Heads of State and Government.

Article XVIII

The functions and conditions of services of the Secretary-General, of the Assistant Secretaries-General and other employees of the Secretariat shall be governed by the provisions of this Charter and the regulations approved by the Assembly of Heads of State and Government.

1. In the performance of their duties the Administrative Secretary-General and the staff shall not seek or receive instructions from any government or from any other authority external to the Organization. They shall refrain from any action which might reflect on their position as international officials responsible only to the Organization.

2. Each member of the Organization undertakes to respect the exclusive character of the responsibilities of the Administrative Secretary-General and the staff and not seek to influence them in the discharge of their responsibilities.

Article XIX COMMISSION OF MEDIATION, CONCILIATION AND ARBITRA-TION

Member States pledge to settle all disputes among themselves by peaceful means and, to this end decide to establish a Commission of Mediation, Conciliation and Arbitration, the composition of which and conditions of service shall be defined by a separate Protocol to be approved by the Assembly of Heads of State and Government. Said Protocol shall be regarded as forming an integral part of the present Charter.

Article XX SPECIALIZED COMMISSIONS

The Assembly shall establish such Specialized Commissions as it may deem necessary, including the following:

1. Economic and Social Commission;
2. Educational and Cultural Commission;
3. Health, Sanitation and Nutrition Commission;

4. Defence Commission;

5. Scientific, Technical and Research Commission.

Article XXI

Each Specialized Commission referred to in Article XX shall be composed of the Ministers concerned or other Ministers or Plenipotentiaries designated by the Governments of the Member States.

Article XXII

The functions of the Specialized Commissions shall be carried out in accordance with the provisions of the present Charter and of the regulations approved by the Council of Ministers.

Article XXIII THE BUDGET

The budget of the Organization prepared by the Administrative Secretary-General shall be approved by the Council of Ministers. The budget shall be provided by contributions from Member States in accordance with the scale of assessment of the United Nations; provided, however, that no Member State shall be assessed an amount exceeding twenty per cent of the yearly regular budget of the Organization. The Member States agree to pay their respective contributions regularly.

Article XXIV SIGNATURE AND RATIFICATION OF CHARTER

1. This Charter shall be open for signature to all independent sovereign African States and shall be ratified by the signatory States in accordance with their respective constitutional processes.

2. The original instrument, done, if possible in African languages, in English and French, all texts being equally authentic, shall be deposited with the Government of Ethiopia which shall transmit certified copies thereof of all independent sovereign African States.

3. Instruments of ratification shall be deposited with the Government of Ethiopia, which shall notify all signatories of each such deposit.

Article XXV ENTRY INTO FORCE

This Charter shall enter into force immediately upon receipt by the Government of Ethiopia of the instruments of ratification from two-thirds of the signatory States.

Article XXVI REGISTRATION OF THE CHARTER

This Charter shall, after due ratification, be registered with the Secretariat of the United Nations through the Government of Ethiopia in conformity with Article 102 of the Charter of the United Nations.

Article XXVII INTERPRETATION OF THE CHARTER

Any question which may arise concerning the interpretation of this Charter shall be decided by a vote of two-thirds of the Assembly of Heads of State and Government of the Organization.

Article XXVIII ADHESION AND ACCESSION

1. Any independent sovereign African State may at any time notify the Administrative Secretary-General of its intention to adhere or accede to this Charter.

2. The Administrative Secretary-General shall, on receipt of such notification, communicate a copy of it to all the Member States. Admission shall be decided by a simple majority of the Member States. The decision of each Member State shall be transmitted to the Administrative Secretary-General, who shall, upon receipt of the required number of votes, communicate the decision to the State concerned.

Article XXIX MISCELLANEOUS

The working languages of the Organization and all its institutions shall be, if possible African languages, English and French.

Article XXX

The Administrative Secretary-General may accept on behalf of the Organization gifts, bequests and other donations made to the Organization, provided that this is approved by the Council of Ministers.

Article XXXI

The Council of Ministers shall decide on the privileges and immunities to be accorded to the personnel of the Secretariat in the respective territories of the Member States.

Article XXXII CESSATION OF MEMBERSHIP

Any State which desires to renounce its membership shall forward a written notification to the Administrative Secretary-General. At the end of one year from the date of such notification, if not withdrawn, the Charter shall cease to apply with respect to the renouncing State, which shall thereby cease to belong to the Organization.

Article XXXIII AMENDMENT OF THE CHARTER

This Charter may be amended or revised if any Member State makes a written request to the Administrative Secretary-General to that effect; provided, however, that the proposed amendment is not submitted to the Assembly for consideration until all the Member States have been duly notified of it and a period of one year has elapsed. Such an amendment will not be effective unless approved by at least two-thirds of all the Member States.

C. LAW OF THE SEA

7. EXTRACTS FROM UNITED NATIONS CONVENTION ON THE LAW OF THE SEA
(UN DOCUMENT A/CONF 62/122 OF OCTOBER 7 1982;
21 ILM 1261 (1982))

{Done at Montego Bay, December 10, 1982}

Part I. Introduction

Article 1 Use of terms and scope

1. For the purposes of this Convention:

(1) "Area" means the sea-bed and ocean floor and subsoil thereof, beyond the limits of national jurisdiction;

(2) "Authority" means the International Sea-Bed Authority;

(3) "activities in the Area" means all activities of exploration for, and exploitation of, the resources of the Area;

(4) "pollution of the marine environment" means the introduction by man, directly or indirectly, of substances or energy into the marine environment, including estuaries, which results or is likely to result in such deleterious effects as harm to living resources and marine life, hazards to human health, hindrance to marine activities, including fishing or other legitimate uses of the sea, impairment of quality for use of sea water and reduction of amenities;

(5) (a) "dumping" means;

   (i) any deliberate disposal of wastes or other matter from vessels, aircraft, platforms or other man-made structures at sea;

any deliberate disposal of vessels, aircraft, platforms or other man-made structures at sea;

   (b) "dumping" does not include:

   (i) the disposal of wastes or other matter incidental to, or derived from the normal operations of vessels, aircraft, platforms or other man-made structures at sea and their equipment, other than wastes or other matter transported by or to vessels, aircraft, platforms or other man-made structures at sea, operating for the purpose of disposal of such matter or derived from the treatment of such wastes or other matter on such vessels, aircraft, platforms or structures;

   (ii) placement of matter for the purpose other than the mere disposal thereof, provided that such placement is not contrary to the aims of this Convention.

2. (1) "States Parties" means States which have consented to be bound by this convention and for which this Convention is in force.

(2) This Convention applies *mutatis mutandis* to the entities referred to in article 305, paragraph 1*(b)*, *(c)*, *(d)*, *(e)* and *(f)*, which become Parties to this Convention in accordance with the conditions relevant to each, and to that extent "States Parties" refers to those entities.

Part II. Territorial sea and contiguous zone

Section 1. General provisions

Article 2.   Legal status of the territorial sea, of the air space over the territorial sea and of its bed and subsoil

1. The sovereignty of a coastal State extends beyond its land territory and internal waters and, in the case of an archipelagic State, its archipelagic waters, to an adjacent belt of sea, described as the territorial sea.

2. This sovereignty extends to the air space over the territorial sea as well as to its bed and subsoil.

3. The sovereignty over the territorial sea is exercised subject to this Convention and to other rules of international law.

Section 2. Limits of the territorial sea

Article 3.   Breadth of the territorial sea

Every State has the right to establish the breadth of its territorial sea up to a limit not exceeding 12 nautical miles, measured from baselines determined in accordance with this Convention.

Article 4.   Outer limit of the territorial sea

The outer limit of the territorial sea is the line every point of which is at a distance from the nearest point of the baseline equal to the breadth of the territorial sea.

Article 5.   Normal baseline

Except where otherwise provided in this Convention, the normal baseline for measuring the breadth of the territorial sea is the low-water line along the coast as marked on large-scale charts officially recognized by the coastal State.

Article 6.   Reefs

In the case of islands situated on atolls or of islands having fringing reefs, the baseline for measuring the breadth of the territorial sea is the seaward low-water line of the reef, as shown by the appropriate symbol on charts officially recognized by the coastal State.

Article 7.   Straight baselines

1. In localities where the coastline is deeply indented and cut into, or if there is a fringe of islands along the coast in its immediate vicinity, the method of straight baselines joining appropriate points may be employed in drawing the baseline from which the breadth of the territorial sea is measured.

2. Where because of the presence of a delta and other natural conditions the coastline is highly unstable, the appropriate points may be selected along the furthest seaward extent of the low-water line and, notwithstanding subsequent regression of the low-water line, the straight baselines shall remain effective until changed by the coastal State in accordance with this Convention.

3. The drawing of straight baselines must not depart to any appreciable extent from the general direction of the coast, and the sea areas lying within the lines must be sufficiently closely linked to the land domain to be subject to the regime of internal waters.

4. Straight baselines shall not be drawn to and from low-tide elevations, unless lighthouses or similar installations which are permanently above sea level have been built on them or except in instances where the drawing of baselines to and from such elevations has received general international recognition.

5. Where the method of straight baselines is applicable under paragraph 1, account may be taken, in determining particular baselines, of economic interests peculiar to the region concerned, the reality and the importance of which are clearly evidenced by long usage.

6. The system of straight baselines may not be applied by a State in such a manner as to cut off the territorial sea of another State from the high seas or an exclusive economic zone.

Article 8. Internal waters

1. Except as provided in Part IV, waters on the landward side of the baseline of the territorial sea form part of the internal waters of the State.

2. Where the establishment of a straight baseline in accordance with the method set forth in article 7 has the effect of enclosing as internal waters areas which had not previously been considered as such, a right of innocent passage as provided in this Convention shall exist in those waters.

Article 9. Mouths of rivers

If a river flows directly into the sea, the baseline shall be a straight line across the mouth of the river between points on the low-water line of its banks.

Article 10. Bays

1. This article relates only to bays the coasts of which belong to a single State.

2. For the purposes of this Convention, a bay is a well-marked indentation whose penetration is in such proportion to the width of its mouth as to contain land-locked waters and constitute more than a mere curvature of the coast. An indentation shall not, however, be regarded as a bay unless its area is as large as, or larger than, that of the semi-circle whose diameter is a line drawn across the mouth of that indentation.

3. For the purpose of measurement, the area of an indentation is that lying between the low-water mark around the shore of the indentation and a line joining the low-water marks of its natural entrance points. Where, because of the presence of islands, an indentation has more than one mouth, the semi-circle shall be drawn on a line as long as the sum total of the lengths of the lines across the different mouths. Islands within an indentation shall be included as if they were part of the water area of the indentation.

4. If the distance between the low-water marks of the natural entrance points of a bay does not exceed 24 nautical miles, a closing line may be drawn between these two low-water marks, and the waters enclosed thereby shall be considered as internal waters.

5. Where the distance between the low-water marks of the natural entrance points of a bay exceeds 24 nautical miles, a straight baseline of 24 nautical miles shall be drawn within the bay in such a manner as to enclose the maximum area of water that is possible with a line of that length.

6. The foregoing provisions do not apply to so-called ''historic'' bays, or in any case where the system of straight baselines provided for in article 7 is applied.

Article 11. Ports

For the purpose of delimiting the territorial sea, the outer-most permanent harbour works which form an integral part of the harbour system are regarded as forming part of the coast. Off-shore installations and artificial islands shall not be considered as permanent harbour works.

Article 12. *Roadsteads*

Roadsteads which are normally used for the loading, unloading and anchoring of ships, and which would otherwise be situated wholly or partly outside the outer limit of the territorial sea, are included in the territorial sea.

Article 13. *Low-tide elevations*

1. A low-tide elevation is a naturally formed area of land which is surrounded by and above water at low tide but submerged at high tide. Where a low-tide elevation is situated wholly or partly at a distance not exceeding the breadth of the territorial sea from the mainland or an island, the low-water line on that elevation may be used as the baseline for measuring the breadth of the territorial sea.

2. Where a low-tide elevation is wholly situated at a distance exceeding the breadth of the territorial sea from the mainland or an island, it has no territorial sea of its own.

Article 14. *Combination of methods for determining baselines*

The coastal State may determine baselines in turn by any of the methods provided for in the foregoing articles to suit different conditions.

Article 15. *Delimitation of the territorial sea between States with opposite or adjacent coasts*

Where the coasts of two States are opposite or adjacent to each other, neither of the two States is entitled, failing agreement between them to the contrary, to extend its territorial sea beyond the median line every point of which is equidistant from the nearest points on the baselines from which the breadth of the territorial sea of each of two States is measured. The above provision does not apply, however, where it is necessary by reason of historic title or other special circumstances to delimit the territorial seas of the two States in a way which is at variance therewith.

Article 16. *Charts and lists of geographical co-ordinates*

1. The baselines for measuring the breadth of the territorial sea determined in accordance with articles 7, 9 and 10, or the limits derived therefrom, and the lines of delimitation drawn in accordance with articles 12 and 15 shall be shown on charts of a scale or scales adequate for ascertaining their position. Alternately, a list of geographical co-ordinates of points, specifying the geodetic datum, may be substituted.

2. The coastal State shall give due publicity to such charts or lists of geographical co-ordinates and shall deposit a copy of each such chart or list with the Secretary-General of the United Nations.

SECTION 3. INNOCENT PASSAGE IN THE TERRITORIAL SEA

SUBSECTION A.   RULES APPLICABLE TO ALL SHIPS

Article 17. *Right of innocent passage*

Subject to this Convention, ships of all States, whether coastal or land-locked, enjoy the right of innocent passage through the territorial sea.

Article 18.   Meaning of passage

1. Passage means navigation through the territorial sea for the purpose of:

(a) traversing that sea without entering internal waters or calling at a roadstead or port facility outside internal waters; or

(b) proceeding to or from internal waters or a call at such roadstead or port facility.

2. Passage shall be continuous and expeditious. However, passage includes stopping and anchoring, but only in so far as the same are incidental to ordinary navigation or are rendered necessary by *force majeure* or distress or for the purpose of rendering assistance to persons, ships or aircraft in danger or distress.

Article 19.   Meaning of innocent passage

1. Passage is innocent so long as it is not prejudicial to the peace, good order or security of the coastal State. Such passage shall take place in conformity with this Convention and with other rules of international law.

2. Passage of a foreign ship shall be considered to be prejudicial to the peace, good order or security of the coastal State if in the territorial sea it engages in any of the following activities:

(a) any threat or use of force against the sovereignty, territorial integrity or political independence of the coastal State, or in any other manner in violation of the principles of international law embodied in the Charter of the United Nations:

(b) any exercise or practice with weapons of any kind;

(c) any act aimed at collecting information to the prejudice of the defence or security of the coastal State;

(d) any act of propaganda aimed at affecting the defence or security of the coastal State;

(e) the launching, landing or taking on board of any aircraft;

(f) the launching, landing or taking on board of any military device;

(g) the loading or unloading of any commodity, currency or person contrary to the customs, fiscal, immigration or sanitary laws and regulations of the coastal State;

(h) any act of wilful and serious pollution contrary to this Convention;

(i) any fishing activities;

(j) the carrying out of research or survey activities;

(k) any act aimed at interfering with any systems of communication or any other facilities or installations of the coastal State;

(l) any other activity not having a direct bearing on passage.

Article 20.   Submarines and other underwater vehicles

In the territorial sea, submarines and other underwater vehicles are required to navigate on the surface and to show their flag.

Article 21.   Laws and regulations of the coastal State relating to innocent passage

1. The coastal State may adopt laws and regulations, in conformity with the provisions of this Convention and other rules of international law, relating to innocent passage through the territorial sea, in respect of all or any of the following:

(a) the safety of navigation and the regulation of maritime traffic;

(b) the protection of navigational aids and facilities and other facilities or installations;

(c) the protection of cables and pipelines;

(d) the conservation of the living resources of the sea;

(e) the prevention of infringement of the fisheries laws and regulations of the coastal State;

(f) the preservation of the environment of the coastal State and the prevention, reduction and control of pollution thereof;

(g) marine scientific research and hydrographic surveys;

(h) the prevention of infringement of the customs, fiscal, immigration or sanitary laws and regulations of the coastal State.

2. Such laws and regulations shall not apply to the design, construction, manning or equipment of foreign ships unless they are giving effect to generally accepted international rules or standards.

3. The coastal State shall give due publicity to all such laws and regulations.

4. Foreign ships exercising the right of innocent passage through the territorial sea shall comply with all such laws and regulations and all generally accepted international regulations relating to the prevention of collisions at sea.

Article 22. Sea lanes and traffic separation schemes in the territorial sea

1. The coastal State may, where necessary having regard to the safety of navigation, require foreign ships exercising the right of innocent passage through its territorial sea to use such sea lanes and traffic separation schemes as it may designate or prescribe for the regulation of the passage of ships.

2. In particular, tankers, nuclear-powered ships and ships carrying nuclear or other inherently dangerous or noxious substances or materials may be required to confine their passage to such sea lanes.

3. In the designation of sea lanes and the prescription of traffic separation schemes under this article, the coastal State shall take into account:

(a) the recommendation of the competent international organization;

(b) any channels customarily used for international navigation;

(c) the special characteristics of particular ships and channels; and

(d) the density of traffic.

4. The coastal State shall clearly indicate such sea lanes and traffic separation schemes on charts to which due publicity shall be given.

Article 23. Foreign nuclear-powered ships and ships carrying nuclear or other inherently dangerous or noxious substances

Foreign nuclear-powered ships and ships carrying nuclear or other inherently dangerous or noxious substances shall, when exercising the right of innocent passage through the territorial sea, carry documents and observe special precautionary measures established for such ships by international agreements.

Article 24. Duties of the coastal State

1. The coastal State shall not hamper the innocent passage of foreign ships through the territorial sea except in accordance with this Convention. In particular, in the application of this Convention or of any laws or regulations adopted in conformity with this Convention, the coastal State shall not:

(a) impose requirements on foreign ships which have the practical effect of denying or impairing the right of innocent passage; or

(b) discriminate in form or in fact against the ships of any State or against ships carrying cargoes to, from or on behalf of any State.

2. The coastal State shall give appropriate publicity to any danger to navigation, of which it has knowledge, within its territorial sea.

Article 25. *Rights of protection of the coastal State*

1. The coastal State may take the necessary steps in its territorial sea to prevent passage which is not innocent.

2. In the case of ships proceeding to internal waters or a call at a port facility outside-internal waters, the coastal State also has the right to take the necessary steps to prevent any breach of the conditions to which admission of those ships to internal waters or such a call is subject.

3. The coastal State may, without discrimination in form or in fact among foreign ships, suspend temporarily in specified areas of its territorial sea the innocent passage of foreign ships if such suspension is essential for the protection of its security, including weapons exercises. Such suspension shall take effect only after having been duly published.

Article 26. *Charges which may be levied upon foreign ships*

1. No charge may be levied upon foreign ships by reason only of their passage through the territorial sea.

2. Charges may be levied upon a foreign ship passing through the territorial sea as payment only for specific services rendered to the ship. These charges shall be levied without discrimination.

SUB-SECTION B. RULES APPLICABLE TO MERCHANT SHIPS AND GOVERNMENT SHIPS OPERATED FOR COMMERCIAL PURPOSES

Article 27. *Criminal jurisdiction on board a foreign ship*

1. The criminal jurisdiction of the coastal State should not be exercised on board a foreign ship passing through the territorial sea to arrest any person or to conduct any investigation in connection with any crime committed on board the ship during its passage, save only in the following cases:

(a) if the consequences of the crime extend to the coastal State;

(b) if the crime is of a kind to disturb the peace of the country or the good order of the territorial sea;

(c) if the assistance of the local authorities has been requested by the master of the ship or by a diplomatic agent or consular officer of the flag State; or

(d) if such measures are necessary for the suppression of illicit traffic in narcotic drugs or psychotropic substances.

2. The above provisions do not affect the right of the coastal State to take any steps authorized by its laws for the purpose of an arrest or investigation on board a foreign ship passing through the territorial sea after leaving internal waters.

3. In the cases provided for in paragraphs 1 and 2, the coastal State shall, if the master so requests, notify a diplomatic agent or consular officer of the flag State before taking

any steps, and shall facilitate contact between such agent or officer and the ship's crew. In cases of emergency this notification may be communicated while the measures are being taken.

4. In considering whether or in what manner an arrest should be made, the local authorities shall have due regard to the interests of navigation.

5. Except as provided in Part XII or with respect to violations of laws and regulations adopted in accordance with Part V, the coastal State may not take any steps on board a foreign ship passing through the territorial sea to arrest any person or to conduct any investigation in connection with any crime committed before the ship entered the territorial sea, if the ship, proceeding from a foreign port, is only passing through the territorial sea without entering internal waters.

Article 28.   Civil jurisdiction in relation to foreign ships

1. The coastal State should not stop or divert a foreign ship passing through the territorial sea for the purpose of exercising civil jurisdiction in relation to a person on board the ship.

2. The coastal State may not levy execution against or arrest the ship for the purpose of any civil proceedings, save only in respect of obligations or liabilities assumed or incurred by the ship itself in the course or for the purpose of its voyage through the waters of the coastal State.

3. Paragraph 2 is without prejudice to the right of the coastal State, in accordance with its laws, to levy execution against or to arrest, for the purpose of any civil proceedings, a foreign ship lying in the territorial sea, or passing through the territorial sea after leaving internal waters.

SUBSECTION C. RULES APPLICABLE TO WARSHIPS AND OTHER GOVERNMENT SHIPS OPERATED FOR NON-COMMERCIAL PURPOSES

Article 29.   Definition of warships

For the purposes of this Convention, ''warship'' means a ship belonging to the armed forces of a State bearing the external marks distinguishing such ships of its nationality, under the command of an officer duly commissioned by the Government of the State and whose name appears in the appropriate service list or its equivalent, and manned by a crew which is under regular armed forces discipline.

Article 30.   Non-compliance by warships with the laws and regulations of the coastal State

If any warship does not comply with the laws and regulations of the coastal State concerning passage through the territorial sea and disregards any request for compliance therewith which is made to it, the coastal State may require it to leave the territorial sea immediately.

Article 31.   Responsibility of the flag State for damage caused by a warship or other government ship operated for non-commercial purposes

The flag State shall bear international responsibility for any loss or damage to the coastal State resulting from the non-compliance by a warship or other government ship operated for non-commercial purposes with the laws and regulations of the coastal State concerning passage through the territorial sea or with the provisions of this Convention or other rules of international law.

Article 32. Immunities of warships and other government ships operated for non-commercial purposes

With such exceptions as are contained in subsection A and in articles 30 and 31, nothing in this Convention affects the immunities of warships and other government ships operated for non-commercial purposes.

SECTION 4. CONTIGUOUS ZONE

Article 33. Contiguous zone

1. In a zone contiguous to its territorial sea, described as the contiguous zone, the coastal State may exercise the control necessary to:

(a) prevent infringement of its customs, fiscal, immigration or sanitary laws and regulations within its territory or territorial sea;

(b) punish infringement of the above laws and regulations committed within its territory or territorial sea.

2. The contiguous zone may not extend beyond 24 nautical miles from the baselines from which the breadth of the territorial sea is measured.

Part III. Straits used for international navigation

SECTION 1. GENERAL PROVISIONS

Article 34. Legal status of waters forming straits used for international navigation

1. The regime of passage through the straits used for international navigation established in this Part shall not in other respects affect the legal status of the waters forming such straits or the exercise by the States bordering the straits of their sovereignty or jurisdiction over such waters and their air space, bed and subsoil.

2. The sovereignty or jurisdiction of the States bordering the straits is exercised subject to this part and to other rules of international law.

Article 35. Scope of this part

Nothing in this Part affects:

(a) any areas of internal waters within a strait, except where the establishment of a straight baseline in accordance with the method set forth in article 7 has the effect of enclosing as internal waters areas which had not previously been considered as such;

(b) the legal status of the waters beyond the territorial seas of States bordering straits as exclusive economic zones or seas; or

(c) the legal regime in straits in which passage is regulated in whole or in part by long-standing international conventions in force specifically relating to such straits.

Article 36. High seas routes or routes through exclusive economic zones through straits used for international navigation

This Part does not apply to a strait used for international navigation if there exists through the strait a route through the high seas or through an exclusive economic zone of similar convenience with respect to navigational and hydrographical characteristics; in such routes, the other relevant parts of this Convention, including the provisions regarding the freedom of navigation and overflight, apply.

Article 37. Scope of this section

This section applies to straits which are used for international navigation between one part of the high seas or an exclusive economic zone and another part of the high seas or an exclusive economic zone.

Article 38. Right of transit passage

1. In straits referred to in article 37, all ships and aircraft enjoy the right of transit passage, which shall not be impeded; except that, if the strait is formed by an island of a State bordering the strait and its mainland, transit passage shall not apply if there exists seaward of the island a route through the high seas or through an exclusive economic zone of similar convenience with respect to navigational and hydrographical characteristics.

2. Transit passage means the exercise in accordance with this Part of the freedom of navigation and overflight solely for the purpose of continuous and expeditious transit of the strait between one part of the high seas or an exclusive economic zone. However, the requirement of continuous and exeditious transit does not preclude passage through the strait for the purpose of entering, leaving or returning from a State bordering the strait, subject to the conditions of entry to that State.

3. Any activity which is not an exercise of the right of transit passage through a strait remains subject to the other applicable provisions of this Convention.

Article 39. Duties of ships and aircraft during transit passage

1. Ships and aircraft, while exercising the right of transit passage, shall:

(a) proceed without delay through or over the strait;

(b) refrain from any threat or use of force against the sovereignty, territorial integrity or political independence of States bordering the strait, or in any other manner in violation of the principles of international law embodied in the Charter of the United Nations;

(c) refrain from any activities other than those incident to their normal modes of continuous and expeditious transit unless rendered necessary by *force majeure* or by distress:

(d) comply with generally accepted international regulations, procedures and practices for the prevention, reduction and control of pollution from ships.

3. Aircraft in transit passage shall:

(a) observe the Rules of the Air established by the International Civil Aviation Organization as they apply to civil aircraft; state aircraft will normally comply with such safety measures and will at all times operate with due regard for the safety of navigation;

(b) at all times monitor the radio frequency assigned by the competent internationally designated air traffic control authority or the appropriate international distress radio frequency.

Article 40. Research and survey activities

During transit passage, foreign ships, including marine scientific research and hydrographic suvey ships, may not carry out any research or survey activities without the prior authorization of the States bordering straits.

Part V. Exclusive economic zone

Article 55.   Specific legal regime of the exclusive economic zone

The exclusive economic zone is an area beyond and adjacent to the territorial sea, subject to the specific legal regime established in this Part, under which the rights and jurisdiction of the coastal State and the rights and freedoms of other States are governed by the relevant provisions of this Convention.

Article 56.   Rights, jurisdiction and duties of the coastal State in the exclusive economic zone

1. In the exclusive economic zone, the coastal State has:

(a) sovereign rights for the purpose of exploring and exploiting, conserving and managing the natural resources, whether living or non-living, of the waters superjacent to the sea-bed and of the sea-bed and its subsoil, and with regard to other activities for the economic exploitation and exploration of the zone, such as the production of energy from the water, currents and winds;

(b) jurisdiction as provided for in the relevant provisions of this Convention with regard to:

  (i)   the establishment and use of artificial islands, installations and structures;

  (ii) marine scientific research;

  (iii) the protection and preservation of the marine environment;

(c) other rights and duties provided for in this Convention.

2. In exercising its rights and performing its duties under this Convention in the exclusive economic zone, the coastal State shall have due regard to the rights and duties of other States and shall act in a manner compatible with the provisions of this Convention.

3. The rights set out in this article with respect to the sea-bed and subsoil shall be exercised in accordance with Part VI.

Article 57.   Breadth of the exclusive economic zone

The exclusive economic zone shall not extend beyond 200 nautical miles from the baselines from which the breadth of the territorial sea is measured.

Article 58.   Rights and duties of other States in the exclusive economic zone

1. In the exclusive economic zone, all States, whether coastal or land-locked, enjoy, subject to the relevant provisions of this Convention, the freedoms referred to in article 87 of navigation and overflight and of the laying of submarine cables and pipelines, and other internationally lawful uses of the sea related to these freedoms, such as those associated with the operation of ships, aircraft and submarine cables and pipelines, and compatible with the other provisions of this Convention.

2. Articles 88 to 115 and other pertinent rules of international law apply to the exclusive economic zone in so far as they are not incompatible with this Part.

3. In exercising their rights and performing their duties under this Convention in the exclusive economic zone, States shall have due regard to the rights and duties of the

coastal State and shall comply with the laws and regulations adopted by the coastal State in accordance with the provisions of this Convention and other rules of international law in so far as they are not incompatible with this Part.

Article 59. Basis for the resolution of conflicts regarding the attribution of rights and jurisdiction in the exclusive economic zone

In cases where this Convention does not attribute rights or jurisdiction to the coastal State or to other States within the exclusive economic zone, and a conflict arises between the interests of the coastal State and any other State or States, the conflict should be resolved on the basis of equity and in the light of all the relevant circumstances, taking into account the respective importance of the interests involved to the parties as well as to the international community as a whole.

Article 60. Artificial islands, installations and structures in the exclusive economic zone

1. In the exclusive economic zone, the coastal State shall have the exclusive right to construct and to authorize and regulate the construction, operation and use of:

(a) artificial islands;

(b) installations and structures for the purposes provided for in article 56 and other economic purposes;

(c) installations and structures which may interfere with the exercise of the rights of the coastal State in the zone.

2. The coastal State shall have exclusive jurisdiction over such artificial islands, installations and structures, including jurisdiction with regard to customs, fiscal, health, safety and immigration laws and regulations.

3. Due notice must be given of the construction of such artificial islands, installations or structures, and permanent means for giving warning of their presence must be maintained. Any installations or structures which are abandoned or disused shall be removed to ensure safety of navigation, taking into account any generally accepted international standards established in this regard by the competent international organization. Such removal shall also have due regard to fishing, the protection of the marine environment and the rights and duties of other States. Appropriate publicity shall be given to the depth, position and dimensions of any installations or structures not entirely removed.

4. The coastal State may, where necessary, establish reasonable safety zones around such artificial islands, installations and structures in which it may take appropriate measures to ensure the safety both of navigation and of the artificial islands, installations and structures.

5. The breadth of the safety zones shall be determined by the coastal State, taking into account applicable international standards. Such zones shall be designed to ensure that they are reasonably related to the nature and function of the artificial islands, installations or structures, and shall not exceed a distance of 500 metres around them, measured from each point of their outer edge, except as authorized by generally accepted international standards or as recommended by the competent international organization. Due notice shall be given of the extent of safety zones.

6. All ships must respect these safety zones and shall comply with generally accepted international standards regarding navigation in the vicinity of artificial islands, installations, structures and safety zones.

7. Artificial islands, installations and structures and the safety zones around them may not be established where interference may be caused to the use of recognized sea lanes concerned with international navigation.

8. Artificial islands, installations and structures do not possess the status of islands. They have no territorial sea of their own, and their presence does not affect the delimitation of the territorial sea, the exclusive economic zone or the continental shelf.

Part VI. Continental Shelf

Article 76. Definition of Continental Shelf

1. The continental shelf of a coastal State comprises the sea-bed and subsoil of the submarine areas that extend beyond its territorial sea throughout the natural prolongation of its land territory to the outer edge of the continental margin, or to a distance of 200 nautical miles from the baselines from which the breadth of the territorial sea is measured where the outer edge of the continental margin does not extend up to that distance.

2. The continental shelf of a coastal State shall not extend beyond the limits provided for in paragraphs 4 to 6.

3. The continental margin comprises the submerged prolongation of the land mass of the coastal State, and consists of the sea-bed and subsoil of the shelf, the slope and the rise. It does not include the deep ocean floor with its oceanic ridges or the subsoil thereof.

4. *(a)* For the purposes of this Convention, the coastal State shall establish the outer edge of the continental margin wherever the margin extends beyond 200 nautical miles from the baselines from which the breadth of the territorial sea is measured, by either:

   (i)   a line delineated in accordance with paragraph 7 by reference to the outermost fixed points at each of which the thickness of sedimentary rocks is at least 1 per cent of the shortest distance from such point to the foot of the continental slope; or

   (ii)   a line delineated in accordance with paragraph 7 by reference to fixed points not more than 60 nautical miles from the foot of the continental slope.

(b) In the absence of evidence to the contrary, the foot of the continental slope shall be determined as the point of maximum change in the gradient at its base.

5. The fixed points comprising the line of the outer limits of the continental shelf on the sea-bed, drawn in accordance with paragraph 4 *(a)* (i) and (ii), either shall not exceed 350 nautical miles from the baselines from which the breadth of the territorial sea is measured or shall not exceed 100 nautical miles from the 2,500-metre isobath, which is a line connecting the depth of 2,500 metres.

6. Notwithstanding the provisions of paragraph 5, on submarine ridges, the outer limit of the continental shelf shall not exceed 350 nautical miles from the baselines from which the breadth of the territorial sea is measured. This paragraph does not apply to submarine elevations that are natural components of the continental margin, such as its plateaux, rises, caps, banks and spurs.

7. The coastal State shall delineate the outer limits of its continental shelf, where that shelf extends beyond 200 nautical miles from the baselines from which the breadth of the territorial sea is measured, by straight lines not exceeding 60 nautical miles in length, connecting fixed points, defined by co-ordinates of latitude and longitude.

8. Information on the limits of the continental shelf beyond 200 nautical miles from the baselines from which the breadth of the territorial sea is measured shall be submitted by the coastal State to the Commission on the Limits of the Continental Shelf set up under Annex II on the basis of equitable geographical representation. The Commission shall make recommendations to coastal States on matters related to the establishment of

the outer limits of their continental shelf. The limits of the shelf established by a coastal State on the basis of these recommendations shall be final and binding.

9. The coastal State shall deposit with the Secretary-General of the United Nations charts and relevant information, including geodetic data, permanently describing the outer limits of its continental shelf. The Secretary-General shall give due publicity thereto.

10. The provisions of this article are without prejudice to the question of delimitation of the continental shelf between States with opposite or adjacent coasts.

Article 77. Rights of the coastal State over the continental shelf

1. The coastal State exercises over the continental shelf sovereign rights for the purpose of exploring it and exploiting its natural resources.

2. The rights referred to in paragraph 1 are exclusive in the sense that if the coastal State does not explore the continental shelf or exploit its natural resources, no one may undertake these activities without the express consent of the coastal State.

3. The rights of the coastal State over the continental shelf do not depend on occupation, effective or notional, or on any express proclamation.

4. The natural resources referred to in this Part consist of the mineral and other non-living resources of the sea-bed and subsoil together with living organisms belonging to sedentary species, that is to say, organisms which, at the harvestable stage, either are immobile on or under the sea-bed or are unable to move except in constant physical contact with the sea-bed or the subsoil.

Article 78. Legal status of the superjacent waters and air space and the rights and freedoms of other States

1. The rights of the coastal State over the continental shelf do not affect the legal status of the superjacent waters or of the air space above those waters.

2. The exercise of the rights of the coastal State over the continental shelf must not infringe or result in any unjustifiable interference with navigation and other rights and freedoms of other States as provided for in this Convention.

Article 79. Submarine cables and pipelines on the continental shelf

1. All States are entitled to lay submarine cables and pipelines on the continental shelf, in accordance with the provisions of this article.

2. Subject to its right to take reasonable measures for the exploration of the continental shelf, the exploitation of its natural resources and the prevention, reduction and control of pollution from pipelines, the coastal State may not impede the laying or maintenance of such cables or pipelines.

3. The delineation of the course for the laying of such pipelines on the continental shelf is subject to the consent of the coastal State.

4. Nothing in this Part affects the right of the coastal State to establish conditions for cables or pipelines entering its territory or territorial sea, or its jurisdiction over cables and pipelines constructed or used in connection with the exploration of its continental shelf or exploitation of its resources or the operations of artificial islands, installations and structures under its jurisdiction.

5. When laying submarine cables or pipelines. States shall have due regard to cables or pipelines already in position. In particular, possibilities of repairing existing cables or pipelines shall not be prejudiced.

Article 80.   Artificial islands, installations and structures on the continental shelf

Article 60 applies *mutatis mutandis* to artificial islands, installations and structures on the continental shelf.

Article 81.   Drilling on the continental shelf

The coastal State shall have the exclusive right to authorize and regulate drilling on the continental shelf for all purposes.

Article 82.   Payments and contributions with respect to the exploitation of the continental shelf beyond 200 nautical miles

1. The coastal State shall make payments or contributions in kind in respect of the exploitation of the non-living resources of the continental shelf beyond 200 nautical miles from the baselines from which the breadth of the territorial sea is measured.

2. The payments and contributions shall be made annually with respect to all production at a site after the first five years of production at that site. For the sixth year, the rate of payment or contribution shall be 1 per cent of the value or volume of production at the site. The rate shall increase by 1 per cent for each subsequent year until the twelfth year and shall remain at 7 per cent thereafter. Production does not include resources used in connection with exploitation.

3. A developing State which is a net importer of a mineral resource produced from its continental shelf is exempt from making such payments or contributions in respect of that mineral resource.

4. The payments or contributions shall be made through the Authority, which shall distribute them to States Parties to this Convention, on the basis of equitable sharing criteria, taking into account the interests and needs of developing States, particularly the least developed and the land-locked among them.

Article 83.   Delimitation of the continental shelf between States with opposite or adjacent coasts

1. The delimitation of the continental shelf between States with opposite or adjacent coasts shall be effected by agreement on the basis of international law, as referred to in Article 38 of the Statute of the International Court of Justice, in order to achieve an equitable solution.

2. If no agreement can be reached within a reasonable period of time, the States concerned shall resort to the procedures provided for in Part XV.

3. Pending agreement as provided for in paragraph 1, the States concerned, in a spirit of understanding and co-operation, shall make every effort to enter into provisional arrangements of a practical nature and, during this transitional period, not to jeopardize or hamper the reaching of the final agreement. Such arrangements shall be without prejudice to the final delimitation.

4. Where there is an agreement in force between the States concerned, questions relating to the delimitation of the continental shelf shall be determined in accordance with the provisions of that agreement.

Article 84.   Charts and lists of geographical co-ordinates

1. Subject to this Part, the outer limit lines of the continental shelf and the lines of delimitation drawn in accordance with article 83 shall be shown on charts of a scale or scales adequate for ascertaining their position. Where appropriate, lists of geographical co-ordinates of points, specifying the geodetic datum, may be substituted for such outer limit lines or lines of delimitation.

2. The coastal State shall give due publicity to such charts or lists of geographical co-ordinates and shall deposit a copy of each such chart or list with the Secretary-General of the United Nations and, in the case of those showing the outer limit lines of the continental shelf, with the Secretary-General of the Authority.

Article 85.   Tunnelling

This Part does not prejudice the right of the coastal State to exploit the subsoil by means of tunnelling, irrespective of the depth of water above the subsoil.

Part VII. High Seas

SECTION 1. GENERAL PROVISIONS

Article 86.   Application of the provisions of this Part

The provisions of this Part apply to all parts of the sea that are not included in the exclusive economic zone, in the territorial sea or in the internal waters of a State, or in the archipelagic waters of an archipelagic State. This article does not entail any abridgement of the freedoms enjoyed by all States in the exclusive economic zone in accordance with article 58.

Article 87.   Freedom of the high seas

1. The high seas are open to all States, whether coastal or land-locked. Freedom of the high seas is exercised under the conditions laid down by this Convention and by other rules of international law. It comprises, *inter alia*, both for coastal and land-locked States:

(a) freedom of navigation;

(b) freedom of overflight;

(c) freedom to lay submarine cables and pipelines, subject to Part VI;

(d) freedom to construct artificial islands and other installations permitted under international law, subject to Part VI;

(e) freedom of fishing, subject to the conditions laid down in section 2;

(f) freedom of scientific research, subject to Parts VI and XIII.

2. These freedoms shall be exercised by all States with due regard for the interests of other States in their exercise of the freedom of the high seas, and also with due regard for the rights under this Convention with respect to activities in the Area.

Article 88.   Reservation of the high seas for peaceful purposes

The high seas shall be reserved for peaceful purposes.

Article 89.   Invalidity of claims of sovereignty over the high seas

No state may validly purport to subject any part of the high seas to its sovereignty.

Article 90. Right of navigation

Every State, whether coastal or land-locked, has the right to sail ships flying its flag on the high seas.

Article 91. Nationality of ships

1. Every State shall fix the conditions for the grant of its nationality to ships, for the registration of ships in its territory and for the right to fly its flag. Ships have the nationality of the State whose flag they are entitled to fly. There must exist a genuine link between the State and the ship.

2. Every State shall issue to ships to which it has granted the right to fly its flag documents to that effect.

Article 92. Status of ships

1. Ships shall sail under the flag of one State only and, save in exceptional cases expressly provided for in international treaties or in this Convention, shall be subject to its exclusive jurisdiction on the high seas. A ship may not change its flag during a voyage or while in a port of call, save in the case of a real transfer of ownership or change of registry.

2. A ship which sails under the flags of two or more States, using them according to convenience, may not claim any of the nationalities in question with respect to any other State, and may be assimilated to a ship without nationality.

Article 93. Ships flying the flag of the United Nations, its specialized agencies and the International Atomic Energy Agency

The preceding articles do not prejudice the question of ships employed on the official service of the United Nations, its specialized agencies or the International Atomic Energy Agency, flying the flag of the Organization.

Article 94. Duties of the flag State

1. Every State shall effectively exercise its jurisdiction and control in administrative, technical and social matters over ships flying its flag.

2. In particular every State shall:

(*a*) maintain a register of ships containing the names and particulars of ships flying its flag, except those which are excluded from generally accepted international regulations on account of their small size; and

(*b*) assume jurisdiction under its internal law over each ship flying its flag and its master, officers and crew in respect of administrative, technical and social matters concerning the ship.

3. Every State shall take such measures for ships flying its flag as are necessary to ensure safety at sea with regard, *inter alia*, to:

(*a*) the construction, equipment and seaworthiness of ships;

(*b*) the manning of ships, labour conditions and the training of crews, taking into account the applicable international instruments;

(*c*) the use of signals, the maintenance of communications and the prevention of collisions.

4. Such measures shall include those necessary to ensure:

(a) that each ship, before registration and thereafter at appropriate intervals, is surveyed by a qualified surveyor of ships, and has on board such charts, nautical publications and navigational equipment and instruments as are appropriate for the safe navigation of the ship;

(b) that each ship is in the charge of a master and officers who possess appropriate qualifications, in particular in seamanship, navigation, communications and marine engineering, and that the crew is appropriate in qualification and numbers for the type, size, machinery and equipment of the ship;

(c) that the master, officers and, to the extent appropriate, the crew are fully conversant with and required to observe the applicable international regulations concerning the safety of life at sea, the prevention of collisions, the prevention, reduction and control of marine pollution, and the maintenance of communications by radio.

5. In taking the measures called for in paragraphs 3 and 4 each State is required to conform to generally accepted international regulations, procedures and practices and to take any steps which may be necessary to secure their observance.

6. A State which has clear grounds to believe that proper jurisdiction and control with respect to a ship have not been exercised may report the facts to the flag State. Upon receiving such a report, the flag State shall investigate the matter and, if appropriate, take any action necessary to remedy the situation.

7. Each State shall cause an inquiry to be held by or before a suitably qualified person or persons into every marine casualty or incident of navigation on the high seas involving a ship flying its flag and causing loss of life or serious injury to nationals of another State or serious damage to ships or installations of another State or to the marine environment. The flag State and the other State shall co-operate in the conduct of any inquiry held by that other State into any such marine casualty or incident of navigation.

Article 95.   Immunity of warships on the high seas

Warships on the high seas have complete immunity from the jurisdiction of any State other than the flag State.

Article 96.   Immunity of ships used only on government non-commercial service

Ships owned or operated by a State and used only on government non-commercial service shall, on the high seas, have complete immunity from the jurisdiction of any State other than the flag State.

Article 97.   Penal jurisdiction in matters of collision or any other incident of navigation

1. In the event of a collision or any other incident of navigation concerning a ship on the high seas, involving the penal or disciplinary responsibility of the master or of any other person in the service of the ship, no penal or disciplinary proceedings may be instituted against such person except before the judicial or administrative authorities either of the flag State or of the State of which such person is a national.

2. In disciplinary matters, the State which has issued a master's certificate or a certificate of competence or license shall alone be competent, after due legal process, to pronounce the withdrawal of such certificate, even if the holder is not a national of the State which issued it.

3. No arrest or detention of the ship, even as a measure of investigation, shall be ordered by any authorities other than those of the flag State.

Article 98.   Duty to render assistance

1. Every State shall require the master of a ship flying its flag, in so far as he can do so without serious danger to the ship, the crew or the passengers:

(a) to render assistance to any person found at sea in danger of being lost;

(b) to proceed with all possible speed to the rescue of persons in distress, if informed of their need of assistance, in so far as such action may reasonably be expected of him;

(c) after a collision, to render assistance to the other ship, its crew and its passengers and, where possible, to inform the other ship of the name of his own ship, its port of registry and the nearest port at which it will call.

2. Every coastal State shall promote the establishment, operation and maintenance of an adequate and effective search and rescue service regarding safety on and over the sea and, where circumstances so require, by way of mutual regional arrangements co-operate with neighbouring States for this purpose.

Article 99.   Prohibition of the transport of slaves

Every State shall take effective measures to prevent and punish the transport of slaves in ships authorized to fly its flag and to prevent the unlawful use of its flag for that purpose. Any slave taking refuge on board any ship, whatever its flag, shall *ipso facto* be free.

Article 100.   Duty to co-operate in the repression of piracy

All States shall co-operate to the fullest possible extent in the repression of piracy on the high seas or in any other place outside the jurisdiction of any State.

Article 101.   Definition of piracy

Piracy consists of any of the following acts:

(a) any illegal acts of violence or detention, or any act of depredation, committed for private ends by the crew or the passengers of a private ship or a private aircraft, and directed:

   (i)   on the high seas, against another ship or aircraft, or against persons or property on board such ship or aircraft;

   (ii) against a ship, aircraft, persons or property in a place outside the jurisdiction of any State;

(b) any act of voluntary participation in the operation of a ship or of an aircraft with knowledge of facts making it a pirate ship or aircraft;

(c) any act of inciting or of intentionally facilitating an act described in subparagraph *(a)* or *(b)*.

Article 102.   Piracy by a warship, government ship or government aircraft whose crew has mutinied

The acts of piracy, as defined in article 101, committed by a warship, government ship or government aircraft whose crew has mutinied and taken control of the ship or aircraft are annilated to acts committed by a private ship or aircraft.

Article 103.   Definition of a pirate ship or aircraft

A ship or aircraft is considered a pirate ship or aircraft if it is intended by the persons in dominant control to be used for the purpose of committing one of the acts referred to in article 101. The same applies if the ship or aircraft has been used to commit any such act, so long as it remains under the control of the persons guilty of that act.

Article 104. *Retention or loss of the nationality of a pirate ship or aircraft*

A ship or aircraft may retain its nationality although it has become a pirate ship or aircraft. The retention or loss of nationality is determined by the law of the State from which such nationality was derived.

Article 105. *Seizure of a pirate ship or aircraft*

On the high seas, or in any other place outside the jurisdiction of any State, every State may seize a pirate ship or aircraft, or a ship or aircraft taken by piracy and under the control of pirates, and arrest the persons and seize the property on board. The courts of the State which carried out the seizure may decide upon the penalties to be imposed, and may also determine the action to be taken with regard to the ships, aircraft or property, subject to the rights of third parties acting in good faith.

Article 106. *Liability for seizure without adequate grounds*

Where the seizure of a ship or aircraft on suspicion of piracy has been effected without adequate grounds, the State making the seizure shall be liable to the State the nationality of which is possessed by the ship or aircraft for any loss or damage caused by the seizure.

Article 107. *Ships and aircraft which are entitled to seize on account of piracy*

A seizure on account of piracy may be carried out only by warships or military aircraft, or other ships or aircraft clearly marked and identifiable as being on government service and authorized to that effect.

Article 108. *Illicit traffic in narcotic drugs or psychotropic substances*

1. All States shall co-operate in the suppression of illicit traffic in narcotic drugs and psychotropic substances engaged in by ships on the high seas contrary to international conventions.

2. Any State which has reasonable grounds for believing that a ship flying its flag is engaged in illicit traffic in narcotic drugs or psychotropic substances may request the co-operation of other States to suppress such traffic.

Article 109. *Unauthorized broadcasting from the high seas*

1. All States shall co-operate in the suppression of unauthorized broadcasting from the high seas.

2. For the purposes of this Convention. ''unauthorized broadcasting'' means the transmission of sound radio or television broadcasts from a ship or installation on the high seas intended for reception by the general public contrary to international regulations, but excluding the transmission of distress calls.

3. Any person engaged in unauthorized broadcasting may be prosecuted before the court of:

(*a*) the flag State of the ship;

(*b*) the State of registry of the installation;

(*c*) the State of which the person is a national;

(d) any State where the transmissions can be received; or

(e) any State where authorized radio communication is suffering interference.

4. On the high seas, a State having jurisdiction in accordance with paragraph 3 may, in conformity with article 110, arrest any person or ship engaged in unauthorized broadcasting and seize the broadcasting apparatus.

Article 110.   Right of visit

1. Except where acts of interference derive from powers conferred by treaty, a warship which encounters on the high seas a foreign ship, other than a ship entitled to complete immunity in accordance with articles 95 and 96, is not justified in boarding it unless there is reasonable ground for suspecting that:

(a) the ship is engaged in piracy;

(b) the ship is engaged in the slave trade;

(c) the ship is engaged in unauthorized broadcasting and the flag State of the warship has jurisdiction under article 109;

(d) the ship is without nationality; or

(e) though flying a foreign flag or refusing to show its flag, the ship is, in reality, of the same nationality as the warship.

2. In the cases provided for in paragraph 1, the warship may proceed to verify the ship's right to fly its flag. To this end, it may send a boat under the command of an officer to the suspected ship. If suspicion remains after the documents have been checked, it may proceed to a further examination on board the ship, which must be carried out with all possible consideration.

3. If the suspicions prove to be unfounded, and provided that the ship boarded has not committed any act justifying them, it shall be compensated for any loss or damage that may have been sustained.

4. These provisions apply *mutatis mutandis* to military aircraft.

5. The provisions also apply to any other authorized ships or aircraft clearly marked and identifiable as being on government service.

Article 111.   Right of hot pursuit

1. The hot pursuit of a foreign ship may be undertaken when the competent authorities of the coastal State have good reason to believe that the ship has violated the laws and regulations of that State. Such pursuit must be commenced when the foreign ship or one of its boats is within the internal waters, the archipelagic waters, the territorial sea or the contiguous zone of the pursuing State, and may only be continued outside the territorial sea or the contiguous zone if the pursuit has not been interrupted. It is not necessary that, at the time when the foreign ship within the territorial sea or the contiguous zone receives the order to stop, the ship giving the order should likewise be within the territorial sea or the contiguous zone. If the foreign ship is within a contiguous zone, as defined in article 33, the pursuit may only be undertaken if there has been a violation of the rights for the protection of which the zone was established.

2. The right of hot pursuit shall apply *mutatis mutandis* to violations in the exclusive economic zone or on the continental shelf, including safety zones around continental shelf installations, of the laws and regulations of the coastal State applicable in accordance with this Convention to the exclusive economic zone or the continental shelf, including such safety zones.

3. The right of hot pursuit ceases as soon as the ship pursued enters the territorial sea of its own State or of a third State.

4. Hot pursuit is not deemed to have begun unless the pursuing ship has satisfied itself by such practicable means as may be available that the ship pursued or one of its boats or other craft working as a team and using the ship pursued as a mother ship is within the limits of the territorial sea, or, as the case may be, within the contiguous zone or the exclusive economic zone or above the continental shelf. The pursuit may only be commenced after a visual or auditory signal to stop has been given at a distance which enables it to be seen or heard by the foreign ship.

5. The right of hot pursuit may be exercised only by warships or military aircraft, or other ships or aircraft clearly marked and identifiable as being on government service and authorized to that effect.

6. Where hot pursuit is effected by an aircraft:

(a) the provisions of paragraph 1 to 4 shall apply *mutatis mutandis*;

(b) the aircraft giving the order to stop must itself actively pursue the ship until a ship or another aircraft of the coastal State, summoned by the aircraft, arrives to take over the pursuit, unless the aircraft is itself able to arrest the ship. It does not suffice to justify an arrest outside the territorial sea that the ship was merely sighted by the aircraft as an offender or suspected offender, if it was not both ordered to stop and pursued by the aircraft itself or other aircraft or ships which continued the pursuit without interruption.

7. The release of a ship arrested within the jurisdiction of a State and escorted to a port of that State for the purposes of an inquiry before the competent authorities may not be claimed solely on the ground that the ship, in the course of its voyage, was escorted across a portion of the exclusive economic zone or the high seas, if the circumstances rendered that necessary.

8. Where a ship has been stopped or arrested outside the territorial sea in circumstances which do not justify the exercise of the right of hot pursuit, it shall be compensated for any loss or damage that may have been thereby sustained.

Article 112.   Right to lay submarine cables and pipelines

1. All States are entitled to lay submarine cables and pipelines on the bed of the high seas beyond the continental shelf.

2. Article 79, paragraph 5, applies to such cables and pipelines.

Article 113.   Breaking or injury of a submarine cable or pipeline

Every State shall adopt the laws and regulations necessary to provide that the breaking or injury by a ship flying its flag or by a person subject to its jurisdiction of a submarine cable beneath the high seas done wilfully or through culpable negligence, in such a manner as to be liable to interrupt or obstruct telegraphic or telephonic communications, and similarly the breaking or injury of a submarine pipeline or high-voltage power cable, shall be a punishable offence. This provision shall apply also to conduct calculated or likely to result in such breaking or injury. However, it shall not apply to any break or injury caused by persons who acted merely with the legitimate object of saving their lives or their ships, after having taken all necessary precautions to avoid such break or injury.

Article 114.   Breaking or injury by owners of a submarine cable or pipeline of another submarine cable or pipeline

Every State shall adopt the laws and regulations necessary to provide that, if persons subject to its jurisdiction who are the owners of a submarine cable or pipeline beneath the high seas, in laying or repairing that cable or pipeline cause a break in or injury to another cable or pipeline, they shall bear the cost of the repairs.

Article 115.   Indemnity for loss incurred in avoiding injury to a submarine cable or pipeline

Every State shall adopt the laws and regulations necessary to ensure that the owners of ships who can prove that they have sacrificed an anchor, a net or any other fishing gear, in order to avoid injuring a submarine cable or pipeline, shall be indemnified by the owner of the cable or pipeline, provided that the owner of the ship has taken all reasonable precautionary measures beforehand.

Part X. Right of Access of Land-Locked States to and from the sea and freedom of transit

Article 124.   Use of terms

1. For the purposes of this Convention:

(a) "land-locked State" means a State which has no sea-coast;

(b) "transit State" means a State, with or without a sea-coast, situated between a land-locked State and the sea, through whose territory traffic in transit passes;

(c) "traffic in transit" means transit of persons, baggage, goods and means of transport across the territory of one or more transit States, when the passage across such territory, with or without trans-shipment, warehousing, breaking bulk or change in the mode of transport, is only a portion of a complete journey which begins or terminates within the territory of the land-locked State;

(d) "means of transport" means:

   (i) railway rolling stock, sea, lake and river craft and road vehicles;

   (ii) where local conditions so require, porters and pack animals.

2. Land-locked States and transit States may, by agreement between them, include as means of transport pipelines and gas lines and means of transport other than those included in paragraph 1.

Article 125.   Right of access to and from the sea and freedom of transit

1. Land-locked States shall have the right of access to and from the sea for the purpose of exercising the rights provided for in this Convention including those relating to the freedom of the high seas and the common heritage of mankind. To this end, land-locked States shall enjoy freedom of transit through the territory of transit States by all means of transport.

2. The terms and modalities for exercising freedom of transit shall be agreed between the land-locked States and transit States concerned through bilateral, subregional or regional agreements.

3. Transit States, in the exercise of their full sovereignty over their territory, shall have the right to take all measures necessary to ensure that the rights and facilities provided for in this Part for land-locked States shall in no way infringe their legitimate interests.

Article 126.   Exclusion of application of the most-favoured-nation clause

The provisions of this Convention, as well as special agreements relating to the exercise of the right of access to and from the sea, establishing rights and facilities on account of the special geographical position of land-locked States, are excluded from the application of the most-favoured-nation clause.

Article 127.   Customs duties, taxes and other charges

1. Traffic in transit shall not be subject to any customs duties, taxes or other charges except charges levied for specific services rendered in connection with such traffic.

2. Means of transport in transit and other facilities provided for and used by land-locked States shall not be subject to taxes or charges higher than those levied for the use of means of transport of the transit State.

Article 128.   Free zones and other customs facilities

For the convenience of traffic in transit, free zones or other customs facilities may be provided at the ports of entry and exit in the transit States, by agreement between those States and the land-locked States.

Article 129.   Co-operation in the construction and improvement of means of transport

Where there are no means of transport in transit States to give effect to the freedom of transit or where the existing means, including the port installations and equipment, are inadequate in any respect, the transit States and land-locked States concerned may co-operate in constructing or improving them.

Article 130.   Measures to avoid or eliminate delays or other difficulties of a technical nature in traffic in transit

1. Transit States shall take all appropriate measures to avoid delays or other difficulties of a technical nature in traffic in transit.

2. Should such delays or difficulties occur, the competent authorities of the transit States and land-locked States concerned shall co-operate towards their expeditious elimination.

Article 131.   Equal treatment in maritime ports

Ships flying the flag of land-locked States shall enjoy treatment equal to that accorded to other foreign ships in maritime ports.

Article 132.   Grant of greater transit facilities

This Convention does not entail in any way the withdrawal of transit facilities which are greater than those provided for in this Convention and which are agreed between States Parties to this Convention or granted by a State Party. This Convention also does not preclude such grant of greater facilities in the future.

Part XI. The area

Section 1. General provisions

Article 133.   Use of terms

For the purposes of this Part:

(a) "resources" means all solid, liquid or gaseous mineral resources *in situ* in the Area at or beneath the sea-bed, including polymetalic nodules;

(b) resources when recovered from the Area, are referred to as "minerals".

Article 134.   Scope of this Part

1. This Part applies to the Area.

2. Activities in the Area shall be governed by the provisions of this Part.

3. The requirements concerning deposit of, and publicity to be given to, the charts or lists of geographical co-ordinates showing the limits referred to in article 1, paragraph 1 (1), are set forth in Part VI.

4. Nothing in this article affects the establishment of the outer limits of the continental shelf in accordance with Part VI or the validity of agreements relating to delimitation between States with opposite or adjacent coasts.

Article 135.   Legal status of the superjacent waters and air space

Neither this Part nor any rights granted or exercised pursuant thereto shall affect the legal status of the waters superjacent to the Area or that of the air space above those waters.

SECTION 2. PRINCIPLES GOVERNING THE AREA

Article 136.   Common heritage of mankind

The Area and its resources are the common heritage of mankind.

Article 137.   Legal status of the Area and its resources

1. No State shall claim or exercise sovereignty or sovereign rights over any part of the Area or its resources, nor shall any State or natural or juridical person appropriate any part thereof. No such claim or exercise of sovereignty or sovereign rights nor such appropriation shall be recognized.

2. All rights in the resources of the Area are vested in mankind as a whole, on whose behalf the Authority shall act. These resources are not subject to alienation. The minerals recovered from the Area, however, may only be alienated in accordance with this Part and the rules, regulations and procedures of the Authority.

3. No State or natural or juridical person shall claim, acquire or exercise rights with respect to the minerals recovered from the Area except in accordance with this Part. Otherwise, no such claim, acquisition or exercise of such rights shall be recognized.

Article 138.   General conduct of States in relation to the Area

The general conduct of States in relation to the Area shall be in accordance with the provisions of this Part, the principles embodied in the Charter of the United Nations and other rules of international law in the interests of maintaining peace and security and promoting international co-operation and mutual understanding.

Article 139.   Responsibility to ensure compliance and liability for damage

1. States Parties shall have the responsibility to ensure that activities in the Area, whether carried out by States Parties, or state enterprises or natural or juridical persons which possess the nationality of States Parties or are effectively controlled by them or their nationals, shall be carried out in conformity with this Part. The same responsibility applies to international organizations for activities in the Area carried out by such organizations.

2. Without prejudice to the rules of international law and Annex III, article 22, damage caused by the failure of a State Party or international organization to carry out

its responsibilities under this Part shall entail liability; States Parties or international organizations acting together shall bear joint and several liability. A State Party shall not however be liable for damage caused by any failure to comply with this Part by a person whom it has sponsored under article 153, paragraph 2(b), if the State Party has taken all necessary and appropriate measures to secure effective compliance under article 153, paragraph 4, and Annex III, article 4, paragraph 4.

3. States Parties that are members of international organizations shall take appropriate measures to ensure the implementation of this article with respect to such organizations.

Article 140.   Benefit of mankind

1. Activities in the Area shall, as specifically provided for in this Part, be carried out for the benefit of mankind as a whole, irrespective of the geographical location of States, whether coastal or land-locked, and taking into particular consideration the interests and needs of developing States and of peoples who have not attained full independence or other self-governing status recognized by the United Nations in accordance with General Assembly resolution 1514 (XV) and other relevant General Assembly resolutions.

2. The Authority shall provide for the equitable sharing of financial and other economic benefits derived from activities in the Area through any appropriate mechanism, on a non-discriminatory basis, in accordance with article 160, paragraph 2 *(f)* (i).

Article 141.   Use of the Area exclusively for peaceful purposes

The Area shall be open to use exclusively for peaceful purposes by all States, whether coastal or land-locked, without discrimination and without prejudice to the other provisions of this Part.

Article 142.   Rights and legitimate interests of coastal States

1. Activities in the area, with respect to resource deposits in the Area which lie across limits of national jurisdiction, shall be conducted with due regard to the rights and legitimate interests of any coastal State across whose jurisdiction such deposits lie.

2. Consultations, including a system of prior notification, shall be maintained with the State concerned, with a view to avoiding infringement of such rights and interests. In cases where activities in the Area may result in the exploitation of resources lying within national jurisdiction, the prior consent of the coastal State concerned shall be required.

3. Neither this Part nor any rights granted or exercised pursuant thereto shall affect the rights of coastal States to take such measures consistent with the relevant provisions of Part XII as may be necessary to prevent, mitigate or eliminate grave and imminent danger to their coastline, or related interests from pollution or threat thereof or from other hazardous occurrences resulting from or caused by any activities in the Area.

Article 143.   Marine scientific research

1. Marine scientific research in the Area shall be carried out exclusively for peaceful purposes and for the benefit of mankind as a whole, in accordance with Part XIII.

2. The Authority may carry out marine scientific research concerning the Area and its resources, and may enter into contracts for that purpose. The Authority shall promote and encourage the conduct of marine scientific research in the Area, and shall co-ordinate and disseminate the results of such research and analysis when available.

3. States Parties may carry out marine scientific research in the Area. States Parties shall promote international co-operation in marine scientific research in the Area by:

(a) participating in international programmes and encouraging co-operation in marine scientific research by personnel of different countries and of the Authority;

(b) ensuring that programmes are developed through the Authority or other international organizations as appropriate for the benefit of developing States and technologically less developed States with a view to:

  (i) strengthening their research capabilities;

  (ii) training their personnel and the personnel of the Authority in the techniques and applications of research;

  (iii) fostering the employment of their qualified personnel in research in the Area;

(c) effectively disseminating the results of research and analysis when available, through the Authority or other international channels when appropriate.

Article 144. Transfer of technology

1. The Authority shall take measures in accordance with this Convention:

(a) to acquire technology and scientific knowledge relating to activities in the Area; and

(b) to promote and encourage the transfer to developing States of such technology and scientific knowledge so that all States Parties benefit therefrom.

2. To this end the Authority and States Parties shall co-operate in promoting the transfer of technology and scientific knowledge relating to activities in the Area so that the Enterprise and all States Parties may benefit therefrom. In particular they shall initiate and promote:

(a) programmes for the transfer of technology to the Enterprise and to developing States with regard to activities in the Area, including *inter alia*, facilitating the access of the enterprise and of developing States to the relevant technology, under fair and reasonable terms and conditions;

(b) measures directed towards the advancement of the technology of the Enterprise and the domestic technology of developing States, particularly by providing opportunities personnel from the Enterprise and from developing States for training in marine science and technology and for their full participation in activities in the Area.

8. THE ANTARCTIC TREATY 1959 (402 UNTS 71)

The Governments of Argentina, Australia, Belgium, Chile, the French Republic, Japan, New Zealand, Norway, the Union of South Africa, the Union of Soviet Socialist Republics, the United Kingdom of Great Britain and Northern Ireland, and the United States of America,

Recognizing that it is in the interest of all mankind that Antarctica shall continue forever to be used exclusively for peaceful purposes and shall not become the scene or object of international discord;

Acknowledging the substantial contributions to scientific knowledge resulting from international cooperation in scientific investigation in Antarctica;

Convinced that the establishment of a firm foundation for the continuation and development of such cooperation on the basis of freedom of scientific investigation in Antarctica as applied during the International Geophysical Year accords with the interests of science and the progress of all mankind;

Convinced also that a treaty ensuring the use of Antarctica for peaceful purposes only and the continuance of international harmony in Antarctica will further the purposes and principles embodied in the Charter of the United Nations;

Have agreed as follows:

Article I

1. Antarctica shall be used for peaceful purposes only. There shall be prohibited, *inter alia*, any measures of a military nature, such as the establishment of military bases and fortifications, the carrying out of military maneuvers, as well as the testing of any type of weapons.

2. The present Treaty shall not prevent the use of military personnel or equipment for scientific research or for any other peaceful purpose.

Article II

Freedom of scientific investigation in Antarctica and cooperation toward that end, as applied during the International Geophysical Year, shall continue, subject to the provisions of the present Treaty.

Article III

1. In order to promote international cooperation in scientific investigation in Antarctica, as provided for in Article II of the present Treaty, the Contracting Parties agree that, to the greatest extent feasible and practicable:

(a) information regarding plans for scientific programs in Antarctica shall be exchanged to permit maximum economy and efficiency of operations;

(b) scientific personnel shall be exchanged in Antarctica between expeditions and stations;

(c) scientific observations and results from Antarctica shall be exchanged and made freely available.

2. In implementing this article, every encouragement shall be given to the establishment of cooperative working relations with those Specialized Agencies of the United Nations and other international organizations having a scientific or technical interest in Antarctica.

Article IV

1. Nothing contained in the present Treaty shall be interpreted as:

(a) a renunciation by any Contracting Party of previously asserted rights of or claims to territorial sovereignty in Antarctica;

(b) a renunciation or diminution by any Contracting Party of any basis of claim to territorial sovereignty in Antarctica which it may wether as a result of its activities or those of its nationals in Antarctica, or otherwise;

(c) prejudicing the position of any Contracting Party as regards its recognition or non-recognition of any other State's right of or claim or basis of claim to territorial sovereignty in Antarctica.

2. No acts or activities taking place while the present Treaty is in force shall constitute a basis for asserting, supporting or denying a claim to territorial sovereignty in Antarctica or create any rights of sovereignty in Antarctica. No new claim, or

enlargement of an existing claim, to territorial sovereignty in Antarctica shall be asserted while the present Treaty is in force.

Article V

1. Any nuclear explosions in Antarctica and the disposal there of radio-active waste material shall be prohibited.

2. In the event of the conclusion of international agreements concerning the use of nuclear energy, including nuclear explosions and the disposal of radioactive waste material, to which all of the Contracting Parties whose representatives are entitled to participate in the meetings provided for under article IX are parties, the rules established under such agreements shall apply in Antarctica.

Article VI

The provisions of the present Treaty shall apply to the area south of 60° South Latitude, including all ice shelves, but nothing in the present Treaty shall prejudice or in any way affect the rights, or the exercise of the rights, of any State under international law with regard to the high seas within that area.

Article VII

1. In order to promote the objectives and ensure the observance of the provisions of the present Treaty, each Contracting Party whose representatives are entitled to participate in the meetings referred to in Article IX of the Treaty shall have the right to designate observers to carry out any inspection provided for by the present Article. Observers shall be nationals of the Contracting Parties which designate them. The names of observers shall be communicated to every other Contracting Party having the right to designate observers, and like notice shall be given of the termination of their appointment.

2. Each observer designated in accordance with the provisions of paragraph 1 of this Article shall have complete freedom of access at any time to any or all areas of Antarctica.

3. All areas of Antarctica, including all stations, installations and equipment within those areas, and all ships and aircraft at points of discharging or embarking cargoes or personnel in Antarctica, shall be open at all times to inspection by any observers designated in accordance with paragraph 1 of this Article.

4. Aerial observation may be carried out at any time over any or all areas of Antarctica by any of the Contracting Parties having the right to designate observers.

5. Each Contracting Party shall, at the time when the present Treaty enters into force for it, inform the other Contracting Parties, and thereafter shall give them notice in advance, of

(a) all expeditions to and within Antarctica, on the part of its ships or nationals, and all expeditions to Antarctica organized in or proceeding from its territory;

(b) all stations in Antarctica occupied by its nationals; and

(c) any military personnel or equipment intended to be introduced by it into Antarctica subject to the conditions prescribed in paragraph 2 of Article I of the present Treaty.

Article VIII

1. In order to facilitate the exercise of their functions under the present Treaty, and without prejudice to the respective positions of the Contracting Parties relating to

jurisdiction over all other persons in Antarctica, observers designated under paragraph 1 of Article VII and scientific personnel exchanged under subparagraph 1 *(b)* of Article III of the Treaty, and members of the staffs accompanying any such persons, shall be subject only to the jurisdiction of the Contracting Party of which they are nationals in respect of all acts or omissions occurring while they are in Antarctica for the purpose of exercising their functions.

2. Without prejudice to the provisions of paragraph 1 of this Article, and pending the adoption of measures in pursuance of subparagraph 1 *(e)* of Article IX, the Contracting Parties concerned in any case of dispute with regard to the exercise of jurisdiction in Antarctica shall immediately consult together with a view to reaching a mutually acceptable solution.

Article IX

1. Representatives of the Contracting Parties named in the preamble to the present Treaty shall meet at the City of Canberra within two months after the date of entry into force of the Treaty, and thereafter at suitable intervals and places, for the purpose of exchanging information, consulting together on matters of common interest pertaining to Antarctica, and formulating and considering, and recommending to their Governments, measures in furtherance of the principles and objectives of the Treaty, including measures regarding:

(a) use of Antarctica for peaceful purposes only;

(b) facilitation of scientific research in Antarctica;

(c) facilitation of international scientific cooperation in Antarctica;

(d) facilitation of the exercise of the rights of inspection provided for in Article VII of the Treaty;

(e) questions relating to the exercise of jurisdiction in Antarctica;

(f) preservation and conservation of living resources in Antarctica.

2. Each Contracting Party which has become a party to the present Treaty by accession under Article XIII shall be entitled to appoint representatives to participate in the meetings referred to in paragraph 1 of the present Article, during such time as that Contracting Party demonstrates its interest in Antarctica by conducting substantial scientific research activity there, such as the establishment of a scientific station or the despatch of a scientific expedition.

3. Reports from the observers referred to in Article VII of the present Treaty shall be transmitted to the representatives of the Contracting Parties participating in the meetings referred to in paragraph 1 of the present Article.

4. The measures referred to in paragraph 1 of this article shall become effective when approved by all the Contracting Parties whose representatives were entitled to participate in the meetings held to consider those measures.

5. Any or all of the rights established in the present Treaty may be exercised as from the date of entry into force of the Treaty whether or not any measures facilitating the exercise of such rights have been proposed, considered or approved as provided in this Article.

Article X

Each of the Contracting Parties undertakes to exert appropriate efforts, consistent with the Charter of the United Nations, to the end that no one engages in any activity in Antarctica contrary to the principles or purposes of the present Treaty.

Article XI

1. If any dispute arises between two or more of the Contracting Parties concerning the interpretation or application of the present treaty, those Contracting Parties shall consult among themselves with a view to having the dispute resolved by negotiation, inquiry, mediation, conciliation, arbitration, judicial settlement or other peaceful means of their own choice.

2. Any dispute of this character not so resolved shall, with the consent, in each case, of all parties to the dispute, be referred to the International Court of Justice for settlement; but failure to reach agreement on reference to the International Court shall not absolve parties to the dispute from the responsibility of continuing to seek to resolve it by any of the various peaceful means referred to in paragraph 1 of this Article.

Article XII

1. *(a)* The present treaty may be modified or amended at any time by unanimous agreement of the Contracting Parties whose representatives are entitled to participate in the meetings provided for under Article IX. Any such modification or amendment shall enter into force when the depositary Government has received notice from all such Contracting Parties that they have ratified it.

(b) Such modification or amendment shall thereafter enter into force as to any other Contracting Party when notice of ratification by it has been received by the depositary Government. Any such Contracting Party from which no notice of ratification is received within a period of two years from the date of entry into force of the modification or amendment in accordance with the provisions of subparagraph 1 *(a)* of this article shall be deemed to have withdrawn from the present treaty on the date of the expiration of such period.

2. *(a)* If after the expiration of thirty years from the date of entry into force of the present Treaty, any of the Contracting Parties whose representatives are entitled to participate in the meetings provided for under Article IX so requests by a communication addressed to the depositary Government, a Conference of all the Contracting Parties shall be held as soon as practicable to review the operation of the Treaty.

(b) Any modification or amendment to the present Treaty which is approved at such a Conference by a majority of the Contracting Parties there represented, including a majority of those whose representatives are entitled to participate in the meetings provided for under Article IX, shall be communicated by the depositary Government to all the Contracting Parties immediately after the termination of the Conference and shall enter into force in accordance with the provisions of paragraph 1 of the present Article.

(c) If any such modification or amendment has not entered into force in accordance with the provisions of subparagraph 1 *(a)* of this Article within a period of two years after the date of its communication to all the Contracting Parties, any Contracting Party may at any time after the expiration of that period give notice to the depositary Government of its withdrawal from the present Treaty; and such withdrawal shall take effect two years after the receipt of the notice by the depositary Government.

Article XIII

1. The present Treaty shall be subject to ratification by the signatory States. It shall be open for accession by any State which is a Member of the United Nations, or by any other State which may be invited to accede to the Treaty with the consent of all the

Contracting Parties whose representatives are entitled to participate in the meetings provided for under Article IX of the Treaty.

2. Ratification of or accession to the present Treaty shall be effected by each State in accordance with its constitutional processes.

3. Instruments of ratification and instruments of accession shall be deposited with the Government of the United States of America, hereby designated as the depositary Government.

4. The depositary Government shall inform all signatory and acceding States of the date of each deposit of an instrument of ratification or accession, and the date of entry into force of the Treaty and of any modification or amendment thereto.

5. Upon the deposit of instruments of ratification by all the signatory States, the present Treaty shall enter into force for those States and for States which have deposited instruments of accession. Thereafter the Treaty shall enter into force for any acceding State upon the deposit of its instrument of accession.

6. The present Treaty shall be registered by the depositary Government pursuant to Article 102 of the Charter of the United Nations.

Article XIV

The present Treaty, done in the English, French, Russian and Spanish languages, each version being equally authentic, shall be deposited in the archives of the Government of the United States of America, which shall transmit duly certified copies thereof to the Governments of the signatory and acceding States.

IN WITNESS WHEREOF, the undersigned Plenipotentiaries, duly authorized, have signed the present Treaty.

DONE at Washington this first day of December, one thousand nine hundred and fifty-nine.

D. LAW OF TREATIES AND DIPLOMATIC IMMUNITY

9. VIENNA CONVENTION ON THE LAW OF TREATIES 1969
(1155 UNTS 331; 8 ILM 679 (1069))

Part I. Introduction

Article 1 *Scope of the present Convention*

The present Convention applies to treaties between States.

Article 2 *Use of terms*

1. For the purposes of the present Convention:

(a) "treaty" means an international agreement concluded between States in written form and governed by international law, whether embodied in a single instrument or in two or more related instruments and whatever its particular designation;

(b) "ratification", "acceptance", "approval" and "accession" mean in each case the international act so named whereby a State establishes on the international plane its consent to be bound by a treaty;

(c) "full powers" means a document emanating from the competent authority of a State designating a person or persons to represent the State for negotiating, adopting or authenticating the text of a treaty, for expressing the consent of the State to be bound by a treaty, or for accomplishing any other act with respect to a treaty;

(d) "reservation" means a unilateral statement, however phrased or named, made by a State, when signing, ratifying, accepting, approving or acceding to a treaty, whereby it purports to exclude or to modify the legal effect of certain provisions of the treaty in their application to that State;

(e) "negotiating State" means a State which took part in the drawing up adoption of the text of the treaty;

(f) "contracting State" means a State which has consented to be bound by the treaty, whether or not the treaty has entered into force;

(g) "partly" means a State which has consented to be bound by the treaty for which the treaty is in force;

(h) "third State" means a State not a party to the treaty;

(i) "international organization" means an intergovernmental organization.

2. The provisions of paragraph 1 regarding the use of terms in the present Convention are without prejudice to the use of those terms or to the meanings which may be given to them in the internal law of any State.

Article 3 *International agreements not within the scope of the present Convention*

The fact that the present Convention does not apply to international agreements concluded between States and other subjects of international law between such other subjects of international law, or to international agreement in written form, shall not affect:

(a) the legal force of such agreements;

(b) the application to them of any of the rules set forth in the present Convention to which they would be subject under international law independently of the Convention;

(c) the application of the Convention to the relations of States as between themselves under international agreements to which other subjects of international law are also parties.

Article 4 *Non-retroactivity of the present Convention*

Without prejudice to the application of any rules set forth in the present Convention to which treaties would be subject under international law independently of the Convention, the Convention applies only to treaties which are concluded by States after the entry into force of the present Convention with regard to such States.

Article 5 *Treaties constituting international organizations and treaties adopted within an international organization*

The present Convention applies to any treaty which is the constituent instrument of an international organization and to any treaty adopted within an international organization without prejudice to any relevant rules of the organization.

Part II. Conclusion and entry into force of treaties

SECTION 1. CONCLUSION OF TREATIES

Article 6 *Capacity of States to conclude treaties*

Every State possesses capacity to conclude treaties.

Article 7 *Full powers*

1. A person is considered as representing a State for the purpose of adopting or authenticating the text of a treaty or for the purpose of expressing the consent of the State to be bound by a treaty if:

(a) he produces appropriate full powers; or

(b) it appears from the practice of the States concerned or from other circumstances that their intention was to consider that person as representing the State for such purposes and to dispense with full powers.

2. In virtue of their functions and without having to produce full powers, the following are considered as representing their State:

(a) Heads of State, Heads of Government and Ministers for Foreign Affairs, for the purpose of performing all acts relating to the conclusion of a treaty;

(b) heads of diplomatic missions, for the purpose of adopting the text of a treaty between the accrediting State and the State to which they are accredited;

(c) representatives accredited by States to an international conference or to an international organization or one of its organs, for the purpose of adopting the text of a treaty in that conference, organization or organ.

Article 8 *Subsequent confirmation of an act performed without authorization*

An act relating to the conclusion of a treaty performed by a person who cannot be considered under article 7 as authorized to represent a state for that purpose is without legal effect unless afterwards confirmed by that State.

Article 9 *Adoption of the text*

1. The adoption of the text of a treaty takes place by the consent of all the States participating in its drawing up except as provided in paragraph 2.

2. The adoption of the text of a treaty at an international conference takes place by the vote of two-thirds of the States present and voting, unless by the same majority they shall decide to apply a different rule.

Article 10 *Authentication of the text*

The text of a treaty is established as authentic and definitive:

(a) by such procedure as may be provided for in the text or agreed upon by the States participating in its drawing up; or

(b) failing such procedure, by the signature, signature *ad referendum* or initialling by the representatives of those States of the text of the treaty or of the final Act of a conference incorporating the text.

Article 11 *Means of expressing consent to be bound by a treaty*

The consent of a State to be bound by a treaty may be expressed by signature, exchange of instruments constituting a treaty, ratification, acceptance, approval or accession, or by any other means if so agreed.

Article 12 *Consent to be bound by a treaty expressed by signature*

1. The consent of a State to be bound by a treaty is expressed by the signature of its representative when:

(a) the treaty provides that signature shall have that effect,

(b) it is otherwise established that the negotiating States were agreed that signature should have that effect, or

(c) the intention of the State to give that effect to the signature appears from the full powers of its representative or was expressed during the negotiation.

2. For the purposes of paragraph 1:

(a) the initialling of a text constitutes a signature of the treaty when it is established that the negotiating States so agreed,

(b) the signature *ad referendum* of a treaty by a representative, if confirmed by his State, constitutes a full signature of the treaty.

Article 13 *Consent to be bound by a treaty expressed by an exchange of instruments constituting a treaty*

The consent of States to be bound by a treaty constituted by instruments exchanged between them is expressed by that exchange when:

(a) the instruments provide that their exchange shall have that effect, or

(b) it is otherwise established that those States were agreed that the exchange of instruments should have that effect.

Article 14 *Consent to be bound by a treaty expressed by ratification, acceptance or approval*

1. The consent of a State to be bound by a treaty is expressed by ratification when:

(a) the treaty provides for such consent to be expressed by means of ratification,

(b) it is otherwise established that the negotiating States were agreed that ratification should be required

(c) the representative of the State has signed the treaty subject to ratification; or

(d) the intention of the State to sign the treaty subject to ratification appears from the full powers of its representative or was expressed during the negotiation.

2. The consent of a State to be bound by a treaty is expressed by acceptance or approval under conditions similar to those which apply to ratification.

Article 15 *Consent to be bound by a treaty expressed by accession*

The consent of a State to be bound by a treaty is expressed by accession when:

(a) the treaty provides that such consent may be expressed by that State by means of accession;

(b) it is otherwise established that the negotiating States were agreed that such consent may be expressed by that State by means of accession; or

(c) all the parties have subsequently agreed that such consent may be expressed by that State by means of accession.

Article 16 *Exchange or deposit of instruments of ratification, acceptance, approval or accession*

Unless the treaty otherwise provides, instruments of ratification, acceptance, approval or accession establish the consent of a State to be bound by a treaty upon:

(a) their exchange between the contracting States;

(b) their deposit with the depositary; or

(c) their notification to the contracting States or to the depositary, if so agreed.

Article 17 *Consent to be bound by part of a treaty and choice of differing provisions*

1. Without prejudice to articles 19 to 23, the consent of a State to be bound by part of a treaty is effective only if the treaty so permits or the other contracting States so agree.

2. The consent of a State to be bound by a treaty which permits a choice between differing provisions is effective only if it is made clear to which of the provisions the consent relates.

Article 18 *Obligation not to defeat the object and purpose of a treaty prior to its entry into force*

A state is obliged to refrain from acts which would defeat the object and purpose of a treaty when:

(a) it has signed the treaty or has exchanged instruments constituting the treaty subject to ratification, acceptance or approval, until it shall have made its intention clear not to become a party to the treaty; or

(b) it has expressed its consent to be bound by the treaty, pending the entry into force of the treaty and provided that such entry into force is not unduly delayed.

SECTION 2. RESERVATIONS

Article 19 *Formulation of reservations*

A State may, when signing, ratifying, accepting, approving or acceding to a treaty, formulate a reservation unless:

(a) the reservation is prohibited by the treaty;

(b) the treaty provides that only specified reservations, which do not include the reservation in question, may be made; or

(c) in cases not falling under sub-paragraphs *(a)* and *(b)*, the reservation is incompatible with the object and purpose of the treaty.

Article 20 *Acceptance of and objection to reservations*

1. A reservation expressly authorized by a treaty does not require any subsequent acceptance by the other contracting States unless the treaty so provides.

2. When it appears from the limited number of the negotiating States and the object and purpose of a treaty that the application of the treaty in its entirety between all the parties is an essential condition of the consent of each one to be bound by the treaty, a reservation requires acceptance by all the parties.

3. When a treaty is a constituent instrument of an international organization and unless it otherwise provides, a reservation requires the acceptance of the competent organ of that organization.

4. In cases not falling under the preceding paragraphs and unless the treaty otherwise provides:

(a) acceptance by another contracting State of a reservation constitutes the reserving State a party to the treaty in relation to that other State if or when the treaty is in force for those States;

(b) an objection by another contracting State to a reservation does not preclude the entry into force of the treaty as between the objecting and reserving States unless a contrary intention is definitely expressed by the objecting State;

(c) an act expressing a State's consent to be bound by the treaty and containing a reservation is effective as soon as at least one other contracting State has accepted the reservation.

5. For the purposes of paragraphs 2 and 4 and unless the treaty otherwise provides, a reservation is considered to have been accepted by a State if it shall have raised no objection to the reservation by the end of a period of twelve months after it was notified of the reservation or by the date on which it expressed its consent to be bound by the treaty, whichever is later.

Article 21 *Legal effects of reservations and of objections to reservations*

1. A reservation established with regard to another party in accordance with articles 19, 20 and 23:

(a) modifies for the reserving State in its relations with that other party the provisions of the treaty to which the reservation relates to the extent of the reservation; and

(b) modifies those provisions to the same extent for that other party in its relations with the reserving State.

2. The reservation does not modify the provisions of the treaty for the other parties to the treaty *inter se*.

3. When a State objecting to a reservation has not opposed the entry into force of the treaty between itself and the reserving State, the provisions to which the reservation relates do not apply as between the two States to the extent of the reservation.

Article 22 *Withdrawal of reservations and of objections to reservations*

1. Unless the treaty otherwise provides, a reservation may be withdrawn at any time and the consent of a State which has accepted the reservation is not required for its withdrawal.

2. Unless the treaty otherwise provides, an objection to a reservation may be withdrawn at any time.

3. Unless the treaty otherwise provides, or it is otherwise agreed:

(a) the withdrawal of a reservation becomes operative in relation to another contracting State only when notice of it has been received by that State;

(b) the withdrawal of an objection to a reservation becomes operative only when notice of it has been received by the State which formulated the reservation.

Article 23 *Procedure regarding reservations*

1. A reservation, an express acceptance of a reservation and an objection to a reservation must be formulated in writing and communicated to the contracting States and other States entitled to become parties to the treaty.

2. If formulated when signing the treaty subject to ratification, acceptance or approval, a reservation must be formally confirmed by the reserving State when expressing its consent to be bound by the treaty. In such a case the reservation shall be considered as having been made on the date of its confirmation.

3. An express acceptance of, or an objection to, a reservation made previously to confirmation of the reservation does not itself require confirmation.

4. The withdrawal of a reservation or of an objection to a reservation must be formulated in writing.

SECTION 3. ENTRY INTO FORCE AND PROVISIONAL APPLICATION OF TREATIES

Article 24 *Entry into force*

1. A treaty enters into force in such manner and upon such date as it may provide or as the negotiating States may agree.

2. Failing any such provision or agreement, a treaty enters into force as soon as consent to be bound by the treaty has been established for all the negotiating States.

3. When the consent of a State to be bound by a treaty is established on a date after the treaty has come into force, the treaty enters into force for that State on that date, unless the treaty otherwise provides.

4. The provisions of a treaty regulating the authentication of its text, the establishment of the consent of States to be bound by the treaty, the manner or date of its entry into force, reservations, the functions of the depositary and other matters arising necessarily before the entry into force of the treaty apply from the time of the adoption of its text.

Article 25 *Provisional application*

1. A treaty or a part of a treaty is applied provisionally pending its entry into force if:

(a) the treaty itself so provides; or

(b) the negotiating States have in some other manner so agreed.

2. Unless the treaty otherwise provides or the negotiating States have otherwise agreed, the provisional application of a treaty or a part of a treaty with respect to a State shall be terminated if that State notifies the other States between which the treaty is being applied provisionally of its intention not to become a party to the treaty.

Part III. Observance, application and interpretation of treaties

Article 26 *Pacta sunt servanda*

Every treaty in force is binding upon the parties to it and must be performed by them in good faith.

Article 27 *Internal law and observance of treaties*

A party may not invoke the provisions of its internal law as justification for its failure to perform a treaty. This rule is without prejudice to article 46.

Article 28 *Non-retroactivity of treaties*

Unless a different intention appears from the treaty or is otherwise established, its provisions do not bind a party in relation to any act or fact which took place or any situation which ceased to exist before the date of the entry into force of the treaty with respect to that party.

Article 29 *Territorial scope of treaties*

Unless a different intention appears from the treaty or is otherwise established, a treaty is binding upon each party in respect of its entire territory.

Article 30 *Application of successive treaties relating to the same subject-matter*

1. Subject to Article 103 of the Charter of the United Nations, the rights and obligations of States parties to successive treaties relating to the same subject-matter shall be determined in accordance with the following paragraphs.

2. When a treaty specifies that it is subject to, or that it is not to be considered as incompatible with, an earlier or later treaty, the provisions of that other treaty prevail.

3. When all the parties to the earlier treaty are parties also to the later treaty but the earlier treaty is not terminated or suspended in operation under article 59, the earlier treaty applies only to the extent that its provisions are compatible with those of the later treaty.

4. When the parties to the later treaty do not include all the parties to the earlier one:

(a) as between States parties to both treaties the same rule applies as in paragraph 3;

(b) as between a State party to both treaties and a State party to only one of the treaties, the treaty to which both States are parties governs their mutual rights and obligations.

5. Paragraph 4 is without prejudice to article 41, or to any question of the termination or suspension of the operation of a treaty under article 60 or to any question of responsibility which may arise for a State from the conclusion or application of a treaty the provisions of which are incompatible with its obligations towards another State under another treaty.

Article 31 *General rule of interpretation*

1. A treaty shall be interpreted in good faith in accordance with the ordinary meaning to be given to the terms of the treaty in their context and in the light of its object and purpose.

2. The context for the purpose of the interpretation of a treaty shall comprise, in addition to the text, including its preamble and annexes:

(a) any agreement relating to the treaty which was made between all the parties in connexion with the conclusion of the treaty;

(b) any instrument which was made by one or more parties in connexion with the conclusion of the treaty and accepted by the other parties as an instrument related to the treaty.

3. There shall be taken into account, together with the context:

(a) any subsequent agreement between the parties regarding the interpretation of the treaty or the application of its provisions;

(b) any subsequent practice in the application of the treaty which establishes the agreement of the parties regarding its interpretation;

(c) any relevant rules of international law applicable in the relations etween the parties.

4. A special meaning shall be given to a form if it is established that the parties so intended.

Article 32 *Supplementary means of interpretation*

Recourse may be had to supplementary means of interpretation, including the preparatory work of the treaty and the circumstances of its conclusion, in order to confirm the meaning resulting from the application of article 31, or to determine the meaning when the interpretation according to article 31:

(a) leaves the meaning ambiguous or obscure; or

(b) leads to a result which is manifestly absurd or unreasonable.

Article 33 *Interpretation of treaties authenticated in two or more languages*

1. When a treaty has been authenticated in two or more languages, the text is equally authoritative in each language, unless the treaty provides or the parties agree that, in case of divergence, a particular text shall prevail.

2. A version of the treaty in a language other than one of those in which the text was authenticated shall be considered an authentic text only if the treaty so provides or the parties so agree.

3. The terms of the treaty are presumed to have the same meaning in each authentic text.

4. Except where a particular text prevails in accordance with paragraph 1, when a comparison of the authentic texts discloses a difference of meaning which the application of articles 31 and 32 does not remove, the meaning which best reconciles the texts, having regard to the object and purpose of the treaty, shall be adopted.

SECTION 4. TREATIES AND THIRD STATES

Article 34 *General rule regarding third States*

A treaty does not create either obligations or rights for a third State without its consent.

Article 35 *Treaties providing for obligations for third States*

An obligation arises for a third State from a provision of a treaty if the parties to the treaty intend the provision to be the means of establishing the obligation and the third State expressly accepts that obligation in writing.

Article 36 *Treaties providing for rights for third States*

1. A right arises for a third State from a provision of a treaty if the parties to the treaty intend the provision to accord that right either to the third State, or to a group of States to which it belongs, or to all States, and the third State assents thereto. Its assent shall be presumed so long as the contrary is not indicated, unless the treaty otherwise provides.

2. A State exercising a right in accordance with paragraph 1 shall comply with the conditions for its exercise provided for in the treaty or established in conformity with the treaty.

Article 37 *Revocation or modification of obligations or rights of third States*

1. When an obligation has arisen for a third State in conformity with article 35, the obligation may be revoked or modified only with the consent of the parties to the treaty and of the third State, unless it is established that they had otherwise agreed.

2. When a right has arisen for a third State in conformity with article 36, the right may not be revoked or modified by the parties if it is established that the right was intended not to be revocable or subject to modification without the consent of the third State.

Article 38 *Rules in a treaty becoming binding on third States through international custom*

Nothing in articles 34 to 37 precludes a rule set forth in a treaty from becoming binding upon a third State as a customary rule of international law, recognized as such.

Part IV. Amendment and modification of treaties

Article 39 *General rule regarding the amendment of treaties*

A treaty may be amended by agreement between the parties. The rules laid down in Part II apply to such an agreement except in so far as the treaty may otherwise provide.

Article 40 *Amendment of multilateral treaties*

1. Unless the treaty otherwise provides, the amendment of multilateral treaties shall be governed by the following paragraphs.

2. Any proposal to amend a multilateral treaty as between all the parties must be notified to all the contracting States, each one of which shall have the right to take part in:

(a) the decision as to the action to be taken in regard to such proposal;

(b) the negotiation and conclusion of any agreement for the amendment of the treaty.

3. Every State entitled to become a party to the treaty shall also be entitled to become a party to the treaty as amended.

4. The amending agreement does not bind any State already a party to the treaty which does not become a party to the amending agreement; article 30, paragraph 4*(b)*, applies in relation to such state.

5. Any State which becomes a party to the treaty after the entry into force of the amending agreement shall, failing an expression of a different intention by that State:

(a) be considered as a party to the treaty as amended; and

(b) be considered as a party to the unamended treaty in relation to any party to the treaty not bound by the amending agreement.

Article 41 *Agreements to modify multilateral treaties between certain of the parties only*

1. Two or more of the parties to a multilateral treaty may conclude an agreement to modify the treaty as between themselves alone if:

(a) the possibility of such a modification is provided for by the treaty; or

(b) the modification in question is not prohibited by the treaty and;

  (i) does not affect the enjoyment by the other parties of their rights under the treaty or the performance of their obligations;

  (ii) does not relate to a provision, derogation from which is incompatible with the effective execution of the object and purpose of the treaty as a whole.

2. Unless in a case falling under paragraph 1*(a)* the treaty otherwise provides, the parties in question shall notify the other parties of their intention to conclude the agreement and of the modification to the treaty for which it provides.

Part V. Invalidity, termination and suspension of the operation of treaties

Section 1. General provisions

Article 42 *Validity and continuance in force of treaties*

1. The validity of a treaty or of the consent of a State to be bound by a treaty may be impeached only through the application of the present Convention.

2. The termination of a treaty, its denunciation or the withdrawal of a party, may take place only as a result of the application of the provisions of the treaty or of the present Convention. The same rule applies to suspension of the operation of a treaty.

Article 43 *Obligations imposed by international law independently of a treaty*

The invalidity, termination or denunciation of a treaty, the withdrawal of a party from it, or the suspension of its operation, as a result of the application of the present Convention or of the provisions of the treaty, shall not in any way impair the duty of any State to fulfil any obligation embodied in the treaty to which it would be subject under international law independently of the treaty.

Article 44 *Separability of treaty provisions*

1. A right of a party, provided for in a treaty or arising under article 56, to denounce, withdraw from or suspend the operation of the treaty may be exercised only with respect to the whole treaty unless the treaty otherwise provides or the parties otherwise agree.

2. A ground for invalidating, terminating, withdrawing from or suspending the operation of a treaty recognized in the present Convention may be invoked only with respect to the whole treaty except as provided in the following paragraphs or in article 60.

3. If the ground relates solely to particular clauses, it may be invoked only with respect to those clauses where:

(a) the said clauses are separable from the remainder of the treaty with regard to their application;

(b) it appears from the treaty or is otherwise established that acceptance of those clauses was not an essential basis of the consent of the other party or parties to be bound by the treaty as a whole; and

(c) continued performance of the remainder of the treaty would not be unjust.

4. In cases falling under articles 49 and 50 the State entitled to invoke the fraud or corruption may do so with respect either to the whole treaty or, subject to paragraph 3, to the particular clauses alone.

5. In cases falling under articles 51, 52 and 53, no separation of the provisions of the treaty is permitted.

Article 45 *Loss of a right to invoke a ground for invalidating, terminating, withdrawing from or suspending the operation of a treaty*

A State may no longer invoke a ground for invalidating, terminating, withdrawing from or suspending the operation of a treaty under articles 46 to 50 or articles 60 and 62 if, after becoming aware of the facts:

(a) it shall have expressly agreed that the treaty is valid or remains in force or continues in operation, as the case may be; or

(b) it must by reason of its conduct be considered as having acquiesced in the validity of the treaty or in its maintenance in force or in operation, as the case may be.

Section 2. Invalidity of treaties

Article 46 *Provisions of internal law regarding competence to conclude treaties*

1. A State may not invoke the fact that its consent to be bound by a treaty has been expressed in violation of a provision of its internal law regarding competence to conclude treaties as invalidating its consent unless that violation was manifest and concerned a rule of its internal law of fundamental importance.

2. A violation is manifest if it would be objectively evident to any State conducting itself in the matter in accordance with normal practice and in good faith.

Article 47 *Specific restrictions on authority to express the consent of a State*

If the authority of a representative to express the consent of a State to be bound by a particular treaty has been made subject to a specific restriction, his omission to observe that restriction may not be invoked as invalidating the consent expressed by him unless the restriction was notified to the other negotiating State prior to his expressing such consent.

Article 48 *Error*

1. A State may invoke an error in a treaty as invalidating its consent to be bound by the treaty if the error relates to a fact or situation which was assumed by that State to exist at the time when the treaty was concluded and formed an essential basis of its consent to be bound by the treaty.

2. Paragraph 1 shall not apply if the State in question contributed by its own conduct to the error or if the circumstances were such as to put that State on notice of a possible error.

3. An error relating only to the wording of the text of a treaty does not affect its validity; article 79 then applies.

Article 49 *Fraud*

If a State has been induced to conclude a treaty by the fraudulent conduct of another negotiating State, the State may invoke the fraud as invalidating its consent to be bound by the treaty.

Article 50 *Corruption of a representative of a State*

If the expression of a State's consent to be bound by a treaty has been procured. through the corruption of its representative directly or indirectly by another negotiating State, the State may invoke such corruption as invalidating its consent to be bound by the treaty.

Article 51 *Coercion of a representative of a State*

The expression of a State's consent to be bound by a treaty which has been procured by the coercion of its representative through acts or threats directed against him shall be without any legal effect.

Article 52 *Coercion of a State by the threat or use of force*

A treaty is void if its conclusion has been procured by the threat or use of force in violation of the principles of international law embodied in the Charter of the United Nations.

Article 53 *Treaties conflicting with a peremptory norm of general international law (jus cogens)*

A treaty is void if, at the time of its conclusion, it conflicts with a peremptory norm of general international law. For the purposes of the present Convention, a peremptory norm of general international law is a norm accepted and recognized by the international community of States as a whole as a norm from which no derogation is permitted and which can be modified only by a subsequent norm of general international law having the same character.

SECTION 3. TERMINATION AND SUSPENSION OF THE OPERATION OF TREATIES

Article 54 *Termination of or withdrawal from a treaty under its provisions or by consent of the parties*

The termination of a treaty or the withdrawal of a party may take place:

(a) in conformity with the provisions of the treaty; or

(b) at any time by consent of all the parties after consultation with the other contracting States.

Article 55 *Reduction of the parties to a multilateral treaty below the number necessary for its entry into force*

Unless the treaty otherwise provides, a multilateral treaty does not terminate by reason only of the fact that the number of the parties falls below the number necessary for its entry into force.

Article 56 *Denunciation of or withdrawal from a treaty containing no provision regarding termination, denunciation or withdrawal*

1. A treaty which contains no provision regarding its termination and which does not provide for denunciation or withdrawal is not subject to denunciation or withdrawal unless:

(a) it is established that the parties intended to admit the possibility of denunciation or withdrawal; or

(b) a right of denunciation or withdrawal may be implied by the nature of the treaty.

2. A party shall give not less than twelve months' notice of its intention to denounce or withdraw from a treaty under paragraph 1.

Article 57 *Suspension of the operation of a treaty under its provisions or by consent of the parties*

The operation of a treaty in regard to all the parties or to a particular party may be suspended:

(a) in conformity with the provisions of the treaty; or

(b) at any time by consent of all the parties after consultation with the other contracting States.

Article 58 *Suspension of the operation of a multilateral treaty by agreement between certain of the parties only*

1. Two or more parties to a multilateral treaty may conclude an agreement to suspend the operation of provisions of the treaty, temporarily and as between themselves alone, if:

(a) the possibility of such a suspension is provided for by the treaty; or

(b) the suspension in question is not prohibited by the treaty and:

    (i) does not affect the enjoyment by the other parties of their rights under the treaty or the performance of their obligations;

    (ii) is not incompatible with the object and purpose of the treaty.

2. Unless in a case falling under paragraph 1*(a)* the treaty otherwise provides, the parties in question shall notify the other parties of their intention to conclude the agreement and of those provisions of the treaty the operation of which they intend to suspend.

Article 59 *Termination or suspension of the operation of a treaty implied by conclusion of a later treaty*

1. A treaty shall be considered as terminated if all the parties to it conclude a later treaty relating to the same subject-matter and:

(a) it appears from the later treaty or is otherwise established that the parties intended that the matter should be governed by that treaty; or

(b) the provisions of the later treaty are so far incompatible with those of the earlier one that the two treaties are not capable of being applied at the same time.

2. The earlier treaty shall be considered as only suspended in operation if it appears from the later treaty or is otherwise established that such was the intention of the parties.

Article 60 *Termination or suspension of the operation of a treaty as a consequence of its breach*

1. A material breach of a bilateral treaty by one of the parties entitles the other to invoke the breach as a ground for terminating the treaty or suspending its operation in whole or in part.

2. A material breach of a multilateral treaty by one of the parties entitles:

(a) the other parties by unanimous agreement to suspend the operation of the treaty in whole or in part or to terminate it either:

(i) in the relations between themselves and the defaulting State, or

(ii) as between all the parties;

(b) a party specially affected by the breach to invoke it as a ground for suspending the operation of the treaty in whole or in part in the relations between itself and the defaulting State;

(c) any party other than the defaulting State to invoke the breach as a ground for suspending the operation of the treaty in whole or in part with respect to itself if the treaty is of such a character that a material breach of its provisions by one party radically changes the position of every party with respect to the further performance of its obligations under the treaty.

3. A material breach of a treaty, for the purposes of this article, consists in:

(a) a repudiation of the treaty not sanctioned by the present Convention; or

(b) the violation of a provision essential to the accomplishment of the object or purpose of the treaty.

4. The foregoing paragraphs are without prejudice to any provision in the treaty applicable in the event of a breach.

5. Paragraphs 1 to 3 do not apply to provisions relating to the protection of the human person contained in treaties of a humanitarian character, in particular to provisions prohibiting any form of reprisals against persons protected by such treaties.

Article 61 *Supervening impossibility of performance*

1. A party may invoke the impossibility of performing a treaty as a ground for terminating or withdrawing from it if the impossibility results from the permanent disappearance or destruction of an object indispensable for the execution of the treaty. If the impossibility is temporary, it may be invoked only as a ground for suspending the operation of the treaty.

2. Impossibility of performance may not be invoked by a party as a ground for terminating, withdrawing from or suspending the operation of a treaty if the impossibility is the result of a breach by that party either of an obligation under the treaty or of any other international obligation owed to any other party to the treaty.

Article 62 *Fundamental change of circumstances*

1. A fundamental change of circumstances which has occurred with regard to those existing at the time of the conclusion of a treaty, and which was not foreseen by the parties, may not be invoked as a ground for terminating or withdrawing from the treaty unless:

(a) the existence of those circumstances constituted an essential basis of the consent of the parties to be bound by the treaty; and

(b) the effect of the change is radically to transform the extent of obligations still to be performed under the treaty.

2. A fundamental change of circumstances may not be invoked as a ground for terminating or withdrawing from a treaty:

(a) if the treaty establishes a boundary; or

(b) if the fundamental change is the result of a breach by the party invoking it either of an obligation under the treaty or of any other international obligation owed to any other party to the treaty.

3. If, under the foregoing paragraphs, a party may invoke a fundamental change of circumstances as a ground for terminating or withdrawing from a treaty it may also invoke the change as a ground for suspending the operation of the treaty.

Article 63 *Severance of diplomatic or consular relations*

The severance of diplomatic or consular relations between parties to a treaty does not affect the legal relations established between them by the treaty except in so far as the existence of diplomatic or consular relations is indispensable for the application of the treaty.

Article 64 *Emergence of a new peremptory norm of general international law (jus cogens)*

If a new peremptory norm of general international law emerges, any existing treaty which is in conflict with that norm becomes void and terminates.

Section 4. Procedure

Article 65 *Procedure to be followed with respect to invalidity, termination, withdrawal from or suspension of the operation of a treaty*

1. A party which, under the provisions of the present Convention, invokes either a defect in its consent to be bound by a treaty or a ground for impeaching the validity of a treaty, terminating it, withdrawing from it or suspending its operation, must notify the other parties of its claim. The notification shall indicate the measure proposed to be taken with respect to the treaty and the reasons therefor.

2. If, after the expiry of a period which, except in cases of special urgency, shall not be less than three months after the receipt of the notification, no party has raised any objection, the party making the notification may carry out in the manner provided in article 67 the measure which it has proposed.

3. If, however, objection has been raised by any other party, the parties shall seek a solution through the means indicated in Article 33 of the Charter of the United Nations.

4. Nothing in the foregoing paragraphs shall affect the rights or obligations of the parties under any provisions in force binding the parties with regard to the settlement of disputes.

5. Without prejudice to article 45, the fact that a State has not previously made the notification prescribed in paragraph 1 shall not prevent it from making such notification in answer to another party claiming performance of the treaty or alleging its violation.

Article 66 *Procedures for judicial settlement, arbitration and conciliation*

If, under paragraph 3 of article 65, no solution has been reached within a period of 12 months following the date on which the objection was raised, the following procedures shall be followed:

(a) any one of the parties to a dispute concerning the application or the interpretation of article 53 or 64 may, by a written application, submit it to the International Court of Justice for a decision unless the parties by common consent agree to submit the dispute to arbitration;

(b) any one of the parties to a dispute concerning the application or the interpretation of any of the other articles in Part V of the present Convention may set in motion the procedure specified in the Annex to the Convention by submitting a request to that effect to the Secretary-General of the United Nations.

Article 67 *Instruments for declaring invalid, terminating, withdrawing from or suspending the operation of a treaty*

1. The notification provided for under article 65 paragraph 1 must be made in writing.

2. Any act declaring invalid, terminating, withdrawing from or suspending the operation of a treaty pursuant to the provisions of the treaty or of paragraphs 2 or 3 of article 65 shall be carried out through an instrument communicated to the other parties. If the instrument is not signed by the Head of State, Head of Government or Minister for Foreign Affairs, the representative of the State communicating it may be called upon to produce full powers.

Article 68 *Revocation of notifications and instruments provided for in articles 65 and 67*

A notification or instrument provided for in articles 65 or 67 may be revoked at any time before it takes effect.

SECTION 5. CONSEQUENCES OF THE INVALIDITY, TERMINATION OR SUSPENSION OF THE OPERATION OF A TREATY

Article 69 *Consequences of the invalidity of a treaty*

1. A treaty the invalidity of which is established under the present Convention is void. The provisions of a void treaty have no legal force.

2. If acts have nevertheless been performed in reliance on such a treaty:

(a) each party may require any other party to establish as far as possible in their mutual relations the position that would have existed if the acts had not been performed;

(b) acts performed in good faith before the invalidity was invoked are not rendered unlawful by reason only of the invalidity of the treaty.

3. In cases falling under articles 49, 50, 51 or 52, paragraph 2 does not apply with respect to the party to which the fraud, the act of corruption or the coercion is imputable.

4. In the case of the invalidity of a particular State's consent to be bound by a multilateral treaty, the foregoing rules apply in the relations between that State and the parties to the treaty.

Article 70 *Consequences of the termination of a treaty*

1. Unless the treaty otherwise provides or the parties otherwise agree, the termination of a treaty under its provisions or in accordance with the present Convention:

(a) releases the parties from any obligation further to perform the treaty;

(b) does not affect any right, obligation or legal situation of the parties created through the execution of the treaty prior to its termination.

2. If a State denounces or withdraws from a multilateral treaty, paragraph 1 applies in the relations between that State and each of the other parties to the treaty from the date when such denunciation or withdrawal takes effect.

Article 71 *Consequences of the invalidity of a treaty which conflicts with a peremptory norm of general international law*

1. In the case of a treaty which is void under article 53 the parties shall:

(a) eliminate as far as possible the consequences of any act performed in reliance on any provision which conflicts with the peremptory norm of general international law; and

(b) bring their mutual relations into conformity with the peremptory norm of general international law.

2. In the case of a treaty which becomes void and terminates under article 64, the termination of the treaty:

(a) releases the parties from any obligation further to perform the treaty;

(b) does not affect any right, obligation or legal situation of the parties created through the execution of the treaty prior to its termination; provided that those rights, obligations or situations may thereafter be maintained only to the extent that their maintenance is not in itself in conflict with the new peremptory norm of general international law.

Article 72 *Consequences of the suspension of the operation of a treaty*

1. Unless the treaty otherwise provides or the parties otherwise agree, the suspension of the operation of a treaty under its provisions or in accordance with the present Convention:

(a) releases the parties between which the operation of the treaty is suspended from the obligation to perform the treaty in their mutual relations during the period of the suspension;

(b) does not otherwise affect the legal relations between the parties established by the treaty.

2. During the period of the suspension the parties shall refrain from acts tending to obstruct the resumption of the operation of the treaty.

Part VI. Miscellaneous provisions

Article 73 *Cases of State succession, State responsibility and outbreak of hostilities*

The provisions of the present Convention shall not prejudge any question that may arise in regard to a treaty from a succession of States or from the international responsibility of a State or from the outbreak of hostilities between States.

Article 74 *Diplomatic and consular relations and the conclusion of treaties*

The severance or absence of diplomatic or consular relations between two or more States does not prevent the conclusion of treaties between those States. The conclusion of a treaty does not in itself affect the situation in regard to diplomatic or consular relations.

Article 75 *Case of an aggressor State*

The provisions of the present Convention are without prejudice to any obligation in relation to a treaty which may arise for an aggressor State in consequence of measures taken in conformity with the Charter of the United Nations with reference to that State's aggression.

Part VII. Depositories, notifications, corrections and registration

Article 76 *Depositaries of treaties*

1. The designation of the depositary of a treaty may be made by the negotiating States, either in the treaty itself or in some other manner. The depositary may be one or

more States, an international organization or the chief administrative officer of the organization.

2. The functions of the depositary of a treaty are international in character and the depositary is under an obligation to act impartially in their performance. In particular, the fact that a treaty has not entered into force between certain of the parties or that a difference has appeared between a State and a depositary with regard to the performance of the latter's functions shall not affect that obligation.

Article 77 *Functions of depositaries*

1. The functions of a depositary, unless otherwise provided in the treaty or agreed by the contracting States, comprise in particular:

(a) keeping custody of the original text of the treaty and of any full powers delivered to the depositary;

(b) preparing certified copies of the original text and preparing any further text of the treaty in such additional languages as may be required by the treaty and transmitting them to the parties and to the States entitled to become parties to the treaty;

(c) receiving any signatures to the treaty and receiving and keeping custody of any instruments, notifications and communications relating to it;

(d) examining whether the signature or any instrument, notification or communication relating to the treaty is in due and proper form and, if need be, bringing the matter to the attention of the State in question;

(e) informing the parties and the States entitled to become parties to the treaty of acts, notifications and communications relating to the treaty;

(f) informing the States entitled to become parties to the treaty when the number of signatures or of instruments of ratification, acceptance, approval or accession required for the entry into force of the treaty has been received or deposited;

(g) registering the treaty with the Secretariat of the United Nations;

(h) performing the functions specified in other provisions of the present Convention.

2. In the event of any difference appearing between a State and the depositary as to the performance of the latter's functions, the depositary shall bring the question to the attention of the signatory States and the contracting States or, where appropriate, of the competent organ of the international organization concerned.

Article 78 *Notifications and communications*

Except as the treaty or the present Convention otherwise provide, any notification or communication to be made by any State under the present Convention shall:

(a) if there is no depositary, be transmitted direct to the States for which it is intended, or if there is a depositary, to the latter;

(b) be considered as having been made by the State in question only upon its receipt by the State to which it was transmitted or, as the case may be, upon its receipt by the depositary,

(c) if transmitted to a depositary, be considered as received by the State for which it was intended only when the latter State has been informed by the depositary in accordance with article 77, paragraph 1*(e)*.

Article 79 *Correction of errors in texts or in certified copies of treaties*

1. Where, after the authentication of the text of a treaty, the signatory States and the contracting States are agreed that it contains an error, the error shall, unless they decide upon some other means of correction, be corrected:

(a) by having the appropriate correction made in the text and causing the correction to be initialled by duly authorized representatives;

(b) by executing or exchanging an instrument or instruments setting out the correction which it has been agreed to make; or

(c) by executing a corrected text of the whole treaty by the same procedure as in the case of the original text.

2. Where the treaty is one for which there is a depositary, the latter shall notify the signatory States and the contracting States of the error and of the proposal to correct it and shall specify an appropriate time-limit within which objection to the proposed correction may be raised. If, on the expiry of the time-limit:

(a) no objection has been raised, the depositary shall make and initial the correction in the text and shall execute a *procès-verbal* of the rectification of the text and communicate a copy of it to the parties and to the States entitled to become parties to the treaty;

(b) an objection has been raised, the depositary shall communicate the objection to the signatory States and to the contracting States.

3. The rules in paragraphs 1 and 2 apply also where the text has been authenticated in two or more languages and it appears that there is a lack of concordance which the signatory States and the contracting States agree should be corrected.

4. The corrected text replaces the defective text *ab initio*, unless the signatory States and the contracting States otherwise decide.

5. The correction of the text of a treaty that has been registered shall be notified to the Secretariat of the United Nations.

6. Where an error is discovered in a certified copy of a treaty, the depositary shall execute a *procès-verbal* specifying the rectification and communicate a copy of it to the signatory States and to the contracting States.

Article 80 *Registration and publication of treaties*

1. Treaties shall, after their entry into force, be transmitted to the Secretariat of the United Nations for registration or filing and recording, as the case may be, and for publication.

2. The designation of a depositary shall constitute authorization for it to perform the acts specified in the preceding paragraph.

Part VIII. Final provision

Article 81 *Signature*

The present Convention shall be open for signature by all States Members of the United Nations or of any of the specialized agencies or of the International Atomic Energy Agency or parties to the Statute of the International Court of Justice, and by any other State invited by the General Assembly of the United Nations to become a party to the Convention, as follows: until 30 November 1969, at the Federal Ministry for Foreign Affairs of the Republic of Austria, and subsequently, until 30 April 1970, at United Nations Headquarters, New York.

Article 82 *Ratification*

The present Convention is subject to ratification. The instruments of ratification shall be deposited with the Secretary-General of the United Nations.

Article 83 *Accession*

The present Convention shall remain open for accession by any State belonging to any of the categories mentioned in article 81. The instruments of accession shall be deposited with the Secretary-General of the United Nations.

Article 84 *Entry into force*

1. The present Convention shall enter into force on the thirtieth day following the date of deposit of the thirty-fifth instrument of ratification or accession.

2. For each State ratifying or acceding to the Convention after the deposit of the thirty-fifth instrument of ratification or accession, the Convention shall enter into force on the thirtieth day after deposit by such State of its instrument of ratification or accession.

Article 85 *Authentic texts*

The original of the present Convention, of which the Chinese, English, French, Russian and Spanish texts are equally authentic, shall be deposited with the Secretary-General of the United Nations.

IN WITNESS WHEREOF the undersigned Plenipotentiaries, being duly authorized thereto by their respective Governments, have signed the present Convention.

DONE AT VIENNA, this twenty-third day of May, one thousand nine hundred and sixty-nine.

10. VIENNA CONVENTION ON DIPLOMATIC RELATIONS, VIENNA, 1961
(500 UNTS 95)

The States Parties to the present Convention,
Recalling that peoples of all nations from ancient times have recognized the status of diplomatic agents,
Having in mind the purposes and principles of the Charter of the United Nations concerning the sovereign equality of States, the maintenance of international peace and security, and the promotion of friendly relations among nations,
Believing that an international convention on diplomatic intercourse, privileges and immunities would contribute to the development of friendly relations among nations, irrespective of their differing constitutional and social systems,
Realizing that the purpose of such privileges and immunities is not to benefit individuals but to ensure the efficient performance of the functions of diplomatic missions as representing States,
Affirming that the rules of customary international law should continue to govern questions not expressly regulated by the provisions of the present Convention,
Have agreed as follows:

Article 1

For the purpose of the present Convention, the following expressions shall have the meanings hereunder assigned to them:
(a) the "head of the mission" is the person charged by the sending State with the duty of acting in that capacity;
(b) the "members of the mission" are the head of the mission and the members of the staff of the mission;

(c) the "members of the staff of the mission" are the members of the diplomatic staff, of the administrative and technical staff and of the service staff of the mission;

(d) the "members of the diplomatic staff" are the members of the staff of the mission having diplomatic rank;

(e) a "diplomatic agent" is the head of the mission or a member of the diplomatic staff of the mission;

(f) the "members of the administrative and technical staff" are the members of the staff of the mission employed in the administrative and technical service of the mission;

(g) the "members of the service staff" are the members of the staff of the mission in the domestic service of the mission;

(h) a "private servant" is a person who is in the domestic service of a member of the mission and who is not an employee of the sending State;

(i) the "premises of the mission" are the buildings or parts of buildings and the land ancillary thereto, irrespective of ownership, used for the purposes of the mission including the residence of the head of the mission.

Article 2

The establishment of diplomatic relations between States, and of permanent diplomatic missions, takes place by mutual consent.

Article 3

1. The functions of a diplomatic mission consist *inter alia* in:

(a) representing the sending State in the receiving State;

(b) protecting in the receiving State the interests of the sending State and of its nationals, within the limits permitted by international law;

(c) negotiating with the Government of the receiving State;

(d) ascertaining by all lawful means conditions and developments in the receiving State, and reporting thereon to the Government of the sending State;

(e) promoting friendly relations between the sending State and the receiving State, and developing their economic, cultural and scientific relations.

2. Nothing in the present Convention shall be construed as preventing the performance of consular functions by a diplomatic mission.

Article 4

1. The sending State must make certain that the *agrément* of the receiving State has been given for the person it proposes to accredit as head of the mission to that State.

2. The receiving State is not obliged to give reasons to the sending State for a refusal of *agrément*.

Article 5

1. The sending State may, after it has given due notification to the receiving States concerned, accredit a head of mission or assign any member of the diplomatic staff, as the case may be, to more than one State, unless there is express objection by any of the receiving States.

2. If the sending State accredits a head of mission to one or more other States it may establish a diplomatic mission headed by a chargé d'affaires ad interim in each State where the head of mission has not his permanent seat.

3. A head of mission or any member of the diplomatic staff of the mission may act as representative of the sending State to any international organization.

Article 6

Two or more States may accredit the same person as head of mission to another State, unless objection is offered by the receiving State.

Article 7

Subject to the provisions of Articles 5, 8, 9 and 11, the sending State may freely appoint the members of the staff of the mission. In the case of military, naval or air attachés, the receiving State may require their names to be submitted beforehand, for its approval.

Article 8

1. Members of the diplomatic staff of the mission should in principle be of the nationality of the sending State.

2. Members of the diplomatic staff of the mission may not be appointed from among persons having the nationality of the receiving State, except with the consent of that State which may be withdrawn at any time.

3. The receiving State may reserve the same right with regard to nationals of a third State who are not also nationals of the sending State.

Article 9

1. The receiving State may at any time and without having to explain its decision, notify the sending State that the head of the mission or any member of the diplomatic staff of the mission is *persona non grata* or that any other member of the staff of the mission is not acceptable. In any such case, the sending State shall, as appropriate, either recall the person concerned or terminate his functions with the mission. A person may be declared *non grata* or not acceptable before arriving in the territory of the receiving State.

2. If the sending State refuses or fails within a reasonable period to carry out its obligations under paragraph 1 of this Article, the receiving State may refuse to recognize the person concerned as a member of the mission.

Article 10

1. The Ministry of Foreign Affairs of the receiving State, or such other ministry as may be agreed, shall be notified of:

(a) the appointment of members of the mission, their arrival and their final departure or the termination of their functions with the mission;

(b) the arrival and final departure of a person belonging to the family of a member of the mission and, where appropriate, the fact that a person becomes or ceases to be a member of the family of a member of the mission;

(c) the arrival and final departure of private servants in the employ of persons referred to in sub-paragraph (a) of this paragraph and, where appropriate, the fact that they are leaving the employ of such persons;

(d) the engagement and discharge of persons resident in the receiving State as members of the mission or private servants entitled to privileges and immunities.

2. Where possible, prior notification of arrival and final departure shall also be given.

Article 11

1. In the absence of specific agreement as to the size of the mission, the receiving State may require that the size of a mission be kept within limits considered by it to be reasonable and normal, having regard to circumstances and conditions in the receiving State and to the needs of the particular mission.

2. The receiving State may equally, within similar bounds and on a non-discriminatory basis, refuse to accept officials of a particular category.

Article 12

The sending State may not, without the prior express consent of the receiving State, establish offices forming part of the mission in localities other than those in which the mission itself is established.

Article 13

1. The head of the mission is considered as having taken up his functions in the receiving State either when he has presented his credentials or when he has notified his arrival and a true copy of his credentials has been presented to the Ministry for Foreign Affairs of the receiving State, or such other ministry as may be agreed, in accordance with the practice prevailing in the receiving State which shall be applied in a uniform manner.

2. The order of presentation of credentials or of a true copy thereof will be determined by the date and time of the arrival of the head of the mission.

Article 14

1. Heads of mission are divided into three classes, namely:
(a) that of ambassadors or nuncios accredited to Heads of State, and other heads of mission of equivalent rank;
(b) that of envoys, ministers and internuncios accredited to Heads of State;
(c) that of chargés d'affaires accredited to Ministers for Foreign Affairs.

2. Except as concerns precedence and etiquette, there shall be no differentiation between heads of mission by reason of their class.

Article 15

The class to which the heads of their missions are to be assigned shall be agreed between States.

Article 16

1. Heads of mission shall take precedence in their respective classes in the order of the date and time of taking up their functions in accordance with Article 13.

2. Alterations in the credentials of a head of mission not involving any change of class shall not affect his precedence.

3. This article is without prejudice to any practice accepted by the receiving State regarding the precedence of the representative of the Holy See.

Article 17

The precedence of the members of the diplomatic staff of the mission shall be notified by the head of the mission to the Ministry for Foreign Affairs or such other ministry as may be agreed,

Article 18

The procedure to be observed in each State for the reception of heads of mission shall be uniform in respect of each class.

Article 19

1. If the post of head of the mission is vacant, or if the head of the mission is unable to perform his functions, a chargé d'affaires ad interim shall act provisionally as head of the mission. The name of the chargé d'affaires ad interim shall be notified, either by the head of the mission or, in case he is unable to do so, by the Ministry for Foreign Affairs of the sending State to the Ministry of Foreign Affairs of the receiving State or such other ministry as may be agreed.

2. In cases where no member of the diplomatic staff of the mission is present in the receiving State, a member of the administrative and technical staff may, with the consent of the receiving State, be designated by the sending State to be in charge of the current administrative affairs of the mission.

Article 20

The mission and its head shall have the right to use the flag and emblem of the sending State on the premises of the mission, including the residence of the head of the mission, and on his means of transport.

Article 21

1. The receiving State shall either facilitate the acquisition on its territory, in accordance with its laws, by the sending State of premises necessary for its mission or assist the latter in obtaining accommodation in some other way.

2. It shall also, where necessary, assist missions in obtaining suitable accommodation for their members.

Article 22

1. The premises of the mission shall be inviolable. The agents of the receiving State may not enter them, except with the consent of the head of the mission.

2. The receiving State is under a special duty to take all appropriate steps to protect the premises of the mission against any intrusion or damage and to prevent any disturbance of the peace of the mission or impairment of its dignity.

3. The premises of the mission, their furnishings and other property thereon and the means of transport of the mission shall be immune from search, requisition, attachment or execution.

Article 23

1. The sending State and the head of the mission shall be exempt from all national, regional or municipal dues and taxes in respect of the premises of the mission, whether owned or leased, other than such as represent payment for specific services rendered.

2. The exemption from taxation referred to in this Article shall not apply to such dues and taxes payable under the law of the receiving State by persons contracting with the sending State or the head of the mission.

Article 24

The archives and documents of the mission shall be inviolable at any time and wherever they may be.

Article 25

The receiving State shall accord full facilities for the performance of the functions of the mission.

Article 26

Subject to its laws and regulations concerning zones entry into which is prohibited or regulated for reasons of national security, the receiving State shall ensure to all members of the mission freedom of movement and travel in its territory.

Article 27

1. The receiving State shall permit and protect free communication on the part of the mission for all official purposes. In communicating with the Government and the other missions and consulates of the sending State, wherever situated, the mission may employ all appropriate means, including diplomatic couriers and messages in code or cipher. However, the mission may install and use a wireless transmitter only with the consent of the receiving State.

2. The official correspondence of the mission shall be inviolable. Official correspondence means all correspondence relating to the mission and its functions.

3. The diplomatic bag shall not be opened or detained.

4. The packages constituting the diplomatic bag must bear visible external marks of their character and may contain only diplomatic documents or articles intended for official use.

5. The diplomatic courier, who shall be provided with an official document indicating his status and the number of packages constituting the diplomatic bag, shall be protected by the receiving State in the performance of his functions. He shall enjoy personal inviolability and shall not be liable to any form of arrest or detention.

6. The sending State or the mission may designate diplomatic couriers *ad hoc*. In such cases the provisions of paragraph 5 of this Article shall also apply, except that the immunities therein mentioned shall cease to apply when such a courier has delivered to the consignee the diplomatic bag in his charge.

7. A diplomatic bag may be entrusted to the captain of a commercial aircraft scheduled to land at an authorized port of entry. He shall be provided with an official document indicating the number of packages constituting the bag but he shall not be considered to be a diplomatic courier. The mission may send one of its members to take possession of the diplomatic bag directly and freely from the captain of the aircraft.

Article 28

The fees and charges levied by the mission in the course of its official duties shall be exempt from all dues and taxes.

Article 29

The person of a diplomatic agent shall be inviolable. He shall not be liable to any form of arrest or detention. The receiving State shall treat him with due respect and shall take all appropriate steps to prevent any attack on his person, freedom or dignity.

Article 30

1. The private residence of a diplomatic agent shall enjoy the same inviolability and protection as the premises of the mission.

2. His papers, correspondence and, except as provided in paragraph 3 of Article 31, his property, shall likewise enjoy inviolability.

Article 31

1. A diplomatic agent shall enjoy immunity from the criminal jurisdiction of the receiving State. He shall also enjoy immunity from its civil and administrative jurisdiction, except in the case of:

(a) a real action relating to private immovable property situated in the territory of the receiving State, unless he holds it on behalf of the sending State for the purposes of the mission;

(b) an action relating to succession in which the diplomatic agent is involved as executor, administrator, heir or legatee as a private person and not on behalf of the sending State;

(c) an action relating to any professional or commercial activity exercised by the diplomatic agent in the receiving State outside his official functions.

2. A diplomatic agent is not obliged to give evidence as a witness.

3. No measures of execution may be taken in respect of a diplomatic agent except in the cases coming under sub-paragraphs *(a)*, *(b)* and *(c)* of paragraph 1 of this Article, and provided that the measures concerned can be taken without infringing the inviolability of his person or of his residence.

4. The immunity of a diplomatic agent from the jurisdiction of the receiving State does not exempt him from the jurisdiction of the sending State.

Article 32

1. The immunity from jurisdiction of diplomatic agents and of persons enjoying immunity under Article 37 may be waived by the sending State.

2. Waiver must always be express.

3. The initiation of proceedings by a diplomatic agent or by a person enjoying immunity from jurisdiction under Article 37 shall preclude him from invoking immunity from jurisdiction in respect of any counter-claim directly connected with the principal claim.

4. Waiver of immunity from jurisdiction in respect of civil or administrative proceedings shall not be held to imply waiver of immunity in respect of the execution of the judgment, for which a separate waiver shall be necessary.

Article 33

1. Subject to the provisions of paragraph 3 of this Article, a diplomatic agent shall with respect to services rendered for the sending State be exempt from social security provisions which may be in force in the receiving State.

2. The exemption provided for in paragraph 1 of this Article shall also apply to private servants who are in the sole employ of a diplomatic agent, on condition:

(a) that they are not nationals of or permanently resident in the receiving State; and

(b) that they are covered by the social security provisions which may be in force in the sending State or a third State.

3. A diplomatic agent who employs persons to whom the exemption provided for in paragraph 2 of this Article does not apply shall observe the obligations which the social security provisions of the receiving State impose upon employers.

4. The exemption provided for in paragraphs 1 and 2 of this Article shall not preclude voluntary participation in the social security system of the receiving State provided that such participation is permitted by that State.

5. The provisions of this Article shall not affect bilateral or multilateral agreements concerning social security concluded previously and shall not prevent the conclusion of such agreements in the future.

Article 34

A diplomatic agent shall be exempt from all dues and taxes, personal or real, national, regional or municipal, except:

(a) indirect taxes of a kind which are normally incorporated in the price of goods or services;

(b) dues and taxes on private immovable property situated in the territory of the receiving State, unless he holds it on behalf of the sending State for the purposes of the mission;

(c) estate, succession or inheritance duties levied by the receiving State, subject to the provisions of paragraph 4 of Article 39;

(d) dues and taxes on private income having its source in the receiving State and capital taxes on investments made in commercial undertakings in the receiving State;

(e) charges levied for specific services rendered;

(f) registration, court or record fees, mortgage dues and stamp duty, with respect to immovable property, subject to the provisions of Article 23.

Article 35

The receiving State shall exempt diplomatic agents from all personal services, from all public service of any kind whatsoever, and from military obligations such as those connected with requisitioning, military contributions and billeting.

Article 36

1. The receiving State shall, in accordance with such laws and regulations as it may adopt, permit entry of and grant exemption from all customs duties, taxes, and related charges other than charges for storage, cartage and similar services, on:

(a) articles for the official use of the mission;

(b) articles for the personal use of a diplomatic agent or members of his family forming part of his household, including articles intended for his establishment.

2. The personal baggage of a diplomatic agent shall be exempt from inspection, unless there are serious grounds for presuming that it contains articles not covered by the exemptions mentioned in paragraph 1 of this Article, or articles the import or export of which is prohibited by the law or controlled by the quarantine regulations of the receiving State. Such inspection shall be conducted only in the presence of the diplomatic agent or of his authorized representative.

Article 37

1. The members of the family of a diplomatic agent forming part of his household shall, if they are not nationals of the receiving State, enjoy the privileges and immunities specified in Articles 29 to 36.

2. Members of the administrative and technical staff of the mission, together with members of their families forming part of their respective households, shall, if they are not nationals of or permanently resident in the receiving State, enjoy the privileges and immunities specified in Articles 29 to 35, except that the immunity from civil and administrative jurisdiction of the receiving State specified in paragraph 1 of Article 31 shall not extend to acts performed outside the course of their duties. They shall also enjoy the privileges specified in Article 36, paragraph 1, in respect of articles imported at the time of first installation.

3. Members of the service staff of the mission who are not nationals of or permanently resident in the receiving State shall enjoy immunity in respect of acts performed in the course of their duties, exemption from dues and taxes on the emoluments they receive by reason of their employment and the exemption contained in Article 33.

4. Private servants of members of the mission shall, if they are not nationals of or permanently resident in the receiving State, be exempt from dues and taxes on the emoluments they receive by reason of their employment. In other respects, they may enjoy privileges and immunities only to the extent admitted by the receiving State. However, the receiving State must exercise its jurisdiction over those persons in such a manner as not to interfere unduly with the performance of the functions of the mission.

Article 38

1. Except insofar as additional privileges and immunities may be granted by the receiving State, a diplomatic agent who is a national of or permanently resident in that State shall enjoy only immunity from jurisdiction, and inviolability, in respect of official acts performed in the exercise of his functions.

2. Other members of the staff of the mission and private servants who are nationals of or permanently resident in the receiving State shall enjoy privileges and immunities only to the extent admitted by the receiving State. However, the receiving State must exercise its jurisdiction over those persons in such a manner as not to interfere unduly with the performance of the functions of the mission.

Article 39

1. Every person entitled to privileges and immunities shall enjoy them from the moment he enters the territory of the receiving State on proceeding to take up his post or, if already in its territory, from the moment when his appointment is notified to the Ministry for Foreign Affairs or such other ministry as may be agreed.

2. When the functions of a person enjoying privileges and immunities have come to an end, such privileges and immunities shall normally cease at the moment when he leaves the country, or on expiry of a reasonable period in which to do so, but shall subsist until that time, even in case of armed conflict. However, with respect to acts performed by such a person in the exercise of his functions as a member of the mission, immunity shall continue to subsist.

3. In case of the death of a member of the mission, the members of his family shall continue to enjoy the privileges and immunities to which they are entitled until the expiry of a reasonable period in which to leave the country.

4. In the event of the death of a member of the mission not a national of or permanently resident in the receiving State or a member of his family forming part of his household, the receiving State shall permit the withdrawal of the movable property of the deceased, with the exception of any property acquired in the country the export

of which was prohibited at the time of his death. Estate, succession and inheritance duties shall not be levied on movable property the presence of which in the receiving State was due solely to the presence there of the deceased as a member of the mission or as a member of the family of a member of the mission.

Article 40

1. If a diplomatic agent passes through or is in the territory of a third State, which has granted him a passport visa if such visa was necessary, while proceeding to take up or to return to his post, or when returning to his own country, the third State shall accord him inviolability and such other immunities as may be required to ensure his transit or return. The same shall apply in the case of any members of his family enjoying privileges or immunities who are accompanying the diplomatic agent, or travelling separately to join him or to return to their country.

2. In circumstances similar to those specified in paragraph 1 of this Article, third States shall not hinder the passage of members of the administrative and technical or service staff of a mission, and of members of their families, through their territories.

3. Third States shall accord to official correspondence and other official communications in transit, including messages in code or cipher, the same freedom and protection as is accorded by the receiving State. They shall accord to diplomatic couriers, who have been granted a passport visa if such visa was necessary, and diplomatic bags in transit the same inviolability and protection as the receiving State is bound to accord.

4. The obligations of third States under paragraphs 1, 2 and 3 of this Article shall also apply to the persons mentioned respectively in those paragraphs, and to official communications and diplomatic bags, whose presence in the territory of the third State is due to *force majeure.*

Article 41

1. Without prejudice to their privileges and immunities, it is the duty of all persons enjoying such privileges and immunities to respect the laws and regulations of the receiving State. They also have a duty not to interfere in the internal affairs of that State.

2. All official business with the receiving State entrusted to the mission by the sending State shall be conducted with or through the Ministry for Foreign Affairs of the receiving State or such other ministry as may be agreed.

3. The premises of the mission must not be used in any manner incompatible with the functions of the mission as laid down in the present Convention or by other rules of general international law or by any special agreements in force between the sending and the receiving State.

Article 42

A diplomatic agent shall not in the receiving State practise for personal profit any professional or commercial activity.

Article 43

The function of a diplomatic agent comes to and end, *inter alia*:

(a) on notification by the sending State to the receiving State that the function of the diplomatic agent has come to an end;

(b) on notification by the receiving State to the sending State that, in accordance with paragraph 2 of Article 9, it refuses to recognize the diplomatic agent as a member of the mission.

Article 44

The receiving State must, even in case of armed conflict, grant facilities in order to enable persons enjoying privileges and immunities, other than nationals of the receiving State, and members of the families of such persons irrespective of their nationality, to leave at the earliest possible moment. It must, in particular, in case of need, place at their disposal the necessary means of transport for themselves and their property.

Article 45

If diplomatic relations are broken off between two States, or if a mission is permanently or temporarily recalled:

(a) the receiving State must, even in case of armed conflict, respect and protect the premises of the mission, together with its property and archives;

(b) the sending State may entrust the custody of the premises of the mission, together with its property and archives, to a third State acceptable to the receiving State;

(c) the sending State may entrust the protection of its interests and those of its nationals to a third State acceptable to the receiving State.

Article 46

A sending State may with the prior consent of a receiving State, and at the request of a third State not represented in the receiving State, undertake the temporary protection of the interests of the third State and of its nationals.

Article 47

1. In the application of the provisions of the present Convention, the receiving State shall not discriminate as between States.

2. However, discrimination shall not be regarded as taking place:

(a) where the receiving State applies any of the provisions of the present Convention restrictively because of a restrictive application of that provision to its mission in the sending State;

(b) where by custom or agreement States extend to each other more favourable treatment than is required by the provisions of the present Convention.

Article 48

The present Convention shall be open for signature by all States Members of the United Nations or of any of the specialized agencies or Parties to the Statute of the International Court of Justice, and by any other State invited by the General Assembly of the United Nations to become a Party to the Convention, as follows: until 31 October 1961 at the Federal Ministry for Foreign Affairs of Austria and subsequently, until 31 March 1962, at the United Nations Headquarters in New York.

Article 49

The present Convention is subject to ratification. The instruments of ratification shall be deposited with the Secretary-General of the United Nations.

Article 50

The present Convention shall remain open for accession by any State belonging to any of the four categories mentioned in Article 48. The instruments of accession shall be deposited with the Secretary-General of the United Nations.

Article 51

1. The present Convention shall enter into force on the thirtieth day following the date of deposit of the twenty-second instrument of ratification or accession with the Secretary-General of the United Nations.

2. For each State ratifying or acceding to the Convention after the deposit of the twenty-second instrument of ratification or accession, the Convention shall enter into force on the thirtieth day after deposit by such State of its instrument of ratification or accession.

Article 52

The Secretary-General of the United Nations shall inform all States belonging to any of the four categories mentioned in Article 48:

(a) of signatures to the present Convention and of the deposit of instruments of ratification or accession, in accordance with Articles 48, 49, and 50;

(b) of the date on which the present Convention will enter into force, in accordance with Article 51.

Article 53

The original of the present Convention, of which the Chinese, English, French, Russian and Spanish texts are equally authentic, shall be deposited with the Secretary-General of the United Nations, who shall send certified copies thereof to all States belonging to any of the four categories mentioned in Article 48.

IN WITNESS WHEREOF the undersigned Plenipotentiaries, being duly authorized thereto by their respective Governments, have signed the present Convention.

DONE at Vienna, this eighteenth day of April one thousand nine hundred and sixty-one.

11. VIENNA CONVENTION ON CONSULAR RELATIONS 596 UNTS 261)

The States Parties to the present Convention,

Recalling that consular relations have been established between peoples since ancient times,

Having in mind the Purposes and Principles of the Charter of the United Nation concerning the sovereign equality of States, the maintenance of international peace and security, and the promotion of friendly relations among nations,

Considering that the United Nations Conference on Diplomatic Intercourse and Immunities adopted the Vienna Convention on Diplomatic Relations which was opened for signature on 18 April 1961,

Believing that an international convention on consular relations, privileges and immunities would also contribute to the development of friendly relations among nations, irrespective of their differing constitutional and social systems,

Realizing that the purpose of such privileges and immunities is not to benefit individuals but to ensure the efficient performance of functions by consular posts on behalf of their respective States,

Affirming that the rules of customary international law continue to govern matters not expressly regulated by the provisions of the present Convention,

Have agreed as follows:

Article 1 DEFINITIONS

1. For the purposes of the present Convention, the following expressions shall have the meanings hereunder assigned to them:

    (a) ''consular post'' means any consulate-general, consulate, vice-consulate or consular agency;

    (b) ''consular district'' means the area assigned to a consular post for the exercise of consular functions;

    (c) ''head of consular post'' means the person charged with the duty of acting in that capacity;

    (d) ''consular officer'' means any person, including the head of a consular post, entrusted in that capacity with the exercise of consular functions;

    (e) ''consular employee'' means any person employed in the administrative or technical service of a consular post;

    (f) ''member of the service staff'' means any person employed in the domestic service of a consular post;

    (g) ''members of the consular post'' means consular officers, consular employees and members of the service staff;

    (h) ''members of the consular staff'' means consular officers, other than the head of a consular post, consular employees and members of the service staff;

    (i) ''member of the private staff'' means a person who is employed exclusively in the private service of a member of the consular post;

    (j) ''consular premises'' means the buildings or parts of buildings and the land ancillary thereto, irrespective of ownership, used exclusively for the purposes of the consular post;

    (k) ''consular archives'' includes all the papers, documents, correspondence, books, films, tapes and registers of the consular post, together with the ciphers and codes, the card-indexes and any article of furniture intended for their protection or safekeeping.

2. Consular officers are of two categories, namely career consular officers and honorary consular officers. The provisions of Chapter II of the present Convention apply to consular posts headed by career consular officers; the provisions of Chapter III govern consular posts headed by honorary consular officers.

3. The particular status of members of the consular posts who are nationals or permanent residents of the receiving State is governed by Article 71 of the present Convention.

CHAPTER I Consular Relations in General

SECTION I. ESTABLISHMENT AND CONDUCT OF CONSULAR RELATIONS

Article 2 ESTABLISHMENT OF CONSULAR RELATIONS

1. The establishment of consular relations between States takes place by mutual consent.

2. The consent given to the establishment of diplomatic relations between two States implies, unless otherwise stated, consent to the establishment of consular relations.

3. The severance of diplomatic relations shall not *ipso facto* involve the severance of consular relations.

Article 3 EXERCISE OF CONSULAR FUNCTIONS

Consular functions are exercised by consular posts. They are also exercised by diplomatic missions in accordance with the provisions of the present Convention.

Article 4 ESTABLISHMENT OF A CONSULAR POST

1. A consular post may be established in the territory of the receiving State only with that State's consent.

2. The seat of the consular post, its classification and the consular district shall be established by the sending State and shall be subject to the approval of the receiving State.

3. Subsequent changes in the seat of the consular post, its classification or the consular district may be made by the sending State only with the consent of the receiving State.

4. The consent of the receiving State shall also be required if a consulate-general or a consulate desires to open a vice-consulate or a consular agency in a locality other than that in which it is itself established.

5. The prior express consent of the receiving State shall also be required for the opening of an office forming part of an existing consular post elsewhere than at the seat thereof.

Article 5 CONSULAR FUNCTIONS

Consular functions consist in:

(*a*) protecting in the receiving State the interests of the sending State and of its nationals, both individuals and bodies corporate, within the limits permitted by international law;

(*b*) furthering the development of commercial, economic, cultural and scientific relations between the sending State and the receiving State and otherwise promoting friendly relations between them in accordance with the provisions of the present Convention;

(*c*) ascertaining by all lawful means conditions and developments in the commercial, economic, cultural and scientific life of the receiving State, reporting thereon to the Government of the sending State and giving information to persons interested;

(*d*) issuing passports and travel documents to nationals of the sending State, and visas or appropriate documents to persons wishing to travel to the sending State;

(*e*) helping and assisting nationals, both individuals and bodies corporate, of the sending State;

(*f*) acting as notary and civil registrar and in capacities of a similar kind, and performing certain functions of an administrative nature, provided that there is nothing contrary thereto in the laws and regulations of the receiving State;

(*g*) safeguarding the interests of nationals, both individuals and bodies corporate, of the sending State in cases of succession *mortis causa* in the territory of the receiving State, in accordance with the laws and regulations of the receiving State;

(*h*) safeguarding, within the limits imposed by the laws and regulations of the receiving State, the interests of minors and other persons lacking full capacity who are nationals of the sending State, particularly where any guardianship or trusteeship is required with respect to such persons;

(*i*) subject to the practices and procedures obtaining in the receiving State, representing or arranging appropriate representation for nationals of the sending State before the tribunals and other authorities of the receiving State, for the purpose of obtaining, in accordance with the laws and regulations of the receiving State, provisional measures for the preservation of the rights and interests of these nationals, where, because of absence or any other reason, such nationals are unable at the proper time to assume the defence of their rights and interests;

(j) transmitting judicial and extra-judicial documents or executing letters rogatory or commissions to take evidence for the courts of the sending State in accordance with international agreements in force or, in the absence of such international agreements, in any other manner compatible with the laws and regulations of the receiving State;

(k) exercising rights of supervision and inspection provided for in the laws and regulations of the sending State in respect of vessels having the nationality of the sending State, and of aircraft registered in that State, and in respect of their crews;

(l) extending assistance to vessels and aircraft mentioned in sub-paragraph *(k)* of this Article and to their crews, taking statements regarding the voyage of a vessel, examining and stamping the ship's papers, and, without prejudice to the powers of the authorities of the receiving State, conducting investigations into any incidents which occurred during the voyage, and settling disputes of any kind between the master, the officers and the seamen in so far as this may be authorized by the laws and regulations of the sending State;

(m) performing any other functions entrusted to a consular post by the sending State which are not prohibited by the laws and regulations of the receiving State or to which no objection is taken by the receiving State or which are referred to in the international agreements in force between the sending State and the receiving State.

Article 6 Exercise of consular functions outside the consular district

A consular officer may, in special circumstances, with the consent of the receiving State, exercise his functions outside his consular district.

Article 7 Exercise of consular functions in a third State

The sending State may, after notifying the States concerned, entrust a consular post established in a particular State with the exercise of consular functions in another State, unless there is express objection by one of the States concerned.

Article 8 Exercise of consular functions on behalf of a third State

Upon appropriate notification to the receiving State, a consular post of the sending State may, unless the receiving State objects, exercise consular functions in the receiving State on behalf of a third State.

Article 9 Classes of heads of consular posts

1. Heads of consular posts are divided into four classes, namely:

    (a) consuls-general;

    (b) consuls;

    (c) vice-consuls;

    (d) consular agents.

2. Paragraph 1 of this Article in no way restricts the right of any of the Contracting Parties to fix the designation of consular officers other than the heads of consular posts.

Article 10 APPOINTMENT AND ADMISSION OF HEADS OF CONSULAR POSTS

1. Heads of consular posts are appointed by the sending State and are admitted to the exercise of their functions by the receiving State.

2. Subject to the provisions of the present Convention, the formalities for the appointment and for the admission of the head of a consular post are determined by the laws, regulations and usages of the sending State and of the receiving State respectively.

Article 11 THE CONSULAR COMMISSION OR NOTIFICATION OF APPOINTMENT

1. The head of a consular post shall be provided by the sending State with a document, in the form of a commission or similar instrument, made out for each appointment, certifying his capacity and showing, as a general rule, his full name, his category and class, the consular district and the seat of the consular post.

2. The sending State shall transmit the commission or similar instrument through the diplomatic or other appropriate channel to the Government of the State in whose territory the head of a consular post is to exercise his functions.

3. If the receiving State agrees, the sending State may, instead of a commission or similar instrument, send to the receiving State a notification containing the particulars required by paragraph 1 of this Article.

Article 12 THE EXEQUATUR

1. The head of a consular post is admitted to the exercise of his functions by an authorization from the receiving State termed an *exequatur*, whatever the form of this authorization.

2. A State which refuses to grant an *exequatur* is not obliged to give to the sending State reasons for such refusal.

3. Subject to the provisions of Articles 13 and 15, the head of a consular post shall not enter upon his duties until he has received an *exequatur*.

Article 13 PROVISIONAL ADMISSION OF HEADS OF CONSULAR POSTS

Pending delivery of the *exequatur*, the head of a consular post may be admitted on a provisional basis to the exercise of his functions. In that case, the provisions of the present Convention shall apply.

Article 14 NOTIFICATION TO THE AUTHORITIES OF THE CONSULAR DISTRICT

As soon as the head of a consular post is admitted even provisionally to the exercise of his functions, the receiving State shall immediately notify the competent authorities of the consular district. It shall also ensure that the necessary measures are taken to enable the head of a consular post to carry out the duties of his office and to have the benefit of the provisions of the present Convention.

Article 15 TEMPORARY EXERCISE OF THE FUNCTIONS OF THE HEAD OF A CONSULAR POST

1. If the head of a consular post is unable to carry out his functions or the position of head of consular post is vacant, an acting head of post may act provisionally as head of the consular post.

2. The full name of the acting head of post shall be notified either by the diplomatic mission of the sending State or, if that State has no such mission in the receiving State, by the head of the consular post, or, if he is unable to do so, by any competent authority

of the sending State, to the Ministry for Foreign Affairs of the receiving State or to the authority designated by that Ministry. As a general rule, this notification shall be given in advance. The receiving State may make the admission as acting head of post of a person who is neither a diplomatic agent nor a consular officer of the sending State in the receiving State conditional on its consent.

3. The competent authorities of the receiving State shall afford assistance and protection to the acting head of post. While he is in charge of the post, the provisions of the present Convention shall apply to him on the same basis as to the head of the consular post concerned. The receiving State shall not, however, be obliged to grant to an acting head of post any facility, privilege or immunity which the head of the consular post enjoys only subject to conditions not fulfilled by the acting head of post.

4. When, in the circumstances referred to in paragraph 1 of this Article, a member of the diplomatic staff of the diplomatic mission of the sending State in the receiving State is designated by the sending State as an acting head of post, he shall, if the receiving State does not object thereto, continue to enjoy diplomatic privileges and immunities.

Article 16 Precedence as between heads of consular posts

1. Heads of consular posts shall rank in each class according to the date of the grant of the *exequatur*.

2. If, however, the head of a consular post before obtaining the *exequatur* is admitted to the exercise of his functions provisionally, his precedence shall be determined according to the date of the provisional admission; this precedence shall be maintained after the granting of the *exequatur*.

3. The order of precedence as between two or more heads of consular posts who obtained the *exequatur* or provisional admission on the same date shall be determined according to the dates on which their commissions or similar instruments or the notifications referred to in paragraph 3 of Article 11 were presented to the receiving State.

4. Acting heads of posts shall rank after all heads of consular posts and, as between themselves, they shall rank according to the dates on which they assumed their functions as acting heads of posts as indicated in the notifications given under paragraph 2 of Article 15.

5. Honorary consular officers who are heads of consular posts shall rank in each class after career heads of consular posts, in the order and according to the rules laid down in the foregoing paragraphs.

6. Heads of consular posts shall have precedence over consular officers not having that status.

Article 17 Performance of diplomatic acts by consular officers

1. In a State where the sending State has no diplomatic mission and is not represented by a diplomatic mission of a third State, a consular officer may, with the consent of the receiving State, and without affecting his consular status, be authorized to perform diplomatic acts. The performance of such acts by a consular officer shall not confer upon him any right to claim diplomatic privileges and immunities.

2. A consular officer may, after notification addressed to the receiving State, act as representative of the sending State to any inter-governmental organization. When so acting, he shall be entitled to enjoy any privileges and immunities accorded to such a representative by customary international law or by international agreements; however, in respect of the performance by him of any consular function, he shall not be entitled

to any greater immunity from jurisdiction than that to which a consular officer is entitled under the present Convention.

Article 18 APPOINTMENT OF THE SAME PERSON BY TWO OR MORE STATES AS A CONSULAR OFFICER

Two or more States may, with the consent of the receiving State, appoint the same person as a consular officer in that State.

Article 19 APPOINTMENT OF MEMBERS OF CONSULAR STAFF

1. Subject to the provisions of Articles 20, 22 and 23, the sending State may freely appoint the members of the consular staff.

2. The full name, category and class of all consular officers, other than the head of a consular post, shall be notified by the sending State to the receiving State in sufficient time for the receiving State, if it so wishes, to exercise its rights under paragraph 3 of Article 23.

3. The sending State may, if required by its laws and regulations, request the receiving State to grant an *exequatur* to a consular officer other than the head of a consular post.

4. The receiving State may, if required by its laws and regulations, grant an *exequatur* to a consular officer other than the head of a consular post.

Article 20 SIZE OF THE CONSULAR STAFF

In the absence of an express agreement as to the size of the consular staff, the receiving State may require that the size of the staff be kept within limits considered by it to be reasonable and normal, having regard to circumstances and conditions in the consular district and to the needs of the particular post.

Article 21 PRECEDENCE AS BETWEEN CONSULAR OFFICERS OF A CONSULAR POST

The order of precedence as between the consular officers of a consular post and any change thereof shall be notified by the diplomatic mission of the sending State or, if that State has no such mission in the receiving State, by the head of the consular post, to the Ministry for Foreign Affairs of the receiving State or to the authority designated by that Ministry.

Article 22 NATIONALITY OF CONSULAR OFFICERS

1. Consular officers should, in principle, have the nationality of the sending State.

2. Consular officers may not be appointed from among persons having the nationality of the receiving State except with the express consent of that State which may be withdrawn at any time.

3. The receiving State may reserve the same right with regard to nationals of a third State who are not also nationals of the sending State.

Article 23 PERSONS DECLARED ''NON GRATA''

1. The receiving State may at any time notify the sending State that a consular officer is *persona non grata* or that any other member of the consular staff is not acceptable. In that event, the sending State shall, as the case may be, either recall the person concerned or terminate his functions with the consular post.

2. If the sending State refuses or fails within a reasonable time to carry out its obligations under paragraph 1 of this Article, the receiving State may, as the case may

be, either withdraw the *exequatur* from the person concerned or cease to consider him as a member of the consular staff.

3. A person appointed as a member of a consular post may be declared unacceptable before arriving in the territory of the receiving State or, if already in the receiving State, before entering on his duties with the consular post. In any such case, the sending State shall withdraw his appointment.

4. In the cases mentioned in paragraphs 1 and 3 of this Article, the receiving State is not obliged to give to the sending State reasons for its decision.

Article 24 NOTIFICATION TO THE RECEIVING STATE OF APPOINTMENTS, ARRIVALS AND DEPARTURES

1. The Ministry for Foreign Affairs of the receiving State or the authority designated by that Ministry shall be notified of:

    (a) the appointment of members of a consular post, their arrival after appointment to the consular post, their final departure or the termination of their functions and any other changes affecting their status that may occur in the course of their service with the consular post;

    (b) the arrival and final departure of a person belonging to the family of a member of a consular post forming part of his household and, where appropriate, the fact that a person becomes or ceases to be such a member of the family;

    (c) the arrival and final departure of members of the private staff and, where appropriate, the termination of their service as such;

    (d) the engagement and discharge of persons resident in the receiving State as members of a consular post or as members of the private staff entitled to privileges and immunities.

2. When possible, prior notification of arrival and final departure shall also be given.

SECTION II. END OF CONSULAR FUNCTIONS

Article 25 TERMINATION OF THE FUNCTIONS OF A MEMBER OF A CONSULAR POST

The functions of a member of a consular post shall come to an end *inter alia*:

    (a) on notification by the sending State to the receiving State that his functions have come to an end;

    (b) on withdrawal of the *exequatur*;

    (c) on notification by the receiving State to the sending State that the receiving State has ceased to consider him as a member of the consular staff.

Article 26 DEPARTURE FROM THE TERRITORY OF THE RECEIVING STATE

The receiving State shall, even in case of armed conflict, grant to members of the consular post and members of the private staff, other than nationals of the receiving State, and to members of their families forming part of their households irrespective of nationality, the necessary time and facilities to enable them to prepare their departure and to leave at the earliest possible moment after the termination of the functions of the members concerned. In particular, it shall, in case of need, place at their disposal the necessary means of transport for themselves and their property other than property acquired in the receiving State the export of which is prohibited at the time of departure.

Article 27 PROTECTION OF CONSULAR PREMISES AND ARCHIVES AND OF THE INTERESTS OF THE SENDING STATE IN EXCEPTIONAL CIRCUMSTANCES

1. In the event of the severance of consular relations between two States:

(a) the receiving State shall, even in case of armed conflict, respect and protect the consular premises, together with the property of the consular post and the consular archives;

(b) the sending State may entrust the custody of the consular premises, together with the property contained therein and the consular archives, to a third State acceptable to the receiving State;

(c) the sending State may entrust the protection of its interests and those of its nationals to a third State acceptable to the receiving State.

2. In the event of the temporary or permanent closure of a consular post, the provisions of sub-paragraph (a) of paragraph 1 of this Article shall apply. In addition,

(a) if the sending State, although not represented in the receiving State by a diplomatic mission, has another consular post in the territory of that State, that consular post may be entrusted with the custody of the premises of the consular post which has been closed, together with the property contained therein and the consular archives, and, with the consent of the receiving State, with the exercise of consular functions in the district of that consular post; or

(b) if the sending State has no diplomatic mission and no other consular post in the receiving State, the provisions of sub-paragraphs (b) and (c) of paragraph 1 of this Article shall apply.

CHAPTER II Facilities, Privileges and Immunities Relating to Consular Posts, Career Consular Officers and other Members of a Consular Post

SECTION I. FACILITIES, PRIVILEGES AND IMMUNITIES RELATING TO A CONSULAR POST

Article 28 FACILITIES FOR THE WORK OF THE CONSULAR POST

The receiving State shall accord full facilities for the performance of the functions of the consular post.

Article 29 USE OF NATIONAL FLAG AND COAT-OF-ARMS

1. The sending State shall have the right to the use of its national flag and coat-of-arms in the receiving State in accordance with the provisions of this Article.

2. The national flag of the sending State may be flown and its coat-of-arms displayed on the building occupied by the consular post and at the entrance door thereof, on the residence of the head of the consular post and on his means of transport when used on official business.

3. In the exercise of the right accorded by this Article regard shall be had to the laws, regulations and usages of the receiving State.

Article 30 ACCOMMODATION

1. The receiving State shall either facilitate the acquisition on its territory, in accordance with its laws and regulations, by the sending State of premises necessary for its consular post or assist the latter in obtaining accommodation in some other way.

2. It shall also, where necessary, assist the consular post in obtaining suitable accommodation for its members.

Article 31 INVIOLABILITY OF THE CONSULAR PREMISES

1. Consular premises shall be inviolable to the extent provided in this Article.

2. The authorities of the receiving State shall not enter that part of the consular premises which is used exclusively for the purpose of the work of the consular post except with the consent of the head of the consular post or of his designee or of the head of the diplomatic mission of the sending State. The consent of the head of the consular post may, however, be assumed in case of fire or other disaster requiring prompt protective action.

3. Subject to the provisions of paragraph 2 of this Article, the receiving State is under a special duty to take all appropriate steps to protect the consular premises against any intrusion or damage and to prevent any disturbance of the peace of the consular post or impairment of its dignity.

4. The consular premises, their furnishings, the property of the consular post and its means of transport shall be immune from any form of requisition for purposes of national defence or public utility. If expropriation is necessary for such purposes, all possible steps shall be taken to avoid impeding the performance of consular functions, and prompt, adequate and effective compensation shall be paid to the sending State.

Article 32 EXEMPTION FROM TAXATION OF CONSULAR PREMISES

1. Consular premises and the residence of the career head of consular post of which the sending State or any person acting on its behalf as the owner or lessee shall be exempt from all national, regional or municipal dues and taxes whatsoever, other than such as represent payment for specific services rendered.

2. The exemption from taxation referred to in paragraph 1 of this Article shall not apply to such dues and taxes if, under the law of the receiving State, they are payable by the person who contracted with the sending State or with the person acting on its behalf.

Article 33 INVIOLABILITY OF THE CONSULAR ARCHIVES AND DOCUMENTS

The consular archives and documents shall be inviolable at all times and wherever they may be.

Article 34 FREEDOM OF MOVEMENT

Subject to its laws and regulations concerning zones entry into which is prohibited or regulated for reasons of national security, the receiving State shall ensure freedom of movement and travel in its territory to all members of the consular post.

Article 35 FREEDOM OF COMMUNICATION

1. The receiving State shall permit and protect freedom of communication on the part of the consular post for all official purposes. In communicating with the Government, the diplomatic missions and other consular posts, wherever situated, of the sending State, the consular post may employ all appropriate means, including diplomatic or consular couriers, diplomatic or consular bags and messages in code or cipher. However, the consular post may install and use a wireless transmitter only with the consent of the receiving State.

2. The official correspondence of the consular post shall be inviolable. Official correspondence means all correspondence relating to the consular post and its functions.

3. The consular bag shall be neither opened nor detained. Nevertheless, if the competent authorities of the receiving State have serious reason to believe that the bag contains something other than the correspondence, documents or articles referred to in paragraph 4 of this Article, they may request that the bag be opened in their presence by an

authorized representative of the sending State. If this request is refused by the authorities of the sending State, the bag shall be returned to its place of origin.

4. The packages constituting the consular bag shall bear visible external marks of their character and may contain only official correspondence and documents or articles intended exclusively for official use.

5. The consular courier shall be provided with an official document indicating his status and the number of packages constituting the consular bag. Except with the consent of the receiving State he shall be neither a national of the receiving State, nor, unless he is a national of the sending State, a permanent resident of the receiving State. In the performance of his functions he shall be protected by the receiving State. He shall enjoy personal inviolability and shall not be liable to any form of arrest or detention.

6. The sending State, its diplomatic missions and its consular posts may designate consular couriers *ad hoc*. In such cases the provisions of paragraph 5 of this Article shall also apply except that the immunities therein mentioned shall cease to apply when such a courier has delivered to the consignee the consular bag in his charge.

7. A consular bag may be entrusted to the captain of a ship or of a commercial aircraft scheduled to land at an authorized port of entry. He shall be provided with an official document indicating the number of packages constituting the bag, but he shall not be considered to be a consular courier. By arrangement with the appropriate local authorities, the consular post may send one of its members to take possession of the bag directly and freely from the captain of the ship or of the aircraft.

Article 36 COMMUNICATION AND CONTACT WITH NATIONALS OF THE SENDING STATE

1. With a view to facilitating the exercise of consular functions relating to nationals of the sending State:

   (a) consular officers shall be free to communicate with nationals of the sending State and to have access to them. Nationals of the sending State shall have the same freedom with respect to communication with and access to consular officers of the sending State;

   (b) if he so requests, the competent authorities of the receiving State shall, without delay, inform the consular post of the sending State if, within its consular district, a national of that State is arrested or committed to prison or to custody pending trial or is detained in any other manner. Any communication addressed to the consular post by the person arrested, in prison, custody or detention shall also be forwarded by the said authorities without delay. The said authorities shall inform the person concerned without delay of his rights under this sub-paragraph;

   (c) consular officers shall have the right to visit a national of the sending State who is in prison, custody or detention, to converse and correspond with him and to arrange for his legal representation. They shall also have the right to visit any national of the sending State who is in prison, custody or detention in their district in pursuance of a judgment. Nevertheless, consular officers shall refrain from taking action on behalf of a national who is in prison, custody or detention if he expressly opposes such action.

2. The rights referred to in paragraph 1 of this Article shall be exercised in conformity with the laws and regulations of the receiving State, subject to the proviso, however, that the said laws and regulations must enable full effect to be given to the purposes for which the rights accorded under this Article are intended.

Article 37 INFORMATION IN CASES OF DEATHS, GUARDIANSHIP OR TRUSTEESHIP, WRECKS AND AIR ACCIDENTS

If the relevant information is available to the competent authorities of the receiving State, such authorities shall have the duty:

(a) in the case of the death of a national of the sending State, to inform without delay the consular post in whose district the death occurred;

(b) to inform the competent consular post without delay of any case where the appointment of a guardian or trustee appears to be in the interests of a minor or other person lacking full capacity who is a national of the sending State. The giving of this information shall, however, be without prejudice to the operation of the laws and regulations of the receiving State concerning such appointments.

(c) if a vessel, having the nationality of the sending State, is wrecked or runs aground in the territorial sea or internal waters of the receiving State, or if an aircraft registered in the sending State suffers an accident on the territory of the receiving State, to inform without delay the consular post nearest to the scene of the occurrence.

Article 38 COMMUNICATION WITH THE AUTHORITIES OF THE RECEIVING STATE

In the exercise of their functions, consular officers may address:

(a) the competent local authorities of their consular district;

(b) the competent central authorities of the receiving State if and to the extent that this is allowed by the laws, regulations and usages of the receiving State or by the relevant international agreements.

Article 39 CONSULAR FEES AND CHARGES

1. The consular post may levy in the territory of the receiving State the fees and charges provided by the laws and regulations of the sending State for consular acts.

2. The sums collected in the form of the fees and charges referred to in paragraph 1 of this Article, and the receipts for such fees and charges, shall be exempt from all dues and taxes in the receiving State.

SECTION II. FACILITIES, PRIVILEGES AND IMMUNITIES RELATING TO CAREER CONSULAR OFFICERS AND OTHER MEMBERS OF A CONSULAR POST

Article 40 PROTECTION OF CONSULAR OFFICERS

The receiving State shall treat consular officers with due respect and shall take all appropriate steps to prevent any attack on their person, freedom or dignity.

Article 41 PERSONAL INVIOLABILITY OF CONSULAR OFFICERS

1. Consular officers shall not be liable to arrest or detention pending trial, except in the case of a grave crime and pursuant to a decision by the competent judicial authority.

2. Except in the case specified in paragraph 1 of this Article, consular officers shall not be committed to prison or liable to any other form of restriction on their personal freedom save in execution of a judicial decision of final effect.

3. If criminal proceedings are instituted against a consular officer, he must appear before the competent authorities. Nevertheless, the proceedings shall be conducted with the

respect due to him by reason of his official position and, except in the case specified in paragraph 1 of this Article, in a manner which will hamper the exercise of consular functions as little as possible. When, in the circumstances mentioned in paragraph 1 of this Article, it has become necessary to detain a consular officer, the proceedings against him shall be instituted with the minimum of delay.

Article 42 NOTIFICATION OF ARREST, DETENTION OR PROSECUTION

In the event of the arrest or detention, pending trial, of a member of the consular staff, or of criminal proceedings being instituted against him, the receiving State shall promptly notify the head of the consular post. Should the latter be himself the object of any such measure, the receiving State shall notify the sending State through the diplomatic channel.

Article 43 IMMUNITY FROM JURISDICTION

1. Consular officers and consular employees shall not be amenable to the jurisdiction of the judicial or administrative authorities of the receiving State in respect of acts performed in the exercise of consular functions.

2. The provisions of paragraph 1 of this Article shall not, however, apply in respect of a civil action either:

  (a) arising out of a contract concluded by a consular officer or a consular employee in which he did not contract expressly or impliedly as an agent of the sending State; or

  (b) by a third party for damage arising from an accident in the receiving State caused by a vehicle, vessel or aircraft.

Article 44 LIABILITY TO GIVE EVIDENCE

1. Members of a consular post may be called upon to attend as witnesses in the course of judicial or administrative proceedings. A consular employee or a member of the service staff shall not, except in the cases mentioned in paragraph 3 of this Article, decline to give evidence. If a consular officer should decline to do so, no coercive measure or penalty may be applied to him.

2. The authority requiring the evidence of a consular officer shall avoid interference with the performance of his functions. It may, when possible, take such evidence at his residence or at the consular post or accept a statement from him in writing.

3. Members of a consular post are under no obligation to give evidence concerning matters connected with the exercise of their functions or to produce official correspondence and documents relating thereto. They are also entitled to decline to give evidence as expert witnesses with regard to the law of the sending State.

Article 45 WAIVER OF PRIVILEGES AND IMMUNITIES

1. The sending State may waive, with regard to a member of the consular post, any of the privileges and immunities provided for in Articles 41, 43 and 44.

2. The waiver shall in all cases be express, except as provided in paragraph 3 of this Article, and shall be communicated to the receiving State in writing.

3. The initiation of proceedings by a consular officer or a consular employee in a matter where he might enjoy immunity from jurisdiction under Article 43 shall preclude him from invoking immunity from jurisdiction in respect of any counter-claim directly connected with the principal claim.

4. The waiver of immunity from jurisdiction for the purposes of civil or administrative proceedings shall not be deemed to imply the wavier of immunity from the measures of execution resulting from the judicial decision; in respect of such measures, a separate waiver shall be necessary.

Article 46 EXEMPTION FROM REGISTRATION OF ALIENS AND RESIDENCE PERMITS

1. Consular officers and consular employees and members of their families forming part of their households shall be exempt from all obligations under the laws and regulations of the receiving State in regard to the registration of aliens and residence permits.

2. The provisions of paragraph 1 of this Article shall not, however, apply to any consular employee who is not a permanent employee of the sending State or who carries on any private gainful occupation in the receiving State or to any member of the family of any such employee.

Article 47 EXEMPTION FROM WORK PERMITS

1. Members of the consular post shall, with respect to services rendered for the sending State, be exempt from any obligations in regard to work permits imposed by the laws and regulations of the receiving State concerning the employment of foreign labour.

2. Members of the private staff of consular officers and of consular employees shall, if they do not carry on any other gainful occupation in the receiving State, be exempt from the obligations referred to in paragraph 1 of this Article.

Article 48 SOCIAL SECURITY EXEMPTION

1. Subject to the provisions of paragraph 3 of this Article, members of the consular post with respect to services rendered by them for the sending State, and members of their families forming part of their households, shall be exempt from social security provisions which may be in force in the receiving State.

2. The exemption provided for in paragraph 1 of this Article shall apply also to members of the private staff who are in the sole employ of members of the consular post, on condition:

    (a) that they are not nationals of or permanently resident in the receiving State; and

    (b) that they are covered by the social security provisions which are in force in the sending State or a third State.

3. Members of the consular post who employ persons to whom the exemption provided for in paragraph 2 of this Article does not apply shall observe the obligations which the social security provisions of the receiving State impose upon employers.

4. The exemption provided for in paragraphs 1 and 2 of this Article shall not preclude voluntary participation in the social security system of the receiving State, provided that such participation is permitted by that State.

Article 49 EXEMPTION FROM TAXATION

1. Consular officers and consular employees and members of their families forming part of their households shall be exempt from all dues and taxes, personal or real, national, regional or municipal, except:

    (a) indirect taxes of a kind which are normally incorporated in the price of goods or services;

(b) dues or taxes on private immovable property situated in the territory of the receiving State, subject to the provisions of Article 32;

(c) estate, succession or inheritance duties, and duties on transfers, levied by the receiving State, subject to the provisions of paragraph (b) of Article 51;

(d) dues and taxes on private income, including capital gains, having its source in the receiving State and capital taxes relating to investments made in commercial or financial undertakings in the receiving State;

(e) charges levied for specific services rendered;

(f) registration, court or record fees, mortgage dues and stamp duties, subject to the provisions of Article 32.

2. Members of the service staff shall be exempt from dues and taxes on the wages which they receive for their services.

3. Members of the consular post who employ persons whose wages or salaries are not exempt from income tax in the receiving State shall observe the obligations which the laws and regulations of that State impose upon employers concerning the levying of income tax.

Article 50 EXEMPTION FROM CUSTOMS DUTIES AND INSPECTION

1. The receiving State shall, in accordance with such laws and regulations as it may adopt, permit entry of and grant exemption from all customs duties, taxes, and related charges other than charges for storage, cartage and similar services, on:

(a) articles for the official use of the consular post;

(b) articles for the personal use of a consular officer or members of his family forming part of his household, including articles intended for his establishment. The articles intended for consumption shall not exceed the quantities necessary for direct utilization by the persons concerned.

2. Consular employees shall enjoy the privileges and exemptions specified in paragraph 1 of this Article in respect of articles imported at the time of first installation.

3. Personal baggage accompanying consular officers and members of their families forming part of their households shall be exempt from inspection. It may be inspected only if there is serious reason to believe that it contains articles other than those referred to in sub-paragraph (b) of paragraph 1 of this Article, or articles the import or export of which is prohibited by the laws and regulations of the receiving State or which are subject to its quarantine laws and regulations. Such inspection shall be carried out in the presence of the consular officer or member of his family concerned.

Article 51 ESTATE OF A MEMBER OF THE CONSULAR POST OR OF A MEMBER OF HIS FAMILY

In the event of the death of a member of the consular post or of a member of his family forming part of his household, the receiving State:

(a) shall permit the export of the movable property of the deceased, with the exception of any such property acquired in the receiving State the export of which was prohibited at the time of his death;

(b) shall not levy national, regional or municipal estate, succession or inheritance duties, and duties on transfers, on movable property the presence of which in the receiving State was due solely to the presence in that State of the deceased as a member of the consular post or as a member of the family of a member of the consular post.

Article 52 EXEMPTION FROM PERSONAL SERVICES AND CONTRIBUTIONS

The receiving State shall exempt members of the consular post and members of their families forming part of their households from all personal services, from all public service of any kind whatsoever, and from military obligations such as those connected with requisitioning, military contributions and billeting.

Article 53 BEGINNING AND END OF CONSULAR PRIVILEGES AND IMMUNITIES

1. Every member of the consular post shall enjoy the privileges and immunities provided in the present Convention from the moment he enters the territory of the receiving State on proceeding to take up his post or, if already in its territory, from the moment when he enters on his duties with the consular post.

2. Members of the family of a member of the consular post forming part of his household and members of his private staff shall receive the privileges and immunities provided in the present Convention from the date from which he enjoys privileges and immunities in accordance with paragraph 1 of this Article or from the date of their entry into the territory of the receiving State or from the date of their becoming a member of such family or private staff, whichever is the latest.

3. When the functions of a member of the consular post have come to an end, his privilege and immunities and those of a member of his family forming part of his household or a member of his private staff shall normally cease at the moment when the person concerned leaves the receiving State or on the expiry of a reasonable period in which to do so, whichever is the sooner, but shall subsist until that time, even in case of armed conflict. In the case of the persons referred to in paragraph 2 of this Article, their privileges and immunities shall come to an end when they cease to belong to the household or to be in the service of a member of the consular post provided, however, that if such persons intend leaving the receiving State within a reasonable period thereafter, their privileges and immunities shall subsist until the time of their departure.

4. However, with respect to acts performed by a consular officer or a consular employee in the exercise of his functions, immunity from jurisdiction shall continue to subsist without limitation of time.

5. In the event of the death of a member of the consular post, the members of his family forming part of his household shall continue to enjoy the privileges and immunities accorded to them until they leave the receiving State or until the expiry of a reasonable period enabling them to do so, whichever is the sooner.

Article 54 OBLIGATIONS OF THIRD STATES

1. If a consular officer passes through or is in the territory of a third State, which has granted him a visa if a visa was necessary, while proceeding to take up or return to his post or when returning to the sending State, the third State shall accord to him all immunities provided for by the other Articles of the present Convention as may be required to ensure his transit or return. The same shall apply in the case of any member of his family forming part of his household enjoying such privileges and immunities who are accompanying the consular officer or travelling separately to join him or to return to the sending State.

2. In circumstances similar to those specified in paragraph 1 of this Article, third States shall not hinder the transit through their territory of other members of the consular post or of members of their families forming part of their households.

3. Third States shall accord to official correspondence and to other official communications in transit, including messages in code or cipher, the same freedom and protection as the receiving State is bound to accord under the present Convention. They shall accord to consular couriers who have been granted a visa, if a visa was necessary, and to consular bags in transit, the same inviolability and protection as the receiving State is bound to accord under the present Convention.

4. The obligations of third States under paragraphs 1, 2 and 3 of this Article shall also apply to the persons mentioned respectively in those paragraphs, and to official communications and to consular bags, whose presence in the territory of the third State is due to *force majeure*.

Article 55

RESPECT FOR THE LAWS AND REGULATIONS OF THE RECEIVING STATE

1. Without prejudice to their privileges and immunities, it is the duty of all persons enjoying such privileges and immunities to respect the laws and regulations of the receiving State. They also have a duty not to interfere in the internal affairs of that State.

2. The consular premises shall not be used in any manner incompatible with the exercise of consular functions.

3. The provisions of paragraph 2 of this Article shall not exclude the possibility of offices of other institutions or agencies being installed in part of the building in which the consular premises are situated, provided that the premises assigned to them are separate from those used by the consular post. In that event, the said offices shall not, for the purposes of the present Convention, be considered to form part of the consular premises.

Article 56 INSURANCE AGAINST THIRD PARTY RISKS

Members of the consular post shall comply with any requirement imposed by the laws and regulations of the receiving State in respect of insurance against third party risks arising from the use of any vehicle, vessel or aircraft.

Article 57 SPECIAL PROVISIONS CONCERNING PRIVATE GAINFUL OCCUPATION

1. Career consular officers shall not carry on for personal profit any professional or commercial activity in the receiving State.

2. Privileges and immunities provided in this Chapter shall not be accorded:
   - (a) to consular employees or to members of the service staff who carry on any private gainful occupation in the receiving State;
   - (b) to members of the family of a person referred to in sub-paragraph (a) of this paragraph or to members of his private staff;
   - (c) to members of the family of a member of a consular post who themselves carry on any private gainful occupation in the receiving State.

CHAPTER III Regime Relating to Honorary Consular Officers and Consular Posts headed by such officers

Article 58 GENERAL PROVISIONS RELATING TO FACILITIES, PRIVILEGES AND IMMUNITIES

1. Articles 28, 29, 30, 34, 35, 36, 37, 38 and 39, paragraph 3 of Article 54 and paragraphs 2 and 3 of Article 55 shall apply to consular posts headed by an honorary

consular officer. In addition, the facilities, privileges and immunities of such consular posts shall be governed by Articles 59, 60, 61 and 62.

2. Articles 42 and 43, paragraph 3 of Article 44, Articles 45 and 53 and paragraph 1 of Article 55 shall apply to honorary consular officers. In addition, the facilities, privileges and immunities of such consular officers shall be governed by Articles 63, 64, 65, 66 and 67.

3. Privileges and immunities provided in the present Convention shall not be accorded to members of the family of an honorary consular officer or of a consular employee employed at a consular post headed by an honorary consular officer.

4. The exchange of consular bags between two consular posts headed by honorary consular officers in different States shall not be allowed without the consent of the two receiving States concerned.

Article 59 PROTECTION OF THE CONSULAR PREMISES

The receiving State shall take such steps as may be necessary to protect the consular premises of a consular post headed by an honorary consular officer against any intrusion or damage and to prevent any disturbance of the peace of the consular post or impairment of its dignity.

Article 60 EXEMPTION FROM TAXATION OF CONSULAR PREMISES

1. Consular premises of a consular post headed by an honorary consular officer of which the sending State is the owner or lessee shall be exempt from all national, regional or municipal dues and taxes whatsoever, other than such as represent payment for specific services rendered.

2. The exemption from taxation referred to in paragraph 1 of this Article shall not apply to such dues and taxes if, under the laws and regulations of the receiving State, they are payable by the person who contracted with the sending State.

Article 61 INVIOLABILITY OF CONSULAR ARCHIVES AND DOCUMENTS

The consular archives and documents of a consular post headed by an honorary consular officer shall be inviolable at all times and wherever they may be, provided that they are kept separate from other papers and documents and, in particular, from the private correspondence of the head of a consular post and of any person working with him, and from the materials, books or documents relating to their profession or trade.

Article 62 EXEMPTION FROM CUSTOMS DUTIES

The receiving State shall, in accordance with such laws and regulations as it may adopt, permit entry of, and grant exemption from all customs duties, taxes, and related charges other than charges for storage, cartage and similar services on the following articles, provided that they are for the official use of a consular post headed by an honorary consular officer: coats-of-arms, flags, signboards, seals and stamps, books, official printed matter, office furniture, office equipment and similar articles supplied by or at the instance of the sending State to the consular post.

Article 63 CRIMINAL PROCEEDINGS

If criminal proceedings are instituted against an honorary consular officer, he must appear before the competent authorities. Nevertheless, the proceedings shall be conducted with the respect due to him by reason of his official position and, except when he is under arrest or detention, in a manner which will hamper the exercise of consular functions as little as possible. When it has become necessary to detain an honorary consular officer, the proceedings against him shall be instituted with the minimum of delay.

Article 64 PROTECTION OF HONORARY CONSULAR OFFICERS

The receiving State is under a duty to accord to an honorary consular officer such protection as may be required by reason of his official position.

Article 65 EXEMPTION FROM REGISTRATION OF ALIENS AND RESIDENCE PERMITS

Honorary consular officers, with the exception of those who carry on for personal profit any professional or commercial activity in the receiving State, shall be exempt from all obligations under the laws and regulations of the receiving State in regard to the registration of aliens and residence permits.

Article 66 EXEMPTION FROM TAXATION

An honorary consular officer shall be exempt from all dues and taxes on the remuneration and emoluments which he receives from the sending State in respect of the exercise of consular functions.

Article 67 EXEMPTION FROM PERSONAL SERVICES AND CONTRIBUTIONS

The receiving State shall exempt honorary consular officers from all personal services and from all public services of any kind whatsoever and from military obligations such as those connected with requisitioning, military contributions and billeting.

Article 68 OPTIONAL CHARACTER OF THE INSTITUTION OF HONORARY CONSULAR OFFICERS

Each State is free to decide whether it will appoint or receive honorary consular officers.

CHAPTER IV General Provisions

Article 69 CONSULAR AGENTS WHO ARE NOT HEADS OF CONSULAR POSTS

1. Each State is free to decide whether it will establish or admit consular agencies conducted by consular agents not designated as heads of consular post by the sending State.

2. The conditions under which the consular agencies referred to in paragraph 1 of this Article may carry on their activities and the privileges and immunities which may be enjoyed by the consular agents in charge of them shall be determined by agreement between the sending State and the receiving State.

Article 70 EXERCISE OF CONSULAR FUNCTIONS BY DIPLOMATIC MISSIONS

1. The provisions of the present Convention apply also, so far as the context permits, to the exercise of consular functions by a diplomatic mission.

2. The names of members of a diplomatic mission assigned to the consular section or otherwise charged with the exercise of the consular functions of the mission shall be notified to the Ministry for Foreign Affairs of the receiving State or to the authority designated by that Ministry.

3. In the exercise of consular functions a diplomatic mission may address:

   (a) the local authorities of the consular district;

   (b) the central authorities of the receiving State if this is allowed by the laws, regulations and usages of the receiving State or by relevant international agreements.

4. The privileges and immunities of the members of a diplomatic mission referred to in paragraph 2 of this Article shall continue to be governed by the rules of international law concerning diplomatic relations.

Article 71 NATIONALS OR PERMANENT RESIDENTS OF THE RECEIVING STATE

1. Except in so far as additional facilities, privileges and immunities may be granted by the receiving State, consular officers who are nationals of or permanently resident in the receiving State shall enjoy only immunity from jurisdiction and personal inviolability in respect of official acts performed in the exercise of their functions, and the privilege provided in paragraph 3 of Article 44. So far as these consular officers are concerned, the receiving State shall likewise be bound by the obligation laid down in Article 42. If criminal proceedings are instituted against such a consular officer, the proceeding shall, except when he is under arrest or detention, be conducted in a manner which will hamper the exercise of consular functions as little as possible.

2. Other members of the consular post who are nationals of or permanently resident in the receiving State and members of their families, as well as members of the families of consular officers referred to in paragraph 1 of this Article, shall enjoy facilities, privileges and immunities only in so far as these are granted to them by the receiving State. Those members of the families of members of the consular post and those members of the private staff who are themselves nationals of or permanently resident in the receiving State shall likewise enjoy facilities, privileges and immunities only in so far as these are granted to them by the receiving State. The receiving State shall, however, exercise its jurisdiction over those persons in such a way as not to hinder unduly the performance of the functions of the consular post.

Article 72 NON-DISCRIMINATION

1. In the application of the provisions of the present Convention the receiving State shall not discriminate as between States.

2. However, discrimination shall not be regarded as taking place:

   (a) where the receiving State applies any of the provisions of the present Convention restrictively because of a restrictive application of that provision to its consular posts in the sending State;

   (b) where by custom or agreement States extend to each other more favourable treatment than is required by the provisions of the present Convention.

Article 73 RELATIONSHIP BETWEEN THE PRESENT CONVENTION AND OTHER INTERNATIONAL AGREEMENTS

1. The provisions of the present Convention shall not affect other international agreements in force as between States parties to them.

2. Nothing in the present Convention shall preclude States from concluding international agreements confirming or supplementing or extending or amplifying the provisions thereof.

CHAPTER V **Final Provisions**

Article 74 SIGNATURE

The present Convention shall be open for signature by all States Members of the United Nations or of any of the specialized agencies or Parties to the Statute of the International Court of Justice, and by any other State invited by the General Assembly of the United Nations to become a Party to the Convention, as follows until 31 October 1963 at the Federal Ministry for Foreign Affairs of the Republic of Austria and subsequently, until 31 March 1964, at the United Nations Headquarters in New York.

Article 75 RATIFICATION

The present Convention is subject to ratification. The instruments of ratification shall be deposited with the Secretary-General of the United Nations.

Article 76 ACCESSION

The present Convention shall remain open for accession by any State belonging to any of the four categories mentioned in Article 74. The instruments of accession shall be deposited with the Secretary-General of the United Nations.

Article 77 ENTRY INTO FORCE

1. The present Convention shall enter into force on the thirtieth day following the date of deposit of the twenty-second instrument of ratification or accession with the Secretary-General of the United Nations.

2. For each State ratifying or acceding to the Convention after the deposit of the twenty-second instrument of ratification or accession, the Convention shall enter into force on the thirtieth day after deposit by such State of its instrument of ratification or accession.

Article 78 NOTIFICATIONS BY THE SECRETARY-GENERAL

The Secretary-General of the United Nations shall inform all States belonging to any of the four categories mentioned in Article 74:

   (a) of signatures to the present Convention and of the deposit of instruments of ratification or accession, in accordance with Articles 74, 75 and 76;

   (b) of the date on which the present Convention will enter into force, in accordance with Article 77.

Article 79 AUTHENTIC TEXTS

The original of the present Convention, of which the Chinese, English, French, Russian and Spanish texts are equally authentic, shall be deposited with the Secretary-General of the United Nations, who shall send certified copies thereof to all States belonging to any of the four categories mentioned in Article 74.

IN WITNESS WHEREOF the undersigned Plenipotentiaries, being duly authorized thereto by their respective Governments, have signed the present Convention.

DONE at Vienna, this twenty-fourth day of April, one thousand nine hundred and sixty-three.

E. INTERNATIONAL ECONOMIC LAW

12. PERMANENT SOVEREIGNTY OVER NATURAL RESOURCES
(GA RES 1803 (XVIII) 1962)

The General Assembly,

Recalling its resolutions 523 (VI) of 12 January 1952 and 626 (VII) of 21 December 1952,

Bearing in mind its resolution 1314 (XIII) of 12 December 1958, by which it established the Commission on Permanent Sovereignty over Natural Resources and instructed it to conduct a full survey of the status of permanent sovereignty over natural wealth and resources as a basic constituent of the right to self-determination, with recommendations, where necessary, for its strengthening, and decided further that, in the conduct of the full survey of the status of the permanent sovereignty of peoples and nations over their natural wealth and resources, due regard should be paid to the rights and duties of States under international law and to the importance of encouraging international co-operation in the economic development of developing countries,

Bearing in mind its resolution 1515 (XV) of 15 December 1960, in which it recommended that the sovereign right of every State to dispose of its wealth and its natural resources should be respected,

Considering that any measure in this respect must be based on the recognition of the inalienable right of all States freely to dispose of their natural wealth and resources in accordance with their national interests, and on respect for the economic independence of States,

Considering that nothing in paragraph 4 below in any way prejudices the position of any Member State on any aspect of the question of the rights and obligations of successor States and Governments in respect of property acquired before the accession to complete sovereignty of countries formerly under colonial rule,

Noting that the subject of succession of States and Governments is being examined as a matter of priority by the International Law Commission.

Considering that it is desirable to promote international co-operation for the economic development of developing countries, and that economic and financial agreements between the developed and the developing countries must be based on the principles of equality and of the right of peoples and nations to self-determination.

Considering that the provisions of economic and technical assistance, loans and increased foreign investment must not be subject to conditions which conflict with the interests of the recipient State,

Considering the benefits to be derived from exchanges of technical and scientific information likely to promote the development and use of such resources and wealth, and the important part which the United Nations and other international organizations are called upon to play in that connexion,

Attaching particular importance to the question of promoting the economic development of developing countries and securing their economic independence,

Noting that the creation and strengthening of the inalienable sovereignty of States over their natural wealth and resources reinforces their economic independence,

Desiring that there should be further consideration by the United Nations of the subject of permanent sovereignty over natural resources in the spirit of international co-operation in the field of economic development, particularly that of the developing countries,

I

1. The right of peoples and nations to permanent sovereignty over their natural wealth and resources must be exercised in the interest of their national development and of the well-being of the people of the State concerned.

2. The exploration, development and disposition of such resources, as well as the import of the foreign capital required for these purposes, should be in conformity with the rules and conditions which the peoples and nations freely consider to be necessary or desirable with regard to the authorization, restriction or prohibition of such activities.

3. In cases where authorization is granted, the capital imported and the earnings on that capital shall be governed by the terms thereof, by the national legislation in force, and by international law. The profits derived must be shared in the proportions freely agreed upon, in each case, between the investors and the recipient State, due care being taken to ensure that there is no impairment, for any reason, of that State's sovereignty over its natural wealth and resources.

4. Nationalization, expropriation or requisitioning shall be based on grounds or reasons of public utility, security or the national interest which are recognized as overriding purely individual or private interests, both domestic and foreign. In such cases the owner shall be paid appropriate compensation, in accordance with the rules in force in the State taking such measures in the exercise of its sovereignty and in accordance with international law. In any case where the question of compensation gives rise to a controversy, the national jurisdiction of the State taking such measures shall be exhausted. However, upon agreement by sovereign States and other parties concerned, settlement of the dispute should be made through arbitration or international adjudication.

5. The free and beneficial exercise of the sovereignty of peoples and nations over their natural resources must be furthered by the mutual respect of States based on their sovereign equality.

6. International co-operation for the economic development of developing countries, whether in the form of public or private capital investments, exchange of goods and services, technical assistance, or exchange of scientific information, shall be such as to further their independent national development and shall be based upon respect for their sovereignty over their natural wealth and resources.

7. Violation of the rights of peoples and nations to sovereignty over their natural wealth and resources is contrary to the spirit and principles of the Charter of the United Nations and hinders the development of international co-operation and the maintenance of peace.

8. Foreign investment agreements freely entered into by or between sovereign States shall be observed in good faith; States and international organizations shall strictly and conscientiously respect the sovereignty of peoples and nations over their natural wealth and resources in accordance with the Charter and the principles set forth in the present resolution.

II

Welcomes the decision of the International Law Commission to speed up its work on the codification of the topic of responsibility of States for the consideration of the General Assembly;

III

Requests the Secretary-General to continue the study of the various aspects of permanent sovereignty over natural resources, taking into account the desire of Member

States to ensure the protection of their sovereign rights while encouraging international co-operation in the field of economic development, and to report to the Economic and Social Council and to the General Assembly, if possible at its eighteenth session.

1194th plenary meeting,
14 December 1962.

13. Declaration on the Establishment of the New International Economic Order 1974
(GA Res 3201 (S-VI) 1974; 13 ILM 715 (1974))

The General Assembly

Adopts the following Declaration:

DECLARATION ON THE ESTABLISHMENT OF A NEW INTERNATIONAL ECONOMIC ORDER

We, the Members of the United Nations,

Having convened a special session of the General Assembly to study for the first time the problems of raw materials and development, devoted to the consideration of the most important economic problems facing the world community,

Bearing in mind the spirit, purposes and principles of the Charter of the United Nations to promote the economic advancement and social progress of all peoples,

Solemnly proclaim our united determination to work urgently for THE ESTABLISHMENT OF A NEW INTERNATIONAL ECONOMIC ORDER based on equity, sovereign equality interdependence, common interest and co-operation among all States, irrespective of their economic and social systems which shall correct inequalities and redress existing injustices, make it possible to eliminate the widening gap between the developed and the developing countries and ensure steadily accelerating economic and social development and peace and justice for present and future generations, and, to that end, declare:

1. The greatest and most significant achievement during the last decades has been the independence from colonial and alien domination of a large number of peoples and nations which has enabled them to become members of the community of free peoples. Technological progress has also been made in all spheres of economic activities in the last three decades, thus providing a solid potential for improving the well-being of all peoples. However, the remaining vestiges of alien and colonial domination, foreign occupation, racial discrimination, *apartheid* and neo-colonialism in all its forms continue to be among the greatest obstacles to the full emancipation and progress of the developing countries and all the peoples involved. The benefits of technological progress are not shared equitably by all members of the international community. The developing countries, which constitute 70 per cent of the world's population, account for only 30 per cent of the world's income. It has proved impossible to achieve an even and balanced development of the international community under the existing international economic order. The gap between the developed and the developing countries continues to widen in a system which was established at a time when most of the developing countries did not even exist as independent States and which perpetuates inequality.

2. The present international economic order is in direct conflict with current developments in international political and economic relations. Since 1970, the world economy has experienced a series of grave crises which have had severe repercussions, especially on the developing countries because of their generally greater

vulnerability to external economic impulses. The developing world has become a powerful factor that makes its influence felt in all fields of international activity. These irreversible changes in the relationship of forces in the world necessitate the active, full and equal participation of the developing countries in the formulation and application of all decisions that concern the international community.

3. All these changes have thrust into prominence the reality of interdependence of all the members of the world community. Current events have brought into sharp focus the realization that the interests of the developed countries and those of the developing countries can no longer be isolated from each other, that there is a close interrelationship between the prosperity of the developed countries and the growth and development of the developing countries, and that the prosperity of the international community as a whole depends upon the prosperity of its constituent parts. International co-operation for development is the shared goal and common duty of all countries. Thus the political, economic and social well-being of present and future generations depends more than ever on co-operation between all the members of the international community on the basis of sovereign equality and the removal of the disequilibrium that exists between them.

4. The new international economic order should be founded on full respect for the following principles:

(a) Sovereign equality of States, self-determination of all peoples, inadmissibility of the acquisition of territories by force, territorial integrity and non-interference in the internal affairs of other States;

(b) The broadest co-operation of all the States members of the international community, based on equity, whereby the prevailing disparities in the world may be banished and prosperity secured for all;

(c) Full and effective participation on the basis of equality of all countries in the solving of world economic problems in the common interest of all countries, bearing in mind the necessity to ensure the accelerated development of all the developing countries, while devoting particular attention to the adoption of special measures in favour of the least developed, land-locked and island developing countries as well as those developing countries most seriously affected by economic crises and natural calamities, without losing sight of the interests of other developing countries;

(d) The right of every country to adopt the economic and social system that it deems the most appropriate for its own development and not to be subjected to discrimination of any kind as a result;

(e) Full permanent sovereignty of every State over its natural resources and all economic activities. In order to safeguard these resources, each State is entitled to exercise effective control over them and their exploitation with means suitable to its own situation, including the right to nationalization or transfer of ownership to its nationals, this right being an expression of the full permanent sovereignty of the State. No State may be subjected to economic, political or any other type of coercion to prevent the free and full exercise of this inalienable right;

(f) The right of all States, territories and peoples under foreign occupation, alien and colonial domination or *apartheid* to restitution and full compensation for the exploitation and depletion of, and damages to, the natural resources and all other resources of those States, territories and peoples;

(g) Regulation and supervision of the activities of transnational corporations by taking measures in the interest of the national economies of the countries where such

transnational corporations operate on the basis of the full sovereignty of those countries;

(h) The right of the developing countries and the peoples of territories under colonial and racial domination and foreign occupation to achieve their liberation and to regain effective control over their natural resources and economic activities;

(i) The extending of assistance to developing countries, peoples and territories which are under colonial and alien domination, foreign occupation, racial discrimination or *apartheid* or are subjected to economic, political or any other type of coercive measures to obtain from them the subordination of the exercise of their sovereign rights and to secure from them advantages of any kind, and to neo-colonialism in all its forms, and which have established or are endeavouring to establish effective control over their natural resources and economic activities that have been or are still under foreign control;

(j) Just and equitable relationship between the prices of raw materials, primary commodities, manufactured and semi-manufactured goods exported by developing countries and the prices of raw materials, primary commodities, manufactures, capital goods and equipment imported by them with the aim of bringing about sustained improvement in their unsatisfactory terms of trade and the expansion of the world economy;

(k) Extension of active assistance to developing countries by the whole international community, free of any political or military conditions;

(l) Ensuring that one of the main aims of the reformed international monetary system shall be the promotion of the development of the developing countries and the adequate flow of real resources to them;

(m) Improving the competitiveness of natural materials facing competition from synthetic substitutes;

(n) Preferential and non-reciprocal treatment for developing countries, wherever feasible, in all fields of international economic co-operation whenever possible;

(o) Securing favourable conditions for the transfer of financial resources to developing countries;

(p) Giving to the developing countries access to the achievements of modern science and technology, and promoting the transfer of technology and the creation of indigenous technology for the benefits of the developing countries in forms and in accordance with procedure which are suited to their economies;

(q) The need for all States to put an end to the waste of natural resources, including food products;

(r) The need for developing countries to concentrate all their resources for the cause of development;

(s) The strengthening, through individual and collective actions, of mutual economic, trade, financial and technical co-operation among the developing countries, mainly on a preferential basis;

(t) Facilitating the role which producers' associations may play within the framework of international co-operation and, in pursuance of their aims, *inter alia* assisting in the promotion of sustained growth of the world economy and accelerating the development of developing countries.

5. The unanimous adoption of the International Development Strategy for the Second United Nations Development Decade was an important step in the promotion of international economic co-operation on a just and equitable basis. The accelerated

implementation of obligations and commitments assumed by the international community within the framework of the Strategy, particularly those concerning imperative development needs of developing countries, would contribute significantly to the fulfilment of the aims and objectives of the present Declaration.

6. The United Nations as a universal organization should be capable of dealing with problems of international economic co-operation in a comprehensive manner and ensuring equally the interests of all countries. It must have an even greater role in the establishment of a new international economic order. The Charter of Economic Rights and Duties of States, for the preparation of which the present Declaration will provide an additional source of inspiration, will constitute a significant contribution in this respect. All the States Members of the United Nations are therefore called upon to exert maximum efforts with a view to securing the implementation of the present Declaration, which is one of the principal guarantees for the creation of better conditions for all peoples to reach a life worthy of human dignity.

7. The present Declaration on the Establishment of a New International Economic Order shall be one of the most important bases of economic relations between all peoples and all nations.

2229th plenary meeting
1 May 1974

14. PROGRAMME OF ACTION ON THE ESTABLISHMENT OF THE NEW ECONOMIC ORDER   (GA RES 3202 (S-VI) 1974)

The General Assembly

Adopts the following Programme of Action:

PROGRAMME OF ACTION ON THE ESTABLISHMENT OF A NEW INTERNA-TIONAL ECONOMIC ORDER

INTRODUCTION

1. In view of the continuing severe economic imbalance in the relations between developed and developing countries, and in the context of the constant and continuing aggravation of the imbalance of the economies of the developing countries and the consequent need for the mitigation of their current economic difficulties, urgent and effective measures need to be taken by the international community to assist the developing countries, while devoting particular attention to the least developed, land-locked and island developing countries and those developing countries most seriously affected by economic crises and natural calamities leading to serious retardation of development processes.

2. With a view to ensuring the application of the Declaration on the Establishment of a New International Economic Order it will be necessary to adopt and implement within a specified period a programme of action of unprecedented scope and to bring about maximum economic co-operation and understanding among all States, particularly between developed and developing countries, based on the principles of dignity and sovereign equality.

I. Fundamental problems of raw materials and primary commodities as related to trade and development

1. *Raw materials*

All efforts should be made:

(a) To put and end to all forms of foreign occupation, racial discrimination, *apartheid*, colonial, neo-colonial and alien domination and exploitation through the exercise of permanent sovereignty over natural resources;

(b) To take measures for the recovery, exploitation, development, marketing and distribution of natural resources, particularly of developing countries, to serve their national interests, to promote collective self-reliance among them and to strengthen mutually beneficial international economic co-operation with a view to bringing about the accelerated development of developing countries;

(c) To facilitate the functioning and to further the aims of producers' associations, including their joint marketing arrangements, orderly commodity trading, improvement in the export income of producing developing countries and in their terms of trade, and sustained growth of the world economy for the benefit of all;

(d) To evolve a just and equitable relationship between the prices of raw materials, primary commodities, manufactured and semi-manufactured goods exported by developing countries and the prices of raw materials, primary commodities, food, manufactured and semi-manufactured goods and capital equipment imported by them, and to work for a link between the prices of exports of developing countries and the prices of their imports from developed countries;

(e) To take measures to reverse the continued trend of stagnation or decline in the real price of several commodities exported by developing countries, despite a general rise in commodity prices, resulting in a decline in the export earnings of these developing countries;

(f) To take measures to expand the markets for natural products in relation to synthetics, taking into account the interests of the developing countries, and to utilize fully the ecological advantages of these products;

(g) To take measures to promote the processing of raw materials in the producer developing countries.

2. *Food*

All efforts should be made:

(a) To take full account of specific problems of developing countries, particularly in times of food shortages, in the international efforts connected with the food problem;

(b) To take into account that, owing to lack of means, some developing countries have vast potentialities of unexploited or underexploited land which, if reclaimed and put into practical use, would contribute considerably to the solution of the food crisis;

(c) By the international community to undertake concrete and speedy measures with a view to arresting desertification, salination and damage by locusts or any other similar phenomenon involving several developing countries, particularly in Africa, and gravely affecting the agricultural production capacity of these countries, and also to assist the developing countries affected by any such phenomenon to develop the affected zones with a view to contributing to the solution of their food problems;

(d) To refrain from damaging or deteriorating natural resources and food resources, especially those derived from the sea, by preventing pollution and taking appropriate steps to protect and reconstitute those resources;

(e) By developed countries, in evolving their policies relating to production, stocks, imports and exports of food, to take full account of the interests of:

   (i) Developing importing countries which cannot afford high prices for their imports;

   (ii) Developing exporting countries which need increased market opportunities for their exports;

(f) To ensure that developing countries can import the necessary quantity of food without undue strain on their foreign exchange resources and without unpredictable deterioration in their balance of payments, and, in this context, that special measures are taken in respect of the least developed, land-locked and island developing countries as well as those developing countries most seriously affected by economic crises and natural calamities;

(g) To ensure that concrete measures to increase food production and storage facilities in developing countries are introduced, *inter alia*, by ensuring an increase in all available essential inputs, including fertilizers, from developed countries on favourable terms;

(h) To promote exports of food products of developing countries through just and equitable arrangements, *inter alia*, by the progressive elimination of such protective and other measures as constitute unfair competition.

3. *General trade*

All efforts should be made:

(a) To take the following measures for the amelioration of terms of trade of developing countries and concrete steps to eliminate chronic trade deficits of developing countries:

   (i) Fulfilment of relevant commitments already undertaken in the United Nations Conference on Trade and Development and in the International Development Strategy for the Second United Nations Development Decade;

   (ii) Improved access to markets, in developed countries through the progressive removal of tariff and non-tariff barriers and of restrictive business practices;

   (iii) Expeditious formulation of commodity agreements where appropriate, in order to regulate as necessary and to stabilize the world markets for raw materials and primary commodities;

   (iv) Preparation of an over-all integrated programme, setting out guidelines and taking into account the current work in this field, for a comprehensive range of commodities of export interest to developing countries;

   (v) Where products of developing countries compete with the domestic production in developed countries, each developed country should facilitate the expansion of imports from developing countries and provide a fair and reasonable opportunity to the developing countries to share in the growth of the market;

   (vi) When the important developed countries derive receipts from customs duties, taxes and other protective measures applied to imports of these products, consideration should be given to the claim of the developing countries that these receipts should be reimbursed in full to the exporting developing countries or devoted to providing additional resources to meet their development needs;

   (vii) Developed countries should make appropriate adjustments in their economies so as to facilitate the expansion and diversification of imports from developing countries and thereby permit a rational, just and equitable international division of labour;

(viii) Setting up general principles for pricing policy for exports of commodities of developing countries, with a view to rectifying and achieving satisfactory terms of trade for them;

(ix) Until satisfactory terms of trade are achieved for all developing countries, consideration should be given to alternative means, including improved compensatory financing schemes for meeting the development needs of the developing countries concerned;

(x) Implementation, improvement and enlargement of the generalized system of preferences for exports of agricultural primary commodities, manufactures and semi-manufactures from developing to developed countries and consideration of its extension to commodities, including those which are processed or semi-processed; developing countries which are or will be sharing their existing tariff advantages in some developed countries as the result of the introduction and eventual enlargement of the generalized system of preferences should, as a matter of urgency, be granted new openings in the markets of other developed countries which should offer them export opportunities that at least compensate for the sharing of those advantages;

(xi) The setting up of buffer stocks within the framework of commodity arrangements and their financing by international financial institutions, wherever necessary, by the developed countries and, when they are able to do so, by the developing countries, with the aim of favouring the producer developing and consumer developing countries and of contributing to the expansion of world trade as a whole;

(xii) In cases where natural materials can satisfy the requirements of the market, new investment for the expansion of the capacity to produce synthetic materials and substitutes should not be made;

(b) To be guided by the principles of non-reciprocity and preferential treatment of developing countries in multilateral trade negotiations between developed and developing countries, and to seek sustained and additional benefits for the international trade of developing countries, so as to achieve a substantial increase in their foreign exchange earnings, diversification of their exports and acceleration of the rate of their economic growth.

4. *Transportation and insurance*

All efforts should be made:

(a) To promote an increasing and equitable participation of developing countries in the world shipping tonnage;

(b) To arrest and reduce the ever-increasing freight rates in order to reduce the costs of imports to, and export from, the developing countries;

(c) To minimize the cost of insurance and reinsurance for developing countries and to assist the growth of domestic insurance and reinsurance markets in developing countries and the establishment to this end, where appropriate, of institutions in these countries or at the regional level;

(d) To ensure the early implementation of the code of conduct for liner conferences;

(e) To take urgent measures to increase the import and export capability of the least developed countries and to offset the disadvantages of the adverse geographic situation and land-locked countries, particularly with regard to their transportation and transit costs, as well as developing island countries in order to increase their trading ability;

(f) By the developed countries to refrain from impairing measures or implementing policies designed to prevent the importation, at equitable prices, of commodities from the developing countries or from frustrating the implementation of legitimate measures and policies adopted by the developing countries in order to improve prices and encourage the export of such commodities.

II. INTERNATIONAL MONETARY SYSTEM AND FINANCING OF THE DEVELOPMENT OF DEVELOPING COUNTRIES

1. *Objectives*

All efforts should be made to reform the international monetary system with, *inter alia*, the following objectives:

(a) Measures to check the inflation already experienced by the developed countries, to prevent it from being transferred to developing countries and to study and devise possible arrangements within the International Monetary Fund to mitigate the effects of inflation in developed countries on the economies of developing countries;

(b) Measures to eliminate the instability of the international monetary system, in particular the uncertainty of the exchange rates, especially as it affects adversely the trade in commodities;

(c) Maintenance of the real value of the currency reserves of the developing countries by preventing their erosion from inflation and exchange rate depreciation of reserve currencies;

(d) Full and effective participation of developing countries in all phases of decision-making for the formulation of an equitable and durable monetary system and adequate participation of developing countries in all bodies entrusted with this reform and, particularly in the proposed Council of Governors of the International Monetary Fund;

(e) Adequate and orderly creation of additional liquidity with particular regard to the needs of the developing countries through the additional allocation of special drawing rights based on the concept of world liquidity needs to be appropriately revised in the light of the new international environment; any creation of international liquidity should be made through international multilateral mechanisms;

(f) Early establishment of a link between special drawing rights and additional development financing in the interest of developing countries, consistent with the monetary characteristics of special drawing rights;

(g) Review by the International Monetary Fund of the relevant provisions in order to ensure effective participation by developing countries in the decision-making process;

(h) Arrangements to promote an increasing net transfer of real resources from the developed to the developing countries;

(i) Review of the methods of operation of the International Monetary Fund, in particular the terms for both credit repayments and "stand-by" arrangements, the system of compensatory financing, and the terms of the financing of commodity buffer stocks, so as to enable the developing countries to make more effective use of them.

2. *Measures*

All efforts should be made to take the following urgent measures to finance the development of developing countries and to meet the balance-of-payment crises in the developing world:

(a) Implementation at an accelerated pace by the developed countries of the time-bound programme, as already laid down in the International Development Strategy

for the Second United Nations Development Decade, for the net amount of financial resource transfers to developing countries; increase in the official component of the net amount of financial resource transfers to developing countries so as to meet and even to exceed the target of the Strategy;

(b) International financing institutions should effectively play their role as development financing banks without discrimination on account of the political or economic system of any member country, assistance being untied;

(c) More effective participation by developing countries, whether recipients or contributors, in the decision-making process in the competent organs of the International Bank for Reconstruction and Development and the International Development Association, through the establishment of a more equitable pattern of voting rights;

(d) Exemption, wherever possible, of the developing countries from all import and capital outflow controls imposed by the developed countries;

(e) Promotion of foreign investment, both public and private, from developed to developing countries in accordance with the needs and requirements in sectors of their economies as determined by the recipient countries;

(f) Appropriate urgent measures, including international action, should be taken to mitigate adverse consequences for the current and future development of developing countries arising from the burden of external debt contracted on hard terms;

(g) Debt renegotiation on a case-by-case basis with a view to concluding agreements on debt cancellation, moratorium, rescheduling or interest subsidization;

(h) International financial institutions should take into account the special situation of each developing country in reorienting their lending policies to suit these urgent needs; there is also need for improvement in practices of international financial institutions in regard to, *inter alia*, development financing and international monetary problems;

(i) Appropriate steps should be taken to give priority to the least developed, land-locked and island developing countries and to the countries most seriously affected by economic crises and natural calamities, in the availability of loans for development purposes which should include more favourable terms and conditions.

3. *Industrialization*

All efforts should be made by the international community to take measures to encourage the industrialization of the developing countries, and to this end:

(a) The developed countries should respond favourably, within the framework of their official aid as well as international financial institutions, to the requests of developing countries for the financing of industrial projects;

(b) The developed countries should encourage investors to finance industrial production projects, particularly export-oriented production, in developing countries, in agreement with the latter and within the context of their laws and regulations;

(c) With a view to bringing about a new international economic structure which should increase the share of the developing countries in world industrial production, the developed countries and the agencies of the United Nations system, in co-operation with the developing countries, should contribute to setting up new industrial capacities including raw materials and commodity-transforming facilities as a matter of priority in the developing countries that produce those raw materials and commodities;

(d) The international community should continue and expand, with the aid of the developed countries and the international institutions, the operational and instruction-oriented technical assistance programmes, including vocational training and manage-

ment development of national personnel of the developing countries, in the light of their special development requirements.

IV. Transfer of technology

All efforts should be made:

(*a*) To formulate an international code of conduct for the transfer of technology corresponding to needs and conditions prevalent in developing countries;

(*b*) To give access on improved terms to modern technology and to adapt that technology, as appropriate, to specific economic, social and ecological conditions and varying stages of development in developing countries;

(*c*) To expand significantly the assistance from developed to developing countries in research and development programmes and in the creation of suitable indigenous technology;

(*d*) To adapt commercial practices governing transfer of technology to the requirements of the developing countries and to prevent abuse of the rights of sellers;

(*e*) To promote international co-operation in research and development in exploration and exploitation, conservation and the legitimate utilization of natural resources and all sources of energy.

In taking the above measures, the special needs of the least developed and land-locked countries should be borne in mind.

V. Regulation and control over the activities of transnational corporations

All efforts should be made to formulate, adopt and implement an international code of conduct for transnational corporations:

(*a*) To prevent interference in the internal affairs of the countries where they operate and their collaboration with racist régimes and colonial administrations;

(*b*) To regulate their activities in host countries, to eliminate restrictive business practices and to conform to the national development plans and objectives of developing countries, and in this context facilitate, as necessary, the review and revision of previously concluded arrangements;

(*c*) To bring about assistance, transfer of technology and management skills to developing countries on equitable and favourable terms;

(*d*) To regulate the repatriation of the profits accruing from their operations, taking into account the legitimate interests of all parties concerned;

(*e*) To promote reinvestment of their profits in developing countries.

VI. Charter of Economic Rights and Duties of States

The Charter of Economic Rights and Duties of States, the draft of which is being prepared by a working group of the United Nations and which the General Assembly has already expressed the intention of adopting at its twenty-ninth regular session, shall constitute an effective instrument towards the establishment of a new system of international economic relations based on equity, sovereign equality, and interdependence of the interests of developed and developing countries. It is therefore of vital importance that the aforementioned Charter be adopted by the General Assembly at its twenty-ninth session.

VII. Promotion of co-operation among developing countries

1. Collective self-reliance and growing co-operation among developing countries will further strengthen their role in the new international economic order. Developing

countries, with a view to expanding co-operation at the regional, subregional and interregional levels, should take further steps, *inter alia*:

(a) To support the establishment and/or improvement of an appropriate mechanism to defend the prices of their exportable commodities and to improve access to and stabilize markets for them. In this context the increasingly effective mobilization by the whole group of oil-exporting countries of their natural resources for the benefit of their economic development is to be welcomed. At the same time there is the paramount need for co-operation among the developing countries in evolving urgently and in a spirit of solidarity all possible means to assist developing countries to cope with the immediate problems resulting from this legitimate and perfectly justified action. The measures already taken in this regard are a positive indication of the evolving co-operation between developing countries:

(b) To protect their inalienable right to permanent sovereignty over their natural resources;

(c) To promote, establish or strengthen economic integration at the regional and subregional levels;

(d) To increase considerably their imports from other development countries;

(e) To ensure that no developing country accords to imports from developed countries more favourable treatment than that accorded to imports from developing countries. Taking into account the existing international agreements, current limitations and possibilities and also their future evolution, preferential treatment should be given to the procurement of import requirements from other developing countries. Wherever possible, preferential treatment should be given to imports from developing countries and the exports of those countries;

(f) To promote close co-operation in the fields of finance, credit relations and monetary issues, including the development of credit relations on a preferential basis and on favourable terms;

(g) To strengthen efforts which are already being made by developing countries to utilize available financial resources for financing development in the developing countries through investment, financing of export-oriented and emergency projects and other long-term assistance;

(h) To promote and establish effective instruments of co-operation in the fields of industry, science and technology, transport, shipping and mass communication media.

2. Developed countries should support initiatives in the regional, subregional and interregional co-operation of developing countries through the extension of financial and technical assistance by more effective and concrete actions, particularly in the field of commercial policy.

VIII. Assistance in the exercise of permanent sovereignty of States over natural resources

All efforts should be made:

(a) To defeat attempts to prevent the free and effective exercise of the rights of every State to full and permanent sovereignty over its natural resources;

(b) To ensure that competent agencies of the United Nations system meet requests for assistance from developing countries in connexion with the operation of nationalized means of production.

IX. Strengthening the role of the United Nations system in the field of international economic co-operation

1. In furtherance of the objectives of the International Development Strategy for the Second United Nations Development Decade and in accordance with the aims and

objectives of the Declaration on the Establishment of a New International Economic Order, all Member States pledge to make full use of the United Nations system in the implementation of the present Programme of Action, jointly adopted by them, in working for the establishment of a new international economic order and thereby strengthening the role of the United Nations in the field of world-wide co-operation for economic and social development.

2. The General Assembly of the United Nations shall conduct an over-all review of the implementation of the Programme of Action as a priority item. All the activities of the United Nations system to be undertaken under the Programme of Action as well as those already planned, such as the World Population Conference, 1974, the World Food Conference, the Second General Conference of the United National Industrial Development Organization and the mid-term review and appraisal of the International Development Strategy for the Second United Nations Development Decade should be so directed as to enable the special session of the General Assembly on development called for under Assembly resolution 3172 (XXVIII) of 17 December 1973, to make its full contribution to the establishment of the new international economic order. All Member States are urged, jointly and individually, to direct their efforts and policies towards the success of that special session.

3. The Economic and Social Council shall define the policy framework and co-ordinate the activities of all organizations, institutions and subsidiary bodies within the United Nations system which shall be entrusted with the task of implementing the present Programme of Action. In order to enable the Economic and Social Council to carry out its tasks effectively:

(a) All organizations, institutions and subsidiary bodies concerned within the United Nations system shall submit to the Economic and Social Council progress reports on the implementation of the Programme of Action within their respective fields of competence as often as necessary, but not less than once a year;

(b) The Economic and Social Council shall examine the progress reports as a matter of urgency, to which end it may be convened, as necessary, in special session or, if need be, may function continuously. It shall draw the attention of the General Assembly to the problems and difficulties arising in connexion with the implementation of the Programme of Action.

4. All organizations, institutions, subsidiary bodies and conferences of the United Nations system are entrusted with the implementation of the Programme of Action. The activities of the United Nations Conference on Trade and Development, as set forth in General Assembly resolution 1995 (XIX) of 30 December 1964, should be strengthened for the purpose of following in collaboration with other competent organizations the development of international trade in raw materials throughout the world.

5. Urgent and effective measures should be taken to review the lending policies of international financial institutions, taking into account the special situation of each developing country, to suit urgent needs, to improve the practices of these institutions in regard to, *inter alia*, development financing and international monetary problems, and to ensure more effective participation by developing countries—whether recipients or contributors—in the decision-making process through appropriate revision of the pattern of voting rights.

6. The developed countries and others in a position to do so should contribute substantially to the various organizations, programmes and funds established within the United Nations system for the purpose of accelerating economic and social development in developing countries.

7. The present Programme of Action complements and strengthens the goals and objectives embodied in the International Development Strategy for the Second United Nations Development Decade as well as the new measures formulated by the General Assembly at its twenty-eighth session to offset the shortfalls in achieving those goals and objectives.

8. The implementation of the Programme of Action should be taken into account at the time of the mid-term review and appraisal of the International Development Strategy for the Second United Nations Development Decade. New commitments, changes, additions and adaptations in the Strategy should be made, as appropriate, taking into account the Declaration on the Establishment of a New International Economic Order and the present Programme of Action.

X. Special Programme

The General Assembly adopts the following Special Programme, including particularly emergency measures to mitigate the difficulties of the developing countries most seriously affected by economic crisis, bearing in mind the particular problem of the least developed and land-locked countries:

The General Assembly,

Taking into account the following considerations:

(*a*) The sharp increase in the prices of their essential imports such as food, fertilizers, energy products, capital goods, equipment and services, including transportation and transit costs, has gravely exacerbated the increasingly adverse terms of trade of a number of developing countries, added to the burden of their foreign debt and, cumulatively created a situation which, if left untended will make it impossible for them to finance their essential imports and development and result in a further deterioration in the levels and conditions of life in these countries. The present crisis is the outcome of all the problems that have accumulated over the years: in the field of trade, in monetary reform, the world-wide inflationary situation, inadequacy and delay in provision of financial assistance and many other similar problems in the economic and development fields. In facing the crisis, this complex situation must be borne in mind so as to ensure that the Special Programme adopted by the international community provides emergency relief and timely assistance to the most seriously affected countries. Simultaneously, steps are being taken to resolve these outstanding problems through a fundamental restructuring of the world economic system, in order to allow these countries while solving the present difficulties to reach an acceptable level of development.

(*b*) The special measures adopted to assist the most seriously affected countries must encompass not only the relief which they require on an emergency basis to maintain their import requirements, but also, beyond that, steps to consciously promote the capacity of these countries to produce and earn more. Unless such a comprehensive approach is adopted, there is every likelihood that the difficulties of the most seriously affected countries may be perpetuated. Nevertheless, the first and most pressing task of the international community is to enable these countries to meet the shortfall in their balance-of-payments positions. But this must be simultaneously supplemented by additional development assistance to maintain and thereafter accelerate their rate of economic development.

(*c*) The countries which have been most seriously affected are precisely those which are at the greatest disadvantage in the world economy: the least developed, the land-locked and other low-income developing countries as well as other developing countries whose economies have been seriously dislocated as a result of the present economic crisis, natural calamities, and foreign aggression and occupation. An indication of the countries thus affected, the level of the impact on their economies and the kind of relief and assistance they require can be assessed on the basis, *inter alia*, of the following criteria:

   (i) Low *per capita* income as a reflection of relative poverty, low productivity, low level of technology and development;

  (ii) Sharp increase in their import cost of essentials relative to export earnings;

 (iii) High ratio of debt servicing to export earnings;

 (iv) Insufficiency in export earnings, comparative inelasticity of export incomes and unavailability of exportable surplus;

  (v) Low level of foreign exchange reserves or their inadequacy for requirements;

 (vi) Adverse impact of higher transportation and transit costs;

(vii) Relative importance of foreign trade in the development process.

(d) The assessment of the extent and nature of the impact on the economies of the most seriously affected countries must be made flexible, keeping in mind the present uncertainty in the world economy, the adjustment policies that may be adopted by the developed countries and the flow of capital and investment. Estimates of the payments situation and needs of these countries can be assessed and projected reliably only on the basis of their average performance over a number of years. Long-term projections, at this time, cannot but be uncertain.

(e) It is important that, in the special measures to mitigate the difficulties of the most seriously affected countries all the developed countries as well as the developing countries should contribute according to their level of development and the capacity and strength of their economies. It is notable that some developing countries, despite their own difficulties and development needs, have shown a willingness to play a concrete and helpful role in ameliorating the difficulties faced by the poorer developing countries. The various initiatives and measures taken recently by certain developing countries with adequate resources on a bilateral and multilateral basis to contribute to alleviating the difficulties of other developing countries are a reflection of their commitment to the principle of effective economic co-operation among developing countries.

(f) The response of the developed countries which have by far the greater capacity to assist the affected countries in overcoming their present difficulties must be commensurate with their responsibilities. Their assistance should be in addition to the presently available levels of aid. They should fulfil and if possible exceed the targets of the International Development Strategy for the Second United Nations Development Decade on financial assistance to the developing countries, especially that relating to official development assistance. They should also give serious consideration to the cancellation of the external debts of the most seriously affected countries. This would provide the simplest and quickest relief to the affected countries. Favourable consideration should also be given to debt moratorium and rescheduling. The current situation should not lead the industrialized countries to adopt what will ultimately prove to be a self-defeating policy aggravating the present crisis.

Recalling the constructive proposals made by His Imperial Majesty the Shahansha of Iran and His Excellency Mr. Houari Boumediène, President of the People's Democratic Republic of Algeria,

1. *Decides* to launch a Special Programme to provide emergency relief and development assistance to the developing countries most seriously affected, as a matter of urgency, and for the period of time necessary, at least until the end of the Second United Nations Development Decade, to help them overcome their present difficulties and to achieve self-sustaining economic development;

2. *Decides* as a first step in the Special Programme to request the Secretary-General to launch an emergency operation to provide timely relief to the most seriously affected developing countries, as defined in subparagraph *(c)* above, with the aim of maintaining unimpaired essential imports for the duration of the coming twelve months and to invite the industrialized countries and other potential contributors to announce their contributions for emergency assistance, or intimate their intention to do so, by 15 June 1974 to be provided through bilateral or multilateral channels, taking into account the commitments and measures of assistance announced or already taken by some countries, and further requests the Secretary-General to report the progress of the emergency operation to the General Assembly at its twenty-ninth session, through the Economic and Social Council at its fifty-seventh session;

3. *Calls upon* the industrialized countries and other potential contributors to extend to the most seriously affected countries immediate relief and assistance which must be of an order of magnitude that is commensurate with the needs of these countries. Such assistance should be in addition to the existing level of aid and provided at a very early date to the maximum possible extent on a grant basis and, where not possible, on soft terms. The disbursement and relevant operational procedures and terms must reflect this exceptional situation. The assistance could be provided either through bilateral or multilateral channels, including such new institutions and facilities that have been or are to be set up. The special measures may include the following:

(a) Special arrangements on particularly favourable terms and conditions including possible subsidies for and assured supplies of essential commodities and goods;

(b) Deferred payments for all or part of imports of essential commodities and goods;

(c) Commodity assistance, including food aid, on a grant basis or deferred payments in local currencies, bearing in mind that this should not adversely affect the exports of developing countries;

(d) Long-term suppliers' credits on easy terms;

(e) Long-term financial assistance on concessionary terms;

(f) Drawings from special International Monetary Fund facilities on concessional terms;

(g) Establishment of a link between the creation of special drawing rights and development assistance, taking into account the additional financial requirements of the most seriously affected countries;

(h) Subsidies, provided bilaterally or multilaterally, for interest on funds available on commercial terms borrowed by the most seriously affected countries;

(i) Debt renegotiation on a case-by-case basis with a view to concluding agreements on debt cancellation, moratorium or rescheduling;

(j) Provision on more favourable terms of capital goods and technical assistance to accelerate the industrialization of the affected countries;

(k) Investment in industrial and development projects on favourable terms;

(l) Subsidizing the additional transit and transport costs, especially of the land-locked countries;

4. *Appeals* to the developed countries to consider favourably the cancellation, moratorium or rescheduling of the debts of the most seriously affected developing countries, on their request, as an important contribution to mitigating the grave and urgent difficulties of these countries;

5. *Decides* to establish a Special Fund under the auspices of the United Nations, through voluntary contributions from industrialized countries and other potential contributors, as a part of the Special Programme, to provide emergency relief and development assistance, which will commence its operations at the latest by 1 January 1975;

6. *Establishes* an *Ad Hoc* Committee on the Special Programme, composed of thirty-six Member States appointed by the President of the General Assembly, after appropriate consultations, bearing in mind the purposes of the Special fund and its terms of reference:

(a) To make recommendations, inter alia, on the scope, machinery and modes of operation of the Special Fund, taking into account the need for:

  (i) Equitable representation on its governing body;

  (ii) Equitable distribution of its resources;

  (iii) Full utilization of the services and facilities of existing international organizations;

  (iv) The possibility of merging the United Nations Capital Development Fund with the operations of the Special Fund;

  (v) A central monitoring body to oversee the various measures being taken both bilaterally and multilaterally;

and, to this end, bearing in mind the different ideas and proposals submitted at the sixth special session, including those put forward by Iran and those made at the 2208th plenary meeting, and the comments thereon, and the possibility of utilizing the Special Fund to provide an alternative channel for normal development assistance after the emergency period;

(b) To monitor, pending commencement of the operations of the Special Fund, the various measures being taken both bilaterally and multilaterally to assist the most seriously affected countries;

(c) To prepare, on the basis of information provided by the countries concerned and by appropriate agencies of the United Nations system, a broad assessment of:

  (i) The magnitude of the difficulties facing the most seriously affected countries;

  (ii) The kind and quantities of the commodities and goods essentially required by them;

  (iii) Their need for financial assistance;

  (iv) Their technical assistance requirements, including especially access to technology;

7. *Requests* the Secretary-General of the United Nations, the Secretary-General of the United Nations Conference on Trade and Development, the President of the International Bank for Reconstruction and Development, the Managing Director of the International Monetary Fund, the Administrator of the United Nations Development Programme and the heads of the other competent international organizations to assist the *Ad Hoc* Committee on the Special Programme in performing the functions assigned to it under paragraph 6 above, and to help, as appropriate, in the operations of the Special Fund;

8. *Requests* the International Monetary Fund to expedite decisions on:

(a) The establishment of an extended special facility with a view to enabling the most seriously affected developing countries to participate in it on favourable terms;

(b) The creation of special drawing rights and the early establishment of the link between their allocation and development financing;

(c) The establishment and operation of the proposed new special facility to extend credits and subsidize interest charges on commercial funds borrowed by Member States, bearing in mind the interests of the developing countries and especially the additional financial requirements of the most seriously affected countries;

9. *Requests* the World Bank Group and the International Monetary Fund to place their managerial, financial and technical services at the disposal of Governments contributing to emergency financial relief so as to enable them to assist without delay in channeling funds to the recipients, making such institutional and procedural changes as may be required;

10. *Invites* the United Nations Development Programme to take the necessary steps, particularly at the country level, to respond on an emergency basis to requests for additional assistance which it may be called upon to render within the framework of the Special Programme;

11. *Requests* the *Ad Hoc* Committee on the Special Programme to submit its report and recommendations to the Economic and Social Council at its fifty-seventh session and invites the Council, on the basis of its consideration of that report, to submit suitable recommendations to the General Assembly at its twenty-ninth session;

12. *Decides* to consider as a matter of high priority at its twenty-ninth session, within the framework of a new international economic order, the question of special measures for the most seriously affected countries.

2229th plenary meeting
1 May 1974

15. CHARTER OF ECONOMIC RIGHTS AND DUTIES OF STATES
(GA RES 3281 (XXIX) 1094; 14 ILM 251 (1975))

CHAPTER I Fundamentals of International Economic Relations

Economic as well as political and other relations among States shall be governed, *inter alia*, by the following principles:

(a) Sovereignty, territorial integrity and political independence of States;
(b) Sovereign equality of all States;
(c) Non-aggression;
(d) Non-intervention;
(e) Mutual and equitable benefit;
(f) Peaceful coexistence;
(g) Equal rights and self-determination of peoples;
(h) Peaceful settlement of disputes;
(i) Remedy of injustices which have been brought about by force and which deprive a nation of the natural means necessary for its normal development;
(j) Fulfilment in good faith of international obligations;
(k) Respect for human rights and fundamental freedoms;
(l) No attempt to seek hegemony and spheres of influence;
(m) Promotion of international social justice;

(n) International co-operation for development;

(o) Free access to and from the sea by land-locked countries within the framework of the above principles.

CHAPTER II Economic Rights and Duties of States

Article 1

Every State has the sovereign and inalienable right to choose its economic system as well as its political, social and cultural systems in accordance with the will of its people, without outside interference, coercion or threat in any form whatsoever.

Article 2

1. Every State has and shall freely exercise full permanent sovereignty, including possession, use and disposal, over all its wealth, natural resources and economic activities.

2. Each State has the right:

(a) To regulate and exercise authority over foreign investment within its national jurisdiction in accordance with its laws and regulations and in conformity with its national objectives and priorities. No State shall be compelled to grant preferential treatment to foreign investment;

(b) To regulate and supervise the activities of transnational corporations within its national jurisdiction and take measures to ensure that such activities comply with its laws, rules and regulations and conform with its economic and social policies. Transnational corporations shall not intervene in the internal affairs of a host State. Every State should, with full regard for its sovereign rights, co-operate with other States in the exercise of the right set forth in this subparagraph;

(c) To nationalize, expropriate or transfer ownership of foreign property, in which case appropriate compensation should be paid by the State adopting such measures, taking into account its relevant laws and regulations and all circumstances that the State considers pertinent. In any case where the question of compensation gives rise to a controversy, it shall be settled under the domestic law of the nationalizing State and by its tribunals, unless it is freely and mutually agreed by all States concerned that other peaceful means be sought on the basis of the sovereign equality of States and in accordance with the principle of free choice of means.

Article 3

In the exploitation of natural resources shared by two or more countries, each State must co-operate on the basis of a system of information and prior consultations in order to achieve optimum use of such resources without causing damage to the legitimate interest of others.

Article 4

Every State has the right to engage in international trade and other forms of economic co-operation irrespective of any differences in political, economic and social systems. No State shall be subjected to discrimination of any kind based solely on such differences. In the pursuit of international trade and other forms of economic co-operation, every State is free to choose the forms of organization of its foreign economic relations and to enter into bilateral and multilateral arrangements consistent with its international obligations and with the needs of international economic co-operation.

Article 5

All States have the right to associate in organizations of primary commodity producers in order to develop their national economies, to achieve stable financing of their development and, in pursuance of their aims, to assist in the promotion of sustained growth of the world economy, in particular accelerating the development of developing countries. Correspondingly all States have the duty to respect that right by refraining from applying economic and political measures that would limit it.

Article 6

It is the duty of States to contribute to the development of international trade of goods, particularly by means of arrangements and by the conclusion of long-term multilateral commodity agreements, where appropriate, and taking into account the interests of producers and consumers. All States share the responsibility to promote the regular flow and access of all commercial goods traded at stable, remunerative and equitable prices, thus contributing to the equitable development of the world economy, taking into account, in particular the interests of developing countries.

Article 7

Every State has the primary responsibility to promote the economic, social and cultural development of its people. To this end, each State has the right and the responsibility to choose its means and goals of development fully to mobilize and use its resources, to implement progressive economic and social reforms and to ensure the full participation of its people in the process and benefits of development. All States have the duty, individually and collectively, to co-operate in order to eliminate obstacles that hinder such mobilization and use.

Article 8

States should co-operate in facilitating more rational and equitable international economic relations and in encouraging structural changes in the context of a balanced world economy in harmony with the needs and interests of all countries, especially developing countries, and should take appropriate measures to this end.

Article 9

All States have the responsibility to co-operate in the economic, social, cultural, scientific and technological fields for the promotion of economic and social progress throughout the world, specially that of the developing countries.

Article 10

All States are juridically equal and, as equal members of the international community, have the right to participate fully and effectively in the international decision-making process in the solution of world economic, financial and monetary problems, *inter alia*, through the appropriate international organizations in accordance with their existing and evolving rules, and to share equitably in the benefits resulting therefrom.

Article 11

All States should co-operate to strengthen and continuously improve the efficiency of international organizations in implementing measures to stimulate the general economic progress of all countries, particularly of developing countries, and therefore should co-operate to adapt them, when appropriate, to the changing needs of international economic co-operation.

Article 12

1. States have the right, in agreement with the parties concerned, to participate in subregional, regional and interregional co-operation in the pursuit of their economic and social development. All States engaged in such co-operation have the duty to ensure that the policies of those groupings to which they belong correspond to the provisions of the present Charter and are outward-looking, consistent with their international obligations and with the needs of international economic co-operation, and have full regard for the legitimate interests of third countries, especially developing countries.

2. In the case of groupings to which the States concerned have transferred or may transfer certain competences as regards matters that come within the scope of the present Charter, its provisions shall also apply to those groupings, in regard to such matters, consistent with the responsibilities of such States as members of such groupings. Those States shall co-operate in the observance by the groupings of the provisions of this Charter.

Article 13

1. Every State has the right to benefit from the advances and developments in science and technology for the acceleration of its economic and social development.

2. All States should promote international scientific and technological co-operation and the transfer of technology, with proper regard for all legitimate interests, including, *inter alia*, the rights and duties of holders, suppliers and recipients of technology. In particular, all States should facilitate the access of developing countries to the achievements of modern science and technology, the transfer of technology and the creation of indigenous technology for the benefit of the developing countries in forms and in accordance with procedures which are suited to their economies and their needs.

3. Accordingly, developed countries should co-operate with the developing countries in the establishment, strengthening and development of their scientific and technological infrastructures and their scientific research and technological activities so as to help to expand and transform the economies of developing countries.

4. All States should co-operate in research with a view to evolving further internationally accepted guidelines or regulations for the transfer of technology, taking fully into account the interests of developing countries.

Article 14

Every State has the duty to co-operate in promoting a steady and increasing expansion and liberalization of world trade and an improvement in the welfare and living standards of all peoples, in particular those of developing countries. Accordingly, all States should co-operate, *inter alia*, towards the progressive dismantling of obstacles to trade and the improvement of the international framework for the conduct of world trade and, to these ends, co-ordinated efforts shall be made to solve in an equitable way the trade problems of all countries, taking into account the specific trade problems of the developing countries. In this connexion, States shall take measures aimed at securing additional benefits for the international trade of developing countries so as to achieve a substantial increase in their foreign exchange earnings, the diversification of their exports, the acceleration of the rate of growth of their trade, taking into account their development needs, an improvement in the possibilities for these countries to participate in the expansion of world trade and a balance more favourable to developing countries in the sharing of the advantages resulting from this expansion, through, in the largest possible measure, a substantial improvement in the conditions of access for the products of interest to the developing countries and, wherever appropriate, measures designed to attain stable, equitable and remunerative prices for primary products.

Article 15

All States have the duty to promote the achievement of general and complete disarmament under effective international control and to utilize the resources released by effective disarmament measures for the economic and social development of countries, allocating a substantial portion of such resources as additional means for the development needs of developing countries.

Article 16

1. It is the right and duty of all States, individually and collectively, to eliminate colonialism, *apartheid*, racial discrimination, neo-colonialism and all forms of foreign aggression, occupation and domination, and the economic and social consequences thereof, as a prerequisite for development. States which practise such coercive policies are economically responsible to the countries, territories and peoples affected for the restitution and full compensation for the exploitation and depletion of, and damages to, the natural and all other resources of those countries, territories and peoples. It is the duty of all States to extend assistance to them.

2. No State has the right to promote or encourage investments that may constitute an obstacle to the liberation of a territory occupied by force.

Article 17

International co-operation for development is the shared goal and common duty of all States. Every State should co-operate with the efforts of developing countries to accelerate their economic and social development by providing favourable external conditions and by extending active assistance to them, consistent with their development needs and objectives, with strict respect for the sovereign equality of States and free of any conditions derogating from their sovereignty.

Article 18

Developed countries should extend, improve and enlarge the system of generalized non-reciprocal and non-discriminatory tariff preferences to the developing countries consistent with the relevant agreed conclusions and relevant decisions as adopted on this subject, in the framework of the competent international organizations. Developed countries should also give serious consideration to the adoption of other differential measures, in areas where this is feasible and appropriate and in ways which will provide special and more favourable treatment, in order to meet the trade and development needs of the developing countries. In the conduct of international economic relations the developed countries should endeavour to avoid measures having a negative effect on the development of the national economies of the developing countries, as promoted by generalized tariff preferences and other generally agreed differential measures in their favour.

Article 19

With a view to accelerating the economic growth of developing countries and bridging the economic gap between developed and developing countries, developed countries should grant generalized preferential, non-reciprocal and non-discriminatory treatment to developing countries in those fields of international economic co-operation where it may be feasible.

Article 20

Developing countries should, in their efforts to increase their over-all trade, give due attention to the possibility of expanding their trade with socialist countries, by granting to these countries conditions for trade not inferior to those granted normally to the developed market economy countries.

Article 21

Developing countries should endeavour to promote the expansion of their mutual trade and to this end may, in accordance with the existing and evolving provisions and procedures of international agreements where applicable, grant trade preferences to other developing countries without being obliged to extend such preferences to developed countries, provided these arrangements do not constitute an impediment to general trade liberalization and expansion.

Article 22

1. All States should respond to the generally recognized or mutually agreed development needs and objectives of developing countries by promoting increased net flows of real resources to the developing countries from all sources, taking into account any obligations and commitments undertaken by the States concerned, in order to reinforce the efforts of developing countries to accelerate their economic and social development.

2. In this context, consistent with the aims and objectives mentioned above and taking into account any obligations and commitments undertaken in this regard, it should be their endeavour to increase the net amount of financial flows from official sources to developing countries and to improve the terms and conditions thereof.

3. The flow of development assistance resources should include economic and technical assistance.

Article 23

To enhance the effective mobilization of their own resources, the developing countries should strengthen their economic co-operation and expand their mutual trade so as to accelerate their economic and social development. All countries, especially developed countries, individually as well as through the competent international organizations of which they are members, should provide appropriate and effective support and co-operation.

Article 24

All States have the duty to conduct their mutual economic relations in a manner which takes into account the interests of other countries. In particular, all States should avoid prejudicing the interests of developing countries.

Article 25

In furtherance of world economic development, the international community, especially its developed members, shall pay special attention to the particular needs and problems of the least developed among the developing countries, of land-locked developing countries and also island developing countries, with a view to helping them to overcome their particular difficulties and thus contribute to their economic and social development.

Article 26

All States have the duty to coexist in tolerance and live together in peace, irrespective of differences in political, economic, social and cultural systems, and to facilitate trade between States having different economic and social systems. International trade should be conducted without prejudice to generalized non-discriminatory and non-reciprocal preferences in favour of developing countries, on the basis of mutual advantage, equitable benefits and the exchange of most-favoured-nation treatment.

Article 27

1. Every State has the right to enjoy fully the benefits of world invisible trade and to engage in the expansion of such trade.

2. World invisible trade, based on efficiency and mutual and equitable benefit, furthering the expansion of the world economy, is the common goal of all States. The role of developing countries in world invisible trade should be enhanced and strengthened consistent with the above objectives, particular attention being paid to the special needs of developing countries.

3. All States should co-operate with developing countries in their endeavours to increase their capacity to earn foreign exchange from invisible transactions, in accordance with the potential and needs of each developing country and consistent with the objectives mentioned above.

Article 28

All States have the duty to co-operate in achieving adjustments in the prices of exports of developing countries in relation to prices of their imports so as to promote just and equitable terms of trade for them, in a manner which is remunerative for producers and equitable for producers and consumers.

CHAPTER III Common Responsibilities Towards the International Community

Article 29

The sea-bed and ocean floor and the subsoil thereof, beyond the limits of national jurisdiction, as well as the resources of the area, are the common heritage of mankind. On the basis of the principles adopted by the General Assembly in resolution 2749 (XXV) of 17 December 1970, all States shall ensure that the exploration of the area and exploitation of its resources are carried out exclusively for peaceful purposes and that the benefits derived therefrom are shared equitably by all States, taking into account the particular interests and needs of developing countries; an international regime applying to the area and its resources and including appropriate international machinery to give effect to its provisions shall be established by an international treaty of a universal character, generally agreed upon.

Article 30

The protection, preservation and enhancement of the environment for the present and future generations is the responsibility of all States. All States shall endeavour to establish their own environmental and developmental policies in conformity with such responsibility. The environmental policies of all States should enhance and not adversely affect the present and future development potential of developing countries. All States have the responsibility to ensure that activities within their jurisdiction or control do not cause damage to the environment of other States or of areas beyond the limits of national jurisdiction. All States should co-operate in evolving international norms and regulations in the field of the environment.

CHAPTER IV Final Provisions

Article 31

All States have the duty to contribute to the balanced expansion of the world economy, taking duly into account the close interrelationship between the well-being of the developed countries and the growth and development of the developing countries, and the fact that the prosperity of the international community as a whole depends upon the prosperity of its constituent parts.

Article 32

No State may use or encourage the use of economic, political or any other type of measures to coerce another State in order to obtain from it the subordination of the exercise of its sovereign rights.

Article 33

1. Nothing in the present Charter shall be construed as impairing or derogating from the provisions of the Charter of the United Nations or actions taken in pursuance thereof.

2. In their interpretation and application, the provisions of the present Charter are interrelated and each provision should be construed in the context of the other provisions.

Article 34

An item on the Charter of Economic Rights and Duties of States shall be included in the agenda of the General Assembly at its thirtieth session, and thereafter on the agenda of every fifth session. In this way a systematic and comprehensive consideration of the implementation of the Charter, covering both progress achieved and any improvements and additions which might become necessary, would be carried out and appropriate measures recommended. Such consideration should take into account the evolution of all the economic, social, legal and other factors related to the principles upon which the present Charter is based and on its purpose.

2315th plenary meeting
12 December 1974

16. Treaty of the Southern African Development Community (SADC)   (32 ILM 122 (1993))

PREAMBLE

We, the heads of State or Government of:
 The People's Republic of Angola
 The Republic of Botswana
 The Kingdom of Lesotho
 The Republic of Malawi
 The Republic of Mozambique
 The Republic of Namibia
 The Kingdom of Swaziland
 The United Republic of Tanzania
 The Republic of Zambia
 The Republic of Zimbabwe

HAVING REGARD to the objectives set forth in "SOUTHERN AFRICA: TOWARD ECONOMIC LIBERATION—A Declaration by the Governments of independent States of Southern Africa, made at Lusaka, on the 1st April, 1980";

IN PURSUANCE of the principles of "TOWARDS A SOUTHERN AFRICAN DEVELOPMENT COMMUNITY—A Declaration made by the Heads of State or Government of Southern Africa at Windhoek, in August, 1992," which affirms our commitment to establish a Development Community in the Region;

DETERMINED to ensure, through common action, the progress and well-being of the peoples of Southern Africa;

CONSCIOUS of our duty to promote the interdependence and integration of our national economies for the harmonious, balanced and equitable development of the Region;

CONVINCED of the need to mobilise our own and international resources to promote the implementation of national, interstate and regional policies, programmes and projects within the framework for economic integration;

DEDICATED to secure, by concerted action, international understanding, support and cooperation;

MINDFUL of the need to involve the peoples of the Region centrally in the process of development and integration, particularly through the guarantee of democratic rights, observance of human rights and the rule of law;

RECOGNISING that, in an increasingly interdependent world, mutual understanding, good neighbourliness, and meaningful cooperation among the countries of the Region are indispensable to the realisation of these ideals;

TAKING INTO ACCOUNT the Lagos Plan of Action and the Final Act of Lagos of April 1980, and the Treaty establishing the African Economic Community signed at Abuja, on the 3rd of June, 1991;

BEARING IN MIND the principles of international law governing relations between States;

HAVING DECIDED TO ESTABLISH AN INTERNATIONAL ORGANISATION TO BE KNOWN AS THE **SOUTHERN AFRICAN DEVELOPMENT COMMUNITY (SADC)**, AND HEREBY AGREE AS FOLLOWS:

CHAPTER I

Article 1 DEFINITIONS

In this Treaty, unless the context otherwise requires:

1. "Treaty" means this Treaty establishing SADC;
2. "Protocol" means an instrument of implementation of this Treaty, having the same legal force as this Treaty;
3. "Community" means the organisation for economic integration established by Article 2 of this Treaty;
4. "Region" means the geographical area of the Member States of SADC;
5. "Member State" means a member of SADC;
6. "Summit" means the Summit of the Heads of State or Government of SADC established by Article 9 of this Treaty;
7. "High Contracting Parties" means States, herein represented by Heads of State or Government or their duly authorised representatives for purposes of the establishment of the Community;
8. "Council" means the Council of Ministers of SADC established by Article 9 of this Treaty;
9. "Secretariat" means the Secretariat of SADC established by Article 9 of this Treaty;
10. "Executive Secretary" means the chief executive officer of SADC appointed under Article 10 (7) of this Treaty;
11. "Commission" means a commission of SADC established by Article 9 of this Treaty;
12. "Tribunal" means the tribunal of the Community established by Article 9 of this Treaty;
13. "Sectoral Committee" means a committee referred to in Article 38 of this Treaty;
14. "Sector Coordinating Unit" means a unit referred to in Article 38 of this Treaty;
15. "Standing Committee" means the Standing Committee of Officials established by Article 9 of this Treaty;
16. "Fund" means resources available at any given time for application to programmes, projects and activities of SADC as provided by Article 26 of this Treaty.

CHAPTER II Establishment and Legal Status

Article 2 ESTABLISHMENT

1. By this Treaty, the High Contracting Parties establish the Southern African Development Community (hereinafter referred to as SADC).
2. The Headquarters of SADC shall be at Gaborone, Republic of Botswana.

Article 3 LEGAL STATUS

1. SADC shall be an international organisation, and shall have legal personality with capacity and power to enter into contract, acquire, own or dispose of movable or immovable property and to sue and be sued.
2. In the territory of each Member State, SADC shall, pursuant to paragraph 1 of this Article, have such legal capacity as is necessary for the proper exercise of its functions.

CHAPTER III **Principles, Objectives and General Undertakings**

Article 4 PRINCIPLES

SADC and its Member States shall act in accordance with the following principles:

(a) sovereign equality of all Member States;

(b) solidarity, peace and security;

(c) human rights, democracy, and the rule of law;

(d) equity, balance and mutual benefit;

(e) peaceful settlement of disputes;

Article 5 OBJECTIVES

1. The objectives of SADC shall be to:

   (a) achieve development and economic growth, alleviate poverty, enhance the standard and quality of life of the peoples of Southern Africa and support the socially disadvantaged through regional integration;

   (b) evolve common political values, systems and institutions;

   (c) promote and defend peace and security;

   (d) promote self-sustaining development on the basis of collective self-reliance, and the interdependence of Member States;

   (e) achieve complementarity between national and regional strategies and programmes;

   (f) promote and maximise productive employment and utilisation of resources of the Region;

   (g) achieve sustainable utilisation of natural resources and effective protection of the environment;

   (h) strengthen and consolidate the long standing historical, social and cultural affinities and links among the peoples of the Region.

2. In order to achieve the objectives set out in paragraph 1 of this Article, SADC shall:

   (a) harmonise political and socio-economic policies and plans of Member States;

   (b) encourage the peoples of the Region and their institutions to take initiatives to develop economic, social and cultural ties across the Region, and to participate fully in the implementation of the programmes and projects of SADC;

   (c) create appropriate institutions and mechanisms for the mobilisation of requisite resources for the implementation of programmes and operations of SADC and its Institutions;

   (d) develop policies aimed at the progressive elimination of obstacles to the free movement of capital and labour, goods and services, and of the peoples of the Region generally, among Member States;

   (e) promote the development of human resources;

   (f) promote the development, transfer and mastery of technology;

   (g) improve economic management and performance through regional cooperation;

   (h) promote the coordination and harmonisation of the international relations of Member States;

   (i) secure international understanding, cooperation and support, and mobilise the inflow if public and private resources into the Region;

(*j*)   develop such other activities as Member States may decide in furtherance of the objectives of this Treaty.

Article 6 GENERAL UNDERTAKINGS

1. Member States undertake to adopt adequate measures to promote the achievement of the objectives of SADC, and shall refrain from taking any measure likely to jeopardise the sustenance of its principles, the achievement of its objectives and the implementation of the provisions of this Treaty.
2. SADC and Member States shall not discriminate against any person on grounds of gender, religion, political views, race, ethnic origin, culture or disability.
3. SADC shall not discriminate against any Member State.
4. Member States shall take all steps necessary to ensure the uniform application of this Treaty.
5. Member States shall take all necessary steps to accord this Treaty the force of national law.
6. Member States shall cooperate with and assist institutions of SADC in the performance of their duties.

CHAPTER IV Membership

Article 7 MEMBERSHIP

States listed in the Preamble hereto shall, upon signature and ratification of this Treaty, be members of SADC.

Article 8 ADMISSION OF NEW MEMBERS

1. Any state not listed in the Preamble to this Treaty may become a member of SADC upon being admitted by the existing members and acceding to this Treaty.
2. The admission of any such state to membership of SADC shall be effected by a unanimous decision of the Summit.
3. The Summit shall determine the procedures for the admission of new members and for accession to this Treaty by such members.
4. Membership of SADC shall not be subject to any reservations.

CHAPTER V Institutions

Article 9 ESTABLISHMENT OF INSTITUTIONS

1. The following Institutions are hereby established:
    (*a*) The Summit of Heads of State or Government;
    (*b*) The Council of Ministers;
    (*c*) Commissions;
    (*d*) The Standing Committee of Officials;
    (*e*) The Secretariat; and
    (*f*) The Tribunal.
2. Other institutions may be established as necessary.

Article 10 THE SUMMIT

1. The Summit shall consist of the Heads of State or Government of all Member States, and shall be the supreme policy-making Institution of SADC.

2. The Summit shall be responsible for the overall policy direction and control of the functions of SADC.

3. The Summit shall adopt legal instruments for the implementation of the provisions of this Treaty; provided that the Summit may delegate this authority to the Council or any other institution of SADC as the Summit may deem appropriate.

4. The Summit shall elect a Chairman and a Vice-Chairman of SADC from among its members for an agreed period, on the basis of rotation.

5. The Summit shall meet at least once a year.

6. The Summit shall decide on the creation of Commissions, other institutions, committees and organs as need arises.

7. The Summit shall appoint the Executive Secretary and the Deputy Executive Secretary, on the recommendation of Council.

8. Unless otherwise provided in this Treaty, the decisions of the Summit shall be by consensus and shall be binding.

Article 11 THE COUNCIL

1. The Council shall consist of one Minister from each Member State, preferably a Minister responsible for economic planning or finance.

2. It shall be the responsibility of the Council to:
   (a) oversee the functioning and development of SADC;
   (b) oversee the implementation of the policies of SADC and the proper execution of its programmes;
   (c) advise the Summit on matters of overall policy and efficient and harmonious functioning and development of SADC;
   (d) approve policies, strategies and work programmes of SADC;
   (e) direct, coordinate and supervise the operations of the institutions of SADC subordinate to it;
   (f) define sectoral areas of cooperation and allocate to Member States responsibility for coordinating sectoral activities, or re-allocate such responsibilities;
   (g) create its own committees as necessary;
   (h) recommend to the Summit persons for appointment to the posts of Executive Secretary and Deputy Executive Secretary;
   (i) determine the Terms and Conditions of Service of the staff of the institutions of SADC;
   (j) convene conferences and other meetings as appropriate, for purposes of promoting the objectives and programmes of SADC; and
   (k) perform such other duties as may be assigned to it by the Summit or this Treaty.

3. The Chairman and Vice-Chairman of the Council shall be appointed by the Member States holding the Chairmanship and the Vice-Chairmanship of SADC respectively.

4. The Council shall meet at least once a year.

5. The Council shall report and be responsible to the Summit.

6. Decisions of the Council shall be by consensus.

Article 12 COMMISSIONS

1. Commissions shall be constituted to guide and coordinate cooperation and integration policies and programmes in designated sectoral areas.

2. The composition, powers, functions, procedures and other matters related to each Commission shall be prescribed by an appropriate protocol approved by the Summit.

3. The Commissions shall work closely with the Secretariat.

4. Commissions shall be responsible and report to the Council.

Article 13 THE STANDING COMMMITTEE OF OFFICIALS

1. The Standing Committee shall consist of one permanent secretary or an official of equivalent rank from each Member State, preferably from a ministry responsible for economic planning or finance.

2. The Standing Committee shall be a technical advisory committee to the Council.

3. The Standing Committee shall be responsible and repot to the Council.

4. The Chairman and Vice-Chairman of the Standing Committee shall be appointed from the Member States holding the Chairmanship and the Vice-Chairmanship, respectively, of the Council.

5. The Standing Committee shall meet at least once a year.

6. Decisions of the Standing Committee shall be by consensus.

Article 14 THE SECRETARIAT

1. The Secretariat shall be the principal executive Institution of SADC, and shall be responsible for:

   (a) strategic planning and management of the programmes of SADC;

   (b) implementation of decisions of the Summit and of the Council;

   (c) organisation and management of SADC meetings;

   (d) financial and general administration;

   (e) representation and promotion of SADC; and

   (f) coordination and harmonisation of the policies and strategies of Member States.

2. The Secretariat shall be headed by the Executive Secretary.

3. The Secretariat shall have such other staff as may be determined by the Council from time to time.

Article 15 THE EXECUTIVE SECRETARY

1. The Executive Secretary shall be responsible to the Council for the following:

   (a) consultation and coordination with the Governments and other institutions of Member States;

   (b) pursuant to the direction of Council or Summit, or on his/her own initiative, undertaking measures aimed at promoting the objectives of SADC and enhancing its performance;

   (c) promotion of cooperation with other organisations for the furtherance of the objectives of SADC;

   (d) organising and servicing meetings of the Summit, the Council, the Standing Committee and any other meetings convened on the direction of the Summit or the Council;

   (e) custodianship of the property of SADC;

   (f) appointment of the staff of the Secretariat, in accordance with procedures, and under Terms and Conditions of Service determined by the Council;

(g) administration and finances of the Secretariat;

(h) preparation of Annual Reports on the activities of SADC and its institutions;

(i) preparation of the Budget and Audited Accounts of SADC for submission to the Council;

(j) diplomatic and other representations of SADC;

(k) public relations and promotion of SADC;

(l) such other functions as may, from time to time, be determined by the Summit and Council.

2. The Executive Secretary shall liaise closely with Commissions, and other institutions, guide, support and monitor the performance of SADC in the various sectors to ensure conformity and harmony with agreed policies, strategies, programmes and projects.

3. The Executive Secretary shall be appointed for four years, and be eligible for appointment for another period not exceeding four years.

Article 16 THE TRIBUNAL

1. The Tribunal shall be constituted to ensure adherence to and the proper interpretation of the provisions of this Treaty and subsidiary instruments and to adjudicate upon such disputes as may be referred to it.

2. The composition, powers, functions, procedures and other related matters governing the Tribunal shall be prescribed in a Protocol adopted by the Summit.

3. Members of the Tribunal shall be appointed for a specified period.

4. The Tribunal shall give advisory opinions on such matters as the Summit or the Council may refer to it.

5. The decisions of the Tribunal shall be final and binding.

Article 17 SPECIFIC UNDERTAKINGS

1. Member States shall respect the international character and responsibilities of SADC, the Executive Secretary and other staff of SADC, and shall not seek to influence them in the discharge of their functions.

2. In the performance of their duties, the members of the Tribunal, the Executive Secretary and the other staff of SADC shall be committed to the international character of SADC, and shall not seek or receive instructions from any Member States, or from any authority external to SADC. They shall refrain from any action incompatible with their positions as international staff responsible only to SADC.

CHAPTER VI Meetings

Article 18 QUORUM

The quorum for all meetings of the Institutions of SADC shall be two-thirds of its Members.

Article 19 DECISIONS

Except as otherwise provided in this Treaty, decisions of the Institutions of SADC shall be taken by consensus.

Article 20 PROCEDURE

Except as otherwise provided in this Treaty, the Institutions of SADC shall determine their own rules of procedure.

CHAPTER VII Cooperation

Article 21 AREAS OF COOPERATION

1. Members States shall cooperate in all areas necessary to foster regional development and integration on the basis of balance, equity and mutual benefit.
2. Member States shall, through appropriate institutions of SADC, coordinate, rationalise and harmonise their overall macro-economic and sectoral policies and strategies, programmes and projects in the areas of cooperation.
3. In accordance with the provisions of this Treaty, Member States agree to cooperate in the areas of:
   (a) food security, land and agriculture;
   (b) infrastructure and services;
   (c) industry, trade, investment and finance;
   (d) human resources development, science and technology;
   (e) natural resources and environment;
   (f) social welfare, information and culture; and
   (g) politics, diplomacy, international relations, peace and security.
4. Additional areas of cooperation may be decided upon by the Council.

Article 22 PROTOCOLS

1. Member States shall conclude such Protocols as may be necessary in each area of cooperation, which shall spell out the objectives and scope of, and institutional mechanisms for, cooperation and integration.
2. Each Protocol shall be approved by the Summit on the recommendation of the Council, and shall thereafter become an integral part of this Treaty.
3. Each Protocol shall be subject to signature and ratification by the parties thereto.

Article 23 NON-GOVERNMENTAL ORGANISATIONS

1. In pursuance of the objectives of this Treaty, SADC shall seek to involve fully, the peoples of the Region and non-governmental organisations in the process of regional integration.
2. SADC shall cooperate with, and support the initiatives of the peoples of the Region and non-governmental organisations, contributing to the objectives of this Treaty in the areas of cooperation in order to foster closer relations among the communities, associations and peoples of the Region.

CHAPTER VIII Relations with other States, Regional and International Organisations

Article 24

1. Subject to the provisions of Article 6 (1), Member States and SADC shall maintain good working relations and other forms of cooperation, and may enter into agreements with

other states, regional and international organisations, whose objectives are compatible with the objectives of SADC and the provisions of this Treaty.

2. Conferences and other meetings may be held between Member States and other Governments and organisations associated with the development efforts of SADC to review policies and strategies, and evaluate the performance of SADC in the implementation of its programmes and projects, identify and agree in future plans of cooperation.

CHAPTER IX Resources, Fund and Assets

Article 25 RESOURCES

1. SADC shall be responsible for the mobilisation of its own and other resources required for the implementation of its programmes and projects.
2. SADC shall create such institutions as may be necessary for the effective mobilisation and efficient application of resources for regional development.
3. Resources acquired by SADC by way of contributions, loans, grants or gifts, shall be the property of SADC.
4. The resources of SADC may be made available to Member States in pursuance of the objectives of this Treaty, on terms and conditions mutually agreed between SADC and the Member States involved.
5. Resources of SADC shall be utilised in the most efficient and equitable manner.

Article 26 FUND

The Fund of SADC shall consist of contributions of Member States, income from SADC enterprises and receipts from regional and non-regional sources.

Article 27 ASSETS

1. Property, both movable and immovable, acquired by or on behalf of SADC shall constitute the assets of SADC, irrespective of their location.
2. Property acquired by Member States, under the auspices of SADC, shall belong to the Member States concerned, subject to provisions of paragraph 3 of this Article, and Articles 25 and 34 of this Treaty.
3. Assets acquired by Member States under the auspices of SADC shall be accessible to all Member States on an equitable basis.

CHAPTER X Financial Provisions

Article 28 THE BUDGET

1. The budget of SADC shall be funded by contributions made by Member States, and such other sources as may be determined by the Council.
2. Member States shall contribute to the budget of SADC in proportions agreed upon by the Council.
3. The Executive Secretary shall cause to be prepared, estimates of revenue and expenditure for the Secretariat and Commissions, and submit them to the Council, not less than three months before the beginning of the financial year.
4. The Council shall approve the estimates of revenue and expenditure before the beginning of the financial year.

5. The financial year of SADC shall be determined by the Council.

Article 29 EXTERNAL AUDIT

1. The Council shall appoint external auditors and shall fix their fees and remuneration at the beginning of each financial year.
2. The Executive Secretary shall cause to be prepared and audited annual statements of accounts for the Secretariat and Commissions, and submit them to the Council for approval.

Article 30 FINANCIAL REGULATIONS

The Executive Secretary shall prepare and submit to the Council for approval financial regulations, standing orders and rules for the management of the affairs of SADC.

CHAPTER XI **Immunities and Privileges**

Article 31

1. SADC, its Institutions and staff shall, in the territory of each Member State, have such immunities and privileges as are necessary for the proper performance of their functions under this Treaty, and which shall be similar to those accorded to comparable international organisations.
2. The immunities and privileges conferred by this Article shall be prescribed in a Protocol.

CHAPTER XII **Settlement of Disputes**

Article 32

Any dispute arising from the interpretation or application of this Treaty, which cannot be settled amicably, shall be referred to the Tribunal.

CHAPTER XIII **Sanctions, Withdrawal and Dissolution**

Article 33 SANCTIONS

1. Sanctions may be imposed against any Member State that:
   (a) persistently fails, without good reason, to fulfil obligations assumed under this Treaty;
   (b) implements policies which undermine the principles and objectives of SADC; or
   (c) is in arrears for more than one year in the payment of contributions to SADC, for reasons other than those caused by natural calamity or exceptional circumstances that gravely affect its economy, and has not secured the dispensation of the Summit.
2. The sanctions shall be determined by the Summit on a case-by-case basis.

Article 34 WITHDRAWAL

1. A Member State wishing to withdraw from SADC shall serve notice of its intention in writing, a year in advance, to the Chairman of SADC, who shall inform other Member States accordingly.

2. At the expiration of the period of notice, the Member State shall, unless the notice is withdrawn, cease to be a member of SADC.

3. During the one year period of notice referred to in paragraph 1 of this Article, the Member State wishing to withdraw from SADC shall comply with the provisions of this Treaty, and shall continue to be bound by its obligations.

4. A Member State which has withdrawn shall not be entitled to claim any property or rights until the dissolution of SADC.

5. Assets of SADC situated in the territory of a Member State which has withdrawn, shall continue to be the property of SADC and be available for its use.

6. The obligations assumed by Member States under this Treaty shall, to the extent necessary to fulfil such obligations, survive the termination of membership by any State.

Article 35 DISSOLUTION

1. The Summit may decide by a resolution supported by three-quarters of all members to dissolve SADC or any of its Institutions, and determine the terms and conditions of dealing with its liabilities and disposal of its assets.

2. A proposal for the dissolution of SADC may be made to the Council by any Member State, for preliminary consideration, provided, however, that such a proposal shall not be submitted for the decision of the Summit until all Member States have been duly notified of it and a period of twelve months has elapsed after the submission to the Council.

CHAPTER XIV Amendment of the Treaty

Article 36

1. An amendment of this Treaty shall be adopted by a decision of three-quarters of all the Members of the Summit.

2. A proposal for the amendment of this Treaty may be made to the Executive Secretary by any Member State for preliminary consideration by the Council, provided, however, that the proposed amendment shall not be submitted to the Council for preliminary consideration until all Member States have been duly notified of it, and a period of three months has elapsed after such notification.

CHAPTER XV Language

Article 37

The working languages of SADC shall be English and Portuguese, and such other languages as the Council may determine.

CHAPTER XVI Saving Provisions

Article 38

A sectoral Committee, Sector Coordinating Unit or any other institution, obligation or arrangement of the Southern African Development Coordination Conference which exists immediately before the coming into force of this Treaty, continues to subsist, operate or bind Member States or SADC as if it were established or undertaken under this Treaty, until the Council or Summit determines otherwise.

CHAPTER XVII Signature, Ratification, Entry into Force, Accession and Depository

Article 39 SIGNATURE

This Treaty shall be signed by the High Contracting Parties.

Article 40 RATIFICATION

This Treaty shall be ratified by the signatory States in accordance with their constitutional procedures.

Article 41 ENTRY INTO FORCE

This Treaty shall enter into force thirty (30) days after the deposit of the instruments of ratification by two thirds of the States listed in the Preamble.

Article 42 ACCESSION

This Treaty shall remain open for accession by any state subject to Article 8 of this Treaty.

Article 43 DEPOSITORY

1. The original texts of this Treaty and Protocols and all instruments of ratification and accession shall be deposited with the Executive Secretary of SADC, who shall transmit certified copies to all Member States.
2. The Executive Secretary shall register this Treaty with the Secretariats of the United Nations Organisation and the Organisation of African Unity.

CHAPTER XVIII Termination of the Memorandum of Understanding

Article 44

This Treaty replaces the Memorandum of Understanding on the Institutions of the Southern African Development Coordination Conference dated 20th July, 1981.

17. DECLARATION ON THE RIGHT TO DEVELOPMENT

(GA RES 41/128 (1986))

The General Assembly,

Having considered the question of the right to development,

Decides to adopt the Declaration on the Right to Development, the text of which is annexed to the present resolution.

97th plenary meetings
4 December 1986

ANNEX

Declaration on the Right to Development

The General Assembly,

Bearing in mind the purposes and principles of the Charter of the United Nations relating to the achievement of international co-operation in solving international problems of an economic, social, cultural or humanitarian nature, and in promoting and encouraging respect for human rights and fundamental freedoms for all without distinction as to race, sex, language or religion,

Recognizing that development is a comprehensive economic, social, cultural and political process, which aims at the constant improvement of the well-being of the entire population and of all individuals on the basis of their active, free and meaningful participation in development and in the fair distribution of benefits resulting therefrom,

Considering that under the provisions of the Universal Declaration of Human Rights everyone is entitled to a social and international order in which the rights and freedoms set forth in that Declaration can be fully realized,

Recalling the provisions of the International Covenant on Economic, Social and Cultural Rights and of the International Covenant on Civil and Political Rights,

Recalling further the relevant agreements, conventions, resolutions, recommendations and other instruments of the United Nations and its specialized agencies concerning the integral development of the human being, economic and social progress and development of all peoples, including those instruments concerning decolonization, the prevention of discrimination, respect for and observance of, human rights and fundamental freedoms, the maintenance of international peace and security and the further promotion of friendly relations and co-operation among States in accordance with the Charter,

Recalling the right of peoples to self-determination, by virtue of which they have the right freely to determine their political status and to pursue their economic, social and cultural development,

Recalling also the right of peoples to exercise, subject to the relevant provisions of both International Covenants on Human Rights, full and complete sovereignty over all their natural wealth and resources,

Mindful of the obligation of States under the Charter to promote universal respect for and observance of human rights and fundamental freedoms for all without distinction of any kind such as race, colour, sex, language, religion, political or other opinion, national or social origin, property, birth or other status,

Considering that the elimination of the massive and flagrant violations of the human rights of the peoples and individuals affected by situations such as those resulting from colonialism, neo-colonialism, *apartheid*, all forms of racism and racial discrimination, foreign domination and occupation, aggression and threats against national sovereignty, national unity and territorial integrity and threats of war would contribute to the establishment of circumstances propitious to the development of a great part of mankind,

Concerned at the existence of serious obstacles to development, as well as to the complete fulfilment of human beings and of peoples, constituted, *inter alia*, by the denial of civil, political, economic, social and cultural rights, and considering that all human rights and fundamental freedoms are indivisible and interdependent and that, in order to promote development, equal attention and urgent consideration should be given to the implementation, promotion and protection of civil, political, economic, social and cultural rights and that, accordingly, the promotion of, respect for and enjoyment of certain human rights and fundamental freedoms cannot justify the denial of other human rights and fundamental freedoms,

Considering that international peace and security are essential elements for the realization of the right to development,

Reaffirming that there is a close relationship between disarmament and development and that progress in the field of development and that resources released through disarmament measures should be devoted to the economic and social development and well-being of all peoples and, in particular, those of the developing countries,

Recognizing that the human person is the central subject of the development process and that development policy should therefore make the human being the main participant and beneficiary of development,

Recognizing that the creation of conditions favourable to the development of peoples and individuals is the primary responsibility of their States,

Aware that efforts at the international level to promote and protect human rights should be accompanied by efforts to establish a new international economic order,

Confirming that the right to development is an inalienable human right and that equality of opportunity for development is a prerogative both of nations and of individuals who make up nations,

Proclaims the following Declaration on the Right to Development:

Article 1

1. The right to development is an inalienable human right by virtue of which every human person and all peoples are entitled to participate in, contribute to, and enjoy economic, social, cultural and political development, in which all human rights and fundamental freedoms can be fully realized.

2. The human right to development also implies the full realization of the right of peoples to self-determination, which includes, subject to the relevant provisions of both International Covenants on Human Rights, the exercise of their inalienable right to full sovereignty over all their natural wealth and resources.

Article 2

1. The human person is the central subject of development and should be the active participant and beneficiary of the right to development.

2. All human beings have a responsibility for development, individually and collectively, taking into account the need for full respect for their human rights and fundamental freedoms as well as their duties to the community, which alone can ensure the free and complete fulfilment of the human being, and they should therefore promote and protect an appropriate political, social and economic order for development.

3. States have the right and the duty to formulate appropriate national development policies that aim at the constant improvement of the well-being of the entire population and of all individuals, on the basis of their active, free and meaningful participation in development and in the fair distribution of the benefits resulting therefrom.

Article 3

1. States have the primary responsibility for the creation of national and international conditions favourable to the realization of the right to development.

2. The realization of the right to development requires full respect for the principles of international law concerning friendly relations and co-operation among States in accordance with the Charter of the United Nations.

3. States have the duty to co-operate with each other in ensuring development and eliminating obstacles to development. States should realize their rights and fulfil their duties in such a manner as to promote a new international economic order based on

sovereign equality, inter-dependence, mutual interest and co-operation among all States, as well as to encourage the observance and realization of human rights.

Article 4

1. States have the duty to take steps, individually and collectively, to formulate international development policies with a view to facilitating the full realization of the right to development.

2. Sustained action is required to promote more rapid development of developing countries. As a complement to the efforts of developing countries, effective international co-operation is essential in providing these countries with appropriate means and facilities to foster their comprehensive development.

Article 5

States shall take resolute steps to eliminate the massive and flagrant violations of the human rights of peoples and human beings affected by situations such as those resulting from *apartheid*, all forms of racism and racial discrimination, colonialism, foreign domination and occupation, aggression, foreign interference and threats against national sovereignty, national unity and territorial integrity, threats of war and refusal to recognize the fundamental right of peoples to self-determination.

Article 6

1. All States should co-operate with a view to promoting, encouraging and strengthening universal respect for and observance of all human rights and fundamental freedoms for all without any distinction as to race, sex, language or religion.

2. All human rights and fundamental freedoms are indivisible and interdependent; equal attention and urgent consideration should be given to the implementation, promotion and protection of civil, political, economic, social and cultural rights.

3. States should take steps to eliminate obstacles to development resulting from failure to observe civil and political rights, as well as economic, social and cultural rights.

Article 7

All States should promote the establishment, maintenance and strengthening of international peace and security and, to that end, should do their utmost to achieve general and complete disarmament under effective international control, as well as to ensure that the resources released by effective disarmament measures are used for comprehensive development, in particular that of the developing countries.

Article 8

1. States should undertake, at the national level, all necessary measures for the realization of the right to development and shall ensure, *inter alia*, equality of opportunity for all in their access to basic resources, education, health services, food, housing, employment and the fair distribution of income. Effective measures should be undertaken to ensure that women have an active role in the development process. Appropriate economic and social reforms should be carried out with a view to eradicating all social injustices.

2. States should encourage popular participation in all spheres as an important factor in development and in the full realization of all human rights.

Article 9

1. All the aspects of the right to development set forth in the present Declaration are indivisible and interdependent and each of them should be considered in the context of the whole.

2. Nothing in the present Declaration shall be construed as being contrary to the purposes and principles of the United Nations, or as implying that any State, group or person has a right to engage in any activity or to perform any act aimed at the violation of the rights set forth in the Universal Declaration of Human Rights and in the International Covenants on Human Rights.

Article 10

Steps should be taken to ensure that full exercise and progressive enhancement of the right to development, including the formulation, adoption and implementation of policy, legislative and other measures at the national and international levels.

F   INTERNATIONAL HUMAN RIGHTS

18.   UNIVERSAL DECLARATION OF HUMAN RIGHTS
(GA RES 217 (111) 1948)

PREAMBLE

Whereas recognition of the inherent dignity and of the equal and inalienable rights of all members of the human family is the foundation of freedom, justice and peace in the world,

Whereas disregard and contempt for human rights have resulted in barbarous acts which have outraged the conscience of mankind, and the advent of a world in which human beings shall enjoy freedom of speech and belief and freedom from fear and want has been proclaimed as the highest aspiration of the common people,

Whereas it is essential, if man is not to be compelled to have recourse, as a last resort, to rebellion against tyranny and oppression, that human rights should be protected by the rule of law,

Whereas it is essential to promote the development of friendly relations between nations,

Whereas the peoples of the United Nations have in the Charter reaffirmed their faith in fundamental human rights, in the dignity and worth of the human person and in the equal rights of men and women and have determined to promote social progress and better standards of life in larger freedom,

Whereas Member States have pledge themselves to achieve, in co-operation with the United Nations, the promotion of universal respect for and observance of human rights and fundamental freedoms,

Whereas a common understanding of these rights and freedoms is of the greatest importance for the full realization of this pledge,

Now, therefore,

The General Assembly

Proclaims this Universal Declaration of Human Rights as a common standard of achievement for all peoples and all nations, to the end that every individual and every organ of society, keeping this Declaration constantly in mind, shall strive by teaching and education to promote respect for these rights and freedoms and by progressive measures, national and international, to secure their universal and effective recognition and observance, both among the peoples of Member States themselves and among the peoples of territories under their jurisdiction.

Article 1 [RIGHT TO DIGNITY]

All human beings are born free and equal in dignity and rights. They are endowed with reason and conscience and should act towards one another in a spirit of brotherhood.

Article 2 [NON-DISCRIMINATION]

Everyone is entitled to all the rights and freedoms set forth in this Declaration, without distinction of any kind, such as race, colour, sex, language, religion, political or other opinion, national or social origin, property, birth or other status.

Furthermore, no distinction shall be made on the basis of the political, jurisdictional or international status of the country or territory to which a person belongs, whether it be independent, trust, non-self-governing or under any other limitation of sovereignty.

Article 3 [RIGHT TO LIFE, LIBERTY AND SECURITY OF PERSON]

Everyone has the right to life, liberty and the security of person.

Article 4 [PROHIBITION OF SLAVERY]

No one shall be held in slavery or servitude; slavery and the slave trade shall be prohibited in all their forms.

Article 5 [PROHIBITION OF TORTURE, CRUEL, INHUMAN OR DEGRADING PUNISHMENT]

No one shall be subjected to torture or to cruel, inhuman or degrading treatment or punishment.

Article 6 [RIGHT TO LEGAL PERSONALITY]

Everyone has the right to recognition everywhere as a person before the law.

Article 7 [EQUALITY BEFORE THE LAW]

All are equal before the law and are entitled without any discrimination to equal protection of the law. All are entitled to equal protection against any discrimination in violation of this Declaration and against any incitement to such discrimination.

Article 8 [RIGHT TO AN EFFECTIVE REMEDY BY A COMPETENT NATIONAL TRIBUNAL]

Everyone has the right to an effective remedy by the competent national tribunals for acts violating the fundamental rights granted him by the constitution or by law.

Article 9 [PROHIBITION OF ARBITRARY ARREST AND DETENTION]

No one shall be subjected to arbitrary arrest, detention or exile.

Article 10 [RIGHT TO A FAIR TRIAL]

Everyone is entitled in full equality to a fair and public hearing by an independent and impartial tribunal, in the determination of his rights and obligations and of any criminal charge against him.

Article 11 [PROHIBITION OF RETROACTIVE OPERATION OF PENAL LEGISLATION]

1. Everyone charged with a penal offence has the right to be presumed innocent until proved guilty according to law in a public trial at which he has had all the guarantees necessary for his defence.

2. No one shall be held guilty of any penal offence on account of any act or omission which did not constitute a penal offence, under national or international law, at the time when it was committed. Nor shall a heavier penalty be imposed than the one that was applicable at the time the penal offence was committed.

Article 12 [Freedom from Arbitrary Interference with Privacy, Family, Home or Correspondence]

No one shall be subjected to arbitrary interference with his privacy, family, home or correspondence, nor to attacks upon his honour and reputation. Everyone has the right to the protection of the law against such interference or attacks.

Article 13 [Freedom of Movement]

1. Everyone has the right to freedom of movement and residence within the borders of each State.

2. Everyone has the right to leave any country, including his own, and to return to his country.

Article 14 [Right to Seek Asylum]

1. Everyone has the right to seek and to enjoy in other countries asylum from persecution.

2. This right may not be invoked in the case of prosecutions genuinely arising from non-political crimes or from acts contrary to the purposes and principles of the United Nations.

Article 15 [Right to a Nationality]

1. Everyone has the right to a nationality.

2. No one shall be arbitrarily deprived of his nationality nor denied the right to change his nationality.

Article 16 [Right to Marry and to Found a Family]

1. Men and women of full age, without any limitation due to race, nationality or religion, have the right to marry and to found a family. They are entitled to equal rights as to marriage, during marriage and at its dissolution.

2. Marriage shall be entered into only with the free and full consent of the intending spouses.

3. The family is the natural and fundamental group unit of society and is entitled to protection by society and the State.

Article 17 [Right to Property]

1. Everyone has the right to own property alone as well as in association with others.

2. No one shall be arbitrarily deprived of his property.

Article 18 [Freedom of Religion, Thought and Conscience]

Everyone has the right to freedom of thought, conscience and religion; this right includes freedom to change his religion or belief, and freedom, either alone or in community with others and in public or private, to manifest his religion or belief in teaching, practice, worship and observance.

Article 19 [Freedom of Expression]

Everyone has the right to freedom of opinion and expression; this right includes freedom to hold opinions without interference and to seek, receive and impart information and ideas through any media and regardless of frontiers.

Article 20 [Freedom of Assembly and Association]

1. Everyone has the right to freedom and peaceful assembly and association.
2. No one may be compelled to belong to an association.

Article 21 [Right to take part in the Public and Political Affairs]

1. Everyone has the right to take part in the government of his country, directly or through freely chosen representatives.
2. Everyone has the right of equal access to public services in his country.
3. The will of the people shall be the basis of the authority of government; this will shall be expressed in periodic and genuine elections which shall be by universal and equal suffrage and shall be held by secret vote or by equivalent free voting procedures.

Article 22 [Right to Social Security]

Everyone, as a member of society, has the right to social security and is entitled to realization, through national effort and international co-operation and in accordance with the organization and resources of each State, of the economic, social and cultural rights indispensable to his dignity and the free development of his personality.

Article 23 [Right to Work and to Equal Pay for Equal Work]

1. Everyone has the right to work, to a choice of employment, to just and favourable conditions of work and to protection against unemployment.
2. Everyone, without any discrimination, has the right to equal pay for equal work.
3. Everyone who works has the right to just and favourable remuneration ensuring for himself and his family an existence worthy of human dignity, and supplemented, if necessary, by all means of social protection.
4. Everyone has the right to form and to join trade unions for the protection of his interests.

Article 24 [Right to Rest and Leisure]

Everyone has the right to rest and leisure including reasonable limitation of working hours and periodic holidays with pay.

Article 25 [Right to an Adequate Living Standard]

1. Everyone has the right to a standard of living adequate for the health and well-being of himself and of his family, including food, clothing, housing and medical care and necessary social services, and the right to security in the event of unemployment, sickness, disability, widowhood, old age or other lack of livelihood in circumstances beyond his control.
2. Motherhood and childhood are entitled to special care and assistance. All children, whether born in or out of wedlock, shall enjoy the same social protection.

Article 26 [Right to Education]

1. Everyone has the right to education. Education shall be free, at least in the elementary and fundamental stages. Elementary education shall be compulsory. Technical and professional education shall be made generally available and higher education shall be equally accessible to all on the basis of merit.

2. Education shall be directed to the full development of the human personality and to the strengthening of respect for human rights and fundamental freedoms. It shall promote understanding, tolerance and friendship among all nations, racial or religious groups, and shall further the activities of the United Nations for the maintenance of peace.

3. Parents have a prior right to choose the kind of education that shall be given to their children.

Article 27 [CULTURAL RIGHTS]

1. Everyone has the right freely to participate in the cultural life of the community, to enjoy the arts and to share in scientific advancement and its benefits.

2. Everyone has the right to the protection of the moral and material interests resulting from any scientific, literary or artistic production of which he is the author.

Article 28

Everyone is entitled to a social and international order in which the rights and freedoms set forth in this Declaration can be fully realized.

Article 29 [LIMITATIONS OF RIGHTS]

1. Everyone has duties to the community in which alone the free and full development of his personality is possible.

2. In the exercise of his rights and freedoms, everyone shall be subject only to such limitations as are determined by law solely for the purpose of securing due recognition and respect for the rights and freedoms of others and of meeting the just requirements of morality, public order and the general welfare in a democratic society.

3. These rights and freedoms may in no case be exercised contrary to the purposes and principles of the United Nations.

Article 30 [PROHIBITION OF MISUSE OF RIGHTS]

Nothing in this Declaration may be interpreted as implying for any State, group or person any right to engage in any activity or to perform any act aimed at the destruction of any of the rights and freedoms set forth herein.

Hundred and eighty-third plenary meeting,
10 December 1948.

19.   INTERNATIONAL COVENANT ON CIVIL AND POLITICAL RIGHTS 1966
(999 UNTS 171; 6 ILM 368 (1967))

The States Parties to the present Covenant,
Considering that, in accordance with the principles proclaimed in the Charter of the United Nations, recognition of the inherent dignity and of the equal and inalienable rights of all members of the human family is the foundation of freedom, justice and peace in the world,
Recognizing that these rights derive from the inherent dignity of the human person,
Recognizing that, in accordance with the Universal Declaration of Human Rights, the ideal of free human beings enjoying civil and political freedom and freedom from fear and want can only be achieved if conditions are created whereby everyone may enjoy his civil and political rights, as well as his economic, social and cultural rights,

Considering the obligation of States under the Charter of the United Nations to promote universal respect for, and observance of, human rights and freedoms,

Realizing that the individual, having duties to other individuals and to the community to which he belongs, is under a responsibility to strive for the promotion and observance of the rights recognized in the present Covenant, Agree upon the following articles:

PART I

Article 1 [RIGHT OF PEOPLES TO SELF DETERMINATION]

1. All peoples have the right of self-determination. By virtue of that right they freely determine their political status and freely pursue their economic, social and cultural development.

2. All peoples may, for their own ends, freely dispose of their natural wealth and resources without prejudice to any obligations arising out of international economic co-operation, based upon the principle of mutual benefit, and international law. In no case may a people be deprived of its own means of subsistence.

3. The States Parties to the present Covenant, including those having responsibility for the administration of Non-Self-Governing and Trust Territories, shall promote the realization of the right of self-determination, and shall respect that right, in conformity with the provisions of the Charter of the United Nations.

PART II

Article 2 [DUTY OF STATES TO TRANSFORM THE TREATY]

1. Each State Party to the present Covenant undertakes to respect and to ensure to all individuals within its territory and subject to its jurisdiction the rights recognized in the present Covenant, without distinction of any kind, such as race, colour, sex, language, religion, political or other opinion, national or social origin, property, birth or other status.

2. Where not already provided for by existing legislative or other measures, each State Party to the present Covenant undertakes to take the necessary steps, in accordance with its constitutional processes and with the provisions of the present Covenant, to adopt such legislative or other measures as may be necessary to give effect to the rights recognized in the present Covenant.

3. Each State Party to the present Covenant undertakes:

(a) To ensure that any person whose rights or freedoms as herein recognized are violated shall have an effective remedy, notwithstanding that the violation has been committed by persons acting in an official capacity;

(b) To ensure that any person claiming such a remedy shall have his right thereto determined by competent judicial, administrative or legislative authorities, or by any other competent authority provided for by the legal system of the State, and to develop the possibilities of judicial remedy;

(c) To ensure that the competent authorities shall enforce such remedies when granted.

Article 3 [EQUALITY OF MEN AND WOMEN IN ENJOYMENT OF RIGHTS]

3. The States Parties to the present Covenant undertake to ensure the equal rights of men and women to the enjoyment of all civil and political rights set forth in the present Covenant.

Article 4 [Derogation in Times of Emergency]

1. In time of public emergency which threatens the life of the nation and the existence of which is officially proclaimed, the States Parties to the present Covenant may take measures derogating from their obligations under the present Covenant to the extent strictly required by the exigencies of the situation, provided that such measures are not inconsistent with their other obligations under international law and do not involve discrimination solely on the ground of race, colour, sex, language, religion or social origin.

2. No derogation from articles 6, 7, 8 (paragraphs 1 and 2), 11, 15, 16 and 18 may be made under this provision.

3. Any State Party to the present Covenant availing itself of the right of derogation shall immediately inform the other States Parties to the present Covenant, through the intermediary of the Secretary-General of the United Nations, of the provisions from which it has derogated and of the reasons by which it was actuated. A further communication shall be made, through the same intermediary, on the date on which it terminates such derogation.

Article 5 [Prohibition of Abuse of Rights]

1. Nothing in the present Covenant may be interpreted as implying for any State, group or person any right to engage in any activity or perform any act aimed at the destruction of any of the rights and freedoms recognized herein or at their limitation to a greater extent than is provided for in the present Covenant.

2. There shall be no restriction upon or derogation from any of the fundamental human rights recognized or existing in any State Party to the present Covenant pursuant to law, conventions, regulations or custom on the pretext that the present Covenant does not recognize such rights or that it recognizes them to a lesser extent.

PART III

Article 6 [Right to Life]

1. Every human being has the inherent right to life. This right shall be protected by law. No one shall be arbitrarily deprived of his life.

2. In countries which have not abolished the death penalty, sentence of death may be imposed only for the most serious crimes in accordance with the law in force at the time of the commission of the crime and not contrary to the provisions of the present Covenant and to the Convention on the Prevention and Punishment of the Crime of Genocide. This penalty can only be carried out pursuant to a final judgement rendered by a competent court.

3. When deprivation of life constitutes the crime of genocide, it is understood that nothing in this article shall authorize any State Party to the present Covenant to derogate in any way from any obligation assumed under the provisions of the Convention on the Prevention and Punishment of the Crime of Genocide.

4. Anyone sentenced to death shall have the right to seek pardon or commutation of the sentence. Amnesty, pardon or commutation of the sentence of death may be granted in all cases.

5. Sentence of death shall not be imposed for crimes committed by persons below eighteen years of age and shall not be carried out on pregnant women.

6. Nothing in this article shall be invoked to delay or to prevent the abolition of capital punishment by any State Party to the present Covenant.

Article 7 [Prohibition of Torture, Cruel, Inhuman or Degrading Punishment or Treatment]

No one shall be subjected to torture or to cruel, inhuman or degrading treatment or punishment. In particular, no one shall be subjected without his free consent to medical or scientific experimentation.

Article 8 [Prohibition of Slavery]

1. No one shall be held in slavery; slavery and the slave-trade in all their forms shall be prohibited.

2. No one shall be held in servitude.

3. *(a)* No one shall be required to perform forced or compulsory labour.

(b) Paragraph 3 *(a)* shall not be held to preclude, in countries where imprisonment with hard labour may be imposed as a punishment for a crime, the performance of hard labour in pursuance of a sentence to such punishment by a competent court.

(c) For the purpose of this paragraph the term "forced or compulsory labour" shall not include:

(i) Any work or service, not referred to in sub-paragraph *(b)*, normally required of a person who is under detention in consequence of a lawful order of a court, or of a person during conditional release from such detention;

(ii) Any service of a military character and, in countries where conscientious objection is recognized, any national service required by law of conscientious objectors;

(iii) Any service exacted in cases of emergency or calamity threatening the life or well-being of the community;

(iv) Any work or service which forms part of normal civil obligations.

Article 9 [Right to Liberty and Security of Person]

1. Everyone has the right to liberty and security of person. No one shall be subjected to arbitrary arrest or detention. No one shall be deprived of his liberty except on such grounds and in accordance with such procedure as are established by law.

2. Anyone who is arrested shall be informed, at the time of arrest, of the reasons for his arrest and shall be promptly informed of any charges against him.

3. Anyone arrested or detained on a criminal charge shall be brought promptly before a judge or other officer authorized by law to exercise judicial power and shall be entitled to trial within a reasonable time or to release. It shall not be the general rule that persons awaiting trial shall be detained in custody, but release may be subject to guarantees to appear for trial, at any other stage of the judicial proceedings, and, should occasion arise, for execution of the judgement.

4. Anyone who is deprived of his liberty by arrest or detention shall be entitled to take proceedings before a court, in order that that court may decide without delay on the lawfulness of his detention and order his release if the detention is not lawful.

5. Anyone who has been the victim of unlawful arrest or detention shall have an enforceable right to compensation.

Article 10 [Right to dignity]

1. All persons deprived of their liberty shall be treated with humanity and with respect for the inherent dignity of the human person.

2. *(a)* Accused persons shall, save in exceptional circumstances, be segregated from convicted persons and shall be subject to separate treatment appropriate to their status as unconvicted persons.

(b) Accused juvenile persons shall be separated from adults and brought as speedily as possible for adjudication.

3. The penitentiary system shall comprise treatment of prisoners the essential aim of which shall be their reformation and social rehabilitation. Juvenile offenders shall be segregated from adults and be accorded treatment appropriate to their age and legal status.

Article 11 [PROHIBITION OF CIVIL IMPRISONMENT]

No one shall be imprisoned merely on the ground of inability to fulfil a contractual obligation.

Article 12 [FREEDOM OF MOVEMENT]

1. Everyone lawfully within the territory of a State shall, within that territory, have the right to liberty of movement and freedom to choose his residence.

2. Everyone shall be free to leave any country, including his own.

3. The above-mentioned rights shall not be subject to any restrictions except those which are provided by law, are necessary to protect national security, public order (*ordre public*), public health or morals or the rights and freedoms of others, and are consistent with the other rights recognized in the present Covenant.

4. No one shall be arbitrarily deprived of the right to enter his own country.

Article 13 [EXPULSION OF ALIENS]

An alien lawfully in the territory of a State Party to the present Covenant may be expelled therefrom only in pursuance of a decision reached in accordance with law and shall, except where compelling reasons of national security otherwise require, be allowed to submit the reasons against his expulsion and to have his case reviewed by, and be represented for the purpose before, the competent authority or a person or persons especially designated by the competent authority.

Article 14 [RIGHT TO A FAIR TRIAL]

1. All persons shall be equal before the courts and tribunals. In the determination of any criminal charge against him, or of his rights and obligations in a suit at law, everyone shall be entitled to a fair and public hearing by a competent, independent and impartial tribunal established by law. The Press and the public may be excluded from all or part of a trial for reasons of morals, public order (*ordre public*) or national security in a democratic society, or when the interest of the private lives of the parties so requires, or to the extent strictly necessary in the opinion of the court in special circumstances where publicity would prejudice the interests of justice; but any judgment rendered in a criminal case or in a suit at law shall be made public except where the interests of juvenile persons otherwise requires or the proceedings concern matrimonial disputes or the guardianship of children.

2. Everyone charged with a criminal offence shall have the right to be presumed innocent until proved guilty according to law.

3. In the determination of any criminal charge against him, everyone shall be entitled to the following minimum guarantees, in full equality:

(a) To be informed promptly and in detail in a language which he understands of the nature and cause of the charge against him;

(b) To have adequate time and facilities for the preparation of his defence and to communicate with counsel of his own choosing;

(c) To be tried without undue delay;

(d) To be tried in his presence, and to defend himself in person or through legal assistance of his own choosing; to be informed, if he does not have legal assistance, of this right; and to have legal assistance assigned to him, in any case where the interests of justice so require, and without payment by him in any such case if he does not have sufficient means to pay for it;

(e) To examine, or have examined, the witnesses against him and to obtain the attendance and examination of witnesses on his behalf under the same conditions as witnesses against him;

(f) To have the free assistance of an interpreter if he cannot understand or speak the language used in court;

(g) Not be compelled to testify against himself or to confess guilt.

4. In the case of juvenile persons, the procedure shall be such as will take account of their age and the desirability of promoting their rehabilitation.

5. Everyone convicted of a crime shall have the right to his conviction and sentence being reviewed by a higher tribunal according to law.

6. When a person has by a final decision been convicted of a criminal offence and when subsequently his conviction has been reversed or he has been pardoned on the ground that a new or newly discovered fact shows conclusively that there has been a miscarriage of justice, the person who has suffered punishment as a result of such conviction shall be compensated according to law, unless it is proved that the non-disclosure of the unknown fact in time is wholly or partly attributable to him.

7. No one shall be liable to be tried or punished again for an offence for which he has already been finally convicted or acquitted in accordance with the law and penal procedure of each country.

Article 15 ['Nulla Peona' Principle]

1. No one shall be held guilty of any criminal offence on account of any act or omission which did not constitute a criminal offence, under national or international law, at the time when it was committed. Nor shall a heavier penalty be imposed than the one that was applicable at the time when the criminal offence was committed. If, subsequent to the commission of the offence, provision is made by law for the imposition of a lighter penalty, the offender shall benefit thereby.

2. Nothing in this article shall prejudice the trial and punishment of any person for any act or omission which, at the time when it was committed, was criminal according to the general principles of law recognized by the community of nations.

Article 16 [Recognotion of Legal Personality of Persons]

Everyone shall have the right to recognition everywhere as a person before the law.

Article 17 [Right to Privacy, Family, Home or Correspondence]

1. No one shall be subjected to arbitrary or unlawful interference with his privacy, family, home or correspondence, nor to unlawful attacks on his honour and reputation.

2. Everyone has the right to the protection of the law. against such interference or attacks.

Article 18 [FREEDOM OF RELIGION, CONSCIENCE AND THOUGHT]

1. Everyone shall have the right to freedom of thought, conscience and religion. This right shall include freedom to have or to adopt a religion or belief of his choice, and freedom, either individually or in community with others and in public or private, to manifest his religion or belief in worship, observance, practice and teaching.

2. No one shall be subject to coercion which would impair his freedom to have or to adopt a religion or belief of his choice.

3. Freedom to manifest one's religion or beliefs may be subject only to such limitations as are prescribed by law and are necessary to protect public safety, order, health, or morals or the fundamental rights and freedoms of others.

4. The States Parties to the present Covenant undertake to have respect for the liberty of parents and, when applicable, legal guardians to ensure the religious and moral education of their children in conformity with their own convictions.

Article 19 [FREEDOM OF EXPRESSION]

1. Everyone shall have the right to hold opinions without interference.

2. Everyone shall have the right to freedom of expression; this right shall include freedom to seek, receive and impart information and ideas of all kinds, regardless of frontiers, either orally, in writing or in print, in the form of art, or through any other media of his choice.

3. The exercise of the rights provided for in paragraph 2 of this article carries with it special duties and responsibilities. It may therefore be subject to certain restrictions, but these shall only be such as are provided by law and are necessary:

(a) For respect of the rights or reputations of others;

(b) For the protection of national security or of public order (*ordre public*), or of public health or morals.

Article 20 [PROHIBITION OF WAR PROPAGANDA]

1. Any propaganda for war shall be prohibited by law.

Any advocacy of national, racial or religious hatred that constitutes incitement to discrimination, hostility or violence shall be prohibited by law.

Article 21 [FREEDOM OF ASSEMBLY]

The right of peaceful assembly shall be recognized. No restrictions may be placed on the exercise of this right other than those imposed in conformity with the law and which are necessary in a democratic society in the interests of national security or public safety, public order (*ordre public*), the protection of public health or morals or the protection of the rights and freedoms of others.

Article 22 [FREEDOM OF ASSOCIATION]

1. Everyone shall have the right to freedom of association with others, including the right to form and join trade unions for the protection of his interests.

2. No restrictions may be placed on the exercise of this right other than those which are prescribed by law and which are necessary in a democratic society in the interests of

national security or public safety, public order (*ordre public*), the protection of public health or morals or the protection of the rights and freedoms of others. This article shall not prevent the imposition of lawful restrictions on members of the armed forces and of the police in their exercise of this right.

3. Nothing in this article shall authorize States Parties to the International Labour Organisation Convention of 1948 concerning freedom of association and protection of the right to organize to take legislative measures which would prejudice, or to apply the law in such a manner as to prejudice, the guarantees provided for in that Convention.

Article 23 [Right to Marry and to Found a Family]

1. The family is the natural and fundamental group unit of society and is entitled to protection by society and the State.

2. The right of men and women of marriageable age to marry and to found a family shall be recognized.

3. No marriage shall be entered into without the free and full consent of the intending spouses.

4. States Parties to the present Covenant shall take appropriate steps to ensure equality of rights and responsibilities of spouses as to marriage, during marriage and at its dissolution. In the case of dissolution, provision shall be made for the necessary protection of any children.

Article 24 [Rights of a Child]

1. Every child shall have, without any discrimination as to race, colour, sex, language, religion, national or social origin, property or birth, the right to such measures of protection as are required by his status as a minor, on the part of his family, society and the State.

2. Every child shall be registered immediately after birth and shall have a name.

3. Every child has the right to acquire a nationality.

Article 25 [Right to Participate in Public Affairs]

Every citizen shall have the right and the opportunity, without any of the distinctions mentioned in article 2 and without unreasonable restrictions:

(a) To take part in the conduct of public affairs, directly or through freely chosen representatives;

(b) To vote and to be elected at genuine periodic elections which shall be by universal and equal suffrage and shall be held by secret ballot, guaranteeing the free expression of the will of the electors;

(c) To have access, on general terms of equality, to public service in his country.

Article 26 [Equality before the Law and Equal Protection]

All persons are equal before the law and are entitled without any discrimination to the equal protection of the law. In this respect, the law shall prohibit any discrimination and guarantee to all persons equal and effective protection against discrimination on any ground such as race, colour, sex, language, religion, political or other opinion, national or social origin, property, birth or other status.

Article 27 [Rights of Minorities]

In those States in which ethnic, religious or linguistic minorities exist, persons belonging to such minorities shall not be denied the right, in community with the other members of their group, to enjoy their own culture, to profess and practise their own religion, or to use their own language.

PART IV

Article 28 [HUMAN RIGHTS COMMITTEE]

1. There shall be established a Human Rights Committee (hereafter referred to in the present Covenant as the Committee). It shall consist of eighteen members and shall carry out the functions hereinafter provided.

2. The Committee shall be composed of nationals of the States Parties to the present Covenant who shall be persons of high moral character and recognized competence in the field of human rights, consideration being given to the usefulness of the participation of some persons having legal experience.

3. The members of the Committee shall be elected and shall serve in their personal capacity.

Article 29 [ELECTION OF MEMBERS OF COMMITTEE]

1. The members of the Committee shall be elected by secret ballot from a list of persons possessing the qualifications prescribed in article 28 and nominated for the purpose by the States Parties to the present Covenant.

2. Each State Party to the present Covenant may nominate not more than two persons. These persons shall be nationals of the nominating State.

3. A person shall be eligible for renomination.

Article 30. 1. The initial election shall be held no later than six months after the date of the entry into force of the present Covenant.

2. At least four months before the date of each election to the Committee, other than an election to fill a vacancy declared in accordance with article 34, the Secretary-General of the United Nations shall address a written invitation to the States Parties to the present Covenant to submit their nominations for membership of the Committee within three months.

3. The Secretary-General of the United Nations shall prepare a list in alphabetical order of all the persons thus nominated, with an indication of the States Parties which have nominated them, and shall submit it to the States Parties to the present Covenant no later than one month before the date of each election.

4. Elections of the members of the Committee shall be held at a meeting of the States Parties to the present Covenant convened by the Secretary-General of the United Nations at the Headquarters of the United Nations. At that meeting, for which two thirds of the States Parties to the present Covenant shall constitute a quorum, the persons elected to the Committee shall be those nominees who obtain the largest number of votes and an absolute majority of the votes of the representatives of States Parties present and voting.

Article 31. 1. The Committee may not include more than one national of the same State.

2. In the election of the Committee, consideration shall be given to equitable geographical distribution of membership and to the representation of the different forms of civilization and of the principal legal systems.

Article 32. 1. The members of the Committee shall be elected for a term of four years. They shall be eligible for re-election if renominated. However, the terms of nine of the members elected at the first election shall expire at the end of two years; immediately after the first election, the names of these nine members shall be chosen by lot by the Chairman of the meeting referred to in article 30, paragraph 4.

2. Elections at the expiry of office shall be held in accordance with the preceding articles of this part of the present Covenant.

Article 33. 1. If, in the unanimous opinion of the other members, a member of the Committee has ceased to carry out his functions for any cause other than absence of a temporary character, the Chairman of the Committee shall notify the Secretary-General of the United Nations, who shall then declare the seat of that member to be vacant.

2. In the event of the death or the resignation of a member of the Committee, the Chairman shall immediately notify the Secretary-General of the United Nations, who shall declare the seat vacant from the date of death or the date on which the resignation takes effect.

Article 34. 1 When a vacancy is declared in accordance with article 33 and if the term of office of the member to be replaced does not expire within six months of the declaration of the vacancy, the Secretary-General of the United Nations shall notify each of the States Parties to the present Covenant, which may within two months submit nominations in accordance with article 29 for the purpose of filling the vacancy.

2. The Secretary-General of the United Nations shall prepare a list in alphabetical order of the persons thus nominated and shall submit it to the States Parties to the present Covenant. The election to fill the vacancy shall then take place in accordance with the relevant provisions of this part of the present Covenant.

3. A member of the Committee elected to fill a vacancy declared in accordance with article 33 shall hold office for the remainder of the term of the member who vacated the seat on the Committee under the provisions of that article.

Article 35. The members of the Committee shall, with the approval of the General Assembly of the United Nations, receive emoluments from United Nations resources on such terms and conditions as the General Assembly may decide, having regard to the importance of the Committee's responsibilities.

Article 36. The Secretary-General of the United Nations shall provide the necessary staff and facilities for the effective performance of the functions of the Committee under the present Covenant.

Article 37. 1. The Secretary-General of the United Nations shall convene the initial meeting of the Committee at the Headquarters of the United Nations.

2. After its initial meeting, the Committee shall meet at such times as shall be provided in its rules of procedure.

3. The Committee shall normally meet at the Headquarters of the United Nations or at the United Nations Office at Geneva.

Article 38. Every member of the Committee shall, before taking up his duties, make a solemn declaration in open committee that he will perform his functions impartially and conscientiously.

Article 39. 1. The Committee shall elect its officers for a term of two years. They may be re-elected.

2. The Committee shall establish its own rules of procedure, but these rules shall provide, *inter alia*, that:

(a) Twelve members shall constitute a quorum;

(b) Decisions of the Committee shall be made by a majority vote of the members present.

Article 40 [SUBMISSION OF REPORTS]

1. The States Parties to the present Covenant undertake to submit reports on the measures they have adopted which give effect to the rights recognized therein and on the progress made in the enjoyment of those rights:

(a) Within one year of the entry into force of the present Covenant for the States Parties concerned;

(b) Thereafter whenever the Committee so requests.

2. All reports shall be submitted to the Secretary-General of the United Nations, who shall transmit them to the Committee for consideration. Reports shall indicate the factors and difficulties, if any, affecting the implementation of the present Covenant.

3. The Secretary-General of the United Nations may, after consultation with the Committee, transmit to the specialized agencies concerned copies of such parts of the reports as may fall within their field of competence.

4. The Committee shall study the reports submitted by the States Parties to the present Covenant. It shall transmit its reports, and such general comments as it may consider appropriate, to the States Parties. The Committee may also transmit to the Economic and Social Council these comments along with the copies of the reports it has received from States Parties to the present Covenant.

5. The States Parties to the present Covenant may submit to the Committee observations on any comments that may be made in accordance with paragraph 4 of this article.

Article 41 [INTER-STATE COMPLAINTS]

1. A State Party to the present Covenant may at any time declare under this article that it recognizes the competence of the Committee to receive and consider communications to the effect that a State Party claims that another State Party is not fulfilling its obligations under the present Covenant. Communications under this article may be received and considered only if submitted by a State Party which has made a declaration recognizing in regard to itself the competence of the Committee. No communication shall be received by the Committee if it concerns a State Party which has not made such a declaration. Communications received under this article shall be dealt with in accordance with the following procedure:

(a) If a State Party to the present Covenant considers that another State Party is not giving effect to the provisions of the present Covenant, it may, by written communication, bring the matter to the attention of that State Party. Within three months after the receipt of the communication, the receiving State shall afford the State which sent the communication an explanation or any other statement in writing clarifying the matter, which should include, to the extent possible and pertinent, reference to domestic procedures and remedies taken, pending, or available in the matter.

(b) If the matter is not adjusted to the satisfaction of both State Parties concerned within six months after the receipt by the receiving State of the initial communication,

either State shall have the right to refer the matter to the Committee, by notice given to the Committee and to the other State.

(c) The Committee shall deal with a matter referred to it only after it has ascertained that all available domestic remedies have been invoked and exhausted in the matter, in conformity with the generally recognized principles of international law. This shall not be the rule where the application of the remedies is unreasonably prolonged.

(d) The Committee shall hold closed meetings when examining communications under this article.

(e) Subject to the provisions of the sub-paragraph *(c)*, the Committee shall make available its good offices to the States Parties concerned with a view to a friendly solution of the matter on the basis of respect for human rights and fundamental freedoms as recognized in the present Covenant.

(f) In any matter referred to it, the Committee may call upon the States Parties concerned, referred to in sub-paragraph *(b)*, to supply any relevant information.

(g) The States Parties concerned, referred to in sub-paragraph *(b)*, shall have the right to be represented when the matter is being considered in the Committee and to make submissions orally and/or in writing.

(h) The Committee shall, within twelve months after the date of receipt of notice under sub-paragraph *(b)*, submit a report:

(i) If a solution within the terms of sub-paragraph *(e)* is reached, the Committee shall confine its report to a brief statement of the facts and of the solution reached;

(ii) If a solution within the terms of sub-paragraph *(e)* is not reached, the Committee shall confine its report to a brief statement of the facts; the written submissions and record of the oral submissions made by the States Parties concerned shall be attached to the report.

In every matter, the report shall be communicated to the States Parties concerned.

2. The provisions of this article shall come into force when ten States Parties to the present Covenant have made declarations under paragraph 1 of this article. Such declarations shall be deposited by the States Parties with the Secretary-General of the United Nations, who shall transmit copies thereof to the other States Parties. A declaration may be withdrawn at any time by notification to the Secretary-General. Such a withdrawal shall not prejudice the consideration of any matter which is the subject of a communication already transmitted under this article; no further communication by any State Party shall be received after the notification of withdrawal of the declaration has been received by the Secretary-General, unless the State Party concerned has made a new declaration.

Article 42 [Conciliation Commission]

1. *(a)* If a matter referred to the Committee in accordance with article 41 is not resolved to the satisfaction of the States Parties concerned, the Committee may, with the prior consent of the States Parties concerned, appoint an *ad hoc* Conciliation Commission (hereinafter referred to as the Commission). The good offices of the Commission shall be made available to the States Parties concerned with a view to an amicable solution of the matter on the basis of respect for the present Covenant.

(b) The Commission shall consist of five persons acceptable to the States Parties concerned. If the States Parties concerned fail to reach agreement within three months on all or part of the composition of the Commission the members of the Commission

concerning whom no agreement has been reached shall be elected by secret ballot by a two-thirds majority vote of the Committee from among its members.

2. The members of the Commission shall serve in their personal capacity. They shall not be nationals of the States Parties concerned, or of a State not party to the present Covenant, or of a State Party which has not made a declaration under article 41.

3. The Commission shall elect its own Chairman and adopt its own rules of procedure.

4. The meetings of the Commission shall normally be held at the Headquarters of the United Nations or at the United Nations Head Office at Geneva. However, they may be held at such other convenient places as the Commission may determine in consultation with the Secretary-General of the United Nations and the States Parties concerned.

5. The secretariat provided in accordance with article 36 shall also service the commissions appointed under this article.

6. The information received and collated by the Committee shall be made available to the Commission and the Commission may call upon the States Parties concerned to supply any other relevant information.

7. When the Commission has fully considered the matter, but in any event not later than twelve months after having been seized of the matter, it shall submit to the Chairman of the Committee a report for communication to the States Parties concerned.

(a) If the Commission is unable to complete its consideration of the matter within twelve months, it shall confine its report to a brief statement of the status of its consideration of the matter.

(b) If an amicable solution to the matter on the basis of respect for human rights as recognized in the present Covenant is reached, the Commission shall confine its report to a brief statement of the facts and of the solution reached.

(c) If a solution within the terms of sub-paragraph *(b)* is not reached, the Commission's report shall embody its findings on all questions of fact relevant to the issues between the States Parties concerned, and its views on the possibilities of an amicable solution of the matter. This report shall also contain the written submissions and a record of the oral submissions made by the States Parties concerned.

(d) If the Commission's report is submitted under sub-paragraph *(c)*, the States Parties concerned shall, within three months of the receipt of the report, notify the Chairman of the Committee whether or not they accept the contents of the report of the Commission.

8. The provisions of this article are without prejudice to the responsibilities of the Committee under article 41.

9. The States Parties concerned shall share equally all the expenses of the members of the Commission in accordance with estimates to be provided by the Secretary-General of the United Nations.

10. The Secretary-General of the United Nations shall be empowered to pay the expenses of the members of the Commission, if necessary, before reimbursement by the States Parties concerned, in accordance with paragraph 9 of this article.

Article 43. The members of the Committee, and of the *ad hoc* conciliation commissions which may be appointed under article 42, shall be entitled to the facilities, privileges and immunities of experts on mission for the United Nations as laid down in the relevant sections of the Convention on the Privileges and Immunities of the United Nations.

Article 44. The provisions for the implementation of the present Covenant shall apply without prejudice to the procedures prescribed in the field of human rights by or under the constituent instruments and the conventions of the United Nations and of the specialized agencies and shall not prevent the States Parties to the present Covenant from having recourse to other procedures for settling a dispute in accordance with general or special international agreements in force between them.

Article 45. The Committee shall submit to the General Assembly of the United Nations through the Economic and Social Council, an annual report on its activities.

PART V

Article 46. Nothing in the present Covenant shall be interpreted as impairing the provisions of the Charter of the United Nations and of the constitutions of the specialized agencies which define the respective responsibilities of the various organs of the United Nations and of the specialized agencies in regard to the matters dealt with in the present Covenant.

Article 47. Nothing in the present Covenant shall be interpreted as impairing the inherent right of all peoples to enjoy and utilize fully and freely their natural wealth and resources.

PART VI

Article 48. 1. The present Covenant is open for signature by any State Member of the United Nations or member of any of its specialized agencies, by any State Party to the Statute of the International Court of Justice, and by any other State which has been invited by the General Assembly of the United Nations to become a party to the present Covenant.

2. The present Covenant is subject to ratification. Instruments of ratification shall be deposited with the Secretary-General of the United Nations.

3. The present Covenant shall be open to accession by any State referred to in paragraph 1 of this article.

4. Accession shall be effected by the deposit of an instrument of accession with the Secretary-General of the United Nations.

5. The Secretary-General of the United Nations shall inform all States which have signed this Covenant or acceded to it of the deposit of each instrument of ratification or accession.

Article 49. 1. The present Covenant shall enter into force three months after the date of the deposit with the Secretary-General of the United Nations of the thirty-fifth instrument of ratification or instrument of accession.

2. For each State ratifying the present Covenant or acceding to it after the deposit of the thirty-fifth instrument of ratification or instrument of accession, the present Covenant shall enter into force three months after the date of the deposit of its own instrument of ratification or instrument of accession.

Article 50. The provisions of the present Covenant shall extend to all parts of federal States without any limitations or exceptions.

Article 51. 1. Any State Party to the present Covenant may propose an amendment and file it with the Secretary-General of the United Nations. The Secretary-General of the United Nations shall thereupon communicate any proposed amendments to the States

Parties to the present Covenant with a request that they notify him whether they favour a conference of States Parties for the purpose of considering and voting upon the proposals. In the event that at least one third of the States Parties favours such a conference, the Secretary-General shall convene the conference under the auspices of the United Nations. Any amendment adopted by a majority of the States Parties present and voting at the conference shall be submitted to the General Assembly of the United Nations for approval.

2. Amendments shall come into force when they have been approved by the General Assembly of the United Nations and accepted by a two-thirds majority of the States Parties to the present Covenant in accordance with their respective constitutional processes.

3. When amendments come into force, they shall be binding on those States Parties which have accepted them, other States Parties still being bound by the provisions of the present Covenant and any earlier amendment which they have accepted.

Article 52. Irrespective of the notifications made under article 48, paragraph 5, the Secretary-General of the United Nations shall inform all States referred to in paragraph 1 of the same article of the following particulars:

(a) Signatures, ratifications and accessions under article 48;

(b) The date of the entry into force of the present Covenant under article 49 and the date of the entry into force of any amendments under article 51.

Article 53. 1. The present Covenant, of which the Chinese, English, French, Russian and Spanish texts are equally authentic, shall be deposited in the archives of the United Nations.

2. The Secretary-General of the United Nations shall transmit certified copies of the present Covenant to all States referred to in article 48.

IN FAITH WHEREOF the undersigned, being duly authorized thereto by their respective Governments, have signed the present Covenant, opened for signature at New York, on the nineteenth day of December, one thousand nine hundred and sixty-six.

20. OPTIONAL PROTOCOL TO THE INTERNATIONAL COVENANT ON CIVIL AND POLITICAL RIGHTS   (999 UNTS 171; 6 ILM 383 (1967))

The States Parties to the present Protocol,

Considering that in order further to achieve the purposes of the Covenant on Civil and Political Rights (hereinafter referred to as the Covenant) and the implementation of its provisions it would be appropriate to enable the Human Rights Committee set up in part IV of the Covenant (hereinafter referred to as the Committee) to receive and consider, as provided in the present Protocol, communications from individuals claiming to be victims of violations of any of the rights set forth in the Covenant,

Have agreed as follows:

Article 1 [INDIVIDUAL COMPLAINT]

A State Party to the Covenant that becomes a party to the present Protocol recognizes the competence of the Committee to receive and consider communications from individuals subject to its jurisdiction who claim to be victims of a violation by that State Party of any of the rights set forth in the Covenant. No communication shall be received by the Committee if it concerns a State Party to the Covenant which is not a party to the present Protocol.

Article 2 [CONDITIONS FOR SUBMISSION]

Subject to the provisions of article 1, individuals who claim that any of their rights enumerated in the Covenant have been violated and who have exhausted all available domestic remedies may submit a written communication to the Committee for consideration.

Article 3 [ANONYMOUS COMPLAINTS]

The Committee shall consider inadmissible any communication under the present Protocol which is anonymous, or which it considers to be an abuse of the right of submission of such communications or to be incompatible with the provisions of the Covenant.

Article 4 [AUDI ALTERAM PARTEM]

1. Subject to the provisions of article 3, the Committee shall bring any communications submitted to it under the present Protocol to the attention of the State Party to the present Protocol alleged to be violating any provision of the Covenant.

2. Within six months, the receiving State shall submit to the Committee written explanations or statements clarifying the matter and the remedy, if any, that may have been taken by that State.

Article 5 [FURTHER CONDITIONS FOR ADMISIBILITY OF INDIVIDUAL COMPLAINTS]

1. The Committee shall consider communications received under the present Protocol in the light of all written information made available to it by the individual and by the State Party concerned.

2. The Committee shall not consider any communication from an individual unless it has ascertained that:

(a) The same matter is not being examined under another procedure of international investigation or settlement;

(b) The individual has exhausted all available domestic remedies.
This shall not be the rule where the application of the remedies is unreasonably prolonged.

3. The Committee shall hold closed meetings when examining communications under the present Protocol.

4. The Committee shall forward its views to the State Party concerned and to the individual.

Article 6 [ANNUAL REPORT]

The Committee shall include in its annual report under article 45 of the Covenant a summary of its activities under the present Protocol.

Article 7 [CHARTER RIGHTS]

Pending the achievement of the objectives of resolution 1514 (XV) adopted by the General Assembly of the United Nations on 14 December 1960 concerning the Declaration on the Granting of Independence to Colonial Countries and Peoples, the provisions of the present Protocol shall in no way limit the right of petition granted to these peoples by the Charter of the United Nations and other international conventions and instruments under the United Nations and its specialized agencies.

Article 8 [Signature, Accession and Ratification]

1. The present Protocol is open for signature by any State which has signed the Covenant.

2. The present Protocol is subject to ratification by any State which has ratified or acceded to the Covenant. Instruments of ratification shall be deposited with the Secretary-General of the United Nations.

3. The present Protocol shall be open to accession by any State which has ratified or acceded to the Covenant.

4. Accession shall be effected by the deposit of an instrument of accession with the Secretary-General of the United Nations.

5. The Secretary-General of the United Nations shall inform all States which have signed the present Protocol or acceded to it of the deposit of each instrument of ratification or accession.

Article 9 [Entry into Force]

1. Subject to the entry into force of the Covenant, the present Protocol shall enter into force three months after the date of the deposit with the Secretary-General of the United Nations of the tenth instrument of ratification or instrument of accession.

2. For each State ratifying the present Protocol or acceding to it after the deposit of the tenth instrument of ratification or instrument of accession, the present Protocol shall enter into force three months after the date of the deposit of its own instrument of ratification or instrument of accession.

Article 10 [Federal Application]

The provisions of the present Protocol shall extend to all parts of federal States without any limitations or exceptions.

Article 11 [Amendment]

1. Any State Party to the present Protocol may propose an amendment and file it with the Secretary-General of the United Nations. The Secretary-General shall thereupon communicate any proposed amendments to the States Parties to the present Protocol with a request that they notify him whether they favour a conference of State Parties for the purpose of considering and voting upon the proposal. In the event that at least one third of the States Parties favours such a conference, the Secretary-General shall convene the conference under the auspices of the United Nations. Any amendment adopted by a majority of the States Parties present and voting at the conference shall be submitted to the General Assembly of the United Nations for approval.

2. Amendments shall come into force when they have been approved by the General Assembly of the United Nations and accepted by a two-thirds majority of the States Parties to the present Protocol in accordance with their respective constitutional processes.

3. When amendments come into force, they shall be binding on those States Parties which have accepted them, other States Parties still being bound by the provisions of the present Protocol and any earlier amendment which they have accepted.

Article 12 [Denunciation]

1. Any State Party may denounce the present Protocol at any time by written notification addressed to the Secretary-General of the United Nations. Denunciation

shall take effect three months after the date of receipt of the notification by the Secretary-General.

2. Denunciation shall be without prejudice to the continued application of the provisions of the present Protocol to any communication submitted under article 2 before the effective date of denunciation.

Article 13

Irrespective of the notifications made under article 8, paragraph 5, of the present Protocol, the Secretary-General of the United Nations shall inform all States referred to in article 48, paragraph 1, of the Covenant of the following particulars:

(a) Signatures, ratifications and accessions under article 8;

(b) The date of the entry into force of the present Protocol under article 9 and the date of the entry into force of any amendments under article 11;

(c) Denunciations under article 12.

Article 14 [AUTHENTIC TEXT]

1. The present Protocol, of which the Chinese, English, French, Russian and Spanish texts are equally authentic, shall be deposited in the archives of the United Nations.

2. The Secretary-General of the United Nations shall transmit certified copies of the present Protocol to all States referred to in article 48 of the Covenant.

21. SECOND OPTIONAL PROTOCOL TO THE INTERNATIONAL COVENANT ON CIVIL AND POLITICAL RIGHTS AIMING AT THE ABOLITION OF THE DEATH PENALTY 1989 (ANNEX GA RES 44/128 1989)

The State Parties to the Present Protocol,

Believing that abolition of the death penalty contributes to enhancement of human dignity and progressive development of human rights,

Recalling article 3 of the Universal Declaration of Human Rights adopted on 10 December 1948 and article 6 of the International Covenant on Civil and Political Rights adopted on 16 December 1966,

Noting that article 6 of the International Covenant on Civil and Political Rights refers to abolition of the death penalty in terms that strongly suggest that abolition is desirable,

Convinced that all measures of abolition of the death penalty should be considered as progress in the enjoyment of the right to life,

Desirous to undertake hereby an international commitment to abolish the death penalty,

Have agreed as follows:

Article 1

1. No one within the jurisdiction of a State Party to the present Optional Protocol shall be executed.
2. Each State Party shall take all necessary measures to abolish the death penalty within its jurisdiction.

Article 2

1. No reservation is admissible to the present Protocol, except for a reservation made at the time of ratification or accession that provides for the application of the death

penalty in time of war pursuant to a conviction for a most serious crime of a military nature committed during wartime.

2. The State Party making such a reservation shall at the time of ratification or accession communicate to the Secretary-General of the United Nations the relevant provisions of its national legislation applicable during wartime.

THE ABOLITION OF THE DEATH PENALTY

3. The State Party having made such a reservation shall notify the Secretary-General of the United Nations of any beginning or ending of a state of war applicable to its territory.

Article 3

The States Parties to the present Protocol shall include in the reports they submit to the Human Rights Committee, in accordance with article 40 of the Covenant, information on the measures that they have adopted to give effect to the present Protocol.

Article 4

With respect to the States Parties to the Covenant that have made a declaration under article 41, the competence of the Human Rights Committee to receive and consider communications when a State Party claims that another State Party is not fulfilling its obligations shall extend to the provisions of the present Protocol, unless the State Party concerned has made a statement to the contrary at the moment of ratification or accession.

Article 5

With respect to the States Parties to the (First) Optional Protocol to the International Covenant on Civil and Political Rights, adopted on 16 December 1966, the competence of the Human Rights Committee to receive and consider communications from individuals subject to its jurisdiction shall extend to the provision of the present Protocol, unless the State Party concerned has made a statement to the contrary at the moment of ratification or accession.

Article 6

1. The provisions of the present Protocol shall apply as additional provisions to the Covenant.

2. Without prejudice to the possibility of a reservation under article 2 of the present Protocol, the right guaranteed in article 1, paragraph 1, of the present Protocol shall not be subject to any derogation under article 4 of the Covenant.

Article 7

1. The present Protocol is open for signature by any State that has signed the Covenant.

2. The present Protocol is subject to ratification by any State that has ratified the Covenant or acceded to it. Instruments of ratification shall be deposited with the Secretary-General of the United Nations.

3. The present Protocol shall be open to accession by any state that has ratified the Covenant or acceded to it.

4. Accession shall be effected by the deposit of an instrument of accession with the Secretary-General of the United Nations.

5. The Secretary-General of the United Nations shall inform all States that have signed the present Protocol or acceded to it of the deposit of each instrument of ratification or accession.

Article 8

1. The present Protocol shall enter into force three months after the date of the deposit with the Secretary-General of the United Nations of the tenth instrument of ratification or accession.

2. For each State ratifying the present Protocol or acceding to it after the deposit of the tenth instrument of ratification or accession, the present Protocol shall enter into force three months after the date of the deposit of its own instrument of ratification or accession.

Article 9

The provisions of the present Protocol shall extend to all parts of federal States without any limitations or exceptions.

Article 10

The Secretary-General of the United Nations shall inform all States referred to in article 48, paragraph 1, of the Covenant of the following particulars:

(a) Reservations, communications and notifications under article 2 of the present Protocol;

(b) Statements made under its article 4 or 5;

(c) Signatures, ratifications and accessions under its article 7;

(d) The date of entry into force of the present Protocol under its article 8.

Article 11

1. The present Protocol, of which the Arabic, Chinese, English, French, Russian and Spanish texts are equally authentic, shall be deposited in the archives of the United Nations.

2. The Secretary-General of the United Nations shall transmit certified copies of the present Protocol to all States referred to in Article 48 of the Covenant.

In Force: July 11, 1991

Ratifications as of February 1, 1993: 14

22. International Covenant on Economic, Social and Cultural Rights UNTS 3 (1967); 6 ILM 360 (1967)

The States Parties to the present Covenant,

Considering that, in accordance with the principles proclaimed in the Charter of the United Nations, recognition of the inherent dignity and of the equal and inalienable rights of all members of the human family is the foundation of freedom, justice and peace in the world,

Recognizing that these rights derive from the inherent dignity of the human person,

Recognizing that, in accordance with the Universal Declaration of Human Rights, the ideal of free human beings enjoying freedom from fear and want can only be achieved if conditions are created whereby everyone may enjoy his economic, social and cultural rights, as well as his civil and political rights,

Considering the obligations of States under the Charter of the United Nations to promote universal respect for, and observance of, human rights and freedoms,

Realizing that the individual, having duties to other individuals and to the community to which he belongs, is under a responsibility to strive for the promotion and observance of the rights recognized in the present Covenant,

Agree upon the following articles:

PART I

Article 1 [RIGHT OF SELF-DETERMINATION]

1. All peoples have the right of self-determination. By virtue of that right they freely determine their political status and freely pursue their economic, social and cultural development.

2. All peoples may, for their own ends, freely dispose of their natural wealth and resources without prejudice to any obligations arising out of international economic co-operation, based upon the principle of mutual benefit, and international law. In no case may a people be deprived of its own means of subsistence.

3. The States Parties to the present Covenant, including those having responsibility for the administration of Non-Self-Governing and Trust Territories, shall promote the realization of the right of self-determination, and shall respect that right, in conformity with the provisions of the Charter of the United Nations.

PART II

Article 2 [PRINCIPLE ON NON-DISCRIMINATION]

1. Each State Party to the present Covenant undertakes to take steps, individually and through international assistance and co-operation, especially economic and technical, to the maximum of its available resources, with a view to achieving progressively the full realization of the rights recognized in the present Covenant by all appropriate means, including particularly the adoption of legislative measures.

2. The States Parties to the present Covenant undertake to guarantee that the rights enunciated in the present Covenant will be exercised without discrimination of any kind as to race, colour, sex, language, religion, political or other opinion, national or social origin, property, birth or other status.

3. Developing countries, with due regard to human rights and their national economy, may determine to what extent they would guarantee the economic rights recogtnized in the present Covenant to non-national. .

Article 3 [EQUAL RIGHT OF MEN AND WOMEN]

The States Parties to the present Covenant undertake to ensure the equal right of men and women to the enjoyment of all economic, social and cultural rights set forth in the present Covenant.

Article 4 [LIMITATIONS]

The States Parties to the present Covenant recognize that, in the enjoyment of those rights provided by the State in conformity with the present Covenant, the State may subject such rights only to such limitations as are determined by law only in so far as this may be compatible with the nature of these rights and solely for the purpose of promoting the general welfare in a democratic society.

Article 5 [No Greater Restrictions or Limitation than Provided]

. Nothing in the present Covenant may be interpreted as implying for any State, group or person any right to engage in any activity or to perform any act aimed at the destruction of any of the rights or freedoms recognized herein, or at their limitation to a greater extent than is provided for in the present Covenant.

2. No restriction upon or derogation from any of the fundamental human rights recognized or existing in any country in virtue of law, conventions, regulations or custom shall be admitted on the pretext that the present Covenant does not recognize such rights or that it recognizes them to a lesser extent.

Part III

Article 6 [Right to Work]

1. The States Parties to the present Covenant recognize the right to work, which includes the right of everyone to the opportunity to gain his living by work which he freely chooses or accepts, and will take appropriate steps to safeguard this right.

2. The steps to be taken by a State Party to the present Covenant to achieve the full realization of this right shall include technical and vocational guidance and training programmes, policies and techniques to achieve steady economic, social and cultural development and full and productive employment under conditions safeguarding fundamental political and economic freedoms to the individual.

Article 7 [Just and Favourable Conditions of Work]

The States Parties to the present Covenant recognize the right of everyone to the enjoyment of just and favourable conditions of work, which ensure, in particular:

(a) remuneration which provides all workers, as a minimum, with:

  (i) fair wages and equal remuneration for work of equal value without distinction of any kind, in particular women being guaranteed conditions of work not inferior to those enjoyed by men, with equal pay for equal work;

  (ii) a decent living for themselves and their families in accordance with the provisions of the present Covenant;

(b) safe and healthy working conditions;

(c) equal opportunity for everyone to be promoted in his employment to an appropriate higher level, subject to no considerations other than those of seniority and competence;

(d) rest, leisure and reasonable limitation of working hours and periodic holidays with pay, as well as remuneration for public holidays.

Article 8 [Trade Union Rights[

1. The States Parties to the present Covenant undertake to ensure:

(a) the right of everyone to form trade unions and join the trade union of his choice, subject only to the rules of the organization concerned, for the promotion and protection of his economic and social interests. No restrictions may be placed on the exercise of this right other than those prescribed by law and which are necessary in a democratic society in the interests of national security or public order or for the protection of the rights and freedoms of others;

(b) the right of trade unions to establish national federations or confederations and the right of the latter to form or join international trade-union organizations;

(c) the right of trade unions to function freely subject to no limitations other than those prescribed by law and which are necessary in a democratic society in the interests of national security or public order or for the protection of the rights and freedoms of others;

(d) the right to strike, provided that it is exercised in conformity with the laws of the particular country.

2. This article shall not prevent the imposition of lawful restrictions on the exercise of these rights by members of the armed forces or of the police or of the administration of the State.

3. Nothing in this article shall authorize States Parties to the International Labour Organization Convention of 1948 concerning Freedom of Association and Protection of the Right to Organize to take legislative measures which would prejudice, or apply the law in such a manner as would prejudice, the guarantees provided for in that Convention.

Article 9 [RIGHT TO SOCIAL SECURITY]

The States Parties to the present Covenant recognize the right of everyone to social security, including social insurance.

Article 10 [PROTECTION OF FAMILY]

The States Parties to the present Covenant recognize that:

1. The widest possible protection and assistance should be accorded to the family, which is the natural and fundamental group unit of society, particularly for its establishment and while it is responsible for the care and education of dependant children. Marriage must be entered into with the free consent of the intending spouses.

2. Special protection should be accorded to mothers during a reasonable period before and after childbirth. During such period working mothers should be accorded paid leave or leave with adequate social security benefits.

3. Special measures of protection and assistance should be taken on behalf of all children and young persons without any discrimination for reasons of parentage or other conditions. Children and young persons should be protected from economic and social exploitation. Their employment in work harmful to their morals or health or dangerous to life or likely to hamper their normal development should be punishable by law. States should also set age limits below which the paid employment of child labour should be prohibited and punishable by law.

Article 11 [RIGHT TO FOOD, CLOTHING AND SHELTER]

The States Parties to the present Covenant recognize the right of everyone to an adequate standard of living for himself and his family, including adequate food, clothing and housing, and to the continuous improvement of living conditions. The States Parties will take appropriate steps to ensure the realization of this right, recognizing to this effect the essential importance of international co-operation based on free consent.

2. The States Parties to the present Covenant, recognizing the fundamental right of everyone to be free from hunger, shall take, individually and through international co-operation, the measures, including specific programmes, which are needed:

(a) to improve methods of production, conservation and distribution of food by making full use of technical and scientific knowledge, by disseminating knowledge

of the principles of nutrition and by developing or reforming agrarian systems in such a way as to achieve the most efficient development and utilization of natural resources;

(b) taking into account the problems of both food-importing and food-exporting countries, to ensure an equitable distribution of world food supplies in relation to need.

Article 12 [RIGHT TO HEALTH]

1. The States Parties to the present Covenant recognize the right of everyone to the enjoyment of the highest attainable standard of physical and mental health.

2. The steps to be taken by the States Parties to the present Covenant to achieve the full realization of this right shall include those necessary for:

(a) the provision for the reduction of the stillbirth-rate and of infant mortality and for the healthy development of the child;

(b) the improvement of all aspects of environmental and industrial hygiene;

(c) the prevention, treatment and control of epidemic, endemic, occupational and other diseases;

(d) the creation of conditions which would assure to all medical service and medical attention in the event of sickness.

Article 13 [RIGHT TO EDUCATION]

1. The States Parties to the present Covenant recognize the right of everyone to education. They agree that education shall be directed to the full development of the human personality and the sense of its dignity, and shall strengthen the respect for human rights and fundamental freedoms. They further agree that education shall enable all persons to participate effectively in a free society, promote understanding, tolerance and friendship among all nations and all racial, ethnic or religious groups, and further the activities of the United Nations for the maintenance of peace.

2. The States Parties to the present Covenant recognize that, with a view to achieving the full realization of this right:

(a) primary education shall be compulsory and available free to all;

(b) secondary education in its different forms, including technical and vocational secondary education, shall be made generally available and accessible to all by every appropriate means, and in particular by the progressive introduction of free education;

(c) higher education shall be made equally accessible to all, on the basis of capacity, by every appropriate means, and in particular by the progressive introduction of free education;

(d) fundamental education shall be encouraged or intensified as far as possible for those persons who have not received or completed the whole period of their primary education;

(e) the development of a system of schools at all levels shall be actively pursued, an adequate fellowship system shall be established, and the material conditions of teaching staff shall be continuously improved.

3. The States Parties to the present Covenant undertake to have respect for the liberty of parents and, when applicable, legal guardians, to choose for their children schools, other than those established by the public authorities, which conform to such minimum

educational standards as may be laid down or approved by the State and to ensure the religious and moral education of their children in conformity with their own convictions.

4. No part of this article shall be construed so as to interfere with the liberty of individuals and bodies to establish and direct educational institutions, subject always to the observance of the principles set forth in paragraph 1 of this article and to the requirement that the education given in such institutions shall conform to such minimum standards as may be laid down by the State.

Article 14 [STATE UNDERTAKING]

Each State Party to the present Covenant which, at the time of becoming a Party, has not been able to secure in its metropolitan territory or other territories under its jurisdiction compulsory primary education, free of charge, undertakes, within two years, to work out and adopt a detailed plan of action for the progressive implementation, within a reasonable number of years, to be fixed in the plan of the principle of compulsory education free of charge for all.

Article 15 [CULTURAL RIGHTS]

1. The States Parties to the present Covenant recognize the right of everyone:

(a) to take part in cultural life;

(b) to enjoy the benefits of scientific progress and its applications;

(c) to benefit from the protection of the moral and material interests resulting from any scientific, literary or artistic production of which he is the author.

2. The steps to be taken by the States Parties to the present Covenant to achieve the full realization of this right shall include those necessary for the conservation, the development and the diffusion of science and culture.

3. The States Parties to the present Covenant undertake to respect the freedom indispensable for scientific research and creative activity.

4. The States Parties to the present Covenant recognize the benefits to be derived from the encouragement and development of international contacts and co-operation in the scientific and cultural fields.

PART IV

Article 16 [REPORTS TO ECOSOC]

1. The States Parties to the present Covenant undertake to submit in conformity with this part of the Covenant reports on the measures which they have adopted and the progress made in achieving the observance of the rights recognized herein.

2. *(a)* All reports shall be submitted to the Secretary-General of the United Nations, who shall transmit copies to the Economic and Social Council for consideration in accordance with the provisions of the present Covenant.

(b) The Secretary-General of the United Nations shall also transmit to the specialized agencies copies of the reports, or any relevant parts therefrom, from States Parties to the present Covenant which are also members of these specialized agencies in so far as these reports, or parts therefrom, relate to any matters which fall within the responsibilities of the said agencies in accordance with their constitutional instruments.

Article 17 [REEPORT]

1. The States Parties to the present Covenant shall furnish their reports in stages, in accordance with a programme to be established by the Economic and Social Council

within one year of the entry into force of the present Covenant after consultation with the States Parties and the specialized agencies concerned.

2. Reports may indicate factors and difficulties affecting the degree of fulfilment of obligations under the present Covenant.

3. Where relevant information has previously been furnished to the United Nations or to any specialized agency by any State Party to the present Covenant, it will not be necessary to reproduce that information, but a precise reference to the information so furnished will suffice.

Article 18 [ROLE OF ECOSOC]

Pursuant to its responsibilities under the Charter of the United Nations in the field of human rights and fundamental freedoms, the Economic and Social Council may make arrangements with the specialized agencies in respect of their reporting to it on the progress made in achieving the observance of the provisions of the present Covenant falling within the scope of their activities. These reports may include particulars of decisions and recommendations on such implementation adopted by their competent organs.

Article 19. The Economic and Social Council may transmit to the Commission on Human Rights for study and general recommendation or as appropriate for information the reports concerning human rights submitted by States in accordance with articles 16 and 17, and those concerning human rights submitted by the specialized agencies in accordance with article 18.

Article 20. The States Parties to the present Covenant and the specialized agencies concerned may submit comments to the Economic and Social Council on any general recommendation under article 19 or reference to such general recommendation in any report of the Commission on Human Rights or any documentation referred to therein.

Article 21. The Economic and Social Council may submit from time to time to the General Assembly reports with recommendations of a general nature and a summary of the information received from the States Parties to the present Covenant and the specialized agencies on the measures taken and the progress made in achieving general observance of the rights recognized in the present Covenant.

Article 22. The Economic and Social Council may bring to the attention of other organs of the United Nations, their subsidiary organs and specialized agencies concerned with furnishing technical assistance any matters arising out of the reports referred to in this part of the present Covenant which may assist such bodies in deciding, each within its field of competence, on the advisability of international measures likely to contribute to the effective progressive implementation of the present Covenant.

Article 23. The States Parties to the present Covenant agree that international action for the achievement of the rights recognized in the present Covenant includes such methods as the conclusion of conventions, the adoption of recommendations, the furnishing of technical assistance and the holding of regional meetings and technical meetings for the purpose of consultation and study organized in conjunction with the Governments concerned.

Article 24. Nothing in the present Covenant shall be interpreted as impairing the provisions of the Charter of the United Nations and of the constitutions of the specialized agencies which define the respective responsibilities of the various organs of the United Nations and of the specialized agencies in regard to the matters dealt with in the present Covenant.

Article 25. Nothing in the present Covenant shall be interpreted as impairing the inherent right of all peoples to enjoy and utilize fully and freely their natural wealth and resources.

PART V

Article 26 [SIGNATURES, RATIFICATION AND ACCESSION]

1. The present Covenant is open for signature by any State Member of the United Nations or member of any of its specialized agencies, by any State Party to the Statute of the International Court of Justice, and by any other State which has been invited by the General Assembly of the United Nations to become a party to the present Covenant.

2. The present Covenant is subject to ratification. Instruments of ratification shall be deposited with the Secretary-General of the United Nations.

3. The present Covenant shall be open to accession by any State referred to in paragraph 1 of this article.

4. Accession shall be effected by the deposit of an instrument of accession with the Secretary-General of the United Nations.

5. The Secretary-General of the United Nations shall inform all States which have signed the present Covenant or acceded to it of the deposit of each instrument of ratification or accession.

Article 27 [ENTRY INTO FORCE]

1. The present Covenant shall enter into force three months after the date of the deposit with the Secretary-General of the United Nations of the thirty-fifth instrument of ratification or instrument of accession.

2. For each State ratifying the present Covenant or acceding to it after the deposit of the thirty-fifth instrument of ratification or instrument of accession, the present Covenant shall enter into force three months after the date of the deposit of its own instrument of ratification or instrument of accession.

Article 28. The provisions of the present Covenant shall extend to all parts of federal States without any limitations or exceptions.

Article 29 [AMENDMENT]

1. Any State Party to the present Covenant may propose an amendment and file it with the Secretary-General of the United Nations. The Secretary-General shall thereupon communicate any proposed amendments to the States Parties to the present Covenant with a request that they notify him whether they favour a conference of States Parties for the purpose of considering and voting upon the proposals. In the event that at least one third of the States Parties favours such a conference, the Secretary-General shall convene the conference under the auspices of the United Nations. Any amendment adopted by a majority of the States Parties present and voting at the conference shall be submitted to the General Assembly of the United Nations for approval.

2. Amendments shall come into force when they have been approved by the General Assembly of the United Nations and accepted by a two-thirds majority of the States Parties to the present Covenant in accordance with their respective constitutional processes.

3. When amendments come into force they shall be binding on those States Parties which have accepted them, other States Parties still being bound by the provisions of the present Covenant and any earlier amendment which they have accepted.

Article 30. Irrespective of the notifications made under article 26, paragraph 5, the Secretary-General of the United Nations shall inform all States referred to in paragraph 1 of the same article of the following particulars:

(a)   signatures, ratifications and accessions under article 26;

(b)   the date of the entry into force of the present Covenant under article 27 and the date of the entry into force of any amendments under article 29.

Article 31.   1.   The present Covenant, of which the Chinese, English, French, Russian and Spanish texts are equally authentic, shall be deposited in the archives of the United Nations.

23.   DECLARATION ON THE GRANTING OF INDEPENDENCE TO COLONIAL COUNTRIES AND PEOPLES   (GA RES 1514 (XV) 1960)

The General Assembly,

Mindful of the determination proclaimed by the peoples of the world in the Charter of the United Nations to reaffirm faith in fundamental human rights, in the dignity and worth of the human person, in the equal rights of men and women and of nations large and small and to promote social progress and better standards of life in larger freedom,

Conscious of the need for the creation of conditions of stability and well-being and peaceful and friendly relations based on respect for the principles of equal rights and self-determination of all peoples, and of universal respect for, and observance of, human rights and fundamental freedoms for all without distinction as to race, sex, language or religion,

Recognizing the passionate yearning for freedom in all dependent peoples and the decisive role of such peoples in the attainment of their independence,

Aware of the increasing conflicts resulting from the denial of or impediments in the way of the freedom of such peoples, which constitute a serious threat to world peace,

Considering the important role of the United Nations in assisting the movement for independence in Trust and Non-Self-Governing Territories,

Recognizing that the peoples of the world ardently desire the end of colonialism in all its manifestations,

Convinced that the continued existence of colonialism prevents the development of international economic co-operation, impedes the social, cultural and economic development of dependent peoples and militates against the United Nations ideal of universal peace,

Affirming that peoples may, for their own ends, freely dispose of their natural wealth and resources without prejudice to any obligations arising out of international economic co-operation, based upon the principle of mutual benefit, and international law,

Believing that the process of liberation is irresistible and irreversible and that, in order to avoid serious crises, an end must be put to colonialism and all practices of segregation and discrimination associated therewith,

Welcoming the emergence in recent years of a large number of dependent territories into freedom and independence, and recognizing the increasingly powerful trends towards freedom in such territories which have not yet attained independence,

Convinced that all peoples have an inalienable right to complete freedom, the exercise of their sovereignty and the integrity of their national territory,

Solemnly proclaims the necessity of bringing to a speedy and unconditional end colonialism in all its forms and manifestations;

And to this end

Declares that:

1. The subjection of peoples to alien subjugation, domination and exploitation constitutes a denial of fundamental human rights, is contrary to the Charter of the United Nations and is an impediment to the promotion of world peace and co-operation.

2. All peoples have the right to self-determination; by virtue of that right they freely determine their political status and freely pursue their economic, social and cultural development.

3. Inadequacy of political, economic, social or educational preparedness should never serve as a pretext for delaying independence.

4. All armed action or repressive measures of all kinds directed against dependent peoples shall cease in order to enable them to exercise peacefully and freely their right to complete independence, and the integrity of their national territory shall be respected.

5. Immediate steps shall be taken, in Trust and Non-Self-Governing Territories or all other territories which have not yet attained independence, to transfer all powers to the peoples of those territories, without any conditions or reservations, in accordance with their freely expressed will and desire, without any distinction as to race, creed or colour, in order to enable them to enjoy complete independence and freedom.

6. Any attempt aimed at the partial or total disruption of the national unity and the territorial integrity of a country is incompatible with the purposes and principles of the Charter of the United Nations.

7. All States shall observe faithfully and strictly the provisions of the Charter of the United Nations, the Universal Declaration of Human Rights and the present Declaration on the basis of equality, non-interference in the internal affairs of all States, and respect for the sovereign rights of all peoples and their territorial integrity.

947th plenary meeting,
14 December 1960.

24. INTERNATIONAL CONVENTION ON THE SUPPRESSION AND PUNISHMENT OF THE CRIME OF *APARTHEID*

(GA RES 3068 (XXVII) 1974; 13 ILM 50 (1974))

The States Parties to the present Convention,

Recalling the provisions of the Charter of the United Nations, in which all Members pledged themselves to take joint and separate action in co-operation with the Organization for the achievement of universal respect for, and observance of, human rights and fundamental freedoms for all without distinction as to race, sex, language or religion,

Considering the Universal Declaration of Human Rights, which states that all human beings are born free and equal in dignity and rights and that everyone is entitled to all the rights and freedoms set forth in the Declaration, without distinction of any kind, such as race, colour or national origin,

Considering the Declaration on the Granting of Independence to Colonial Countries and Peoples, in which the General Assembly stated that the process of liberation is irresistible and irreversible and that, in the interests of human dignity, progress and justice, an end must be put to colonialism and all practices of segregation and discrimination associated therewith,

Observing that, in accordance with the International Convention on the Elimination of All Forms of Racial Discrimination, States particularly condemn racial segregation and *apartheid* and undertake to prevent, prohibit and eradicate all practices of this nature in territories under their jurisdiction,

Observing that, in the Convention on the Prevention and Punishment of the Crime of Genocide, certain acts which may also be qualified as acts of *apartheid* constitute a crime under international law,

Observing that, in the Convention on the Non-Applicability of Statutory Limitations to War Crimes and Crimes Against Humanity, "inhuman acts resulting from the policy of *apartheid*" are qualified as crimes against humanity,

Observing that the General Assembly of the United Nations has adopted a number of resolutions in which the policies and practices of *apartheid* are condemned as a crime against humanity,

Observing that the Security Council has emphasized that *apartheid* and its continued intensification and expansion seriously disturb and threaten international peace and security,

Convinced that an International Convention on the Suppression and Punishment of the Crime of *Apartheid* would make it possible to take more effective measures at the international and national levels with a view to the suppression and punishment of the crime of *apartheid*,

Have agreed as follows:

Article I

1. The States Parties to the present Convention declare that *apartheid* is a crime against humanity and that inhuman acts resulting from the policies and practices of *apartheid* and similar policies and practices of racial segregation and discrimination, as defined in article II of the Convention, are crimes violating the principles of international law, in particular the purposes and principles of the Charter of the United Nations, and constituting a serious threat to international peace and security.

2. The States Parties to the present Convention declare criminal those organizations, institutions and individuals committing the crime of *apartheid*.

Article II

For the purpose of the present Convention, the term "the crime of *apartheid*", which shall include similar policies and practices of racial segregation and discrimination as practised in southern Africa, shall apply to the following inhuman acts committed for the purpose of establishing and maintaining domination by one racial group of persons over any other racial group of persons and systematically oppressing them:

(a) Denial to a member or members of a racial group or groups of the right to life and liberty of person:

 (i) By murder of members of a racial group or groups;

 (ii) By the infliction upon the members of a racial group or groups of serious bodily and mental harm, by the infringement of their freedom or dignity, or by subjecting them to torture or to cruel, inhuman or degrading treatment or punishment;

(iii) By arbitrary arrest and illegal imprisonment of the members of a racial group or groups;

(b) Deliberate imposition on a racial group or groups of living conditions calculated to cause its or their physical destruction in whole or in part;

(c) Any legislative measures and other measures calculated to prevent a racial group or groups from participation in the political, social, economic and cultural life of the country and the deliberate creation of conditions preventing the full development of such a group or groups, in particular by denying to members of a racial group or groups basic human rights and freedoms, including the right to work, the right to form recognized trade unions, the right to education, the right to leave and to return to their country, the right to a nationality, the right to freedom of movement and residence, the right to freedom of opinion and expression and the right to freedom of peaceful assembly and association;

(d) Any measures, including legislative measures, designed to divide the population along racial lines by the creation of separate reserves and ghettos for the members of a racial group or groups, the prohibition of mixed marriages among members of various racial groups, the expropriation of landed property belonging to a racial group or groups or to members thereof;

(e) Exploitation of the labour of the members of a racial group or groups, in particular by submitting them to forced labour;

(f) Persecution of organizations and persons, by depriving them of fundamental rights and freedoms, because they oppose *apartheid.*

Article III

International criminal responsibility shall apply, irrespective of the motive involved, to individuals, members of organizations and institutions and representatives of the State, whether residing in the territory of the State in which the acts are perpetrated or in some other State, whenever they:

(a) Commit, participate in, directly incite or conspire in the commission of the acts mentioned in article II of the present Convention;

(b) Directly abet, encourage or co-operate in the commission of the crime of *apartheid.*

Article IV

The States Parties to the present Convention undertake:

(a) To adopt any legislative or other measures necessary to suppress as well as to prevent any encouragement of the crime of *apartheid* and similar segregationist policies or their manifestations and to punish persons guilty of that crime;

(b) To adopt legislative, judicial and administrative measures to prosecute, bring to trial and punish in accordance with their jurisdiction persons responsible for, or accused of, the acts defined in article II of the present Convention, whether or not such persons reside in the territory of the State in which the acts are committed or are nationals of that State or of some other State or are stateless persons.

Article V

Persons charged with the acts enumerated in article II of the present Convention may be tried by competent tribunal of any State Party to the Convention which may acquire jurisdiction over the person of the accused or by an international penal tribunal having jurisdiction with respect to those States Parties which shall have accepted its jurisdiction.

Article VI

The States Parties to the present Convention undertake to accept and carry out in accordance with the Charter of the United Nations the decisions taken by the Security

Council aimed at the prevention, suppression and punishment of the crime of *apartheid*, and to co-operate in the implementation of decisions adopted by other competent organs of the United Nations with a view to achieving the purposes of the Convention.

Article VII

1. The States Parties to the present Convention undertake to submit periodic reports to the group established under article IX on the legislative, judicial, administrative or other measures that they have adopted and that give effect to the provisions of the Convention.

2. Copies of the reports shall be transmitted through the Secretary-General of the United Nations to the Special Committee on *Apartheid*.

Article VIII

Any State Party to the present Convention may call upon any competent organ of the United Nations to take such action under the Charter of the United Nations as it considers appropriate for the prevention and suppression of the crime of *apartheid*.

Article IX

1. The Chairman of the Commission on Human Rights shall appoint a group consisting of three members of the Commission on Human Rights, who are also representatives of States Parties to the present Convention, to consider reports submitted by States Parties in accordance with article VII.

2. If, among the members of the Commission on Human Rights, there are no representatives of States Parties to the present Convention or if there are fewer than three such representatives, the Secretary-General of the United Nations shall, after consulting all States Parties to the Convention, designate a representative of the State Party or representatives of the States Parties which are not members of the Commission on Human Rights to take part in the work of the group established in accordance with paragraph 1 of this article, until such time as representatives of the States Parties to the Convention are elected to the Commission on Human Rights.

3. The group may meet for a period of not more than five days, either before the opening or after the closing of the session of the Commission on Human Rights, to consider the reports submitted in accordance with article VII.

Article X

1. The States Parties to the present Convention empower the Commission on Human Rights:

(a) To request United Nations organs, when transmitting copies of petitions under article 15 of the International Convention on the Elimination of All Forms of Racial Discrimination, to draw its attention to complaints concerning acts which are enumerated in article II of the present Convention;

(b) To prepare, on the basis of reports from competent organs of the United Nations and periodic reports from States Parties to the present Convention, a list of individuals, organizations, institutions and representatives of States which are alleged to be responsible for the crimes enumerated in article II of the Convention, as well as those against whom legal proceedings have been undertaken by States Parties to the Convention;

(c) To request information from the competent United Nations organs concerning measures taken by the authorities responsible for the administration of Trust and Non-Self-Governing Territories, and all other Territories to which General Assembly resolution 1514 (XV) of 14 December 1960 applies, with regard to such individuals alleged to be responsible for crimes under article II of the Convention who are believed to be under their territorial and administrative jurisdiction.

2. Pending the achievement of the objectives of the Declaration on the Granting of Independence to Colonial Countries and Peoples, contained in General Assembly resolution 1514 (XV), the provisions of the present Convention shall in no way limit the right of petition granted to those peoples by other international instruments or by the United Nations and its specialized agencies.

Article XI

1. Acts enumerated in article II of the present Convention shall not be considered political crimes for the purpose of extradition.

2. The States Parties to the present Convention undertake in such cases to grant extradition in accordance with their legislation and with the treaties in force.

Article XII

Disputes between States Parties arising out of the interpretation, application or implementation of the present Convention which have not been settled by negotiation shall, at the request of the States Parties to the dispute, be brought before the International Court of Justice, save where the parties to the dispute have agreed on some other form of settlement.

Article XIII

The present Convention is open for signature by all States. Any State which does not sign the Convention before its entry into force may accede to it.

Article XIV

1. The present Convention is subject to ratification. Instruments of ratification shall be deposited with the Secretary-General of the United Nations.

2. Accession shall be effected by the deposit of an instrument of accession with the Secretary-General of the United Nations.

Article XV

1. The present Convention shall enter into force on the thirtieth day after the date of the deposit with the Secretary-General of the United Nations of the twentieth instrument of ratification or accession.

2. For each State ratifying the present Convention or acceding to it after the deposit of the twentieth instrument of ratification or instrument of accession, the Convention shall come into force on the thirtieth day after the date of the deposit of its own instrument of ratification or instrument of accession.

Article XVI

A State Party may denounce the present Convention by written notification to the Secretary-General of the United Nations. Denunciation shall take effect one year after the date of receipt of the notification by the Secretary-General.

Article XVII

1. A request for the revision of the present Convention may be made at any time by any State Party by means of a notification in writing addressed to the Secretary-General of the United Nations.

2. The General Assembly of the United Nations shall decide upon the steps, if any, to be taken in respect of such request.

Article XVIII

The Secretary-General of the United Nations shall inform all States of the following particulars:

(a) Signatures, ratifications and accessions under articles XIII and XIV;

(b) The date of entry into force of the present Convention under article XV;

(c) Denunciations under article XVI;

(d) Notifications under article XVII.

Article XIX

1. The present Convention, of which the Chinese, English, French, Russian and Spanish texts are equally authentic, shall be deposited in the archives of the United Nations.

2. The Secretary-General of the United Nations shall transmit certified copies of the present Convention to all States.

25. INTERNATIONAL CONVENTION ON THE ELIMINATION OF ALL FORMS OF RACIAL DISCRIMINATION 1966

(660 UNTS 195; 5 ILM 352 (1966))

The States Parties to this Convention,

Considering that the Charter of the United Nations is based on the principles of the dignity and equality inherent in all human beings, and that all Member States have pledged themselves to take joint and separate action, in co-operation with the Organization, for the achievement of one of the purposes of the United Nations which is to promote and encourage universal respect for and observance of human rights and fundamental freedoms for all, without distinction as to race, sex, language or religion,

Considering that the Universal Declaration of Human Rights proclaims that all human beings are born free and equal in dignity and rights and that everyone is entitled to all the rights and freedoms set out therein, without distinction of any kind, in particular as to race, colour or national origin,

Considering that all human beings are equal before the law and are entitled to equal protection of the law against any discrimination and against any incitement to discrimination,

Considering that the United Nations has condemned colonialism and all practices of segregation and discrimination associated therewith, in whatever form and wherever they exist, and that the Declaration on the Granting of Independence to Colonial Countries and Peoples of 14 December 1960 (General Assembly resolution 1514 (XV)) has affirmed and solemnly proclaimed the necessity of bringing them to a speedy and unconditional end,

Considering that the United Nations Declaration on the Elimination of All Forms of Racial Discrimination of 20 November 1963 (General Assembly resolution 1904 (XVIII)) solemnly affirms the necessity of speedily eliminating racial discrimination throughout the world in all its forms and manifestations and of securing understanding of and respect for the dignity of the human person,

Convinced that any doctrine of superiority based on racial differentiation is scientifically false, morally condemnable, socially unjust and dangerous, and that there is no justification for racial discrimination, in theory or in practice, anywhere,

Reaffirming that discrimination between human beings on the grounds of race, colour or ethnic origin is an obstacle to friendly and peaceful relations among nations and is capable of disturbing peace and security among peoples and the harmony of persons living side by side even within one and the same State,

Convinced that the existence of racial barriers is repugnant to the ideals of any human society,

Alarmed by manifestations of racial discrimination still in evidence in some areas of the world and by governmental policies based on racial superiority or hatred, such as policies of *apartheid*, segregation or separation,

Resolved to adopt all necessary measures for speedily eliminating racial discrimination in all its forms and manifestations, and to prevent and combat racist doctrines and practices in order to promote understanding between races and to build an international community free from all forms of racial segregation and racial discrimination,

Bearing in mind the Convention concerning Discrimination in respect of Employment and Occupation adopted by the International Labour Organization in 1958, and the Convention against Discrimination in Education adopted by the United Nations Educational, Scientific and Cultural Organization in 1960,

Desiring to implement the principles embodied in the United Nations Declaration on the Elimination of All Forms of Racial Discrimination and to secure the earliest adoption of practical measures to that end,

Have agreed as follows:

PART I

Article I

1. In this Convention, the term "racial discrimination" shall mean any distinction, exclusion, restriction or preference based on race, colour, descent, or national or ethnic origin which has the purpose or effect of nullifying or impairing the recognition, enjoyment or exercise, on an equal footing, of human rights and fundamental freedoms in the political, economic, social, cultural or any other field of public life.

2. This Convention shall not apply to distinctions, exclusions, restrictions or preferences made by a State Party to this Convention between citizens and non-citizens.

3. Nothing in this Convention may be interpreted as affecting in any way the legal provisions of States Parties concerning nationality, citizenship or naturalization, provided that such provisions do not discriminate against any particular nationality.

4. Special measures taken for the sole purpose of securing adequate advancement of certain racial or ethnic groups or individuals requiring such protection as may be necessary in order to ensure such groups or individuals equal enjoyment or exercise of human rights and fundamental freedoms shall not be deemed racial discrimination, provided, however, that such measures do not, as a consequence, lead to the maintenance

of separate rights for different racial groups and that they shall not be continued after the objectives for which they were taken have been achieved.

Article 2

1. States Parties condemn racial discrimination and undertake to pursue by all appropriate means and without delay a policy of eliminating racial discrimination in all its forms and promoting understanding among all races, and, to this end:

(a) Each State Party undertakes to engage in no act or practice of racial discrimination against persons, groups of persons or institutions and to ensure that all public authorities and public institutions, national and local, shall act in conformity with this obligation;

(b) Each State Party undertakes not to sponsor, defend or support racial discrimination by any persons or organization;

(c) Each State Party shall take effective measures to review governmental, national and local policies, and to amend, rescind or nullify any laws and regulations which have the effect of creating or perpetuating racial discrimination wherever it exists;

(d) Each State Party shall prohibit and bring to an end, by all appropriate means, including legislation as required by circumstances, racial discrimination by any persons, group or organization;

(e) Each State Party undertakes to encourage, where appropriate, integrationist multi-racial organizations and movements and other means of eliminating barriers between races, and to discourage anything which tends to strengthen racial division.

2. States Parties shall, when the circumstances so warrant, take, in the social, economic, cultural and other fields, special and concrete measures to ensure the adequate development and protection of certain racial groups or individuals belonging to them, for the purpose of guaranteeing them the full and equal enjoyment of human rights and fundamental freedoms. These measures shall in no case entail as a consequence the maintenance of unequal or separate rights for different racial groups after the objectives for which they were taken have been achieved.

Article 3

States Parties particularly condemn racial segregation and *apartheid* and undertake to prevent, prohibit and eradicate all practices of this nature in territories under their jurisdiction.

Article 4

States Parties condemn all propaganda and all organizations which are based on ideas or theories of superiority of one race or group of persons of one colour or ethnic origin, or which attempt to justify or promote racial hatred and discrimination in any form, and undertake to adopt immediate and positive measures designed to eradicate all incitement to, or acts of, such discrimination and, to this end, with due regard to the principles embodied in the Universal Declaration of Human Rights and the rights expressly set forth in article 5 of this Convention, *inter alia*:

(a) Shall declare an offence punishable by law all dissemination of ideas based on racial superiority or hatred, incitement to racial discrimination, as well as all acts of violence or incitement to such acts against any race or group of persons of another colour or ethnic origin, and also the provision of any assistance to racist activities, including the financing thereof;

(b) Shall declare illegal and prohibit organizations, and also organized and all other propaganda activities, which promote and incite racial discrimination, and shall recognize participation in such organizations or activities as an offence punishable by law;

(c) Shall not permit public authorities or public institutions, national or local, to promote or incite racial discrimination.

Article 5

In compliance with the fundamental obligations laid down in article 2 of this Convention, States Parties undertake to prohibit and to eliminate racial discrimination in all its forms and to guarantee the right of everyone, without distinction as to race, colour, or national or ethnic origin, to equality before the law, notably in the enjoyment of the following rights:

(a) The right to equal treatment before the tribunals and all other organs administering justice;

(b) The right to security of person and protection by the State against violence or bodily harm, whether inflicted by government officials or by any individual, group or institution;

(c) Political rights, in particular the rights to participate in elections—to vote and to stand for election—on the basis of universal and equal suffrage, to take part in the Government as well as in the conduct of public affairs at any level and to have equal access to public service;

(d) Other civil rights, in particular:

  (i) The right to freedom of movement and residence within the border of the State;

  (ii) The right to leave any country, including one's own, and to return to one's country;

  (iii) The right to nationality;

  (iv) The right to marriage and choice of spouse;

  (v) The right to own property alone as well as in association with others;

  (vi) The right to inherit;

  (vii) The right to freedom of thought, conscience and religion;

  (viii) The right to freedom of opinion and expression;

  (ix) The right to freedom of peaceful assembly and association;

(e) Economic, social and cultural rights, in particular:

  (i) The rights to work, to free choice of employment, to just and favourable conditions of work, to protection against unemployment, to equal pay for equal work, to just and favourable remuneration;

  (ii) The right to form and join trade unions;

  (iii) The right to housing;

  (iv) The right to public health, medical care, social security and social services;

  (v) The right to education and training;

  (vi) The right to equal participation in cultural activities;

(f) The right of access to any place or service intended for use by the general public, such as transport, hotels, restaurants, cafés, theatres and parks.

Article 6

States Parties shall assure to everyone within their jurisdiction effective protection and remedies, through the competent national tribunals and other State institutions, against any acts of racial discrimination which violate his human rights and fundamental freedoms contrary to this Convention, as well as the right to seek from such tribunals just and adequate reparation or satisfaction for any damage suffered as a result of such discrimination.

Article 7

States Parties undertake to adopt immediate and effective measures, particularly in the fields of teaching, education, culture and information, with a view to combating prejudices which lead to racial discrimination and to promoting understanding, tolerance and friendship among nations and racial or ethnical groups, as well as to propagating the purposes and principles of the Charter of the United Nations, the Universal Declaration of Human Rights, the United Nations Declaration on the Elimination of All Forms of Racial Discrimination, and this Convention.

PART II

Article 8

1. There shall be established a Committee on the Elimination of Racial Discrimination (hereinafter referred to as the Committee) consisting of eighteen experts of high moral standing and acknowledged impartiality elected by States Parties from among their nationals, who shall serve in their personal capacity, consideration being given to equitable geographical distribution and to the representation of the different forms of civilization as well as of the principal legal systems.

2. The members of the Committee shall be elected by secret ballot from a list of persons nominated by the States Parties. Each State Party may nominate one person from among its own nationals.

3. The initial election shall be held six months after the date of the entry into force of this Convention. At least three months before the date of each election the Secretary-General of the United Nations shall address a letter to the States Parties inviting them to submit their nominations within two months. The Secretary-General shall prepare a list in alphabetical order of all persons thus nominated, indicating the States Parties which have nominated them, and shall submit it to the States Parties.

4. Elections of the members of the Committee shall be held at a meeting of States Parties convened by the Secretary-General at United Nations Headquarters. At that meeting, for which two-thirds of the States Parties shall constitute a quorum, the persons elected to the Committee shall be those nominees who obtain the largest number of votes and an absolute majority of the votes of the representatives of States Parties present and voting.

5. *(a)* The members of the Committee shall be elected for a term of four years. However, the terms of nine of the members elected at the first election shall expire at the end of two years; immediately after the first election the names of these nine members shall be chosen by lot by the Chairman of the Committee.

(b) For the filling of casual vacancies, the State Party whose expert has ceased to function as a member of the Committee shall appoint another expert from among its nationals, subject to the approval of the Committee.

6.   States Parties shall be responsible for the expenses of the members of the Committee while they are in performance of Committee duties.

Article 9

1.   States Parties undertake to submit to the Secretary-General of the United Nations, for consideration by the Committee, a report on the legislative, judicial, administrative or other measures which they have adopted and which give effect to the provisions of this Convention: *(a)* within one year after the entry into force of the Convention for the State concerned; and *(b)* thereafter every two years and whenever the Committee so requests. The Committee may request further information from the States Parties.

2.   The Committee shall report annually, through the Secretary-General, to the General Assembly of the United Nations on is activities and may make suggestions and general recommendations based on the examination of the reports and information received from the States Parties. Such suggestions and general recommendations shall be reported to the General Assembly together with comments, if any, from States Parties.

Article 10

1.   The Committee shall adopt its own rules of procedure.

2.   The Committee shall elect its officers for a term of two years.

3.   The secretariat of the Committee shall be provided by the Secretary-General of the United Nations.

4.   The meetings of the Committee shall normally be held at United Nations Headquarters.

Article 11

1.   If a State Party considers that another State Party is not giving effect to the provisions of this Convention, it may bring the matter to the attention of the Committee. The Committee shall then transmit the communication to the State Party concerned. Within three months, the receiving State shall submit to the Committee written explanations or statements clarifying the matter and the remedy, if any, that may have been taken by that State.

2.   If the matter is not adjusted to the satisfaction of both parties, either by bilateral negotiations or by any other procedure open to them, within six months after the receipt by the receiving State of the initial communication, either State shall have the right to refer the matter again to the Committee by notifying the Committee and also the other State.

3.   The Committee shall deal with a matter referred to it in accordance with paragraph 2 of this article after it has ascertained that all available domestic remedies have been invoked and exhausted in the case, in conformity with the generally recognized principles of international law. This shall not be the rule where the application of the remedies is unreasonably prolonged.

4.   In any matter referred to it, the Committee may call upon the States Parties concerned to supply any other relevant information.

5.   When any matter arising out of this article is being considered by the Committee, the States Parties concerned shall be entitled to send a representative to take part in the proceedings of the Committee, without voting rights, while the matter is under consideration.

Article 12

1. *(a)* After the Committee has obtained and collated all the information it deems necessary, the Chairman shall appoint an *ad hoc* Conciliation Commission (hereinafter referred to as the Commission) comprising five persons who may or may not be members of the Committee. The members of the Commission shall be appointed with the unanimous consent of the parties to the dispute, and its good offices shall be made available to the States concerned with a view to an amicable solution of the matter on the basis of respect for this Convention.

(b) If the States Parties to the dispute fail to reach agreement within three months on all or part of the composition of the Commission, the members of the Commission not agreed upon by the States Parties to the dispute shall be elected by secret ballot by a two-thirds majority vote of the Committee from among its own members.

2. The members of the Commission shall serve in their personal capacity. They shall not be nationals of the States Parties to the dispute or of a State not Party to this Convention.

3. The Commission shall elect its own Chairman and adopt its own rules of procedure.

4. The meetings of the Commission shall normally be held at United Nations Headquarters or at any other convenient place as determined by the Commission.

5. The secretariat provided in accordance with article 10, paragraph 3, of this Convention shall also service the Commission whenever a dispute among States Parties brings the Commission into being.

6. The States Parties to the dispute shall share equally all the expenses of the members of the Commission in accordance with estimates to be provided by the Secretary-General of the United Nations.

7. The Secretary-General shall be empowered to pay the expenses of the members of the Commission, if necessary, before reimbursement by the States Parties to the dispute in accordance with paragraph 6 of this article.

8. The information obtained and collated by the Committee shall be made available to the Commission, and the Commission may call upon the States concerned to supply any other relevant information.

Article 13

1. When the Commission has fully considered the matter, it shall prepare and submit to the Chairman of the Committee a report embodying its findings on all questions of fact relevant to the issue between the parties and containing such recommendations as it may think proper for the amicable solution of the dispute.

2. The Chairman of the Committee shall communicate the report of the Commission to each of the States Parties to the dispute. These States will, within three months, inform the Chairman of the Committee whether or not they accept the recommendations contained in the report of the Commission.

3. After the period provided for in paragraph 2 of this article, the Chairman of the Committee shall communicate the report of the Commission and the declarations of the States Parties concerned to the other States Parties to this Convention.

Article 14

1. A State Party may at any time declare that it recognizes the competence of the Committee to receive and consider communications from individuals or groups of

individuals within its jurisdiction claiming to be victims of a violation by that State Party of any of the rights set forth in this Convention. No communication shall be received by the Committee if it concerns a State Party which has not made such a declaration.

2.   Any State Party which makes a declaration as provided for in paragraph 1 of this article may establish or indicate a body within its national legal order which shall be competent to receive and consider petitions from individuals and groups of individuals within its jurisdiction who claim to be victims of a violation of any of the rights set forth in this Convention and who have exhausted other available local remedies.

3.   A declaration made in accordance with paragraph 1 of this article and the name of any body established or indicated in accordance with paragraph 2 of this article shall be deposited by the State Party concerned with the Secretary-General of the United Nations, who shall transmit copies thereof to the other States Parties. A declaration may be withdrawn at any time by notification to the Secretary-General, but such a withdrawal shall not affect communications pending before the Committee.

4.   A register of petitions shall be kept by the body established or indicated in accordance with paragraph 2 of this article, and certified copies of the register shall be filed annually through appropriate channels with the Secretary-General on the under-standing that the contents shall not be publicly disclosed.

5.   In the event of failure to obtain satisfaction from the body established or indicated in accordance with paragraph 2 of this article, the petitioner shall have the right to communicate the matter to the Committee within six months.

6.   *(a)* The Committee shall confidentially bring any communication referred to it to the attention of the State Party alleged to be violating any provision of this Convention, but the identity of the individual or groups of individuals concerned shall not be revealed without his or their express consent. The Committee shall not receive anonymous communications.

   (b) Within three months, the receiving State shall submit to the Committee written explanations or statements clarifying the matter and the remedy, if any, that may have been taken by that State.

7.   *(a)* The Committee shall consider communications in the light of all information made available to it by the State Party concerned and by the petitioner. The Committee shall not consider any communication from a petitioner unless it has ascertained that the petitioner has exhausted all available domestic remedies. However, this shall not be the rule where the application of the remedies is unreasonably prolonged.

   (b) The Committee shall forward its suggestions and recommendations, if any, to the State Party concerned and to the petitioner.

8.   The Committee shall include in its annual report a summary of such communica-tions and, where appropriate, a summary of the explanations and statements of the States Parties concerned and of its own suggestions and recommendations.

9.   The Committee shall be competent to exercise the functions provided for in this article only when at least ten States Parties to this Convention are bound by declarations in accordance with paragraph 1 of this article.

Article 15

1.   Pending the achievement of the objectives of the Declaration on the Granting of Independence to Colonial Countries and Peoples, contained in General Assembly resolution 1514 (XV) of 14 December 1960, the provisions of this Convention shall in

no way limit the right of petition granted to these peoples by other international instruments or by the United Nations and its specialized agencies.

2. *(a)* The Committee established under article 8, paragraph 1, of this Convention shall receive copies of the petitions from, and submit expressions of opinion and recommendations on these petitions to, the bodies of the United Nations which deal with matters directly related to the principles and objectives of this Convention in their consideration of petitions from the inhabitants of Trust and Non-Self-Governing Territories and all other territories to which General Assembly resolution 114 (XV) applies, relating to matters covered by this Convention which are before these bodies.

(b) The Committee shall receive from the competent bodies of the United Nations copies of the reports concerning the legislative, judicial, administrative or other measures directly related to the principles and objectives of this Convention applied by the administering Powers within the Territories mentioned in sub-paragraph *(a)* of this paragraph, and shall express opinions and make recommendations to these bodies.

3. The Committee shall include in its report to the General Assembly, a summary of the petitions and reports it has received from United Nations bodies, and the expressions of opinion and recommendations of the Committee relating to the said petitions and reports.

4. The Committee shall request from the Secretary-General of the United Nations all information relevant to the objectives of this Convention and available to him regarding the Territories mentioned in paragraph 2*(a)* of this article.

Article 16

The provisions of this Convention concerning the settlement of disputes or complaints shall be applied without prejudice to other procedures for settling disputes or complaints in the field of discrimination laid down in the constituent instruments of, or in conventions adopted by, the United Nations and its specialized agencies, and shall not prevent the States Parties from having recourse to other procedures for settling a dispute in accordance with general or special international agreements in force between them.

Part III

Article 17

1. This Convention is open for signature by any State Member of the United Nations or member of any of its specialized agencies, by any State Party to the Statute of the International Court of Justice, and by any other State which has been invited by the General Assembly of the United Nations to become a Party to this Convention.

2. This Convention is subject to ratification. Instruments of ratification shall be deposited with the Secretary-General of the United Nations.

Article 18

1. This Convention shall be open to accession by any State referred to in article 17, paragraph 1, of the Convention.

2. Accession shall be effected by the deposit of an instrument of accession with the Secretary-General of the United Nations.

Article 19

1. This Convention shall enter into force on the thirtieth day after the date of the deposit with the Secretary-General of the United Nations of the twenty-seventh instrument of ratification or instrument of accession.

2. For each State ratifying this Convention or acceding to it after the deposit of the twenty-seventh instrument of ratification or instrument of accession, the Convention shall enter into force on the thirtieth day after the date of the deposit of its own instrument of ratification or instrument of accession.

Article 20

1. The Secretary-General of the United Nations shall receive and circulate to all States which are or may become Parties to this Convention reservations made by States at the time of ratification or accession. Any State which objects to the reservation shall, within a period of ninety days from the date of the said communication, notify the Secretary-General that it does not accept it.

2. A reservation incompatible with the object and purpose of this Convention shall not be permitted, nor shall a reservation the effect of which would inhibit the operation of any of the bodies established by this Convention be allowed. A reservation shall be considered incompatible or inhibitive if at least two-thirds of the States Parties to this Convention object to it.

3. Reservations may be withdrawn at any time by notification to this effect addressed to the Secretary-General. Such notification shall take effect on the date on which it is received.

Article 21

A State Party may denounce this Convention by written notification to the Secretary-General of the United Nations. Denunciation shall take effect one year after the date of receipt of the notification by the Secretary-General.

Article 22

Any dispute between two or more States Parties with respect to the interpretation or application of this Convention, which is not settled by negotiation or by the procedures expressly provided for in this Convention, shall, at the request of any of the parties to the dispute, be referred to the International Court of Justice for decision, unless the disputants agree to another mode of settlement.

Article 23

1. A request for the revision of this Convention may be made at any time by any State Party by means of a notification in writing addressed to the Secretary-General of the United Nations.

2. The General Assembly of the United Nations shall decide upon the steps, if any, to be taken in respect of such a request.

Article 24

The Secretary-General of the United Nations shall inform all States referred to in article 17, paragraph 1, of this Convention of the following particulars:

    (a) Signatures, ratifications and accessions under articles 17 and 18;

    (b) The date of entry into force of this Convention under article 19;

    (c) Communications and declarations received under articles 14, 20 and 23;

    (d) Denunciations under article 21.

Article 25

1.   This Convention, of which the Chinese, English, French, Russian and Spanish texts are equally authentic, shall be deposited in the archives of the United Nations.

2.   The Secretary-General of the United Nations shall transmit certified copies of this Convention to all States belonging to any of the categories mentioned in article 17, paragraph 1, of the Convention.

IN FAITH WHEREOF the undersigned, being duly authorized thereto by their respective Governments, have signed the present Convention, opened for signature at New York, on the seventh day of March, one thousand nine hundred and sixty-six.

26.   CONVENTION ON THE ELIMINATION OF ALL FORMS OF DISCRIMINATION AGAINST WOMEN   (GA RES 34/180 1979 19 ILM 33 (1980))

The States Parties to the present Convention,

Noting that the Charter of the United Nations reaffirms faith in fundamental human rights, in the dignity and worth of the human person and in the equal rights of men and women,

Noting that the Universal Declaration of Human Rights affirms the principle of the inadmissibility of discrimination and proclaims that all human beings are born free and equal in dignity and rights and that everyone is entitled to all the rights and freedoms set forth therein, without distinction of any kind, including distinction based on sex,

Noting that the States Parties to the International Covenants on Human Rights have the obligation to ensure the equal right of men and women to enjoy all economic, social, cultural, civil and political rights,

Considering the international conventions concluded under the auspices of the United Nations and the specialized agencies promoting equality of rights of men and women,

Noting also the resolutions, declarations and recommendations adopted by the United Nations and the specialized agencies promoting equality of rights of men and women,

Concerned, however, that despite these various instruments extensive discrimination against women continues to exist.

Recalling that discrimination against women violates the principle of equality of rights and respect for human dignity, is an obstacle to the participation of women, on equal terms with men, in the political, social, economic and cultural life of their countries, hampers the growth of the prosperity of society and the family and make more difficult the full development of the potentialities of women in the service of their countries and of humanity,

Concerned that in situations of poverty women have the least access to food, health, education, training and opportunities for employment and other needs,

Convinced that the establishment of the new international economic order based on equality and justice will contribute significantly towards the promotion of equality between men and women,

Emphasizing that the eradication of *apartheid*, all forms of racism, racial discrimination, colonialism, neo-colonialism, aggression, foreign occupation and domination and interference in the internal affairs of States is essential to the full enjoyment of the rights of men and women,

Affirming that the strengthening of international peace and security, the relaxation of international tension, mutual co-operation among all States irrespective of their social and economic systems, general and complete disarmament, in particular nuclear disarmament under strict and effective international control, the affirmation of the principles of justice, equality and mutual benefit in relations among countries and the realization of the right of peoples under alien and colonial domination and foreign occupation to self-determination and independence, as well as respect for national sovereignty and territorial integrity, will promote social progress and development and as a consequence will contribute to the attainment of full equality between men and women,

Convinced that the full and complete development of a country, the welfare of the world and the cause of peace requires the maximum participation of women on equal terms with men in all fields,

Bearing in mind the great contribution of women to the welfare of the family and to the development of society, so far not fully recognized, the social significance of maternity and the role of both parents in the family and in the upbringing of children, and aware that the role of women in procreation should not be a basis for discrimination but that the upbringing of children requires a sharing of responsibility between men and women and society as a whole,

Aware that a change in the traditional role of men as well as the role of women in society and in the family is needed to achieve full equality between men and women,

Determined to implement the principles set forth in the Declaration on the Elimination of Discrimination against Women and, for that purpose, to adopt the measures required for the elimination of such discrimination in all its forms and manifestations,

Have agreed on the following:

PART I

Article 1 [DEFINITION]

For the purposes of the present Convention, the term "discrimination against women" shall mean any distinction, exclusion or restriction made on the basis of sex which has the effect or purpose of impairing or nullifying the recognition, enjoyment or exercise by women, irrespective of their marital status, on a basis of equality of men and women, of human rights and fundamental freedoms in the political, economic, social, cultural, civil or any other field.

Article 2 [STATE UNDERTAKINGS]

States Parties condemn discrimination against women in all its forms, agree to pursue by all appropriate means and without delay a policy of eliminating discrimination against women and, to this end, undertake:

(a) To embody the principle of the equality of men and women in their national constitutions or other appropriate legislation if not yet incorporated therein and to ensure, through law and other appropriate means, the practical realization of this principle;

(b) To adopt appropriate legislation and other measures, including sanctions where appropriate, prohibiting all discrimination against women;

(c) To establish legal protection of the rights of women on an equal basis with men and to ensure through competent national tribunals and other public institutions the effective protection of women against any act of discrimination;

(d) To refrain from engaging in any act or practice of discrimination against women and to ensure that public authorities and institutions shall act in conformity with this obligation;

(e) To take all appropriate measures to eliminate discrimination against women by any person, organization or enterprise;

(f) To take all appropriate measures, including legislation, to modify or abolish existing laws, regulations, customs and practices which constitute discrimination against women;

(g) To repeal all national penal provisions which constitute discrimination against women.

Article 3

States Parties shall take in all fields, in particular in the political, social, economic and cultural fields, all appropriate measures, including legislation, to ensure the full development and advancement of women, for the purpose of guaranteeing them the exercise and enjoyment of human rights and fundamental freedoms on a basis of equality with men.

Article 4 [AFFIRMATIVE ACTION]

1. Adoption by States Parties of temporary special measures aimed at accelerating *de facto* equality between men and women shall not be considered discrimination as defined in the present Convention, but shall in no way entail as a consequence the maintenance of unequal or separate standards; these measures shall be discontinued when the objectives of equality of opportunity and treatment have been achieved.

2. Adoption by States Parties of special measures, including those measures contained in the present Convention, aimed at protecting maternity shall not be considered discriminatory.

Article 5 [SOCIETAL EDUCATION]

States Parties shall take all appropriate measures:

(a) To modify the social and cultural patterns of conduct of men and women, with a view to achieving the elimination of prejudices and customary and all other practices which are based on the idea of the inferiority or the superiority of either of the sexes or on stereotyped roles for men and women;

(b) To ensure that family education includes a proper understanding of maternity as a social function and the recognition of the common responsibility of men and women in the upbringing and development of their children, it being understood that the interests of the children is the primordial consideration in all cases.

Article 6 [TRAFFIC, EXPLOITATION AND PROSTITUTION]

States Parties shall take all appropriate measures, including legislation, to suppress all forms of traffic in women and exploitation or prostitution of women.

PART II

Article 7 [MEASURES TO ENSURE EQUAL PARTICIPATION INTERNALLY]

States Parties shall take all appropriate measures to eliminate discrimination against women in the political and public life of the country and, in particular, shall ensure to women, on equal terms with men, the right:

(a) To vote in all elections and public referenda and to be eligible for election to all publicly elected bodies;

(b) To participate in the formulation of government policy and the implementation thereof and to hold public office and perform all public functions at all levels of government;

(c) To participate in non-governmental organizations and associations concerned with the public and political life of the country.

Article 8 [MEASURES TO ENSURE EQUAL PARTICIPATION IN INTERNATIONAL ORGANISATIONS]

States Parties shall take all appropriate measures to ensure to women, on equal terms with men and without any discrimination, the opportunity to represent their Governments at the international level and to participate in the work of international organizations.

Article 9 [RIGHT TO RETAIN NATIONALITY]

1. States Parties shall grant women equal rights with men to acquire, change or retain their nationality. They shall ensure in particular that neither marriage to an alien nor change of nationality by the husband during marriage shall automatically change the nationality of the wife, render her stateless or force upon her the nationality of the husband.

2. States Parties shall grant women equal rights with men with respect to the nationality of their children.

PART III

Article 10 [EQUALITY IN FIELD OF EDUCATION]

States Parties shall take all appropriate measures to eliminate discrimination against women in order to ensure to them equal rights with men in the field of education and in particular to ensure, on a basis of equality of men and women:

(a) The same conditions for career and vocational guidance, for access to studies and for the achievement of diplomas in educational establishments of all categories in rural was well as in urban areas; this equality shall be ensured in pre-school, general, technical, professional and higher technical education, as well as in all types of vocational training;

(b) Access to the same curricula, the same examinations, teaching staff with qualifications of the same standard and school premises and equipment of the same quality;

(c) The elimination of any stereotyped concept of the roles of men and women at all levels and in all forms of education by encouraging co-education and other types of education which will help to achieve this aim and, in particular, by the revision of textbooks and school programmes and the adaptation of teaching methods;

(d) The same opportunities to benefit from scholarships and other study grants;

(e) The same opportunities for access to programmes of continuing education, including adult and functional literacy programmes, particularly those aimed at reducing, at the earliest possible time, any gap in education existing between men and women;

(f) The reduction of female student drop-out rates and the organization of programmes for girls and women who have left school prematurely;

(g) The same opportunities to participate actively in sports and physical education;

(h) Access to specific educational information to help to ensure the health and well-being of families, including information and advice on family planning.

Article 11 [EMPLOYMENT]

1. States Parties shall take all appropriate measures to eliminate discrimination against women in the field of employment in order to ensure, on a basis of equality of men and women, the same rights, in particular:

(a) The right to work as an inalienable right of all human beings;

(b) The right to the same employment opportunities, including the application of the same criteria for selection in matters of employment;

(c) The right to free choice of profession and employment, the right to promotion, job security and all benefits and conditions of service and the right to receive vocational training and retraining, including apprenticeships, advanced vocational training and recurrent training;

(d) The right to equal remuneration, including benefits, and to equal treatment in respect of work of equal value, as well as equality of treatment in the evaluation of the quality of work;

(e) The right to social security, particularly in cases of retirement, unemployment, sickness, invalidity and old age and other incapacity to work, as well as the right to paid leave;

(f) The right to protection of health and to safety in working conditions, including the safeguarding of the function of reproduction.

2. In order to prevent discrimination against women on the grounds of marriage or maternity and to ensure their effective right to work, States Parties shall take appropriate measures:

(a) To prohibit, subject to the imposition of sanctions, dismissal on the grounds of pregnancy or of maternity leave and discrimination in dismissals on the basis of marital status;

(b) To introduce maternity leave with pay or with comparable social benefits without loss of former employment, seniority or social allowances;

(c) To encourage the provision of the necessary supporting social services to enable parents to combine family obligations with work responsibilities and participation in public life, in particular through promoting the establishment and development of a network of child-care facilities;

(d) To provide special protection to women during pregnancy in types of work proved to be harmful to them.

3. Protective legislation relating to matters covered in this article shall be reviewed periodically in the light of scientific and technological knowledge and shall be revised, repealed or extended as necessary.

Article 12 [HEALTH CARE]

1. States Parties shall take all appropriate measures to eliminate discrimination against women in the field of health care in order to ensure, on a basis of equality of men and women, access to health care services, including those related to family planning.

2. Notwithstanding the provisions of paragraph 1 of this article, States Parties shall ensure to women appropriate services in connexion with pregnancy, confinement and the post-natal period, granting free services where necessary, as well as adequate nutrition during pregnancy and lactation.

Article 13 [Equality in Economic and Social Life]

States Parties shall take all appropriate measures to eliminate discrimination against women in other areas of economic and social life in order to ensure, on a basis of equality of men and women, the same rights, in particular:

(a) The right to family benefits;

(b) The right to bank loans, mortgages and other forms of financial credit;

(c) The right to participate in recreational activities, sports and all aspects of cultural life.

Article 14 [Rural Women]

1. States Parties shall take into account the particular problems faced by rural women and the significant roles which rural women play in the economic survival of their families, including their work in the non-monetized sectors of the economy, and shall take all appropriate measures to ensure the application of the provisions of the present Convention to women in rural areas.

2. States Parties shall take all appropriate measures to eliminate discrimination against women in rural areas in order to ensure, on a basis of equality of men and women, that they participate in and benefit from rural development and, in particular, shall ensure to such women the right:

(a) To participate in the elaboration and implementation of development planning at all levels;

(b) To have access to adequate health care facilities, including information, counselling and services in family planning;

(c) To benefit directly from social security programmes;

(d) To obtain all types of training and education, formal and non-formal, including that relating to functional literacy, as well as, *inter alia*, the benefit of all community and extension services, in order to increase their technical proficiency;

(e) To organize self-help groups and co-operatives in order to obtain equal access to economic opportunities through employment or self-employment;

(f) To participate in all community activities;

(g) To have access to agricultural credit and loans, marketing facilities, appropriate technology and equal treatment in land and agrarian reform as well as in land resettlement schemes;

(h) To enjoy adequate living conditions, particularly in relation to housing, sanitation, electricity and water supply, transport and communications.

Part IV

Article 15 [Women as Legal Subjects]

1. States Parties shall accord to women equality with men before the law.

2. States Parties shall accord to women, in civil matters, a legal capacity identical to that of men and the same opportunities to exercise that capacity. In particular, they shall give women equal rights to conclude contracts and to administer property and shall treat them equally in all stages of procedure in courts and tribunals.

3. States Parties agree that all contracts and all other private instruments of any kind with a legal effect which is directed at restricting the legal capacity of women shall be deemed null and void.

4. States Parties shall accord to men and women the same rights with regard to the law relating to the movement of persons and the freedom to choose their residence and domicile.

Article 16 [EQUALITY IN MARRIAGE OF FAMILY RELATIONS]

1. States Parties shall take all appropriate measures to eliminate discrimination against women in all matters, relating to marriage and family relations and in particular shall ensure, on a basis of equality of men and women:

(a) The same right to enter into marriage;

(b) The same right freely to choose a spouse and to enter into marriage only with their free and full consent;

(c) The same rights and responsibilities during marriage and at its dissolution;

(d) The same rights and responsibilities as parents, irrespective of their marital status, in matters relating to their children; in all cases the interests of the children shall be paramount;

(e) The same rights to decide freely and responsibly on the number and spacing of their children and to have access to the information, education and means to enable them to exercise these rights;

(f) The same rights and responsibilities with regard to guardianship, wardship, trusteeship and adoption of children, or similar institutions where these concepts exist in national legislation; in all cases the interests of the children shall be paramount;

(g) The same personal rights as husband and wife, including the right to choose a family name, a profession and an occupation;

(h) The same rights for both spouses in respect of the ownership, acquisition, management, administration, enjoyment and disposition of property, whether free of charge or for a valuable consideration.

2. The betrothal and the marriage of a child shall have no legal effect, and all necessary action, including legislation, shall be taken to specify a minimum age for marriage and to make the registration of marriages in an official registry compulsory.

PART V

Article 17 [ESTABLISHMENT OF COMMITTEE ON THE ELIMINATION OF DISCRIMINATION AGAINST WOMEN]

1. For the purpose of considering the progress made in the implementation of the present Convention, there shall be established a Committee on the Elimination of Discrimination against Women (hereinafter referred to as the Committee) consisting, at the time of entry into force of the Convention, of eighteen and, after ratification of or accession to the Convention by the thirty-fifth State Party, of twenty-three experts of high moral standing and competence in the field covered by the Convention. The experts shall be elected by States Parties from among their nationals and shall serve in their personal capacity, consideration being given to equitable geographical distribution and to the representation of the different forms of civilization as well as the principal legal systems.

2. The members of the Committee shall be elected by secret ballot from a list of persons nominated by States Parties. Each State Party may nominate one person from among its own nationals.

3. The initial election shall be held six months after the date of the entry into force of the present Convention. At least three months before the date of each election the

Secretary-General of the United Nations shall address a letter to the States Parties inviting them to submit their nominations within two months. The Secretary-General shall prepare a list in alphabetical order of all persons thus nominated, indicating the States Parties which have nominated them, and shall submit it to the States Parties.

4. Elections of the members of the Committee shall be held at a meeting of States Parties convened by the Secretary-General at United Nations Headquarters. At that meeting, for which two thirds of the States Parties shall constitute a quorum, the persons elected to the Committee shall be those nominees who obtain the largest number of votes and an absolute majority of the votes of the representatives of States Parties present and voting.

5. The members of the Committee shall be elected for a term of four years. However, the terms of nine of the members elected at the first election shall expire at the end of two years; immediately after the first election the names of these nine members shall be chosen by lot by the Chairman of the Committee.

6. The election of the five additional members of the Committee shall be held in accordance with the provisions of paragraphs 2, 3 and 4 of this article, following the thirty-fifth ratification or accession. The terms of two of the additional members elected on this occasion shall expire at the end of two years, the names of these two members having been chosen by lot by the Chairman of the Committee.

7. For the filing of casual vacancies, the State Party whose expert has ceased to function as a member of the Committee shall appoint another expert from among its nationals, subject to the approval of the Committee.

8. The members of the Committee shall, with the approval of the General Assembly, receive emoluments from United Nations resources on such terms and conditions as the Assembly may decide, having regard to the importance of the Committee's responsibilities.

9. The Secretary-General of the United Nations shall provide the necessary staff and facilities for the effective performance of the functions of the Committee under the present Convention.

Article 18 [REPORTS]

1. States Parties undertake to submit to the Secretary-General of the United Nations, for consideration by the Committee, a report on the legislative, judicial, administrative or other measures which they have adopted to give effect to the provisions of the present Convention and on the progress made in this respect:

(*a*) Within one year after the entry into force for the State concerned;

(*b*) Thereafter at least every four years and further whenever the Committee so requests.

2. Reports may indicate factors and difficulties affecting the degree of fulfilment of obligations under the present Convention.

Article 19

1. The Committee shall adopt its own rules of procedure.

2. The Committee shall elect its officers for a term of two years.

Article 20

1. The Committee shall normally meet for a period of not more than two weeks annually in order to consider the reports submitted in accordance with article 18 of the present Convention.

2. The meetings of the Committee shall normally be held at United Nations Headquarters or at any other convenient place as determined by the Committee.

Article 21

1. The Committee shall, through the Economic and Social Council, report annually to the General Assembly of the United Nations on its activities and may make suggestions and general recommendations based on the examination of reports and information received from the States Parties. Such suggestions and general recommendations shall be included in the report of the Committee together with comments, if any, from States Parties.

2. The Secretary-General of the United Nations shall transmit the reports of the Committee to the Commission on the Status of Women for its information.

Article 22

The specialized agencies shall be entitled to be represented at the consideration of the implementation of such provisions of the present Convention as fall within the scope of their activities. The Committee may invite the specialized agencies to submit reports on the implementation of the Convention in areas falling within the scope of their activities.

Part VI

Article 23

Nothing in the present Convention shall affect any provisions that are more conducive to the achievement of equality between men and women which may be contained:

(a) In the legislation of a State Party; or

(b) In any other international convention, treaty or agreement in force for that State.

Article 24

States Parties undertake to adopt all necessary measures at the national level aimed at achieving the full realization of the rights recognized in the present Convention.

Article 25 [Signature, Ratification and Accession]

1. The present Convention shall be open for signature by all States.

2. The Secretary-General of the United Nations is designated as the depositary of the present Convention.

3. The present Convention is subject to ratification. Instruments of ratification shall be deposited with the Secretary-General of the United Nations.

4. The present Convention shall be open to accession by all States. Accession shall be effected by the deposit of an instrument of accession with the Secretary-General of the United Nations.

Article 26 [Revision]

1. A request for the revision of the present Convention may be made at any time by any State party by means of a notification in writing addressed to the Secretary-General of the United Nations.

2. The General Assembly of the United Nations shall decide upon the steps, if any, to be taken in respect of such a request.

Article 27 [ENTRY INTO FORCE]

1. The present Convention shall enter into force on the thirtieth day after the date of deposit with the Secretary-General of the United Nations of the twentieth instrument of ratification or accession.

2. For each State ratifying the present Convention or acceding to it after deposit of the twentieth instrument of ratification or accession, the Convention shall enter into force on the thirtieth day after the date of the deposit of its own instrument of ratification or accession.

Article 28 [RESERVATIONS]

1. The Secretary-General of the United Nations shall receive and circulate to all States the text of reservations made by States at the time of ratification or accession.

2. A reservation incompatible with the object and purpose of the present Convention shall not be permitted.

3. Reservations may be withdrawn at any time by notification to this effect addressed to the Secretary-General of the United Nations, who shall then inform all States thereof. Such notification shall take effect on the date on which it is received.

Article 29 [DISPUTE SETTLEMENT]

1. Any dispute between two or more States Parties concerning the interpretation or application of the present Convention which is not settled by negotiation shall, at the request of one of them, be submitted to arbitration. If within six months from the date of the request for arbitration the parties are unable to agree on the organization of the arbitration, any one of those parties may refer the dispute to the International Court of Justice by request in conformity with the Statute of the Court.

2. Each State Party may at the time of signature or ratification of the present Convention or accession thereto declare that it does not consider itself bound by paragraph 1 of this article. The other States Parties shall not be bound by that paragraph with respect to any State Party which has made such a reservation.

3. Any State Party which has made a reservation in accordance with paragraph 2 of this article may at any time withdraw that reservation by notification to the Secretary-General of the United Nations.

Article 30

The present Convention, the Arabic, Chinese, English, French, Russian and Spanish texts of which are equally authentic, shall be deposited with the Secretary-General of the United Nations.

IN WITNESS WHEREOF the undersigned, duly authorized, have signed the present Convention.

27. CONVENTION AGAINST TORTURE AND OTHER CRUEL, INHUMAN OR DEGRADING TREATMENT OR PUNISHMENT   (24 ILM 535)

The States Parties to this Convention,

Considering that, in accordance with the principles proclaimed in the Charter of the United Nations, recognition of the equal and inalienable rights of all members of the human family is the foundation of freedom, justice and peace in the world.

Recognizing that those rights derive from the inherent dignity of the human person,

Considering the obligation of States under the Charter, in particular Article 55, to promote universal respect for, and observance of, human rights and fundamental freedoms,

Having regard to article 5 of the Universal Declaration of Human Rights and article 7 of the International Covenant on Civil and Political Rights, both of which provide that no one shall be subjected to torture or to cruel, inhuman or degrading treatment or punishment,

Having regard also to the Declaration on the Protection of All Persons from Being Subjected to Torture and Other Cruel, Inhuman or Degrading Treatment or Punishment, adopted by the General Assembly on 9 December 1975,

Desiring to make more effective the struggle against torture and other cruel, inhuman or degrading treatment or punishment throughout the world,

Have agreed as follows:

PART I

Article 1

1. For the purposes of this Convention, the term "torture" means any act by which severe pain or suffering, whether physical or mental, is intentionally inflicted on a person for such purposes as obtaining from him or a third person information or a confession, punishing him for an act he or a third person has committed or is suspected of having committed, or intimidating or coercing him or a third person, or for any reason based on discrimination of any kind, when such pain or suffering is inflicted by or at the instigation of or with the consent or acquiescence of a public official or other person acting in an official capacity. It does not include pain or suffering arising only from, inherent in or incidental to lawful sanctions.

2. This article is without prejudice to any international instrument or national legislation which does or may contain provisions of wider application.

Article 2

1. Each State Party shall take effective legislative, administrative, judicial or other measures to prevent acts of torture in any territory under its jurisdiction.

2. No exceptional circumstances whatsoever, whether a state of war or a threat of war, internal political instability or any other public emergency, may be invoked as a justification of torture.

3. An order from a superior officer or a public authority may not be invoked as a justification of torture.

Article 3

1. No State Party shall expel, return ("*refouler*") or extradite a person to another State where there are substantial grounds for believing that he would be in danger of being subjected to torture.

2. For the purpose of determining whether there are such grounds, the competent authorities shall take into account all relevant considerations including, where applicable, the existence in the State concerned, of a consistent pattern of gross, flagrant or mass violations of human rights.

Article 4

1. Each State Party shall ensure that all acts of torture are offences under its criminal law. The same shall apply to an attempt to commit torture and to an act by any person which constitutes complicity or participation in torture.

2. Each State Party shall make these offences punishable by appropriate penalties which take into account their grave nature.

Article 5

1. Each State Party shall take such measures as may be necessary to establish its jurisdiction over the offences referred to in article 4 in the following cases:

   (a) When the offences are committed in any territory under its jurisdiction or on board a ship or aircraft registered in that State;

   (b) When the alleged offender is a national of that State;

   (c) When the victim is a national of that State if that State considers it appropriate.

2. Each State Party shall likewise take such measures as may be necessary to establish its jurisdiction over such offences in cases where the alleged offender is present in any territory under its jurisdiction and it does not extradite him pursuant to article 8 to any of the States mentioned in paragraph 1 of this article.

3. This Convention does not exclude any criminal jurisdiction exercised in accordance with internal law.

Article 6

1. Upon being satisfied, after an examination of information available to it, that the circumstances so warrant, any State Party in whose territory a person alleged to have committed any offence referred to in article 4 is present shall take him into custody or take other legal measures to ensure his presence. The custody and other legal measures shall be as provided in the law of that State but may be continued only for such time as is necessary to enable any criminal or extradition proceedings to be instituted.

2. Such State shall immediately make a preliminary inquiry into the facts.

3. Any person in custody pursuant to paragraph 1 of this article shall be assisted in communicating immediately with the nearest appropriate representative of the State of which he is a national, or, if he is a stateless person, with the representative of the State where he usually resides.

4. When a State, pursuant to this article, has taken a person into custody, it shall immediately notify the States referred to in article 5, paragraph 1, of the fact that such person is in custody and of the circumstances which warrant his detention. The State which makes the preliminary inquiry contemplated in paragraph 2 of this article shall promptly report its findings to the said States and shall indicate whether it intends to exercise jurisdiction.

Article 7

1. The State Party in the territory under whose jurisdiction a person alleged to have committed any offence referred to in article 4 is found shall in the cases contemplated in article 5, if it does not extradite him, submit the case to its competent authorities for the purpose of prosecution.

2. These authorities shall take their decision in the same manner as in the case of any ordinary offence of a serious nature under the law of that State. In the cases referred to in article 5, paragraph 2, the standards of evidence required for prosecution and conviction shall in no way be less stringent than those which apply in the cases referred to in article 5, paragraph 1.

3. Any person regarding whom proceedings are brought in connection with any of the offences referred to in article 4 shall be guaranteed fair treatment at all stages of the proceedings.

Article 8

1. The offences referred to in article 4 shall be deemed to be included as extraditable offences in any extradition treaty existing between States Parties. States Parties undertake to include such offences as extraditable offences in every extradition treaty to be concluded between them.

2. If a State Party which makes extradition conditional on the existence of a treaty receives a request for extradition from another State Party with which it has no extradition treaty, it may consider this Convention as the legal basis for extradition in respect of such offences. Extradition shall be subject to the other conditions provided by the law of the requested State.

3. States Parties which do not make extradition conditional on the existence of a treaty shall recognize such offences as extraditable offences between themselves subject to the conditions provided by the law of the requested State.

4. Such offences shall be treated, for the purpose of extradition between States Parties, as if they had been committed not only in the place in which they occurred but also in the territories of the States required to establish their jurisdiction in accordance with article 5, paragraph 1.

Article 9

1. States Parties shall afford one another the greatest measure of assistance in connection with criminal proceedings brought in respect of any of the offences referred to in article 4, including the supply of all evidence at their disposal necessary for the proceedings.

2. States Parties shall carry out their obligations under paragraph 1 of this article in conformity with any treaties on mutual judicial assistance that may exist between them.

Article 10

1. Each State Party shall ensure that education and information regarding the prohibition against torture are fully included in the training of law enforcement personnel, civil or military, medical personnel, public officials and other persons who may be involved in the custody, interrogation or treatment of any individual subjected to any form of arrest, detention or imprisonment.

2. Each State Party shall include this prohibition in the rules or instructions issued in regard to the duties and functions of any such persons.

Article 11

Each State Party shall keep under systematic review interrogation rules, instructions, methods and practices as well as arrangements for the custody and treatment of persons subjected to any form of arrest, detention or imprisonment in any territory under its jurisdiction, with a view to preventing any cases of torture.

Article 12

Each State Party shall ensure that its competent authorities proceed to a prompt and impartial investigation, wherever there is reasonable ground to believe that an act of torture has been committed in any territory under its jurisdiction.

Article 13

Each State Party shall ensure that any individual who alleges he has been subjected to torture in any territory under its jurisdiction has the right to complain to, and to have his case promptly and impartially examined by, its competent authorities, Steps shall be taken to ensure that the complainant and witnesses are protected against all ill-treatment or intimidation as a consequence of his complaint or any evidence given.

Article 14

1. Each State Party shall ensure in its legal system that the victim of an act of torture obtains redress and has an enforceable right to fair and adequate compensation, including the means for as full rehabilitation as possible. In the event of the death of the victim as a result of an act of torture, his dependants shall be entitled to compensation.

2. Nothing in this article shall affect any right of the victim or other persons to compensation which may exist under national law.

Article 15

Each State Party shall ensure that any statement which is established to have been made as a result of torture shall not be invoked as evidence in any proceedings, except against a person accused of torture as evidence that the statement was made.

Article 16

1. Each State Party shall undertake to prevent in any territory under its jurisdiction other acts of cruel, inhuman or degrading treatment or punishment which do not amount to torture as defined in article 1, when such acts are committed by or at the instigation of or with the consent or acquiescence of a public official or other person acting in an official capacity. In particular, the obligations contained in articles 10, 11, 12, and 13 shall apply with the substitution for references to torture of reference to other forms of cruel, inhuman or degrading treatment or punishment.

2. The provisions of this Convention are without prejudice to the provisions of any other international instrument or national law which prohibits cruel, inhuman or degrading treatment or punishment or which relates to extradition or expulsion.

PART II

Article 17

1. There shall be established a Committee against Torture (hereinafter referred to as the Committee) which shall carry out the functions hereinafter provided. The Committee shall consist of ten experts of high moral standing and recognized competence in the field of human rights, who shall serve in their personal capacity. The experts shall be elected by the States Parties, consideration being given to equitable geographical distribution and to the usefulness of the participation of some persons having legal experience.

2. The members of the Committee shall be elected by secret ballot from a list of persons nominated by States Parties. Each State Party may nominate one person from among its own nationals. States Parties shall bear in mind the usefulness of nominating persons who are also members of the Human Rights Committee established under the International Covenant on Civil and Political Rights and who are willing to serve on the Committee against Torture.

3. Elections of the members of the Committee shall be held at biennial meetings of States Parties convened by the Secretary-General of the United Nations. At those meetings, for which two thirds of the States Parties shall constitute a quorum, the

persons elected to the Committee shall be those who obtain the largest number of votes and an absolute majority of the votes of the representatives of States Parties present and voting.

4. The initial election shall be held no later than six months after the date of the entry into force of this Convention. At least four months before the date of each election, the Secretary-General of the United Nations shall address a letter to the States Parties inviting them to submit their nominations within three months. The Secretary-General shall prepare a list in alphabetical order of all persons thus nominated, indicating the States Parties which have nominated them, and shall submit it to the States Parties.

5. The members of the Committee shall be elected for a term of four years. They shall be eligible for re-election if renominated. However, the term of five of the members elected at the first election shall expire at the end of two years, immediately after the first election the names of these five members shall be chosen by lot by the chairman of the meeting referred to in paragraph 3 of this article.

6. If a member of the Committee dies or resigns or for any other cause can no longer perform his Committee duties, the State Party which nominated him shall appoint another expert from among its nationals to serve for the remainder of his term, subject to the approval of the majority of the States Parties. The approval shall be considered given unless half or more of the States Parties respond negatively within six weeks after having been informed by the Secretary-General of the United Nations of the proposed appointment.

7. States Parties shall be responsible for the expenses of the members of the Committee while they are in performance of Committee duties.

Article 18

1. The Committee shall elect its officers for a term of two years. They may be re-elected.

2. The Committee shall establish its own rules of procedure, but these rules shall provide, *inter alia*, that:

(a) Six members shall constitute a quorum;

(b) Decisions of the Committee shall be made by a majority vote of the members present.

3. The Secretary-General of the United Nations shall provide the necessary staff and facilities for the effective performance of the functions of the Committee under this Convention.

4. The Secretary-General of the United Nations shall convene the initial meeting of the Committee. After its initial meeting, the Committee shall meet at such times as shall be provided in its rules of procedure.

5. The States Parties shall be responsible for expenses incurred in connection with the holding of meetings of the States Parties and of the Committee, including reimbursement to the United Nations for any expenses, such as the cost of staff and facilities, incurred by the United Nations pursuant to paragraph 3 of this article.

Article 19

1. The States Parties shall submit to the Committee, through the Secretary-General of the United Nations, reports on the measures they have taken to give effect to their undertakings under this Convention, within one year after the entry into force of the Convention for the State Party concerned. Thereafter the States Parties shall submit

supplementary reports every four years on any new measures taken and such other reports as the Committee may request.

2. The Secretary-General of the United Nations shall transmit the reports to all States Parties.

3. Each report shall be considered by the Committee which may make such general comments on the report as it may consider appropriate and shall forward these to the State Party concerned. That State Party may respond with any observations it chooses to the Committee.

4. The Committee may, at its discretion, decide to include any comments made by it in accordance with paragraph 3 of this article, together with the observations thereon received from the State Party concerned, in its annual report made in accordance with article 24. If so requested by the State Party concerned, the Committee may also include a copy of the report submitted under paragraph 1 of this article.

Article 20

1. If the Committee receives reliable information which appears to it to contain well-founded indications that torture is being systematically practised in the territory of a State Party, the Committee shall invite that State Party to co-operate in the examination of the information and to this end to submit observations with regard to the information concerned.

2. Taking into account any observations which may have been submitted by the State Party concerned, as well as any other relevant information available to it, the Committee may, if it decides that this is warranted, designate one or more of its members to make a confidential inquiry and to report to the Committee urgently.

3. If an inquiry is made in accordance with paragraph 2 of this article, the Committee shall seek the co-operation of the State Party concerned. In agreement with that State Party, such an inquiry may include a visit to its territory.

4. After examining the findings of its member or members submitted in accordance with paragraph 2 of this article, the Committee shall transmit these findings to the State Party concerned together with any comments or suggestions which seem appropriate in view of the situation.

5. All the proceedings of the Committee referred to in paragraphs 1 to 4 of this article shall be confidential, and at all stages of the proceedings the co-operation of the State Party shall be sought. After such proceedings have been completed with regard to an inquiry made in accordance with paragraph 2, the Committee may, after consultations with the State Party concerned, decide to include a summary account of the results of the proceedings in its annual report made in accordance with article 24.

Article 21

1. A State Party to this Convention may at any time declare under this article that it recognizes the competence of the Committee to receive and consider communications to the effect that a State Party claims that another State Party is not fulfilling its obligations under this Convention. Such communications may be received and considered according to the procedures laid down in this article only if submitted by a State Party which has made a declaration recognizing in regard to itself the competence of the Committee. No communication shall be dealt with by the Committee under this article if it concerns a State Party which has not made such a declaration. Communications received under this article shall be dealt with in accordance with the following procedure:

(a) If a State Party considers that another State Party is not giving effect to the provisions of this Convention, it may, by written communication, bring the matter to the attention of that State Party. Within three months after the receipt of the communication the receiving State shall afford the State which sent the communication an explanation or any other statement in writing clarifying the matter, which should include, to the extent possible and pertinent, reference to domestic procedures and remedies taken, pending or available in the matter;

(b) If the matter is not adjusted to the satisfaction of both States Parties concerned within six months after the receipt by the receiving State of the initial communication, either State shall have the right to refer the matter to the Committee, by notice given to the Committee and to the other State;

(c) The Committee shall deal with a matter referred to it under this article only after it has ascertained that all domestic remedies have been invoked and exhausted in the matter, in conformity with the generally recognized principles of international law. This shall not be the rule where the application of the remedies is unreasonably prolonged or is unlikely to bring effective relief to the person who is the victim of the violation of this Convention;

(d) The Committee shall hold closed meetings when examining communications under this article;

(e) Subject to the provisions of subparagraph *(c)*, the Committee shall make available its good offices to the States Parties concerned with a view to a friendly solution of the matter on the basis of respect for the obligations provided for in this Convention. For this purpose, the Committee may, when appropriate, set up an *ad hoc* conciliation commission;

(f) In any matter referred to it under this article, the Committee may call upon the States Parties concerned, referred to in subparagraph *(b)*, to supply any relevant information;

(g) The States Parties concerned, referred to in subparagraph *(b)*, shall have the right to be represented when the matter is being considered by the Committee and to make submissions orally and/or in writing.

(h) The Committee shall, within twelve months after the date of receipt of notice under subparagraph *(b)*, submit a report:

  (i) If a solution within the terms of subparagraph *(e)* is reached, the Committee shall confine its report to a brief statement of the facts and of the solution reached;

  (ii) If a solution within the terms of subparagraph *(e)* is not reached, the Committee shall confine its report to a brief statement of the facts; the written submissions and record of the oral submissions made by the States Parties concerned shall be attached to the report. In every matter, the report shall be communicated to the States Parties concerned.

2. The provisions of this article shall come into force when five States Parties to this Convention have made declarations under paragraph 1 of this article. Such declarations shall be deposited by the States Parties with the Secretary-General of the United Nations, who shall transmit copies thereof to the other States Parties. A declaration may be withdrawn at any time by notification to the Secretary-General. Such a withdrawal shall not prejudice the consideration of any matter which is the subject of a communication already transmitted under this article; no further communication by any State Party shall be received under this article after the notification of withdrawal of the declaration has been received by the Secretary-General, unless the State Party concerned has made a new declaration.

Article 22

1. A State Party to this Convention may at any time declare under this article that it recognizes the competence of the Committee to receive and consider communications from or on behalf of individuals subject to its jurisdiction who claim to be victims of a violation by a State Party of the provisions of the Convention. No communication shall be received by the Committee if it concerns a State Party which has not made such a declaration.

2. The Committee shall consider inadmissible any communication under this article which is anonymous or which it considers to be an abuse of the right of submission of such communications or to be incompatible with the provisions of this Convention.

3. Subject to the provisions of paragraph 2, the Committee shall bring any communications submitted to it under this article to the attention of the State Party to this Convention which has made a declaration under paragraph 1 and is alleged to be violating any provisions of the Convention. Within six months, the receiving State shall submit to the Committee written explanations or statements clarifying the matter and the remedy, if any, that may have been taken by that State.

4. The Committee shall consider communications received under this article in the light of all information made available to it by or on behalf of the individual and by the State Party concerned.

5. The Committee shall not consider any communications from an individual under this article unless it has ascertained that:

(a) The same matter has not been, and is not being, examined under another procedure of international investigation or settlement;

(b) The individual has exhausted all available domestic remedies; this shall not be the rule where the application of the remedies is unreasonably prolonged or is unlikely to bring effective relief to the person who is the victim of the violation of this Convention.

6. The Committee shall hold closed meetings when examining communications under this article.

7. The Committee shall forward its views to the State Party concerned and to the individual.

8. The provisions of this article shall come into force when five States Parties to this Convention have made declarations under paragraph 1 of this article. Such declarations shall be deposited by the States Parties with the Secretary-General of the United Nations, who shall transmit copies thereof to the other States Parties. A declaration may be withdrawn at any time by notification to the Secretary-General. Such a withdrawal shall not prejudice the consideration of any matter which is the subject of a communication already transmitted under this article; no further communication by or on behalf of an individual shall be received under this article after the notification of withdrawal of the declaration has been received by the Secretary-General, unless the State Party has made a new declaration.

Article 23

The members of the Committee and of the *ad hoc* conciliation commissions which may be appointed under article 21, paragraph 1 *(e)*, shall be entitled to the facilities, privileges and immunities of experts on mission for the United Nations as laid down in the relevant sections of the Convention on the Privileges and Immunities of the United Nations.

Article 24

The Committee shall submit an annual report on its activities under this Convention to the States Parties and to the General Assembly of the United Nations.

PART III

Article 25

1. This Convention is open for signature by all States.

2. This Convention is subject to ratification. Instruments of ratification shall be deposited with the Secretary-General of the United Nations.

Article 26

This Convention is open to accession by all States. Accession shall be effected by the deposit of an instrument of accession with the Secretary-General of the United Nations.

Article 27

1. This Convention shall enter into force on the thirtieth day after the date of the deposit with the Secretary-General of the United Nations of the twentieth instrument of ratification or accession.

2. For each State ratifying this Convention or acceding to it after the deposit of the twentieth instrument of ratification or accession, the Convention shall enter into force on the thirtieth day after the date of the deposit of its own instrument of ratification or accession.

Article 28

1. Each State may, at the time of signature or ratification of this Convention or accession thereto, declare that it does not recognize the competence of the Committee provided for in article 20.

2. Any State Party having made a reservation in accordance with paragraph 1 of this article may, at any time, withdraw this reservation by notification to the Secretary-General of the United Nations.

Article 29

1. Any State Party to this Convention may propose an amendment and file it with the Secretary-General of the United Nations. The Secretary-General shall thereupon communicate the proposed amendment to the States Parties with a request that they notify him whether they favour a conference of States Parties for the purpose of considering and voting upon the proposal. In the event that within four months from the date of such communication at least one third of the States Parties favours such a conference, the Secretary-General shall convene the conference under the auspices of the United Nations. Any amendment adopted by a majority of the States Parties present and voting at the conference shall be submitted by the Secretary-General to all the States Parties for acceptance.

2. An amendment adopted in accordance with paragraph 1 of this article shall enter into force when two thirds of the States Parties to this Convention have notified the Secretary-General of the United Nations that they have accepted it in accordance with their respective constitutional processes.

3. When amendments enter into force, they shall be binding on those States Parties which have accepted them, other States Parties still being bound by the provisions of this Convention and any earlier amendments which they have accepted.

Article 30

1. Any dispute between two or more States Parties concerning the interpretation or application of this Convention which cannot be settled through negotiation shall, at the request of one of them, be submitted to arbitration. If within six months from the date of the request for arbitration the Parties are unable to agree on the organization of the arbitration, any one of those Parties may refer the dispute to the International Court of Justice by request in conformity with the Statute of the Court.

2. Each State may, at the time of signature or ratification of this Convention or accession thereto, declare that it does not consider itself bound by paragraph 1 of this article. The other States Parties shall not be bound by paragraph 1 of this article with respect to any State Party having made such a reservation.

3. Any State Party having made a reservation in accordance with paragraph 2 of this article may at any time withdraw this reservation by notification to the Secretary-General of the United Nations.

Article 31

1. A State Party may denounce this Convention by written notification to the Secretary-General of the United Nations. Denunciation becomes effective one year after the date of receipt of the notification by the Secretary-General.

2. Such a denunciation shall not have the effect of releasing the State Party from its obligations under this Convention in regard to any act or omission which occurs prior to the date at which the denunciation becomes effective, nor shall denunciation prejudice in any way the continued consideration of any matter which is already under consideration by the Committee prior to the date at which the denunciation becomes effective.

3. Following the date at which the denunciation of a State Party becomes effective, the Committee shall not commence consideration of any new matter regarding that State.

Article 32

The Secretary-General of the United Nations shall inform all States Members of the United Nations and all States which have signed this Convention or acceded to it of the following:

(a) Signatures, ratifications and accessions under articles 25 and 26;

(b) The date of entry into force of this Convention under article 27 and the date of the entry into force of any amendments under article 29;

(c) Denunciations under article 31.

Article 33

1. This Convention, of which the Arabic, Chinese, English, French, Russian and Spanish texts are equally authentic, shall be deposited with the Secretary-General of the United Nations.

2. The Secretary-General of the United Nations shall transmit certified copies of this Convention to all States.

28. CONVENTION ON THE PREVENTION AND PUNISHMENT OF THE CRIME OF GENOCIDE.   (GA RES 260 (III); 78 UNTS 277)

.THE CONTRACTING PARTIES,

HAVING CONSIDERED the declaration made by the General Assembly of the United Nations in its resolution 96 (I) dated 11 December 1946 that genocide is a crime under international law, contrary to the spirit and aims of the United Nations and condemned by the civilized world;

RECOGNIZING that at all periods of history genocide has inflicted great losses on humanity; and

BEING CONVINCED that, in order to liberate mankind from such an odious scourge, international co-operation is required,

HEREBY AGREE AS HEREINAFTER PROVIDED:

Article I

The Contracting Parties confirm that genocide, whether committed in time of peace or in time of war, is a crime under international law which they undertake to prevent and to punish.

Article II

In the present Convention, genocide means any of the following acts committed with intent to destroy, in whole or in part, a national, ethnical, racial or religious group, as such;

   (a) Killing members of the group;

   (b) Causing serious bodily or mental harm to members of the group;

   (c) Deliberately inflicting on the group conditions of life calculated to bring about its physical destruction in whole or in part;

   (d) Imposing measures intended to prevent births within the group;

   (e) Forcibly transferring children of the group to another group.

Article III

The following acts shall be punishable:

   (a) Genocide;

   (b) Conspiracy to commit genocide;

   (c) Direct and public incitement to commit genocide;

   (d) Attempt to commit genocide;

   (e) Complicity in genocide.

Article IV

Persons committing genocide or any of the other acts enumerated in article III shall be punished, whether they are constitutionally responsible rulers, public officials or private individuals.

Article V

The Contracting Parties undertake to enact, in accordance with their respective Constitutions, the necessary legislation to give effect to the provisions of the present

Convention and, in particular, to provide effective penalties for persons guilty of genocide or of any of the other acts enumerated in article III.

Article VI

Persons charged with genocide or any of the other acts enumerated in article III shall be tried by a competent tribunal of the State in the territory of which the act was committed, or by such international penal tribunal as may have jurisdiction with respect to those Contracting Parties which shall have accepted its jurisdiction.

Article VII

Genocide and the other acts enumerated in article III shall not be considered as political crimes for the purpose of extradition.

The Contracting Parties pledge themselves in such cases to grant extradition in accordance with their laws and treaties in force.

Article VIII

Any Contracting Party may call upon the competent organs of the United Nations to take such action under the Charter of the United Nations as they consider appropriate for the prevention and suppression of acts of genocide or any of the other acts enumerated in article III.

Article IX

Disputes between the Contracting Parties relating to the interpretation, application or fulfilment of the present Convention, including those relating to the responsibility of a State for genocide or for any of the other acts enumerated in article III, shall be submitted to the International Court of Justice at the request of any of the parties to the dispute.

Article X

The present Convention, of which the Chinese, English, French, Russian and Spanish texts are equally authentic, shall bear the date of 9 December 1948.

Article XI

The present Convention shall be open until 31 December 1949 for signature on behalf of any Member of the United Nations and of any non-member State to which an invitation to sign has been addressed by the General Assembly.

The present Convention shall be ratified, and the instruments of ratification shall be deposited with the Secretary-General of the United Nations.

After 1 January 1950 the present Convention may be acceded to on behalf of any Member of the United Nations and of any non-member State which has received an invitation as aforesaid.

Instruments of accession shall be deposited with the Secretary-General of the United Nations.

Article XII

Any Contracting Party may at any time, by notification addressed to the Secretary-General of the United Nations, extend the application of the present Convention to all or any of the territories for the conduct of whose foreign relations that Contracting Party is responsible.

Article XIII

On the day when the first twenty instruments of ratification or accession have been deposited, the Secretary-General shall draw up a *procès-verbal* and transmit a copy thereof to each Member of the United Nations and to each of the non-member States contemplated in article XI.

The present Convention shall come into force on the ninetieth day following the date of deposit of the twentieth instrument of ratification or accession.

Any ratification or accession effected subsequent to the latter date shall become effective on the ninetieth day following the deposit of the instrument of ratification or accession.

Article XIV

The present Convention shall remain in effect for a period of ten years as from the date of its coming into force.

It shall thereafter remain in force for successive periods of five years for such Contracting Parties as have not denounced it at least six months before the expiration of the current period.

Denunciation shall be effected by a written notification addressed to the Secretary-General of the United Nations.

Article XV

If, as a result of denunciations, the number of Parties to the present Convention should become less than sixteen, the Convention shall cease to be in force as from the date on which the last of these denunciations shall become effective.

Article XVI

A request for the revision of the present Convention may be made at any time by any Contracting Party by means of a notification in writing addressed to the Secretary-General.

The General Assembly shall decide upon the steps, if any, to be taken in respect of such request.

Article XVII

The Secretary-General of the United Nations shall notify all Members of the United Nations and the non-member States contemplated in article XI of the following:
- *(a)* Signatures, ratifications and accessions received in accordance with article XI;
- *(b)* Notifications received in accordance with article XII;
- *(c)* The date upon which the present Convention comes into force in accordance with article XIII;
- *(d)* Denunciations received in accordance with article XIV;
- *(e)* The abrogation of the Convention in accordance with article XV;
- *(f)* Notifications received in accordance with article XVI.

Article XVIII

The original of the present Convention shall be deposited in the archives of the United Nations.

A certified copy of the Convention shall be transmitted to each Member of the United Nations and to each of the non-member States contemplated in article XI.

Article XIX

The present Convention shall be registered by the Secretary-General of the United Nations on the date of its coming into force.

29. CONVENTION ON THE NON-APPLICABILITY OF STATUTORY LIMITATIONS TO WAR CRIMES AND CRIMES AGAINST HUMANITY
(GA RES 2391 (XXIII) 1068; 8 ILM 68 (1969))

PREAMBLE

The States Parties to the present Convention,

Recalling resolutions of the General Assembly of the United Nations 3 (I) of 13 February 1946 and 170 (II) of 31 October 1947 on the extradition and punishment of war criminals, resolution 95 (I) of 11 December 1946 affirming the principles of international law recognized by the Charter of the International Military Tribunal, Nürnberg, and the judgment of the Tribunal, and resolutions 2184 (XXI) of 12 December 1966 and 2202 (XXI) of 16 December 1966 which expressly condemned as crimes against humanity the violation of the economic and political rights of the indigenous population on the one hand and the policies of *apartheid* on the other,

Recalling resolutions of the Economic and Social Council of the United Nations 1074 D (XXXIX) of 28 July 1965 and 1158 (XLI) of 5 August 1966 on the punishment of war criminals and of persons who have committed crimes against humanity,

Noting that none of the solemn declarations, instruments or conventions relating to the prosecution and punishment of war crimes and crimes against humanity made provisions for a period of limitation,

Considering that war crimes and crimes against humanity are among the gravest crimes in international law,

Convinced that the effective punishment of war crimes and crimes against humanity is an important element in the prevention of such crimes, the protection of human rights and fundamental freedoms, the encouragement of confidence, the furtherance of co-operation among peoples and the promotion of international peace and security,

Noting that the application to war crimes and crimes against humanity of the rules of municipal law relating to the period of limitation for ordinary crimes is a matter of serious concern to world public opinion, since it prevents the prosecution and punishment of persons responsible for those crimes,

Recognising that it is necessary and timely to affirm in international law, through this Convention, the principle that there is no period of limitation for war crimes and crimes against humanity, and to secure its universal application.

Have agreed as follows:

Article I

No statutory limitation shall apply to the following crimes, irrespective of the date of their commission:

(a) War crimes as they are defined in the Charter of the International Military Tribunal, Nürnberg, of 8 August 1945 and confirmed by resolutions 3 (I) of 13 February 1946 and 95 (I) of 11 December 1946 of the General Assembly of the United Nations, particularly the ''grave breaches'' enumerated in the Geneva Conventions of 12 August 1949 for the protection of war victims;

(b) Crimes against humanity whether committed in time of war or in time of peace as they are defined in the Charter of the International Military Tribunal, Nürnberg, of 8 August 1945 and confirmed by resolutions 3 (I) of 13 February 1946 and 95 (I) of 11 December 1946 of the General Assembly of the United Nations, eviction by armed attack or occupation and inhuman acts resulting from the policy of *apartheid*, and the crime of genocide as defined in the 1948 Convention on the Prevention and Punishment of the Crime of Genocide, even if such acts do not constitute a violation of the domestic law of the country in which they were committed.

Article II

If any of the crimes mentioned in article I is committed, the provisons of this Convention shall apply to representatives of the State authority and private individuals who, as principals or accomplices, participate in or who directly incite others to the commission of any of those crimes, or who conspire to commit them, irrespective of the degree of completion, and to representatives of the State authority who tolerate their commission.

Article III

The States Parties to the present Convention undertake to adopt all necessary domestic measures, legislative or otherwise, with a view to making possible the extradition, in accordance with international law, of the persons referred to in article II of this Convention.

Article IV

The States Parties to the present Convention undertake to adopt, in accordance with their respective constitutional processes, any legislative or other measures necessary to ensure that statutory or other limitations shall not apply to the prosecution and punishment of the crimes referred to in articles I and II of this Convention and that, where they exist, such limitations shall be abolished.

Article V

This Convention shall, until 31 December 1969, be open for signature by any State Member of the United Nations or member of any of its specialized agencies or of the International Atomic Energy Agency, by any State Party to the Statute of the International Court of Justice, and by any other State which has been invited by the General Assembly of the United Nations to become a party to this Convention.

Article VI

This Convention is subject to ratification. Instruments of ratification shall be deposited with the Secretary-General of the United Nations.

Article VII

This Convention shall be open to accession by any State referred to in article V. Instruments of accession shall be deposited with the Secretary-General of the United Nations.

Article VIII

1. This Convention shall enter into force on the ninetieth day after the day of the deposit with the Secretary-General of the United Nations of the tenth instrument of ratification or accession.

2. For each State ratifying this Convention or acceding to it after the deposit of the tenth instrument of ratification or accession, the Convention shall enter into force on the ninetieth day after the date of the deposit of its own instrument of ratification or accession.

Article IX

1. After the expiry of a period of ten years from the date on which this Convention enters into force, a request for the revision of the Convention may be made at any time by any Contracting Party by means of a notification in writing addressed to the Secretary-General of the United Nations.

2. The General Assembly of the United Nations shall decide upon the steps, if any, to be taken in respect of such a request.

Article X

1. This Convention shall be deposited with the Secretary-General of the United Nations.

2. The Secretary-General of the United Nations shall transmit certified copies of this Convention to all States referred to in article V.

3. The Secretary-General of the United Nations shall inform all States referred to in article V of the following particulars:

(a) Signatures of this Convention, and instruments of ratification and accession deposited under articles V, VI and VII;

(b) The date of entry into force of this Convention in accordance with article VIII;

(c) Communications received under article IX.

Article XI

This Convention, of which the Chinese, English, French, Russian and Spanish texts are equally authentic, shall bear the date of 26 November 1968.

IN WITNESS WHEREOF the undersigned, being duly authorized for that purpose, have signed this Convention.

30. CONVENTION RELATING TO THE STATUS OF REFUGEES
(GA RES 429 (V) 1950; 189 UNTS 137)

CHAPTER I General Provisions

Article 1

For the purposes of the present Convention, the term ''refugee'' shall apply to any person who:

(1) Has been considered a refugee under the Arrangements of 12 May 1926 and 30 June 1928 or under the Conventions of 28 October 1933 and 10 February 1938, the Protocol of 14 September 1939 or the Constitution of the International Refugee Organization;

Decisions of non-eligibility taken by the International Refugee Organization during the period of its activities shall not prevent the status of refugee being accorded to persons who fulfil the conditions of paragraph 2 of this section;

(2) As a result of events occurring before 1 January 1951 and owing to well-founded fear of being persecuted for reasons of race, religion, nationality, membership of a particular social group or political opinion, is outside the country of his nationality and is unable or, owing to such fear, is unwilling to avail himself of the protection of that country; or who, not having a nationality and being outside the country of his former habitual residence as a result of such events, is unable or, owing to such fear, is unwilling to return to it.

In the case of a person who has more than one nationality, the term "the country of his nationality" shall mean each of the countries of which he is a national, and a person shall not be deemed to be lacking the protection of the country of his nationality if, without any valid reason based on well-founded fear, he has not availed himself of the protection of one of the countries of which he is a national.

B. (1) For the purposes of this Convention, the words "events occurring before 1 January 1951" in article 1, section A, shall be understood to mean either

(a) "events occurring in Europe before 1 January 1951"; or

(b) "events occurring in Europe or elsewhere before 1 January 1951";

and each Contracting State shall make a declaration at the time of signature, ratification or accession, specifying which of these meanings it applies for the purpose of its obligations under this Convention.

(2) Any Contracting State which has adopted alternative (a) may at any time extend its obligations by adopting alternative (b) by means of a notification addressed to the Secretary-General of the United Nations.

C. This Convention shall cease to apply to any person falling under the terms of section A if:

(1) He has voluntarily re-availed himself of the protection of the country of his nationality; or

(2) Having lost his nationality, he has voluntarily re-acquired it; or

(3) He has acquired a new nationality, and enjoys the protection of the country of his new nationality; or

(4) He has voluntarily re-established himself in the country which he left or outside which he remained owing to fear of persecution; or

(5) He can no longer, because the circumstances in connexion with which he has been recognized as a refugee have ceased to exist, continue to refuse to avail himself of the protection of the country of his nationality;

Provided that this paragraph shall not apply to a refugee falling under section A(1) of this article who is able to invoke compelling reasons arising out of previous persecution for refusing to avail himself of the protection of the country of nationality;

(6) Being a person who has no nationality he is, because the circumstances in connexion with which he has been recognized as a refugee have ceased to exist, able to return to the country of his former habitual residence;

Provided that this paragraph shall not apply to a refugee falling under section A(1) of this article who is able to invoke compelling reasons arising out of previous persecution for refusing to return to the country of his former habitual residence.

D.   This Convention should not apply to persons who are at present receiving from organs or agencies of the United Nations other than the United Nations High Commissioner for Refugees protection or assistance.

When such protection or assistance has ceased for any reason, without the position of such persons being definitively settled in accordance with the relevant resolutions adopted by the General Assembly of the United Nations, these persons shall *ipso facto* be entitled to the benefits of this Convention.

E.   This Convention shall not apply to a person who is recognized by the competent authorities of the country in which he has taken residence as having the rights and obligations which are attached to the possession of the nationality of that country.

F.   The provisions of this Convention shall not apply to any person with respect to whom there are serious reasons for considering that:

(a) He has committed a crime against peace, a war crime, or a crime against humanity, as defined in the international instruments drawn up to make provision in respect of such crimes;

(b) He has committed a serious non-political crime outside the country of refuge prior to his admission to that country as a refugee;

(c) He has been guilty of acts contrary to the purposes and principles of the United Nations.

Article 2 GENERAL OBLIGATIONS

Every refugee has duties to the country in which he finds himself, which require in particular that he conform to its laws and regulations as well as to measures taken for the maintenance of public order.

Article 3 NON-DISCRIMINATION

The Contracting States shall apply the provisions of this Convention to refugees without discrimination as to race, religion or country of origin.

Article 4 RELIGION

The Contracting States shall accord to refugees within their territories treatment at least as favourable as that accorded to their nationals with respect to freedom to practice their religion and freedom as regards the religious education of their children.

Article 5 RIGHTS GRANTED APART FROM THIS CONVENTION

Nothing in this Convention shall be deemed to impair any rights and benefits granted by a Contracting State to refugees apart from this Convention.

Article 6 THE TERM "IN THE SAME CIRCUMSTANCES"

For the purpose of this Convention, the term "in the same circumstances" implies that any requirements (including requirements as to length and conditions of sojourn or residence) which the particular individual would have to fulfil for the enjoyment of the right in question, if he were not a refugee, must be fulfilled by him, with the exception of requirements which by their nature a refugee is incapable of fulfilling.

Article 7 EXEMPTION FROM RECIPROCITY

1.   Except where this Convention contains more favourable provisions, a Contracting State shall accord to refugees the same treatment as is accorded to aliens generally.

2.   After a period of three years' residence, all refugees shall enjoy exemption from legislative reciprocity in the territory of the Contracting State.

3.   Each Contracting State shall continue to accord to refugees the rights and benefits to which they were already entitled, in the absence of reciprocity, at the date of entry into force of this Convention for that State.

4.   The Contracting States shall consider favourably the possibility of according to refugees, in the absence of reciprocity, rights and benefits beyond those to which they are entitled according to paragraphs 2 and 3, and to extending exemptions from reciprocity to refugees who do not fulfil the conditions provided for in paragraphs 2 and 3.

5.   The provisions of paragraphs 2 and 3 apply both to the rights and benefits referred to in articles 13, 18, 19, 21 and 22 of this Convention and to rights and benefits for which this Convention does not provide.

Article 8 EXEMPTION FROM EXCEPTIONAL MEASURES

With regard to exceptional measures which may be taken against the person, property or interests of nationals of a foreign State, the Contracting State shall not apply such measures to a refugee who is formally a national of the said State solely on account of such nationality. Contracting States which, under their legislation, are prevented from applying the general principle expressed in this article, shall, in appropriate cases, grant exemptions in favour of such refugees.

Article 9 PROVISIONAL MEASURES

Nothing in this Convention shall prevent a Contracting State, in time of war or other grave and exceptional circumstances, from taking provisionally measures which it considers to be essential to the national security in the case of a particular person, pending a determination by the Contracting State that that person is in fact a refugee and that the continuance of such measures is necessary in his case in the interests of national security.

Article 10 CONTINUITY OF RESIDENCE

1.   Where a refugee has been forcibly displaced during the Second World War and removed to the territory of a Contracting State, and is resident there, the period of such enforced sojourn shall be considered to have been lawful residence within that territory.

2.   Where a refugee has been forcibly displaced during the Second World War from the territory of a Contracting State and has, prior to the date of entry into force of this Convention, returned there for the purpose of taking up residence, the period of residence before and after such enforced displacement shall be regarded as one uninterrupted period for any purposes for which uninterrupted residence is required.

Article 11 REFUGEE SEAMEN

In the case of refugees regularly serving as crew members on board a ship flying the flag of a Contracting State, that State shall give sympathetic consideration to their establishment on its territory and the issue of travel documents to them or their temporary admission to its territory particularly with a view to facilitating their establishment in another country.

CHAPTER II Juridical Status

Article 12 PERSONAL STATUS

1. The personal status of a refugee shall be governed by the law of the country of his domicile or, if he has no domicile, by the law of the country of his residence.

2. Rights previously acquired by a refugee and dependent on personal status, more particularly rights attaching to marriage, shall be respected by a Contracting State, subject to compliance, if this be necessary, with the formalities required by the law of that State, provided that the right in question is one which would have been recognized by the law of that State had he not become a refugee.

Article 13 MOVABLE AND IMMOVABLE PROPERTY

The Contracting State shall accord to a refugee treatment as favourable as possible and, in any event, not less favourable than that accorded to aliens generally in the same circumstances, as regards the acquisition of movable and immovable property and other rights pertaining thereto, and to leases and other contracts relating to movable and immovable property.

Article 14 ARTISTIC RIGHTS AND INDUSTRIAL PROPERTY

In respect of the protection of industrial property, such as inventions, designs or models, trade marks, trade names, and of rights in literary, artistic and scientific works, a refugee shall be accorded in the country in which he has his habitual residence the same protection as is accorded to nationals of that country. In the territory of any other Contracting State, he shall be accorded the same protection as is accorded in that territory to nationals of the country in which he has his habitual residence.

Article 15 RIGHT OF ASSOCIATION

As regards non-political and non-profit-making associations and trade unions the Contracting States shall accord to refugees lawfully staying in their territory the most favourable treatment accorded to nationals of a foreign country, in the same circumstances.

Article 16 ACCESS TO COURTS

1. A refugee shall have free access to the courts of law on the territory of all Contracting States.

2. A refugee shall enjoy in the Contracting State in which he has his habitual residence the same treatment as a national in matters pertaining to access to the Courts, including legal assistance and exemption from *cautio judicatum solvi*.

3. A refugee shall be accorded in the matters referred to in paragraph 2 in countries other than that in which he has his habitual residence the treatment granted to a national of the country of his habitual residence.

CHAPTER III Gainful Employment

Article 17 WAGE-EARNING EMPLOYMENT

1. The Contracting State shall accord to refugees lawfully staying in their territory the most favourable treatment accorded to nationals of a foreign country in the same circumstances, as regards the right to engage in wage-earning employment.

2.   In any case, restrictive measures imposed on aliens or the employment of aliens for the protection of the national labour market shall not be applied to a refugee who was already exempt from them at the date of entry into force of this Convention for the Contracting States concerned, or who fulfils one of the following conditions:

   (a) He has completed three years' residence in the country.

   (b) He has a spouse possessing the nationality of the country of residence. A refugee may not invoke the benefit of this provision if he has abandoned his spouse;

   (c) He has one or more children possessing the nationality of the country of residence.

3.   The Contracting States shall give sympathetic consideration to assimilating the rights of all refugees with regard to wage-earning employment to those of nationals, and in particular of those refugees who have entered their territory pursuant to programmes of labour recruitment or under immigration schemes.

Article 18 SELF-EMPLOYMENT

The Contracting States shall accord to a refugee lawfully in their territory treatment as favourable as possible and, in any event, not less favourable than that accorded to aliens generally in the same circumstances, as regards the right to engage on his own account in agriculture, industry, handicrafts and commerce and to establish commercial and industrial companies.

Article 19 liberal professions

1.   Each Contracting State shall accord to refugees lawfully staying in their territory who hold diplomas recognized by the competent authorities of that State, and who are desirous of practising a liberal profession, treatment as favourable as possible and, in any event, no less favourable than that accorded to aliens generally in the same circumstances.

2.   The Contracting States shall use their best endeavours consistently with their laws and constitutions to secure the settlement of such refugees in the territories, other than the metropolitan territory, for whose international relations they are responsible.

CHAPTER IV Welfare

Article 20 RATIONING

Where a rationing system exists, which applies to the population at large and regulates the general distribution of products in short supply, refugees shall be accorded the same treatment as nationals.

Article 21 HOUSING

As regards housing, the Contracting States, in so far as the matter is regulated by laws or regulations or is subject to the control of public authorities, shall accord to refugees lawfully staying in their territory treatment as favourable as possible and, in any event, not less favourable than that accorded to aliens generally in the same circumstances.

Article 22 PUBLIC EDUCATION

1.   The Contracting State shall accord to refugees the same treatment as is accorded to nationals with respect to elementary education.

2.   The Contracting States shall accord to refugees treatment as favourable as possible, and, in any event, not less favourable than that accorded to aliens generally in the same circumstances, with respect to education other than elementary education and, in particular, as regards access to studies, the recognition of foreign school certificates, diplomas and degrees, the remission of fees and charges and the award of scholarships.

Article 23 PUBLIC RELIEF

The Contracting States shall accord to refugees lawfully staying in their territory the same treatment with respect to public relief and assistance as is accorded to their nationals.

Article 24 LABOUR LEGISLATION AND SOCIAL SECURITY

1.   The Contracting States shall accord to refugees lawfully staying in their territory the same treatment as is accorded to nationals in respect of the following matters:

    (a) In so far as such matters are governed by laws or regulations or are subject to the control of administrative authorities: remuneration, including family allowances where these form part of remuneration, hours of work, overtime arrangements, holidays with pay, restrictions on home work, minimum age of employment, apprenticeship and training, women's work and the work of young persons, and the enjoyment of the benefits of collective bargaining;

    (b) Social security (legal provisions in respect of employment, injury, occupational diseases, maternity, sickness, disability, old age, death, unemployment, family responsibilities and any other contingency which, according to national laws or regulations, is covered by a social security scheme), subject to the following limitations:

        (i) There may be appropriate arrangements for the maintenance of acquired rights and rights in course of acquisition;

        (ii) National laws or regulations of the country of residence may prescribe special arrangements concerning benefits or portions of benefits which are payable wholly out of public funds, and concerning allowances paid to persons who do not fulfil the contribution conditions prescribed for the award of a normal pension.

2.   The right to compensation for the death of a refugee resulting from employment injury or from occupational disease shall not be affected by the fact that the residence of the beneficiary is outside the territory of the Contracting State.

3.   The Contracting States shall extend to refugees the benefits of agreements concluded between them, or which may be concluded between them in the future, concerning the maintenance of acquired rights and rights in the process of acquisition in regard to social security, subject only to the conditions which apply to nationals of the States signatory to the agreements in question.

4.   The Contracting States will give sympathetic consideration to extending to refugees so far as possible the benefits of similar agreements which may at any time be in force between such Contracting States and non-contracting States.

CHAPTER V Administrative Measures

Article 25 ADMINISTRATIVE ASSISTANCE

1.   When the exercise of a right by a refugee would normally require the assistance of authorities of a foreign country to whom he cannot have recourse, the Contracting States

in whose territory he is residing shall arrange that such assistance be afforded to him by their own authorities or by an international authority.

2.   The authority or authorities mentioned in paragraph 1 shall deliver or cause to be delivered under their supervision to refugees such documents or certifications as would normally be delivered to aliens by or through their national authorities.

3.   Documents or certifications so delivered shall stand in the stead of the official instruments delivered to aliens by or through their national authorities, and shall be given credence in the absence of proof to the contrary.

4.   Subject to such exceptional treatment as may be granted to indigent persons, fees may be charged for the services mentioned herein, but such fees shall be moderate and commensurate with those charged to nationals for similar services.

5.   The provisions of this article shall be without prejudice to articles 27 and 28.

Article 26 FREEDOM OF MOVEMENT

Each Contracting State shall accord to refugees lawfully in its territory the right to choose their place of residence and to move freely within its territory, subject to any regulations applicable to aliens generally in the same circumstances.

Article 27 IDENTITY PAPERS

The Contracting States shall issue identity papers to any refugee in their territory who does not possess a valid travel document.

Article 28 TRAVEL DOCUMENTS

1.   The Contracting States shall issue to refugees lawfully staying in their territory travel documents for the purpose of travel outside their territory, unless compelling reasons of national security or public order otherwise require, and the provisions of the Schedule to this Convention shall apply with respect to such documents. The Contracting States may issue such a travel document to any other refugee in their territory; they shall in particular give sympathetic consideration to the issue of such a travel document to refugees in their territory who are unable to obtain a travel document from the country of their lawful residence.

2.   Travel documents issued to refugees under previous international agreements by parties thereto shall be recognized and treated by the Contracting States in the same way as if they had been issued pursuant to this article.

Article 29 FISCAL CHARGES

1.   The Contracting States shall not impose upon refugees duties, charges or taxes, of any description whatsoever, other or higher than those which are or may be levied on their nationals in similar situations.

2.   Nothing in the above paragraph shall prevent the application to refugees of the laws and regulations concerning charges in respect of the issue to aliens of administrative documents including identity papers.

Article 30 TRANSFER OF ASSETS

1.   A Contracting State shall, in conformity with its laws and regulations, permit refugees to transfer assets which they have brought into its territory, to another country where they have been admitted for the purposes of resettlement.

2.   A Contracting State shall give sympathetic consideration to the application of refugees for permission to transfer assets wherever they may be and which are necessary for their resettlement in another country to which they have been admitted.

Article 31 REFUGEES UNLAWFULLY IN THE COUNTRY OF REFUGE

1.   The Contracting States shall not impose penalties, on account of their illegal entry or presence, on refugees who, coming directly from a territory where their life or freedom was threatened in the sense of article 1, enter or are present in their territory without authorization, provided they present themselves without delay to the authorities and show good cause for their illegal entry or presence.

2.   The Contracting States shall not apply to the movements of such refugees restrictions other than those which are necessary and such restrictions shall only be applied until their status in the country is regularized or they obtain admission into another country. The Contracting States shall allow such refugees a reasonable period and all the necessary facilities to obtain admission into another country.

Article 32 EXPULSION

1.   The Contracting States shall not expel a refugee lawfully in their territory save on grounds of national security or public order.

2.   The expulsion of such a refugee shall be only in pursuance of a decision reached in accordance with due process of law. Except where compelling reasons of national security otherwise require, the refugee shall be allowed to submit evidence to clear himself, and to appeal to and be represented for the purpose before competent authority or a person or persons specially designated by the competent authority.

3.   The Contracting States shall allow such a refugee a reasonable period within which to seek legal admission into another territory. The Contracting States reserve the right to apply during that period such internal measures as they may deem necessary.

Article 33 PROHIBITION OF EXPULSION OR RETURN (''REFOULEMENT'')

1.   No Contracting State shall expel or return (''refouler'') a refugee in any manner whatsoever to the frontiers of territories where his life or freedom would be threatened on account of his race, religion, nationality, membership of a particular social group or political opinion.

2.   The benefit of the present provision may not, however, be claimed by a refugee whom there are reasonable grounds for regarding as a danger to the security of the country in which he is, or who, having been convicted by a final judgment of a particularly serious crime, constitutes a danger to the community of that country.

Article 34 NATURALIZATION

The Contracting States shall as far as possible facilitate the assimilation and naturalization of refugees. They shall in particular make every effort to expedite naturalization proceedings and to reduce as far as possible the charges and costs of such proceedings.

CHAPTER VI Executory and Transitory Provisions

Article 35 CO-OPERATION OF THE NATIONAL AUTHORITIES WITH THE UNITED NATIONS

1.   The Contracting States undertake to co-operate with the Office of the United Nations High Commissioner for Refugees, or any other agency of the United Nations

which may succeed it, in the exercise of its functions, and shall in particular facilitate its duty of supervising the application of the provisions of this Convention.

2. In order to enable the Office of the High Commissioner or any other agency of the United Nations which may succeed it, to make reports to the competent organs of the United Nations, the Contracting States undertake to provide them in the appropriate form with information and statistical data requested concerning:

> *(a)* the conditions of refugees,
>
> *(b)* the implementation of this Convention, and
>
> *(c)* laws, regulations and decrees which are, or may hereafter be, in force relating to refugees.

Article 36 INFORMATION ON NATIONAL LEGISLATION

The Contracting States shall communicate to the Secretary-General of the United Nations the laws and regulations which they may adopt to ensure the application of this Convention.

Article 37 RELATION TO PREVIOUS CONVENTIONS

Without prejudice to article 28, paragraph 2, of this Convention, this Convention replaces as between parties to it, the Arrangements of 5 July 1922, 31 May 1924, 12 May 1926, 30 June 1928 and 30 July 1935, the Conventions of 28 October 1933 and 10 February 1938, the Protocol of 14 September 1939 and the Agreement of 15 October 1946.

CHAPTER VII Final Clauses

Article 38 SETTLEMENT OF DISPUTES

Any disputes between parties to this Convention relating to its interpretation or application, which cannot be settled by other means, shall be referred to the International Court of Justice at the request of any one of the parties to the dispute.

Article 39 SIGNATURE, RATIFICATION AND ACCESSION

1. This Convention shall be opened for signature at Geneva on 28 July 1951 and shall thereafter be deposited with the Secretary-General of the United Nations. It shall be open for signature at the European Office of the United Nations from 28 July to 31 August 1951 and shall be re-opened for signature at the Headquarters of the United Nations from 17 September 1951 to 31 December 1952.

2. This Convention shall be open for signature on behalf of all States Members of the United Nations, and also on behalf of any other State invited to attend the Conference of Plenipotentiaries on the Status of Refugees and Stateless Persons or to which an invitation to sign will have been addressed by the General Assembly. It shall be ratified and the instruments of ratification shall be deposited with the Secretary-General of the United Nations.

3. The Convention shall be open from 28 July 1951 for accession by the States referred to in paragraph 2 of this article. Accession shall be effected by the deposit of an instrument of accession with the Secretary-General of the United Nations.

Article 40 TERRITORIAL APPLICATION CLAUSE

1. Any State may, at the time of signature, ratification or accession, declare that this Convention shall extend to all or any of the territories for the international relations of

which it is responsible. Such a declaration shall take effect when the Convention enters into force for the State concerned.

2.   At any time thereafter any such extension shall be made by notification addressed to the Secretary-General of the United Nations and shall take effect as from the ninetieth day after the day of receipt by the Secretary-General of the United Nations of this notification, or as from the date of entry into force of the Convention for the State concerned, whichever is the later.

3.   With respect to those territories to which this Convention is not extended at the time of signature, ratification or accession, each State concerned shall consider the possibility of taking the necessary steps in order to extend the application of this Convention to such territories, subject, where necessary for constitutional reasons, to the consent of the Governments of such territories.

Article 41 FEDERAL CLAUSE

In the case of a Federal or non-unitary State, the following provisions shall apply:

(a)   With respect to those articles of this Convention, that come within the legislative jurisdiction of the federal legislative authority, the obligations of the Federal Government shall to this extent be the same as those of Parties which are not Federal States;

(b)   With respect to those articles of this Convention that come within the legislative jurisdiction of constituent States, provinces or cantons which are not, under the constitutional system of the federation, bound to take legislative action, the Federal Government shall bring such articles with a favourable recommendation to the notice of the appropriate authorities of states, provinces or cantons at the earliest possible moment.

(c)   A Federal State Party to this Convention shall, at the request of any other Contracting State transmitted through the Secretary-General of the United Nations, supply a statement of the law and practice of the Federation and its constituent units in regard to any particular provision of the Convention showing the extent to which effect has been given to that provision by legislative or other action.

Article 42 RESERVATIONS

1.   At the time of signature, ratification or accession, any State may make reservations to articles in the Convention other than to articles 1, 3, 4, 16(1), 33, 36–46 inclusive.

2.   Any State making a reservation in accordance with paragraph 1 of this article may at any time withdraw the reservation by a communication to that effect addressed to the Secretary-General of the United Nations.

Article 43 ENTRY INTO FORCE

1.   The Convention shall come into force on the nineteenth day following the day of deposit of the sixth instrument of ratification or accession.

2.   For each State ratifying or acceding to the Convention after the deposit of the sixth instrument of ratification or accession, the Convention shall enter into force on the nineteenth day following the date of deposit by such State of its instrument of ratification or accession.

Article 44 DENUNCIATION

1.   Any Contracting State may denounce this Convention at any time by a notification addressed to the Secretary-General of the United Nations.

2. Such denunciation shall take effect for the Contracting State concerned one year from the date upon which it is received by the Secretary-General of the United Nations.

3. Any State which has made a declaration or notification under article 40 may, at any time thereafter, by a notification to the Secretary-General of the United Nations, declare that the Convention shall cease to extend to such territory one year after the date of receipt of the notification by the Secretary-General.

Article 45 REVISION

1. Any Contracting State may request revision of this Convention at any time by a notification addressed to the Secretary-General of the United Nations.

2. The General Assembly of the United Nations shall recommend the steps, if any, to be taken in respect of such request.

Article 46 NOTIFICATION BY THE SECRETARY-GENERAL OF THE UNITED NATIONS

The Secretary-General of the United Nations shall inform all Members of the United Nations and non-member States referred to in article 39:

(a) Of declarations and notifications in accordance with section B of article 1;

(b) Of signatures, ratifications and accessions in accordance with article 39;

(c) Of declarations and notifications in accordance with article 40;

(d) Of reservations and withdrawals in accordance with article 42;

(e) Of the date on which this Convention will come into force in accordance with article 43;

(f) Of denunciations and notifications in accordance with article 44;

(g) Of requests for revision in accordance with article 45.

IN FAITH WHEREOF the undersigned, duly authorised, have signed this Convention on behalf of their respective Governments.

DONE at Geneva, this twenty-eight day of July, one thousand nine hundred and fifty-one, in a single copy, of which the English and French texts are equally authentic and which shall remain deposited in the archives of the United Nations, and certified true copies of which shall be delivered to all Members of the United Nations and to the non-member States referred to in article 39.

31. PROTOCOL RELATING TO THE STATUS OF REFUGEES
(606 UNTS 267; 6 ILM 78)

The States Parties to the present Protocol,

Considering that the Convention relating to the Status of Refugees done at Geneva on 28 July 1951 (hereinafter referred to as the Convention) covers only those persons who have become refugees as a result of events occurring before 1 January 1951,

Considering that new refugee situations have arisen since the Convention was adopted and that the refugees concerned may therefore not fall within the scope of the Convention,

Considering that it is desirable that equal status should be enjoyed by all refugees covered by the definition in the Convention irrespective of the dateline 1 January 1951,

Have agreed as follows:

Article I GENERAL PROVISION

1. The States Parties to the present Protocol undertake to apply articles 2 to 34 inclusive of the Convention to refugees as hereinafter defined.

2. For the purposes of the present Protocol, the term ''refugee'' shall, except as regards the application of paragraph 3 of this article, mean any person within the definition of article 1 of the Convention as if the words ''As a result of events occurring before 1 January 1951 and . . . '' and the words ''. . . as a result of such events''; in article 1A(2) were omitted.

3. The present Protocol shall be applied by the States Parties hereto without any geographic limitation, save that existing declarations made by States already Parties to the Convention in accordance with article 1B(1)(*a*) of the Convention, shall, unless extended under article 1B(2) thereof, apply also under the present Protocol.

Article II Co-operation of the national authorities with the United Nations

1. The States Parties to the present Protocol undertake to co-operate with the Office of the United Nations High Commissioner for Refugees, or any other agency of the United Nations which may succeed it, in the exercise of its functions, and shall in particular facilitate its duty of supervising the application of the provisions of the present Protocol.

2. In order to enable the Office of the High Commissioner, or any other agency of the United Nations which may succeed it, to make reports to the competent organs of the United Nations, the States Parties to the present Protocol undertake to provide them with the information and statistical data requested, in the appropriate form, concerning:

> (*a*) The condition of refugees;
>
> (*b*) The implementation of the present Protocol;
>
> (*c*) Laws, regulations and decrees which are, or may hereafter be, in force relating to refugees.

Article III Information on national legislation

The States Parties to the present Protocol shall communicate to the Secretary-General of the United Nations the laws and regulations which they may adopt to ensure the application of the present Protocol.

Article IV Settlement of disputes

Any dispute between States Parties to the present Protocol which relates to its interpretation or application and which cannot be settled by other means shall be referred to the International Court of Justice at the request of any one of the Parties.

Article V Accession

The present Protocol shall be open for accession on behalf of all States Parties to the Convention and of any other State Member of the United Nations or member of any of the specialized agencies or to which an invitation to accede may have been addressed by the General Assembly of the United Nations. Accession shall be effected by the deposit of an instrument of accession with the Secretary-General of the United Nations.

Article VI Federal clause

In the case of a Federal or non-unitary State, the following provisions shall apply:

(*a*) With respect to those articles of the Convention to be applied in accordance with article I, paragraph 1, of the present Protocol that come within the legislative jurisdiction of the federal legislative authority, the obligations of the Federal Government shall to this extent be the same as those of States Parties which are not Federal States;

(b) With respect to those articles of the Convention to be applied in accordance with article I, paragraph 1, of the present Protocol that come within the legislative jurisdiction of constituent States, provinces or cantons which are not, under the constitutional system of the federation, bound to take legislative action, the Federal Government shall bring such articles with a favourable recommendation to the notice of the appropriate authorities of States, provinces or cantons at the earliest possible moment;

(c) A Federal State Party to the present Protocol shall, at the request of any other State Party hereto transmitted through the Secretary-General of the United Nations, supply a statement of the law and practice of the Federation and its constituent units in regard to any particular provision of the Convention to be applied in accordance with article I, paragraph 1, of the present Protocol, showing the extent to which effect has been given to that provision by legislative or other action.

Article VII RESERVATIONS AND DECLARATIONS

1.   At the time of accession, any State may make reservations in respect of article IV of the present Protocol and in respect of the application in accordance with article I of the present Protocol of any provisions of the Convention other than those contained in articles 1, 3, 4, 16(1) and 33 thereof, provided that in the case of a State Party to the Convention reservations made under this article shall not extend to refugees in respect of whom the Convention applies.

2.   Reservations made by States Parties to the Convention in accordance with article 42 thereof shall, unless withdrawn, be applicable in relation to their obligations under the present Protocol.

3.   Any State making a reservation in accordance with paragraph 1 of this article may at any time withdraw such reservation by a communication to that effect addressed to the Secretary-General of the United Nations.

4.   Declaration made under article 40, paragraphs 1 and 2, of the Convention by a State Party thereto which accedes to the present Protocol shall be deemed to apply in respect of the present Protocol, unless upon accession a notification to the contrary is addressed by the State Party concerned to the Secretary-General of the United Nations. The provisions of article 40, paragraphs 2 and 3, and of article 44, paragraph 3, of the Convention shall be deemed to apply *mutatis mutandis* to the present Protocol.

Article VIII ENTRY INTO FORCE

1.   The present Protocol shall come into force on the day of deposit of the sixth instrument of accession.

2.   For each State acceding to the Protocol after the deposit of the sixth instrument of accession, the Protocol shall come into force on the date of deposit by such State of its instrument of accession.

Article IX DENUNCIATION

1.   Any State Party hereto may denounce this Protocol at any time by a notification addressed to the Secretary-General of the United Nations.

2.   Such denunciation shall take effect for the State Party concerned one year from the date on which it is received by the Secretary-General of the United Nations.

Article X NOTIFICATION BY THE SECRETARY-GENERAL OF THE UNITED NATIONS

The Secretary-General of the United Nations shall inform the States referred to in article V above of the date of entry into force, accessions, reservations and withdrawals of reservations to and denunciations of the present Protocol, and of declarations and notifications hereto.

Article XI DEPOSIT IN THE SECRETARIAT OF THE UNITED NATIONS

A copy of the present Protocol, of which the Chinese, English, French, Russian and Spanish texts are equally authentic, signed by the President of the General Assembly and by the Secretary-General of the United Nations, shall be deposited in the archives of the Secretariat of the United Nations. The Secretary-General will transmit certified copies thereof to all States Members of the United Nations and to the other States referred to in article V above.

32. STATUTE OF THE OFFICE OF THE UN COMMISSIONER FOR REFUGEES (GA RES 428 (V) 1950)

CHAPTER I General provisions

1. The United Nations High Commissioner for Refugees, acting under the authority of the General Assembly, shall assume the function of providing international protection, under the auspices of the United Nations, to refugees who fall within the scope of the present Statute and of seeking permanent solutions for the problem of refugees by assisting governments and, subject to the approval of the governments concerned, private organizations to facilitate the voluntary repatriation of such refugees, or their assimilation within new national communities.

In the exercise of his functions, more particularly when difficulties arise, and for instance with regard to any controversy concerning the international status of these persons, the High Commissioner shall request the opinion of an advisory committee on refugees if it is created.

2. The work of the High Commissioner shall be of an entirely non-political character; it shall be humanitarian and social and shall relate, as a rule, to groups and categories of refugees.

3. The High Commissioner shall follow policy directives given him by the General Assembly or the Economic and Social Council.

4. The Economic and Social Council may decide, after hearing the views of the High Commissioner on the subject, to establish an advisory committee on refugees, which shall consist of representatives of States Members and States non-members of the United nations, to be selected by the Council on the basis of their demonstrated interest in and devotion to the solution of the refugee problem.

5. The General Assembly shall review, not later than at its eighth regular session, the arrangements for the Office of the High Commissioner with a view to determining whether the Office should be continued beyond 31 December 1953.

CHAPTER II Functions of the High Commissioner

6. The competence of the High Commissioner shall extend to:

A. (i) Any person who has been considered a refugee under the Arrangements of 12 May 1926 and 30 June 1928 or under the Conventions of 28 October 1933 and 10 February 1938, the Protocol of 14 September 1939 or the Constitution of the International Refugee Organization;

(ii) Any person who, as a result of events occurring before 1 January 1951 and owing to well-founded fear of being persecuted for reasons of race, religion, nationality or political opinion, is outside the country of his nationality and is unable or, owing to such fear or for reasons other than personal convenience, is unwilling to avail himself of the protection of that country; or who, not having a nationality and being outside the country of his former habitual residence, is unable or, owing to such fear or for reasons other than personal convenience, is unwilling to return to it.

Decisions as to eligibility taken by the International Refugee Organization during the period of its activities shall not prevent the status of refugee being accorded to persons who fulfil the conditions of the present paragraph;

The competence of the High Commissioner shall cease to apply to any person defined in section A above if:

(a) He has voluntarily re-availed himself of the protection of the country of his nationality; or

(b) Having lost his nationality, he has voluntarily re-acquired it; or

(c) He has acquired a new nationality, and enjoys the protection of the country of his new nationality; or

(d) He has voluntarily re-established himself in the country which he left or outside which he remained owing to fear of persecution; or

(e) He can no longer, because the circumstances in connexion with which he has been recognized as a refugee have ceased to exist, claim grounds other than those of personal convenience for continuing to refuse to avail himself of the protection of the country of his nationality. Reasons of a purely economic character may not be invoked; or

(f) Being a person who has no nationality, he can no longer, because the circumstances in connexion with which he has been recognized as a refugee have ceased to exist and he is able to return to the country of his former habitual residence, claim grounds other than those of personal convenience for continuing to refuse to return to that country;

B. Any other person who is outside the country of his nationality or, if he has no nationality, the country of his former habitual residence, because he has or had well-founded fear of persecution by reason of his race, religion, nationality or political opinion and is unable or, because of such fear, is unwilling to avail himself of the protection of the government of the country of his nationality, or, if he has no nationality, to return to the country of his former habitual residence.

7. Provided that the competence of the High Commissioner as defined in paragraph 6 above shall not extend to a person:

(a) Who is a national of more than one country unless he satisfies the provisions of the preceding paragraph in relation to each of the countries of which he is a national; or

(b) Who is recognized by the competent authorities of the country in which he has taken residence as having the rights and obligations which are attached to the possession of the nationality of that country; or

(c) Who continues to receive from other organs or agencies of the United Nations protection or assistance; or

(d) In respect of whom there are serious reasons for considering that he has committed a crime covered by the provisions of treaties of extradition or a crime mentioned in article VI of the London Charter of the International Military Tribunal or by the provisions of article 14, paragraph 2, of the Universal Declaration of Human Rights.

8. The High Commissioner shall provide for the protection of refugees falling under the competence of his Office by:

(a) Promoting the conclusion and ratification of international conventions for the protection of refugees, supervising their application and proposing amendments thereto;

(b) Promoting through special agreements with governments the execution of any measures calculated to improve the situation of refugees and to reduce the number requiring protection;

(c) Assisting governmental and private efforts to promote voluntary repatriation or assimilation within new national communities;

(d) Promoting the admission of refugees, not excluding those in the most destitute categories, to the territories of States;

(e) Endeavouring to obtain permission for refugees to transfer their assets and especially those necessary for their resettlement;

(f) Obtaining from governments information concerning the number and conditions of refugees in their territories and the laws and regulations concerning them;

(g) Keeping in close touch with the governments and inter-governmental organizations concerned;

(h) Establishing contact in such manner as he may think best with private organizations dealing with refugee questions;

(i) Facilitating the co-ordination of the efforts of private organizations concerned with the welfare of refugees.

9. The High Commissioner shall engage in such additional activities, including repatriation and resettlement, as the General Assembly may determine, within the limits of the resources placed at his disposal.

10. The High Commissioner shall administer any funds, public or private, which he receives for assistance to refugees, and shall distribute them among the private and, as appropriate, public agencies which he deems best qualifiedto administer such assistance.

The High Commissioner may reject any offers which he does not consider appropriate or which cannot be utilized.

The High Commissioner shall not appeal to governments for funds or make a general appeal, without the prior approval of the General Assembly.

The High Commissioner shall include in his annual report a statement of his activities in this field.

11. The High Commissioner shall be entitled to present his views before the General Assembly, the Economic and Social Council and their subsidiary bodies.

The High Commissioner shall report annually to the General Assembly through the Economic and Social Council; his report shall be considered as a separate item on the agenda of the General Assembly.

12. The High Commissioner may invite the co-operation of the various specialized agencies.

CHAPTER III · Organization and finances

13. The High Commissioner shall be elected by the General Assembly on the nomination of the Secretary-General. The terms of appointment of the High Commissioner shall be proposed by the Secretary-General and approved by the General Assembly. The High Commissioner shall be elected for a term of three years, from 1 January 1951.

14. The High Commissioner shall appoint, for the same term, a Deputy High Commissioner of a nationality other than his own.

15. *(a)* Within the limits of the budgetary appropriations provided, the staff of the Office of the High Commissioner shall be appointed by the High Commissioner and shall be responsible to him in the exercise of their functions.

(b) Such staff shall be chosen from persons devoted to the purposes of the Office of the High Commissioner.

(c) Their conditions of employment shall be those provided under the staff regulations adopted by the General Assembly and the rules promulgated thereunder by the Secretary-General.

(d) Provision may also be made to permit the employment of personnel without compensation.

16. The High Commissioner shall consult the governments of the countries of residence of refugees as to the need for appointing representatives therein. In any country recognizing such need, there may be appointed a representative approved by the government of that country. Subject to the foregoing, the same representative may serve in more than one country.

17. The High Commissioner and the Secretary-General shall make appropriate arrangements for liaison and consultation on matters of mutual interest.

18. The Secretary-General shall provide the High Commissioner with all necessary facilities within budgetary limitations.

19. The Office of the High Commissioner shall be located in Geneva, Switzerland.

20. The Office of the High Commissioner shall be financed under the budget of the United Nations. Unless the General Assembly subsequently decides otherwise, no expenditure, other than administrative expenditures relating to the functioning of the office of the High Commissioner, shall be borne on the budget of the United Nations, and all other expenditures relating to the activities of the High Commissioner shall be financed by voluntary contributions.

21. The administration of the office of the High Commissioner shall be subject to the Financial Regulations of the United Nations and to the financial rules promulgated thereunder by the Secretary-General.

22. Transactions relating to the High Commissioner's funds shall be subject to audit by the United Nations Board of Auditors, provided that the Board may accept audited accounts from the agencies to which funds have been allocated. Administrative arrangements for the custody of such funds and their allocation shall be agreed between the High Commissioner and the Secretary-General in accordance with the Financial Regulations of the United Nations and rules promulgated thereunder by the Secretary-General.

33. DECLARATION ON TERRITORIAL ASYLUM

(GA RES 2312 (XXII) 1967)

The General Assembly,

Recalling its resolutions 1839 (XVII) of 19 December 1962, 2100 (XX) of 20 December 1965 and 2203 (XXI) of 16 December 1966 concerning a declaration on the right of asylum,

Considering the work of codification to be undertaken by the International Law Commission in accordance with General Assembly resolution 1400 (XIV) of 21 November 1959,

Adopts the following Declaration:

The General Assembly,

Noting that the purposes proclaimed in the Charter of the United Nations are to maintain international peace and security, to develop friendly relations among all nations and to achieve international co-operation in solving international problems of an economic, social, cultural or humanitarian character and in promoting and encouraging respect for human rights and for fundamental freedoms for all without distinction as to race, sex, language or religion.

Mindful of the Universal Declaration of Human Rights, which declares in article 14 that:

"1. Everyone has the right to seek and to enjoy in other countries asylum from persecution.

"2. This right may not be invoked in the case of prosecutions genuinely arising from non-political crimes or from acts contrary to the purposes and principles of the United Nations",

Recalling also article 13, paragraph 2, of the Universal Declaration of Human Rights, which states:

"Everyone has the right to leave any country, including his own, and to return to his country",

Recognizing that the grant of asylum by a State to persons entitled to invoke article 14 of the Universal Declaration of Human Rights is a peaceful and humanitarian act and that, as such, it cannot be regarded as unfriendly by any other State,

Recommends that, without prejudice to existing instruments dealing with asylum and the status of refugees and stateless persons, States should base themselves in their practices relating to territorial asylum on the following principles:

Article 1

1. Asylum granted by a State, in the exercise of its sovereignty, to persons entitled to invoke article 14 of the Universal Declaration of Human Rights, including persons struggling against colonialism, shall be respected by all other States.

2. The right to seek and to enjoy asylum may not be invoked by any person with respect to whom there are serious reasons for considering that he has committed a crime against peace, a war crime or a crime against humanity, as defined in the international instruments drawn up to make provision in respect of such crimes.

3. It shall rest with the State granting asylum to evaluate the grounds for the grant of asylum.

Article 2

1. The situation of persons referred to in article 1, paragraph 1, is, without prejudice to the sovereignty of States and the purposes and principles of the United Nations, of concern to the international community.

2. Where a State finds difficulty in granting or continuing to grant asylum, States individually or jointly or through the United Nations shall consider, in a spirit of international solidarity, appropriate measures to lighten the burden on that State.

Article 3

1. No person referred to in article 1, paragraph 1, shall be subjected to measures such as rejection at the frontier or if he has already entered the territory in which he seeks asylum, expulsion or compulsory return to any State where he may be subjected to persecution.

2. Exception may be made to the foregoing principle only for overriding reasons of national security or in order to safeguard the population, as in the case of a mass influx of persons.

3. Should a State decide in any case that exception to the principle stated in paragraph 1 of this article would be justified, it shall consider the possibility of granting to the person concerned, under such conditions as it may deem appropriate, an opportunity, whether by way of provisional asylum or otherwise, of going to another State.

Article 4

States granting asylum shall not permit persons who have received asylum to engage in activities contrary to the purposes and principles of the United Nations.

1631st plenary meeting
14 December 1967.

34. Declaration on the Human Rights of Individuals Who are not Nationals of the Country in which They Live

(GA Res 40/144 1985)

The General Assembly,

Considering that the Charter of the United Nations encourages universal respect for and observance of the human rights and fundamental freedoms of all human beings, without distinction as to race, sex, language or religion,

Considering that the Universal Declaration of Human Rights proclaims that all human beings are born free and equal in dignity and rights and that everyone is entitled to all the rights and freedoms set forth in that Declaration, without distinction of any kind, such as race, colour, sex, language, religion, political or other opinion, national or social origin, property, birth or other status,

Considering that the Universal Declaration of Human Rights proclaims further that everyone has the right to recognition everywhere as a person before the law, that all are equal before the law and entitled without any discrimination to equal protection of the law, and that all are entitled to equal protection against any discrimination in violation of that Declaration and against any incitement to such discrimination.

Being aware that the States Parties to the International Covenants on Human Rights undertake to guarantee that the rights enunciated in these Covenants will be exercised without discrimination of any kind as to race, colour, sex, language, religion, political or other opinion, national or social origin, property, birth or other status,

Conscious that, with improving communications and the development of peaceful and friendly relations among countries, individuals increasingly live in countries of which they are not nationals,

Reaffirming the purposes and principles of the Charter of the United Nations,

Recognizing that the protection of human rights and fundamental freedoms provided for in international instruments should also be ensured for individuals who are not nationals of the country in which they live,

Proclaims this Declaration:

Article 1

For the purposes of this Declaration, the term "alien" shall apply, with due regard to qualifications made in subsequent articles, to any individual who is not a national of the State in which he or she is present.

Article 2

1. Nothing in this Declaration shall be interpreted as legitimizing the illegal entry into and presence in a State of any alien, nor shall any provision be interpreted as restricting the right of any State to promulgate laws and regulations concerning the entry of aliens and the terms and conditions of their stay or to establish differences between nationals and aliens. However, such laws and regulations shall not be incompatible with the international legal obligations of that State, including those in the field of human rights.

2. This Declaration shall not prejudice the enjoyment of the rights accorded by domestic law and of the rights which under international law a State is obliged to accord to aliens, even where this Declaration does not recognize such rights or recognizes them to a lesser extent.

Article 3

Every State shall make public its national legislation or regulations affecting aliens.

Article 4

Aliens shall observe the laws of the State in which they reside or are present and regard with respect the customs and traditions of the people of that State.

Article 5

1. Aliens shall enjoy, in accordance with domestic law and subject to the relevant international obligations of the State in which they are present, in particular the following rights:

(a) The right to life and security of person; no alien shall be subjected to arbitrary arrest or detention; no alien shall be deprived of his or her liberty except on such grounds and in accordance with such procedures as are established by law;

(b) The right to protection against arbitrary or unlawful interference with privacy, family, home or correspondence;

(c) The right to be equal before the courts, tribunals and all other organs and authorities administering justice and, when necessary, to free assistance of an interpreter in criminal proceedings and, when prescribed by law, other proceedings;

(d) The right to choose a spouse, to marry, to found a family;

(e) The right to freedom of thought, opinion, conscience and religion; the right to manifest their religion or beliefs, subject only to such limitations as are prescribed by law and are necessary to protect public safety, order, health or morals or the fundamental rights and freedoms of others;

(f) The right to retain their own language, culture and tradition;

(g) The right to transfer abroad earnings, savings or other personal monetary assets, subject to domestic currency regulations.

2. Subject to such restrictions as are prescribed by law and which are necessary in a democratic society to protect national security, public safety, public order, public health or morals or the rights and freedoms of others, and which are consistent with the other

rights recognized in the relevant international instruments and those set forth in this Declaration, aliens shall enjoy the following rights:

(a) The right to leave the country;

(b) The right to freedom of expression;

(c) The right to peaceful assembly;

(d) The right to own property alone as well as in association with others, subject to domestic law.

3. Subject to the provisions referred to in paragraph 2, aliens lawfully in the territory of a State shall enjoy the right to liberty of movement and freedom to choose their residence within the borders of the State.

4. Subject to national legislation and due authorization, the spouse and minor or dependant children of an alien lawfully residing in the territory of a State shall be admitted to accompany, join and stay with the alien.

Article 6

No alien shall be subjected to torture or to cruel, inhuman or degrading treatment or punishment and, in particular, no alien shall be subjected without his or her free consent to medical or scientific experimentation.

Article 7

An alien lawfully in the territory of a State may be expelled therefrom only in pursuance of a decision reached in accordance with law and shall, except where compelling reasons of national security otherwise require, be allowed to submit the reasons why he or she should not be expelled and to have the case reviewed by, and be represented for the purpose before, the competent authority or a person or persons specially designated by the competent authority. Individual or collective expulsion of such aliens on grounds of race, colour, religion, culture, descent or national or ethnic origin is prohibited.

Article 8

1. Aliens lawfully residing in the territory of a State shall also enjoy, in accordance with the national laws, the following rights, subject to their obligations under article 4:

(a) The right to safe and healthy working conditions, to fair wages and equal remuneration for work of equal value without distinction of any kind, in particular, women being guaranteed conditions of work not inferior to those enjoyed by men, with equal pay for equal work;

(b) The right to join trade unions and other organizations or associations of their choice and to participate in their activities. No restrictions may be placed on the exercise of this right other than those prescribed by law and which are necessary, in a democratic society, in the interests of national security or public order or for the protection of the rights and freedoms of others;

(c) The right to health protection, medical care, social security, social services, education, rest and leisure, provided that they fulfil the requirements under the relevant regulations for participation and that undue strain is not placed on the resources of the State.

2. With a view to protecting the rights of aliens carrying on lawful paid activities in the country in which they are present, such rights may be specified by the Governments concerned in multilateral or bilateral conventions.

Article 9

No alien shall be arbitrarily deprived of his or her lawfully acquired assets.

Article 10

Any alien shall be free at any time to communicate with the consulate or diplomatic mission of the State of which he or she is a national or, in the absence thereof, with the consulate or diplomatic mission of any other State entrusted with the protection of the interests of the State of which he or she is a national in the State where he or she resides.

35. CONVENTION ON THE RIGHTS OF THE CHILD
(GA RES 25/44 1989; 28 ILM 1448)

PREAMBLE

The States Parties to the present Convention,

Considering that, in accordance with the principles proclaimed in the Charter of the United Nations, recognition of the inherent dignity and of the equal and inalienable rights of all members of the human family is the foundation of freedom, justice and peace in the world.

Bearing in mind that the peoples of the United Nations have, in the Charter, reaffirmed their faith in fundamental human rights and in the dignity and worth of the human person, and have determined to promote social progress and better standards of life in larger freedom,

Recognizing that the United Nations has, in the Universal Declaration of Human Rights and in the International Covenants on Human Rights, proclaimed and agreed that everyone is entitled to all the rights and freedoms set forth therein, without distinction of any kind, such as race, colour, sex, language, religion, political or other opinion, national or social origin, property, birth or other status,

Recalling that, in the Universal Declaration of Human Rights, the United Nations has proclaimed that childhood is entitled to special care and assistance.

Convinced that the family, as the fundamental group of society and the natural environment for the growth and well-being of all its members and particularly children, should be afforded the necessary protection and assistance so that it can fully assume its responsibilities within the community,

Recognizing that the child, for the full and harmonious development of his or her personality, should grow up in a family environment, in an atmosphere of happiness, love and understanding,

Considering that the child should be fully prepared to live an individual life in society, and brought up in the spirit of the ideals proclaimed in the Charter of the United Nations, and in particular in the spirit of peace, dignity, tolerance, freedom, equality and solidarity,

Bearing in mind that the need to extend particular care to the child has been stated in the Geneva Declaration of the Rights of the Child of 1924 and in the Declaration of the Rights of the Child adopted by the General Assembly on 20 November 1959 and recognized in the Universal Declaration of Human Rights, in the International Covenant on Civil and Political Rights (in particular in articles 23 and 24), in the International Covenant on Economic, Social and Cultural Rights (in particular in article 10) and in the statutes and relevant instruments of specialized agencies and international organizations concerned with the welfare of children,

Bearing in mind that, as indicated in the Declaration of the Rights of the Child, "the child, by reason of his physical and mental immaturity, needs special safeguards and care, including appropriate legal protection, before as well as after birth",

Recalling the provisions of the Declaration on Social and Legal Principles Relating to the Protection and Welfare of Children with Special Reference to Foster Placement and Adoption Nationally and Internationally; the United Nations Standard Minimum Rules for the Administration of Juvenile Justice (The Beijing Rules); and the Declaration on the Protection of Women and Children in Emergency and Armed Conflict,

Recognizing that, in all countries in the world, there are children living in exceptionally difficult conditions, and that such children need special consideration.

Taking due account of the importance of the traditions and cultural values of each people for the protection and harmonious development of the child,

Recognizing the importance of international co-operation for improving the living conditions of children in every country, in particular in the developing countries,

Have agreed as follows:

PART I

Article 1 [DEFINITION OF CHILD]

For the purposes of the present Convention, a child means every human being below the age of eighteen years unless, under the law applicable to the child, majority is attained earlier.

Article 2 [PRINCIPLE OF NON-DISCRIMINATION]

1. States Parties shall respect and ensure the rights set forth in the present Convention to each child within their jurisdiction without discrimination of any kind, irrespective of the child's or his or her parent's or legal guardian's race, colour, sex, language, religion, political or other opinion, national, ethnic or social origin, property, disability, birth or other status.

2. States Parties shall take all appropriate measures to ensure that the child is protected against all forms of discrimination or punishment on the basis of the status, activities, expressed opinions, or beliefs of the child's parents, legal guardians, or family members.

Article 3 [INTERESTS OF THE CHILD ARE PRIMARY]

1. In all actions concerning children, whether undertaken by public or private social welfare institutions, courts of law, administrative authorities or legislative bodies, the best interests of the child shall be a primary consideration.

2. States Parties undertake to ensure the child such protection and care as is necessary for his or her well-being, taking into account the rights and duties of his or her parents, legal guardians, or other individuals legally responsible for him or her, and, to this end, shall take all appropriate legislative and administrative measures.

3. States Parties shall ensure that the institutions, services and facilities responsible for the care or protection of children shall conform with the standards established by competent authorities, particularly in the areas of safety, health, in the number and suitability of their staff, as well as competent supervision.

Article 4

States Parties shall undertake all appropriate legislative, administrative, and other measures for the implementation of the rights recognized in the present Convention.

With regard to economic, social and cultural rights, States Parties shall undertake such measures to the maximum extent of their available resources and, where needed, within the framework of international co-operation.

Article 5 [RIGHTS AND DUTIES OF PARENTS]

States Parties shall respect the responsibilities, rights and duties of parents or, where applicable, the members of the extended family or community as provided for by local custom, legal guardians or other persons legally responsible for the child, to provide, in a manner consistent with the evolving capacities of the child, appropriate direction and guidance in the exercise by the child of the rights recognized in the present Convention.

Article 6 [RIGHT TO LIFE]

1. States Parties recognize that every child has the inherent right to life.

2. States Parties shall ensure to the maximum extent possible the survival and development of the child.

Article 7 [RIGHT TO A NAME AND NATIONALITY]

1. The child shall be registered immediately after birth and shall have the right from birth to a name, the right to acquire a nationality and, as far as possible, the right to know and be cared for by his or her parents.

2. States Parties shall ensure the implementation of these rights in accordance with their national law and their obligations under the relevant international instruments in this field, in particular where the child would otherwise be stateless.

Article 8 [RIGHT TO IDENTITY]

1. States Parties undertake to respect the right of the child to preserve his or her identity, including nationality, name and family relations as recognized by law without unlawful interference.

2. Where a child is illegally deprived of some or all of the elements of his or her identity, States Parties shall provide appropriate assistance and protection, with a view to speedily re-establishing his or her identity.

Article 9 [RIGHT NOT TO BE SEPARATED FROM PARENTS]

1. States Parties shall ensure that a child shall not be separated from his or her parents against their will, except when competent authorities subject to judicial review determine, in accordance with applicable law and procedures, that such separation is necessary for the best interests of the child. Such determination may be necessary in a particular case such as one involving abuse or neglect of the child by the parents, or one where the parents are living separately and a decision must be made as to the child's place of residence.

2. In any proceedings pursuant to paragraph 1 of the present article, all interested parties shall be given an opportunity to participate in the proceedings and make their views known.

3. States Parties shall respect the right of the child who is separated from one or both parents to maintain personal relations and direct contact with both parents on a regular basis, except if it is contrary to the child's best interests.

4. Where such separation results from any action initiated by a State Party, such as the detention, imprisonment, exile, deportation or death (including death arising from any

cause while the person is in the custody of the State) of one or both parents or of the child, that State Party shall, upon request, provide the parents, the child or, if appropriate, another member of the family with the essential information concerning the whereabouts of the absent member(s) of the family unless the provision of the information would be detrimental to the well-being of the child. States Parties shall further ensure that the submission of such a request shall of itself entail no adverse consequences for the person(s) concerned.

Article 10 [REUNIFICATION OF FAMILIES]

1. In accordance with the obligation of States Parties under article 9, paragraph 1, applications by a child or his or her parents to enter or leave a State Party for the purpose of family reunification shall be dealt with by States Parties in a positive, humane and expeditious manner. States Parties shall further ensure that the submission of such a request shall entail no adverse consequences for the applicants and for the members of their family.

2. A child whose parents reside in different States shall have the right to maintain on a regular basis, save in exceptional circumstances, personal relations and direct contacts with both parents. Towards that end and in accordance with the obligation of States Parties under article 9, paragraph 1, States Parties shall respect the right of the child and his or her parents to leave any country, including their own, and to enter their own country. The right to leave any country shall be subject only to such restrictions as are prescribed by law and which are necessary to protect the national security, public order (*ordre public*), public health or morals or the rights and freedoms of others and are consistent with the other rights recognized in the present Convention.

Article 11 [ILLICIT TRANSFER OF CHILDREN]

1. States Parties shall take measures to combat the illicit transfer and non-return of children abroad.

2. To this end, States Parties shall promote the conclusion of bilateral or multilateral agreements or accession to existing agreements.

Article 12 [RIGHT OF CHILDREN TO BE HEARD]

1. States Parties shall assure to the child who is capable of forming his or her own views the right to express those views freely in all matters affecting the child, the views of the child being given due weight in accordance with the age and maturity of the child.

2. For this purpose, the child shall in particular be provided the opportunity to be heard in any judicial and administrative proceedings affecting the child, either directly, or through a representative or an appropriate body, in a manner consistent with the procedural rules of national law.

Article 13 [FREEDOM OF EXPRESSION]

1. The child shall have the right to freedom of expression; this right shall include freedom to seek, receive and impart information and ideas of all kinds, regardless of frontiers, either orally, in writing or in print, in the form of art, or through any other media of the child's choice.

2. The exercise of this right may be subject to certain restrictions, but these shall only be such as are provided by law and are necessary:

(*a*) For respect of the rights or reputations of others; or *(b)* For the protection of national security or of public order (*ordre public*), or of public health or morals.

Article 14 [Freedom of Thought, Conscience and Religion]

1. States Parties shall respect the right of the child to freedom of thought, conscience and religion.

2. States Parties shall respect the rights and duties of the parents and, when applicable, legal guardians, to provide direction to the child in the exercise of his or her right in a manner consistent with the evolving capacities of the child.

3. Freedom to manifest one's religion or beliefs may be subject only to such limitations as are prescribed by law and are necessary to protect public safety, order, health or morals, or the fundamental rights and freedoms of others.

Article 15 [Freedom of Association]

1. States Parties recognize the rights of the child to freedom of association and to freedom of peaceful assembly.

2. No restrictions may be placed on the exercise of these rights other than those imposed in conformity with the law and which are necessary in a democratic society in the interests of national security or public safety, public order (*ordre public*), the protection of public health or morals or the protection of the rights and freedoms of others.

Article 16 [Prohibition of Arbitrary Interference with Privacy, Home and Correspondence and Children]

1. No child shall be subjected to arbitrary or unlawful interference with his or her privacy, family, home or correspondence, nor to unlawful attacks on his or her honour and reputation.

2. The child has the right to the protection of the law against such interference or attacks.

Article 17 [Promotion of Social, Spiritual and moral Well-being of Children]

States Parties recognize the important function performed by the mass media and shall ensure that the child has access to education and material from a diversity of national and international sources, especially those aimed at the promotion of his or her social, spiritual and moral well-being and physical and mental health. To this end, States Parties shall:

(a) Encourage the mass media to disseminate information and material of social and cultural benefit to the child and in accordance with the spirit of article 29;

(b) Encourage international co-operation in the production, exchange and dissemination of such information and material from a diversity of cultural, national and international sources;

(c) Encourage the production and dissemination of children's books;

(d) Encourage the mass media to have particular regard to the linguistic needs of the child who belongs to a minority group or who is indigenous;

(e) Encourage the development of appropriate guidelines for the protection of the child from information and material injurious to his or her well-being, bearing in mind the provisions of articles 13 and 18.

Article 18 [Parental Responsibility]

1. States Parties shall use their best efforts to ensure recognition of the principle that both parents have common responsibilities for the upbringing and development of the child. Parents or, as the case may be, legal guardians have the primary responsibility for the upbringing and development of the child. The best interests of the child will be their basic concern.

2. For the purpose of guaranteeing and promoting the rights set forth in the present Convention, States Parties shall render appropriate assistance to parents and legal guardians in the performance of their child-rearing responsibilities and shall ensure the development of institutions, facilities and services for the care of children.

3. States Parties shall take all appropriate measures to ensure that children of working parents have the right to benefit from child-care services and facilities for which they are eligible.

Article 19 [Protection of Children from Abuse]

1. States Parties shall take all appropriate legislative, administrative, social and educational measures to protect the child from all forms of physical or mental violence, injury or abuse, neglect or negligent treatment, maltreatment or exploitation, including sexual abuse, while in the care of parent(s), legal guardian(s) or any other person who has the care of the child.

2. Such protective measures should, as appropriate, include effective procedures for the establishment of social programmes to provide necessary support for the child and for those who have the care of the child, as well as for other forms of prevention and for identification, reporting, referral, investigation, treatment and follow-up of instances of child maltreatment described heretofore, and, as appropriate, for judicial involvement.

Article 20 [Special State Protection]

1. A child temporarily or permanently deprived of his or her family environment, or in whose own best interests cannot be allowed to remain in that environment, shall be entitled to special protection and assistance provided by the State.

2. States Parties shall in accordance with their national laws ensure alternative care for such a child.

3. Such care could include, *inter alia*, foster placement, *kafalah* of Islamic law, adoption or, if necessary, placement in suitable institutions for the care of children. When considering solutions, due regard shall be paid to the desirability of continuity in a child's upbringing and to the child's ethnic, religious, cultural and linguistic background.

Article 21 [Protection in Case of Adoption]

States Parties that recognize and/or permit the system of adoption shall ensure that the best interests of the child shall be the paramount consideration and they shall:

(a) Ensure that the adoption of a child is authorized only by competent authorities who determine, in accordance with applicable law and procedures and on the basis of all pertinent and reliable information, that the adoption is permissible in view of the child's status concerning parents, relatives and legal guardians and that, if required, the persons concerned have given their informed consent to the adoption on the basis of such counselling as may be necessary;

(b) Recognize the inter-country adoption may be considered as an alternative means of the child's care, if the child cannot be placed in a foster or an adoptive family or cannot in any suitable manner be cared for in the child's country of origin;

(c) Ensure that the child concerned by inter-country adoption enjoys safeguards and standards equivalent to those existing in the case of national adoption;

(d) Take all appropriate measures to ensure that, in inter-country adoption, the placement does not result in improper financial gain for those involved in it;

(e) Promote, where appropriate, the objectives of the present article by concluding bilateral or multilateral arrangements or agreements, and endeavour, within this framework, to ensure that the placement of the child in another country is carried out by competent authorities or organs.

Article 22 [Rights of Refugee Children]

1. States Parties shall take appropriate measures to ensure that a child who is seeking refugee status or who is considered a refugee in accordance with applicable international or domestic law and procedures shall, whether unaccompanied or accompanied by his or her parents or by any other person, receive appropriate protection and humanitarian assistance in the enjoyment of applicable rights set forth in the present Convention and in other international human rights or humanitarian instruments to which the said States are Parties.

2. For this purpose, States Parties shall provide, as they consider appropriate, co-operation in any efforts by the United Nations and other competent intergovernmental organizations or non-governmental organizations co-operating with the United Nations to protect and assist such a child and to trace the parents or other members of the family of any refugee child in order to obtain information necessary for reunification with his or her family. In cases where no parents or other members of the family can be found, the child shall be accorded the same protection as any other child permanently, or temporarily deprived of his or her family environment for any reason, as set forth in the present Convention.

Article 23 [Rights of disabled Children]

1. States Parties recognize that a mentally or physically disabled child should enjoy a full and decent life, in conditions which ensure dignity, promote self-reliance and facilitate the child's active participation in the community.

2. States Parties recognize the right of the disabled child to special care and shall encourage and ensure the extension, subject to available resources, to the eligible child and those responsible for his or her care, of assistance for which application is made and which is appropriate to the child's condition and to the circumstances of the parents or others caring for the child.

3. Recognizing the special needs of a disabled child, assistance extended in accordance with paragraph 2 of the present article shall be provided free of charge, whenever possible, taking into account the financial resources of the parents or others caring for the child, and shall be designed to ensure that the disabled child has effective access to and receives education, training, health care services, rehabilitation services, preparation for employment and recreation opportunities in a manner conducive to the child's achieving the fullest possible social integration and individual development, including his or her cultural and spiritual development.

4. States Parties shall promote, in the spirit of international co-operation, the exchange of appropriate information in the field of preventive health care and of

medical, psychological and functional treatment of disabled children, including dissemination of and access to information concerning methods of rehabilitation, education and vocational services, with the aim of enabling States Parties to improve their capabilities and skills and to widen their experience in these areas. In this regard, particular account shall be taken of the needs of developing countries.

Article 24 [RIGHT TO ATTAINABLE STANDARD OF HEALTH]

1. States Parties recognize the right of the child to the enjoyment of the highest attainable standard of health and to facilities for the treatment of illness and rehabilitation of health. States Parties shall strive to ensure that no child is deprived of his or her right of access to such health care services.

2. States Parties shall pursue full implementation of this right and, in particular, shall take appropriate measures:

(a) To diminish infant and child mortality;

(b) To ensure the provision of necessary medical assistance and health care to all children with emphasis on the development of primary health care;

(c) To combat disease and malnutrition, including within the framework of primary health care, through, *inter alia*, the application of readily available technology and through the provision of adequate nutritious food and clean drinking-water, taking into consideration the dangers and risks of environmental pollution;

(d) To ensure appropriate pre-natal and post-natal health care for mothers;

(e) To ensure that all segments of society, in particular parents and children, are informed, have access to education and are supported in the use of basic knowledge of child health and nutrition, the advantages of breast-feeding, hygiene and environmental sanitation and the prevention of accidents;

(f) To develop preventive health care, guidance for parents and family planning education and services.

3. States Parties shall take all effective and appropriate measures with a view to abolishing traditional practices prejudicial to the health of children.

4. States Parties undertake to promote and encourage international co-operation with a view to achieving progressively the full realization of the right recognized in the present article. In this regard, particular account shall be taken of the needs of developing countries.

Article 25 [PERIODIC REVIEW]

States Parties recognize the right of a child who has been placed by the competent authorities for the purposes of care, protection or treatment of his or her physical or mental health to a periodic review of the treatment provided to the child and all other circumstances relevant to his or her placement.

Article 26 [RIGHT TO SOCIAL SECURITY]

1. States Parties shall recognize for every child the right to benefit from social security, including social insurance, and shall take the necessary measures to achieve the full realization of this right in accordance with their national law.

2. The benefits should, where appropriate, be granted, taking into account the resources and the circumstances of the child and persons having responsibility for the maintenance of the child, as well as any other consideration relevant to an application for benefits made by or on behalf of the child.

Article 27 [Right to an Adequate Standard of Living]

1. States Parties recognize the right of every child to a standard of living adequate for the child's physical, mental, spiritual, moral and social development.

2. The parent(s) or others responsible for the child have the primary responsibility to secure, within their abilities and financial capacities, the conditions of living necessary for the child's development.

3. States Parties, in accordance with national conditions and within their means, shall take appropriate measures to assist parents and others responsible for the child to implement this right and shall in case of need provide material assistance and support programmes, particularly with regard to nutrition, clothing and housing.

4. States Parties shall take all appropriate measures to secure the recovery of maintenance for the child from the parents or other persons having financial responsibility for the child, both within the State Party and from abroad. In particular, where the person having financial responsibility for the child lives in a State different from that of the child, States Parties shall promote the accession to international agreements or the conclusion of such agreements, as well as the making of other appropriate arrangements.

Article 28 [Right to Education]

1. States Parties recognize the right of the child to education, and with a view to achieving this right progressively and on the basis of equal opportunity, they shall, in particular:

(a) Make primary education compulsory and available free to all;

(b) Encourage the development of different forms of secondary education, including general and vocational education, make them available and accessible to every child, and take appropriate measures such as the introduction of free education and offering financial assistance in case of need;

(c) Make higher education accessible to all on the basis of capacity by every appropriate means;

(d) Make educational and vocational information and guidance available and accessible to all children;

(e) Take measures to encourage regular attendance at schools and the reduction of drop-out rates.

2. States Parties shall take all appropriate measures to ensure that school discipline is administered in a manner consistent with the child's human dignity and in conformity with the present Convention.

3. States Parties shall promote and encourage international co-operation in matters relating to education, in particular with a view to contributing to the elimination of ignorance and illiteracy throughout the world and facilitating access to scientific and technical knowledge and modern teaching methods. In this regard, particular account shall be taken of the needs of developing countries.

Article 29 [Aim of Education]

1. States Parties agree that the education of the child shall be directed to:

(a) The development of the child's personality, talents and mental and physical abilities to their fullest potential;

(b) The development of respect for human rights and fundamental freedoms, and for the principles enshrined in the Charter of the United Nations;

(c) The development of respect for the child's parents, his or her own cultural identity, language and values, for the national values of the country in which the child is living, the country from which he or she may originate, and for civilizations different from his or her own;

(d) The preparation of the child for responsible life in a free society, in the spirit of understanding, peace, tolerance, equality of sexes, and friendship among all peoples, ethnic, national and religious groups and persons of indigenous origin;

(e) The development of respect for the natural environment.

2. No part of the present article or article 28 shall be construed so as to interfere with the liberty of individuals and bodies to establish and direct educational institutions, subject always to the observance of the principles set forth in paragraph 1 of the present article and to the requirements that the education given in such institutions shall conform to such minimum standards as may be laid down by the State.

Article 30 [RIGHTS OF CHILDREN OF MINORITIES]

In those States in which ethnic, religious or linguistic minorities or persons of indigenous origin exist, a child belonging to such a minority or who is indigenous shall not be denied the right, in community with other members of his or her group, to enjoy his or her own culture, to profess and practise his or her own religion, or to use his or her own language.

Article 31 [CULTURAL, ARTISTIC, RECREATIONAL ACTIVITY]

1. States Parties recognize the right of the child to rest and leisure, to engage in play and recreational activities appropriate to the age of the child and to participate freely in cultural life and the arts.

2. States Parties shall respect and promote the right of the child to participate fully in cultural and artistic life and shall encourage the provision of appropriate and equal opportunities for cultural, artistic, recreational and leisure activity.

Article 32 [PROHIBITION OF ECONOMIC EXPLOITATION OF CHILDREN]

1. States Parties recognize the right of the child to be protected from economic exploitation and from performing any work that is likely to be hazardous or to interfere with the child's education, or to be harmful to the child's health or physical, mental, spiritual, moral or social development.

2. States Parties shall take legislative, administrative, social and educational measures to ensure the implementation of the present article. To this end, and having regard to the relevant provisions of other international instruments. States Parties shall in particular:

(a) Provide for a minimum age or minimum ages for admission to employment;

(b) Provide for appropriate regulation of the hours and conditions of employment;

(c) Provide for appropriate penalties or other sanctions to ensure the effective enforcement of the present article.

Article 33 [PROTECTION OF CHILDREN FROM ILLICIT USE AND TRAFFICKING OF DRUGS]

States Parties shall take all appropriate measures, including legislative, administrative, social and educational measures, to protect children from the illicit use of narcotic drugs and psychotropic substances as defined in the relevant international treaties, and to prevent the use of children in the illicit production and trafficking of such substances.

Article 34 [Protection of Children from Sexual Exploitation]

States Parties undertake to protect the child from all forms of sexual exploitation and sexual abuse. For these purposes, States Parties shall in particular take all appropriate national, bilateral and multilateral measures to prevent:

(a) The inducement or coercion of a child to engage in any unlawful sexual activity;

(b) The exploitative use of children in prostitution or other unlawful sexual practices;

(c) The exploitative use of children in pornographic performances and materials.

Article 35 [Prevention of Abduction and Sale of Children]

States Parties shall take all appropriate national, bilateral and multilateral measures to prevent the abduction of, the sale of or traffic in children for any purpose or in any form.

Article 36

States Parties shall protect the child against all other forms of exploitation prejudicial to any aspects of the child's welfare.

Article 37 [Protection of Children in Detention]

States Parties shall ensure that:

(a) No child shall be subjected to torture or other cruel, inhuman or degrading treatment or punishment. Neither capital punishment nor life imprisonment without possibility of release shall be imposed for offences committed by persons below eighteen years of age;

(b) No child shall be deprived of his or her liberty unlawfully or arbitrarily. The arrest, detention or imprisonment of a child shall be in conformity with the law and shall be used only as a measure of last resort and for the shortest appropriate period of time;

(c) Every child deprived of liberty shall be treated with humanity and respect for the inherent dignity of the human person, and in a manner which takes into account the needs of persons of his or her age. In particular, every child deprived of liberty shall be separated from adults unless it is considered in the child's best interest not to do so and shall have the right to maintain contact with his or her family through correspondence and visits, save in exceptional circumstances.

(d) Every child deprived of his or her liberty shall have the right to prompt access to legal and other appropriate assistance, as well as the right to challenge the legality of the deprivation of his or her liberty before a court or other competent, independent and impartial authority, and to a prompt decision on any such action.

Article 38 [Protection of Children in Times of Armed Conflict]

1. States Parties undertake to respect and to ensure respect for rules of international humanitarian law applicable to them in armed conflicts which are relevant to the child.

2. States Parties shall take all feasible measures to ensure that persons who have not attained the age of fifteen years do not take a direct part in hostilities.

3. States Parties shall refrain from recruiting any person who has not attained the age of fifteen years into their armed forces. In recruiting among those persons who have attained the age of fifteen years but who have not attained the age of eighteen years, States Parties shall endeavour to give priority to those who are oldest.

4. In accordance with their obligations under international humanitarian law to protect the civilian population in armed conflicts, States Parties shall take all feasible measures to ensure protection and care of children who are affected by an armed conflict.

Article 39 [Rehabilitation of Children]

States Parties shall take all appropriate measures to promote physical and psychological recovery and social reintegration of a child victim of: any form of neglect, exploitation, or abuse; torture or any other form of cruel, inhuman or degrading treatment or punishment; or armed conflicts. Such recovery and reintegration shall take place in an environment which fosters the health, self-respect and dignity of the child.

Article 40 [Rights of children Accused of having Committed an Offence]

1. States Parties recognize the right of every child alleged as, accused of, or recognized as having infringed the penal law to be treated in a manner consistent with the promotion of the child's sense of dignity and worth, which reinforces the child's respect for the human rights and fundamental freedoms of others and which takes into account the child's age and the desirability of promoting the child's reintegration and the child's assuming a constructive role in society.

2. To this end, and having regard to the relevant provisions of international instruments, States Parties shall, in particular, ensure that:

(a) No child shall be alleged as, be accused of, or recognized as having infringed the penal law by reason of acts or omissions that were not prohibited by national or international law at the time they were committed;

(b) Every child alleged as or accused of having infringed the penal law has at least the following guarantees:

(i) To be presumed innocent until proven guilty according to law;

(ii) To be informed promptly and directly of the charges against him or her, and, if appropriate, through his or her parents or legal guardians, and to have legal or other appropriate assistance in the preparation and presentation of his or her defence;

(iii) To have the matter determined without delay by a competent, independent and impartial authority or judicial body in a fair hearing according to law, in the presence of legal or other appropriate assistance and, unless it is considered not to be in the best interest of the child, in particular, taking into account his or her age or situation, his or her parents or legal guardians;

(iv) Not to be compelled to give testimony or to confess guilt; to examine or have examined adverse witnesses and to obtain the participation and examination of witnesses on his or her behalf under conditions of equality;

(v) If considered to have infringed the penal law, to have this decision and any measures imposed in consequence thereof reviewed by a higher competent, independent and impartial authority or judicial body according to law;

(vi) To have the free assistance of an interpreter if the child cannot understand or speak the language used;

(vii) To have his or her privacy fully respected at all stages of the proceedings.

3. States Parties shall seek to promote the establishment of laws, procedures, authorities and institutions specifically applicable to children alleged as, accused of, or recognized as having infringed the penal law, and, in particular:

(a) The establishment of a minimum age below which children shall be presumed not to have the capacity to infringe the penal law;

(b) Whenever appropriate and desirable, measures for dealing with such children without resorting to judicial proceedings, providing that human rights and legal safeguards are fully respected.

4. A variety of dispositions such as care, guidance and supervision orders; counselling; probation; foster care; education and vocational training programmes and other alternatives to institutional care shall be available to ensure that children are dealt with in a manner appropriate to their well-being and proportionate both to their circumstances and the offence.

Article 41

Nothing in the present Convention shall affect any provisions which are more conducive to the realization of the rights of the child and which may be contained in:

(a) The law of a State Party; or

(b) International law in force for that State.

PART II

Article 42 [DISSEMINATION OF INFORMATION]

States Parties undertake to make the principles and provisions of the Convention widely known, by appropriate and active means, to adults and children alike.

Article 43 [COMMITTEE ON THE RIGHTS OF THE CHILD]

1. For the purpose of examining the progress made by States Parties in achieving the realization of the obligations undertaken in the present Convention, there shall be established a Committee on the Rights of the Child, which shall carry out the functions hereinafter provided.

2. The Committee shall consist of ten experts of high moral standing and recognized competence in the field covered by this Convention. The members of the Committee shall be elected by States Parties from among their nationals and shall serve in their personal capacity, consideration being given to equitable geographical distribution, as well as to the principal legal systems.

3. The members of the Commitee shall be elected by secret ballot from a list of persons nominated by States Parties. Each State Party may nominate one person from among its own nationals.

4. The initial election to the Committee shall be held no later than six months after the date of the entry into force of the present Convention and thereafter every second year. At least four months before the date of each election, the Secretary-General of the United Nations shall address a letter to States Parties inviting them to submit their nominations within two months. The Secretary-General shall subsequently prepare a list in alphabetical order of all persons thus nominated, indicating States Parties which have nominated them, and shall submit it to the States Parties to the present Convention.

5. The elections shall be held at meetings of States Parties convened by the Secretary-General at United Nations Headquarters. At those meetings, for which two thirds of States Parties shall constitute a quorum, the persons elected to the Committee shall be those who obtain the largest number of votes and an absolute majority of the votes of the representatives of States Parties present and voting.

6. The members of the Committee shall be elected for a term of four years. They shall be eligible for re-election if renominated. The term of five of the members elected at the first elections shall expire at the end of two years, immediately after the first election, the names of these five members shall be chosen by lot by the Chairman of the meeting.

7. If a member of the Committee dies or resigns or declares that for any other cause he or she can no longer perform the duties of the Committee, the State Party which nominated the member shall appoint another expert from among its nationals to serve for the remainder of the term, subject to the approval of the Committee.

8. The Committee shall establish its own rules of procedure.

9. The Committee shall elect its officers for a period of two years.

10. The meetings of the Committee shall normally be held at United Nations Headquarters or at any other convenient place as determined by the Committee. The Committee shall normally meet annually. The duration of the meetings of the Committee shall be determined, and reviewed, if necessary, by a meeting of the States Parties to the present Convention, subject to the approval of the General Assembly.

11. The Secretary-General of the United Nations shall provide the necessary staff and facilities for the effective performance of the functions of the Committee under the present Convention.

12. With the approval of the General Assembly, the members of the Committee established under the present Convention shall receive emoluments from United Nations resources on such terms and conditions as the Assembly may decide.

Article 44 [REPORTS]

1. States Parties undertake to submit to the Committee, through the Secretary-General of the United Nations, reports on the measures they have adopted which give effect to the rights recognized herein and on the progress made on the enjoyment of those rights;

(a) Within two years of the entry into force of the Convention for the State Party concerned;

(b) Thereafter every five years.

2. Reports made under the present article shall indicate factors and difficulties, if any, affecting the degree of fulfilment of the obligations under the present Convention. Reports shall also contain sufficient information to provide the Committee with a comprehensive understanding of the implementation of the Convention in the country concerned.

3. A State Party which has submitted a comprehensive initial report to the Committee need not, in its subsequent reports submitted in accordance with paragraph 1 *(b)* of the present article, repeat basic information previously provided.

4. The Committee may request from States Parties further information relevant to the implementation of the Convention.

5. The Committee shall submit to the General Assembly, through the Economic and Social Council, every two years, reports on its activities.

6. States Parties shall make their reports widely available to the public in their own countries.

Article 45

In order to foster the effective implementation of the Convention and to encourage international co-operation in the field covered by the Convention:

(a) The specialized agencies, the United Nations Children's Fund and other United Nations organs shall be entitled to be represented at the consideration of the implementation of such provisions of the present Convention as fall within the scope of their mandate. The Committee may invite the specialized agencies, the United Nations

Children's Fund and other competent bodies as it may consider appropriate to provide expert advice on the implementation of the Convention in areas falling within the scope of their respective mandates. The Committee may invite the specialized agencies, the United Nations Children's Fund and other United Nations organs to submit reports on the implementation of the Convention in areas falling within the scope of their activities;

(b) The Committee shall transmit, as it may consider appropriate, to the specialized agencies, the United Nations Children's Fund and other competent bodies any reports from States Parties that contain a request, or indicate a need, for technical advice or assistance, along with the Committee's observations and suggestions, if any, on these requests or indications;

(c) The Committee may recommend to the General Assembly that it request the Secretary-General to undertake on its behalf studies on specific issues relating to the rights of the child;

(d) The Committee may make suggestions and general recommendations based on information received pursuant to articles 44 and 45 of the present Convention. Such suggestions and general recommendations shall be transmitted to any State Party concerned and reported to the General Assembly, together with comments, if any, from States Parties.

PART III

Article 46 [SIGNATURE]

The present Convention shall be open for signature by all States.

Article 47 [RATIFICATION]

The present Convention is subject to ratification. Instruments of ratification shall be deposited with the Secretary-General of the United Nations.

Article 48 [ACCESSION]

The present Convention shall remain open for accession by any State. The instruments of accession shall be deposited with the Secretary-General of the United Nations.

Article 49 [ENTRY INTO FORCE]

1. The present Convention shall enter into force on the thirtieth day following the date of deposit with the Secretary-General of the United Nations of the twentieth instrument of ratification or accession.

2. For each State ratifying or acceding to the Convention after the deposit of the twentieth instrument of ratification or accession, the Convention shall enter into force on the thirtieth day after the deposit by such State of its instrument of ratification or accession.

Article 50 [AMENDMENT]

1. Any State Party may propose an amendment and file it with the Secretary-General of the United Nations. The Secretary-General shall thereupon communicate the proposed amendment to States Parties, with a request that they indicate whether they favour a conference of States Parties for the purpose of considering and voting upon the proposals. In the event that, within four months from the date of such communication, at least one third of the States Parties favour such a conference, the Secretary-General

shall convene the conference under the auspices of the United Nations. Any amendment adopted by a majority of States Parties present and voting at the conference shall be submitted to the General Assembly for approval.

2. An amendment adopted in accordance with paragraph 1 of the present article shall enter into force when it has been approved by the General Assembly of the United Nations and accepted by a two-thirds majority of States Parties.

3. When an amendment enters into force, it shall be binding on those States Parties which have accepted it, other States Parties still being bound by the provisions of the present Convention and any earlier amendmens which they have accepted.

Article 51 [RESERVATIONS]

1. The Seccretary-General of the United Nations shall receive and circulate to all States the text of reservations made by States at the time of ratification of accession.

2. A reservation incompatible with the object and purpose of the present Convention shall not be permitted.

3. Reservations may be withdrawn at any time by notification to that effect addressed to the Secretary-General of the United Nations, who shall then inform all States. Such notification shall take effect on the date on which it is received by the Secretary-General.

Article 52 [DENUNCIATION]

A State Party may denounce the present Convention by written notification to the Secretary-General of the United Nations. Denunciation becomes effective one year after the date of receipt of the notification by the Secretary-General.

Article 53 [DEPOSITORY]

The Secretary-General of the United Nations is designated as the depositary of the present Convention.

Article 54

The original of the present Convention, of which the Arabic, Chinese, English, French, Russian and Spanish texts are equally authentic, shall be deposited with the Secretary-General of the United Nations.

IN WITNESS THEREOF the undersigned plenipotentiaries, being duly authorized thereto by their respective Governments, have signed the present Convention.

G. REGIONAL INSTRUMENTS

36. THE AFRICAN CHARTER ON HUMAN AND PEOPLES' RIGHTS
(21 ILM 58 (1082))

PREAMBLE

The African States members of the Organization of African Unity, parties to the present convention entitled "African Charter on Human and Peoples' Rights",

Recalling Decision 115 (XVI) of the Assembly of Heads of State and Government at its Sixteenth Ordinary Session held in Monrovia, Liberia, from 17 to 20 July 1979 on the preparation of a "preliminary draft on an African Charter on Human and Peoples' Rights providing *inter alia* for the establishment of bodies to promote and protect human and peoples' rights";

Considering the Charter of the Organization of African Unity, which stipulates that "freedom, equality, justice and dignity are essential objectives for the achievement of the legitimate aspirations of the African peoples";

Reaffirming the pledge they solemnly made in Article 2 of the said Charter to eradicate all forms of colonialism from Africa, to coordinate and intensify their cooperation and efforts to achieve a better life for the peoples of Africa and to promote international cooperation having due regard to the Charter of the United Nations and the Universal Declaration of Human Rights;

Taking into consideration the virtues of their historical tradition and the values of African civilization which should inspire and characterize their reflection on the concept of human and peoples' rights;

Recognizing on the one hand, that fundamental human rights stem from the attributes of human beings, which justifies their national and international protection and on the other hand that the reality and respect of peoples rights should necessarily guarantee human rights;

Considering that the enjoyment of rights and freedoms also implies the performance of duties on the part of everyone;

Convinced that it is henceforth essential to pay particular attention to the right to development and that civil and political rights cannot be dissociated from economic, social and cultural rights in their conception as well as universality and that the satisfaction of economic, social and cultural rights is a guarantee for the enjoyment of civil and political rights;

Conscious of their duty to achieve the total liberation of Africa, the peoples of which are still struggling for their dignity and genuine independence, and undertaking to eliminate colonialism, neo-colonialism, apartheid, zionism and to dismantle aggressive foreign military bases and all forms of discrimination, particularly those based on race, ethnic group, colour, sex, language, religion or political opinion;

Reaffirming their adherence to the principles of human and peoples' rights and freedoms contained in the declarations, conventions and other instruments adopted by the Organization of African Unity, the Movement of Non-Aligned Countries and the United Nations;

Firmly convinced of their duty to promote and protect human and peoples' rights and freedoms taking into account the importance traditionally attached to these rights and freedoms in Africa;

HAVE AGREED AS FOLLOWS:

Part I. Rights and duties

CHAPTER I Human and Peoples' Rights

Article 1 [CHARTER NOT SELF EXECUTING]

The Member States of the Organization of African Unity parties to the present Charter shall recognize the rights, duties and freedoms enshrined in this Charter and shall undertake to adopt legislative or other measures to give effect to them.

Article 2 [NON-DISCRIMINATION]

Every individual shall be entitled to the enjoyment of the rights and freedoms recognized and guaranteed in the present Charter without distinction of any kind such as race, ethnic group, color, sex, language, religion, political or any other opinion, national and social origin, fortune, birth or other status.

Article 3 [EQUALITY BEFORE THE LAW AND EQUAL PROTECTION OF THE LAW]

1. Every individual shall be equal before the law.
2. Every individual shall be entitled to equal protection of the law.

Article 4 [RIGHT TO LIFE]

Human beings are inviolable. Every human being shall be entitled to respect for his life and the integrity of his person. No one may be arbitrarily deprived of this right.

Article 5 [RIGHT TO DIGNITY AND FREEDOM FROM SLAVERY, TORTURE AND INHUMAN PUNISHMENT]

Every individual shall have the right to the respect of the dignity inherent in a human being and to the recognition of his legal status. All forms of exploitation and degradation of man particularly slavery, slave trade, torture, cruel, inhuman or degrading punishment and treatment shall be prohibited.

Article 6 [RIGHT TO LIBERTY AND SECURITY OF PERSON]

Every individual shall have the right to liberty and to the security of his person. No one may be deprived of his freedom except for reasons and conditions previously laid down by law. In particular, no one may be arbitrarily arrested or detained.

Article 7 [RIGHT TO A FAIR TRIAL AND ACCESS TO COURTS]

1. Every individual shall have the right to have his cause heard. This comprises:
   (a) the right to an appeal to competent national organs against acts of violating his fundamental rights as recognized and guaranteed by conventions, laws, regulations and customs in force;
   (b) the right to be presumed innocent until proved guilty by a competent court or tribunal;
   (c) the right to defence, including the right to be defended by counsel of his choice;
   (d) the right to be tried within a reasonable time by an impartial court or tribunal.
2. No one may be condemned for an act or omission which did not constitute a legally punishable offence at the time it was committed. No penalty may be inflicted for an offence for which no provision was made at the time it was committed. Punishment is personal and can be imposed only on the offender.

Article 8 [Freedom of Religion and Conscience]

Freedom of conscience, the profession and free practice of religion shall be guaranteed. No one may, subject to law and order, be submitted to measures restricting the exercise of these freedoms.

Article 9 [Freedom of Expression and Information]

1. Every individual shall have the right to receive information.
2. Every individual shall have the right to express and disseminate his opinions within the law.

Article 10 [Freedom of Association]

1. Every individual shall have the right to free association provided that he abides by the law.
2. Subject to the obligation of solidarity provided for in Article 29 no one may be compelled to join an association.

Article 11 [Freedom of Assembly]

Every individual shall have the right to assemble freely with others. The exercise of this right shall be subject only to necessary restrictions provided for by law in particular those enacted in the interest of national security, the safety, health, ethics and rights and freedoms of others.

Article 12 [Freedom of Movement of Nationals and Right of Asylum]

1. Every individual shall have the right to freedom of movement and residence within the borders of a State provided he abides by the law.
2. Every individual shall have the right to leave any country including his own, and to return to his country. This right may only be subject to restrictions, provided for by law for the protection of national security, law and order, public health or morality.
3. Every individual shall have the right, when persecuted, to seek and obtain asylum in other countries in accordance with laws of those countries and international conventions.
4. A non-national legally admitted in a territory of a State Party to the present Charter, may only be expelled from it by virtue of a decision taken in accordance with the law.
5. The mass expulsion of non-nationals shall be prohibited. Mass expulsion shall be that which is aimed at national, racial, ethnic or religious groups.

Article 13 [Right to Participate in the Political and Public Affairs]

1. Every citizen shall have the right to participate freely in the government of his country, either directly or through freely chosen representatives in accordance with the provisions of the law.
2. Every citizen shall have the right of equal access to the public service of his country.
3. Every individual shall have the right of access to public property and services in strict equality of all persons before the law.

Article 14 [Property Rights]

The right to property shall be guaranteed. It may only be encroached upon in the interest of public need or in the general interest of the community and in accordance with the provisions of appropriate laws.

Article 15 [Equal Pay for Equal Work]

Every individual shall have the right to work under equitable and satisfactory conditions, and shall receive equal pay for equal work.

Article 16 [Right to Attainable Health]

1. Every individual shall have the right to enjoy the best attainable state of physical and mental health.
2. States parties to the present Charter shall take the necessary measures to protect the health of their people and to ensure that they receive medical attention when they are sick.

Article 17 [Right to Education]

1. Every individual shall have the right to education.
2. Every individual may freely take part in the cultural life of his community.
3. The promotion and protection of morals and traditional values recognized by the community shall be the duty of the State.

Article 18 [Family and Elimination of Discrimination against Women]

1. The family shall be the natural unit and basis of society. It shall be protected by the State which shall take care of its physical health and moral.
2. The State shall have the duty to assist the family which is the custodian of morals and traditional values recognized by the community.
3. The State shall ensure the elimination of every discrimination against women and also censure the protection of the rights of the woman and the child as stipulated in international declarations and conventions.
4. The aged and the disabled shall also have the right to special measures of protection in keeping with their physical or moral needs.

Article 19 [Equality of Peoples]

All peoples shall be equal; they shall enjoy the same respect and shall have the same rights. Nothing shall justify the domination of a people by another.

Article 20 [Right of Peoples to Self Determination]

1. All peoples shall have the right to existence. They shall have the unquestionable and inalienable right to self-determination. They shall freely determine their political status and shall pursue their economic and social development according to the policy they have freely chosen.
2. Colonized or oppressed peoples shall have the right to free themselves from the bonds of domination by resorting to any means recognized by the international community.

3. All peoples shall have the right to the assistance of the States parties to the present Charter in their liberation struggle against foreign domination, be it political, economic or cultural.

Article 21 [Right of Peoples to Freely Dispose of their Wealth and Natural Resources]

1. All peoples shall freely dispose of their wealth and natural resources. This right shall be exercised in the exclusive interest of the people. In no case shall a people be deprived of it.
2. In case of spoliation the dispossessed people shall have the right to the lawful recovery of its property as well as to an adequate compensation.
3. The free disposal of wealth and natural resources shall be exercised without prejudice to the obligation of promoting international economic cooperation based on mutual respect, equitable exchange and the principles of international law.
4. States Parties to the present Charter shall individually and collectively exercise the right to free disposal of their wealth and natural resources with a view to strengthening African unity and solidarity.
5. States Parties to the present Charter shall undertake to eliminate all forms of foreign economic exploitation particularly that practiced by international monopolies so as to enable their peoples to fully benefit from the advantages derived from their national resources.

Article 22 [Right to Development]

1. All peoples shall have the right to their economic, social and cultural development with due regard to their freedom and identity and in the equal enjoyment of the common heritage of mankind.
2. States shall have the duty, individually or collectively, to ensure the exercise of the right to development.

Article 23 [Right of Peoples to National and International Peace and Security]

1. All peoples shall have the right to national and international peace and security. The principles of solidarity and friendly relations implicitly affirmed by the Charter of the United Nations and reaffirmed by that of the Organization of African Unity shall govern relations between States.
2. For the purpose of strengthening peace, solidarity and friendly relations, States Parties to the present Charter shall ensure that:
    (a) any individual enjoying the right of asylum under Article 12 of the present Charter shall not engage in subversive activities against his country of origin or any other State Party to the present Charter;
    (b) their territories shall not be used as bases for subversive or terrorist activities against the people of any other State Party to the present Charter.

Article 24 [Right to a Favourable Environment]

All peoples shall have the right to a general satisfactory environment favorable to their development.

Article 25 [Duty of the State to Promote the Charter]

States Parties to the present Charter shall have the duty to promote and ensure through teaching, education and publication, the respect of the rights and freedoms contained in the present Charter and to see to it that these freedoms and rights as well as corresponding obligations and duties are understood.

Article 26 [DUTY OF STATES TO GUARANTEE INDEPENDENCE OF THE COURTS]

States parties to the present Charter shall have the duty to guarantee the independence of the Courts and shall allow the establishment and improvement of appropriate national institutions entrusted with the promotion and protection of the rights and freedoms guaranteed by the present Charter.

CHAPTER II **Duties**

Article 27 [INDIVIDUAL'S DUTY TO FAMILY AND COMMUNITY]

1. Every individual shall have duties towards his family and society, the State and other legally recognized communities and the international community.
2. The rights and freedoms of each individual shall be exercised with due regard to the rights of others, collective security, morality and common interest.

Article 28 [DUTY TO RESPECT AND CONSIDER FELLOW BEINGS]

Every individual shall have the duty to respect and consider his fellow beings without discrimination, and to maintain relations aimed at promoting, safeguarding and reinforcing mutual respect and tolerance.

Article 29 [INDIVIDUALS DUTY TO PRESERVE POSITIVE AFRICAN CULTURAL VALUES]

The individual shall also have the duty:

1. To preserve the harmonious development of the family and to work for the cohesion and respect of the family; to respect his parents at all times, to maintain them in case of need;
2. To serve his national community by placing his physical and intellectual abilities at its service;
3. Not to compromise the security of the State whose national or resident he is;
4. To preserve and strengthen social and national solidarity, particularly when the latter is threatened;
5. To preserve and strengthen the national independence and the territorial integrity of his country and to contribute to its defence in accordance with the law;
6. To work to the best of his abilities and competence, and to pay taxes imposed by law in the interest of the society;
7. To preserve and strengthen positive African cultural values in his relations with other members of the society, in the spirit of tolerance, dialogue and consultation and, in general, to contribute to the promotion of the moral well-being of society;
8. To contribute to the best of his abilities, at all times and at all levels, to the promotion and achievement of African Unity.

Part II. Measures of safeguard

CHAPTER I Establishment and Organization of the African Commission on Human and Peoples' Rights

Article 30 [ESTABLISHMENT OF COMMISSION]

An African Commission on Human and Peoples' Rights, hereinafter called "the Commission", shall be established within the Organization of African Unity to promote human and peoples' rights and ensure their protection in Africa.

Article 31 [COMPOSITION OF COMMISSION]

1. The Commission shall consist of eleven members chosen from amongst African personalities of the highest reputation, known for their high morality, integrity, impartiality and competence in matters of human and peoples' rights; particular consideration being given to persons having legal experience.
2. The members of the Commission shall serve in their personal capacity.

Article 32

The Commission shall not include more than one national of the same State.

Article 33

The members of the Commission shall be elected by secret ballot by the Assembly of Heads of State and Government, from a list of persons nominated by the States parties to the present Charter.

Article 34

Each State Party to the present Charter may not nominate more than two candidates. The candidates must have the nationality of one of the States Parties to the present Charter. When two candidates are nominated by a State, one of them may not be a national of that State.

Article 35

1. The Secretary General of the Organization of African Unity shall invite States Parties to the present Charter at least four months before the elections to nominate candidates;
2. The Secretary General of the Organization of African Unity shall make an alphabetical list of the persons thus nominated and communicate it to the Heads of State and Government at least one month before the elections.

Article 36 [TERM OF OFFICE OF MEMBERS]

The members of the Commission shall be elected for a six year period and shall be eligible for re-election. However, the term of office of four of the members elected at the first election shall terminate after two years and the term of office of the three others, at the end of four years.

Article 37

Immediately after the first election, the Chairman of the Assembly of Heads of State and Government of the Organization of African Unity shall draw lots to decide the names of those members referred to in Article 36.

Article 38 [SOLEMN DECLARATION]

After their election, the members of the Commission shall make a solemn declaration to discharge their duties impartially and faithfully.

Article 39 [VACANCIES]

1. In case of death or resignation of a member of the Commission, the Chairman of the Commission shall immediately inform the Secretary General of the Organization of African Unity, who shall declare the seat vacant from the date of death or from the date on which the resignation takes effect.
2. If, in the unanimous opinion of other members of the Commission, a member has stopped discharging his duties for any reason other than a temporary absence, the Chairman of the Commission shall inform the Secretary General of the Organization of African Unity, who shall then declare the seat vacant.
3. In each of the cases anticipated above, the Assembly of Heads of State and Government shall replace the member whose seat became vacant for the remaining period of his term unless the period is less than six months.

Article 40

Every member of the Commission shall be in office until the date his successor assumes office.

Article 41

The Secretary General of the Organization of African Unity shall appoint the Secretary of the Commission. He shall also provide the staff and services necessary for the effective discharge of the duties of the Commission. The Organization of African Unity shall bear the costs of the staff and services.

Article 42

1. The Commission shall elect its Chairman and Vice Chairman for a two year period. They shall be eligible for re-election.
2. The Commission shall lay down its rules of procedure.
3. Seven members shall form a quorum.
4. In case of an equality of votes, the Chairman shall have a casting vote.
5. The Secretary General may attend the meetings of the Commission. He shall neither participate in deliberations nor shall he be entitled to vote. The Chairman of the Commission may, however, invite him to speak.

Article 43 [DIPLOMATIC STATUS]

In discharging their duties, members of the Commission shall enjoy diplomatic privileges and immunities provided for in the General Convention on the Privileges and Immunities of the Organization of African Unity.

Article 44 [REMUNERATION]

Provision shall be made for the emoluments and allowances of the members of the Commission in the Regular Budget of the Organization of African Unity.

CHAPTER II **Mandate of the Commission**

Article 45 [FUNCTIONS]

The functions of the Commission shall be:

1. To promote Human and Peoples' Rights and in particular:
    (a) to collect documents, undertake studies and researches on African problems in the field of human and peoples' rights, organize seminars, symposia and conferences, disseminate information, encourage national and local institutions concerned with human and peoples' rights, and should the case arise, give its views or make recommendations to Governments.
    (b) to formulate and lay down, principles and rules aimed at solving legal problems relating to human and peoples' rights and fundamental freedoms upon which African Governments may base their legislations.
    (c) co-operate with other African and international institutions concerned with the promotion and protection of human and peoples' rights.
2. Ensure the protection of human and peoples' rights under conditions laid down by the present Charter.
3. Interpret all the provisions of the present Charter at the request of a State party, an institution of the OAU or an African Organization recognized by the OAU.
4. Perform any other tasks which may be entrusted to it by the Assembly of Heads of State and Government.

CHAPTER III **Procedure of the Commission**

Article 46

The Commission may resort to any appropriate method of investigation; it may hear from the Secretary General of the Organization of African Unity or any other person capable of enlightening it.

COMMUNICATION FROM STATES

Article 47

If a State Party to the present Charter has good reasons to believe that another State Party to this Charter has violated the provisions of the Charter, it may draw, by written communication, the attention of that State to the matter. This communication shall also be addressed to the Secretary General of the OAU and to the Chairman of the Commission. Within three months of the receipt of the communication, the State to which the communication is addressed shall give the enquiring State written explanation or statement elucidating the matter. This should include as much as possible relevant information relating to the laws and rules of procedure applied and applicable, and the redress already given or course of action available.

Article 48 [DISPUTE RESOLUTION]

If within three months from the date on which the original communication is received by the State to which it is addressed, the issue is not settled to the satisfaction of the two States involved through bilateral negotiation or by any other peaceful procedure, either State shall have the right to submit the matter to the Commission through the Chairman and shall notify the other States involved.

Article 49 [DIRECT ACCESS]

Notwithstanding the provisions of Article 47, if a State party to the present Charter considers that another State party has violated the provisions of the Charter, it may refer the matter directly to the Commission by addressing a communication to the Chairman, to the Secretary General of the Organization of African Unity and the State concerned.

Article 50 [EXHAUSTION OF LOCAL REMEDIES]

The Commission can only deal with a matter submitted to it after making sure that all local remedies, if they exist, have been exhausted, unless it is obvious to the Commission that the procedure of achieving these remedies would be unduly prolonged.

Article 51

1. The Commission may ask the States concerned to provide it with all relevant information.
2. When the Commission is considering the matter, States concerned may be represented before it and submit written or oral representation.

Article 52 [REPORT OF FINDINGS]

After having obtained from the States concerned and from other sources all the information it deems necessary and after having tried all appropriate means to reach an amicable solution based on the respect of Human and Peoples' Rights, the Commission shall prepare, within a reasonable period of time from the notification referred to in Article 48, a report stating the facts and its findings. This report shall be sent to the States concerned and communicated to the Assembly of Heads of State and Government.

Article 53 [RECOMMENDATIONS]

While transmitting its report, the Commission may make to the Assembly of Heads of State and Government such recommendations as it deems useful.

Article 54

The Commission shall submit to each ordinary Session of the Assembly of Heads of State and Government a report on its activities.

OTHER COMMUNICATIONS

Article 55

1. Before each Session, the Secretary of the Commission shall make a list of the communications other than those of States Parties to the present Charter and transmit them to the members of the Commission, who shall indicate which communications should be considered by the Commission.
2. A communication shall be considered by the Commission if a simple majority of its members so decide.

Article 56

Communications relating to human and peoples' rights referred to in Article 55 received by the Commission, shall be considered if they:
1. Indicate their authors even if the latter request anonymity,

2. Are compatible with the Charter of the Organization of African Unity or with the present Charter,

3. Are not written in disparaging or insulting language directed against the State concerned and its institutions or to the Organization of African Unity,

4. Are not based exclusively on news disseminated through the mass media,

5. Are sent after exhausting local remedies, if any, unless it is obvious that this procedure is unduly prolonged,

6. Are submitted within a reasonable period from the time local remedies are exhausted or from the date the Commission is seized of the matter, and

7. Do not deal with cases which have been settled by these States involved in accordance with the principles of the Charter of the United Nations, or the Charter of the Organization of African Unity or the provisions of the present Charter.

Article 57

Prior to any substantive consideration, all communications shall be brought to the knowledge of the State concerned by the Chairman of the Commission.

Article 58

1. When it appears after deliberations of the Commission that one or more communications apparently relate to special cases which reveal the existence of a series of serious or massive violations of human and peoples' rights, the Commission shall draw the attention of the Assembly of Heads of State and Government to these special cases.

2. The Assembly of Heads of State and Government may then request the Commission to undertake an in-depth study of these cases and make a factual report, accompanied by its findings and recommendations.

3. A case of emergency duly noticed by the Commission shall be submitted by the latter to the Chairman of the Assembly of Heads of State and Government who may request an in-depth study.

Article 59 [CONFIDENTIALITY]

1. All measures taken within the provisions of the present Chapter shall remain confidential until such a time as the Assembly of Heads of State and Government shall otherwise decide.

2. However, the report shall be published by the Chairman of the Commission upon the decision of the Assembly of Heads of State and Government.

3. The report on the activities of the Commission shall be published by its Chairman after it has been considered by the Assembly of Heads of State and Government.

CHAPTER IV Applicable Principles

Article 60 [GUIDING PRINCIPLES]

The Commission shall draw inspiration from international law on human and peoples' rights, particularly from the provisions of various African instruments on human and peoples' rights, the Charter of the United Nations, the Charter of the Organization of African Unity, the Universal Declaration of Human Rights, other instruments adopted by the United Nations and by African countries in the field of human and peoples' rights as well as from the provisions of various instruments adopted within the Specialized Agencies of the United Nations of which the parties to the present Charter are members.

Article 61 [Subsidiary Measures]

The Commission shall also take into consideration, as subsidiary measures to determine the principles of law, other general or special inter-national conventions, laying down rules expressly recognized by member states of the Organization of African Unity, African practices consistent with international norms on human and peoples' rights, customs generally accepted as law, general principles of law recognized by African states as well as legal precedents and doctrine.

Article 62 [Reporting]

Each state party shall undertake to submit every two years, from the date the present Charter comes into force, a report on the legislative or other measures taken with a view to giving effect to the rights and freedoms recognized and guaranteed by the present Charter.

Article 63 [Signature, Ratification, Adherence]

1. The present Charter shall be open to signature, ratification or adherence of the member states of the Organization of African Unity.
2. The instruments of ratification or adherence to the present Charter shall be deposited with the Secretary General of the Organization of African Unity.
3. The present Charter shall come into force three months after the reception by the Secretary General of the instruments of ratification or adherence of a simple majority of the member states of the Organization of African Unity.

Part III. General provisions

Article 64

1. After the coming into force of the present Charter, members of the Commission shall be elected in accordance with the relevant Articles of the present Charter.
2. The Secretary General of the Organization of African Unity shall convene the first meeting of the Commission at the Headquarters of the Organization within three months of the constitution of the Commission. Thereafter, the Commission shall be convened by its Chairman whenever necessary but at least once a year.

Article 65 [Coming into Force]

For each of the States that will ratify or adhere to the present Charter after its coming into force, the Charter shall take effect three months after the date of the deposit by that State of its instrument of ratification or adherence.

Article 66 [Protocols]

Special protocols or agreements may, if necessary, supplement the provisions of the present Charter.

Article 67

The Secretary General of the Organization of African Unity shall inform member states of the Organization of the deposit of each instrument of ratification or adherence.

Article 68 [Amendment]

The present Charter may be amended if a State party makes a written request to that effect to the Secretary General of the Organization of African Unity. The Assembly of Heads of State and Government may only consider the draft amendment after all the States Parties have been duly informed of it and the Commission has given its opinion on it at the request of the sponsoring State. The amendment shall be approved by a simple majority of the States Parties. It shall come into force for each State which has accepted it in accordance with its constitutional procedure three months after the Secretary General has received notice of the acceptance.

European Convention for the Protection of Human Rights and Fundamental Freedoms   (213 UNTS 221; European TS 5)

The Governments signatory hereto, being Members of the Council of Europe,

Considering the Universal Declaration of Human Rights proclaimed by the General Assembly of the United Nations on 10th December 1948;

Considering that this Declaration aims at securing the universal and effective recognition and observance of the Rights therein declared;

Considering that the aim of the Council of Europe is the achievement of greater unity between its Members and that one of the methods by which that aim is to be pursued is the maintenance and further realisation of Human Rights and Fundamental Freedoms;

Reaffirming their profound belief in those Fundamental Freedoms which are the foundation of justice and peace in the world and are best maintained on the one hand by an effective political democracy and on the other by a common understanding and observance of the Human Rights upon which they depend;

Being resolved, as the Governments of European countries which are like-minded and have a common heritage of political traditions, ideals, freedom and the rule of law, to take the first steps for the collective enforcement of certain of the Rights stated in the Universal Declaration;

Have agreed as follows:

Article 1

The High Contracting Parties shall secure to everyone within their jurisdiction the rights and freedoms defined in Section I of this Convention.

Section I

Article 2 [Right to Life]

(1) Everyone's right to life shall be protected by law. No one shall be deprived of his life intentionally save in the execution of a sentence of a court following his conviction of a crime for which this penalty is provided by law.

(2) Deprivation of life shall not be regarded as inflicted in contravention of this Article when it results from the use of force which is no more than absolutely necessary:

(a) in defence of any person from unlawful violence;

(b) in order to effect a lawful arrest or to prevent the escape of a person lawfully detained;

(c) in action lawfully taken for the purpose of quelling a riot or insurrection.

Article 3 [PROHIBITION OF TORTURE OR INHUMAN OR DEGRADING TREATMENT OR PUNISHMENT]

No one shall be subjected to torture or to inhuman or degrading treatment or punishment.

Article 4 [PROHIBITION OF SLAVERY, SERVITUDE AND FORCED OR COMPULSORY LABOUR]

(1) No one shall be held in slavery or servitude.

(2) No one shall be required to perform forced or compulsory labour.

(3) For the purpose of this Article the term "forced or compulsory labour" shall not include:

(*a*) any work required to be done in the ordinary course of detention imposed according to the provisions of Article 5 of this Convention or during conditional release from such detention;

(*b*) any service of a military character or, in a case of conscientious objectors in countries where they are recognised, service exacted instead of compulsory military service;

Article 5 [RIGHT TO LIBERTY AND SECURITY OF PERSON]

1. Everyone has the right to liberty and security of person. No one shall be deprived of his liberty save in the following cases and in accordance with a procedure prescribed by law:

(*a*) the lawful detention of a person after conviction by a competent court;

(*b*) the lawful arrest or detention of a person for non-compliance with the lawful order of a court or in order to secure the fulfilment of any obligation prescribed by law;

(*c*) the lawful arrest or detention of a person effected for the purpose of bringing him before the competent legal authority on reasonable suspicion of having committed an offence or when it is reasonably considered necessary to prevent his committing an offence or fleeing after having done so;

(*d*) the detention of a minor by lawful order for the purpose of educational supervision or his lawful detention for the purpose of bringing him before the competent legal authority;

(*e*) the lawful detention of persons for the prevention of the spreading of infectious diseases, of persons of unsound mind, alcoholics or drug addicts or vagrants;

(*f*) the lawful arrest or detention of a person to prevent his effecting an unauthorised entry into the country or of a person against whom action is being taken with a view to deportation or extradition.

2. Everyone who is arrested shall be informed promptly, in a language which he understands, of the reasons for his arrest and of any charge against him.

3. Everyone arrested or detained in accordance with the provisions of paragraph 1(*c*) of this Article shall be brought promptly before a judge or other officer authorised by law to exercise judicial power and shall be entitled to trial within a reasonable time or to release pending trial. Release may be conditioned by guarantees to appear for trial.

4. Everyone who is deprived of his liberty by arrest or detention shall be entitled to take proceedings by which the lawfulness of his detention shall be decided speedily by a court and his release ordered if the detention is not lawful.

(5) Everyone who has been the victim of arrest or detention in contravention of the provisions of this Article shall have an enforceable right to compensation.

Article 6 [Right to a Fair Trial]

(1) In the determination of his civil rights and obligations or of any criminal charge against him, everyone is entitled to a fair and public hearing within a reasonable time by an independent and impartial tribunal established by law. Judgment shall be pronounced publicly but the press and public may be excluded from all or part of the trial in the interests of morals, public order or national security in a democratic society, where the interests of juveniles or the protection of the private life of the parties so require, or to the extent strictly necessary in the opinion of the court in special circumstances where publicity would pejudice the interests of justice.

(2) Everyone charged with a criminal offence shall be presumed innocent until proved guilty according to law.

(3) Everyone charged with a criminal offence has the following minimum rights:

(a) to be informed promptly, in a language which he understands and in detail, of the nature and cause of the accusation against him;

(b) to have adequate time and facilities for the preparation of his defence;

(c) to defend himself in person or through legal assistance of his own choosing or, if he has not sufficient means to pay for legal assistance, to be given it free when the interests of justice so require;

(d) to examine or have examined witnesses against him and to obtain the attendance and examination of witnesses on his behalf under the same conditions as witnesses against him;

(e) to have the free assistance of an interpreter if he cannot understand or speak the language used in court.

Article 7 [Nulla Poena, Nullum Crimen Sine Praevi Lege Poenali]

(1) No one shall be held guilty of any criminal offence on account of any act or omission which did not constitute a criminal offence under national or international law at the time when it was committed. Nor shall a heavier penalty be imposed than the one that was applicable at the time the criminal offence was committed.

(2) This Article shall not prejudice the trial and punishment of any person for any act or omission which, at the time when it was committed, was criminal according to the general principles of law recognised by civilised nations.

Article 8 [Right to Respect for Private and Family Life, Home and Correspondence]

(1) Everyone has the right to respect for his private and family life, his home and his correspondence.

(2) There shall be no interference by a public authority with the exercise of this right except such as is in accordance with the law and is necessary in a democratic society in the interests of national security, public safety or the economic well-being of the country, for the prevention of disorder or crime, for the protection of health or morals, or for the protection of the rights and freedoms of others.

Article 9 [Freedom of Religion, Conscience and Thought]

(1) Everyone has the right to freedom of thought, conscience and religion; this right includes freedom to change his religion or belief and freedom, either alone or in community with others and in public or private, to manifest his religion or belief, in worship, teaching, practice and observance.

(2) Freedom to manifest one's religion or beliefs shall be subject only to such limitations as are prescribed by law and are necessary in a democratic society in the interests of public safety, for the protection of public order, health or morals, or for the protection of the rights and freedoms of others.

Article 10 [FREEDOM OF EXPRESSION]

(1) Everyone has the right to freedom of expression. This right shall include freedom to hold opinions and to receive and impart information and ideas without interference by public authority and regardless of frontiers. This Article shall not prevent States from requiring the licensing of broadcasting, television or cinema enterprises.

(2) The exercise of these freedoms, since it carries with it duties and responsibilities, may be subject to such formalities, conditions, restrictions or penalties as are prescribed by law and are necessary in a democratic society, in the interests of national security, territorial integrity or public safety, for the prevention of disorder or crime, for the protection of health or morals, for the protection of the reputation or rights of others, for preventing the disclosure of information received in confidence, or for maintaining the authority and impartiality of the judiciary.

Article 11 [FREEDOM OF ASSEMBLY AND ASSOCIATION]

(1) Everyone has the right to freedom of peaceful assembly and to freedom of association with others, including the right to form and to join trade unions for the protection of his interests.

(2) No restrictions shall be placed on the exercise of these rights other than such as are prescribed by law and are necessary in a democratic society in the interests of national security or public safety, for the prevention of disorder or crime, for the protection of health or morals or for the protection of the rights and freedoms of others. This Article shall not prevent the imposition of lawful restrictions on the exercise of these rights by members of the armed forces, of the police or of the administration of the State.

Article 12 [RIGHT TO MARRY AND TO FOUND A FAMILY]

Men and women of marriageable age have the right to marry and to found a family, according to the national laws governing the exercise of this right.

Article 13 [RIGHT TO AN EFFECTIVE REMEDY BEFORE A NATIONAL AUTHORITY]

Everyone whose rights and freedoms as set forth in this Convention are violated shall have an effective remedy before a national authority notwithstanding that the violation has been committed by persons acting in an official capacity.

Article 14 [NON DISCRIMINATION PRINCIPLE]

The enjoyment of rights and freedoms set forth in this Convention shall be secured without discrimination on any ground such as sex, race, colour, language, religion, political or other opinion, national or social origin, association with a national minority, property, birth or other status.

Article 15 [DEROGATION IN TIME OF EMERGENCY]

(1) In time of war or other public emergency threatening the life of the nation any High Contracting Party may take measures derogating from its obligations under this

Convention to the extent strictly required by the exigencies of the situation, provided that such measures are not inconsistent with its other obligations under international law.

(2) No derogation from Article 2, except in respect of deaths resulting from lawful acts of war, or from Articles 3, 4 (paragraph 1) and 7 shall be made under this provision.

(3) Any High Contracting Party availing itself of this right of derogation shall keep the Secretary-General of the Council of Europe fully informed of the measures which it has taken and the reasons therefor. It shall also inform the Secretary-General of the Council of Europe when such measures have ceased to operate and the provisions of the Convention are again being fully executed.

Article 16 [Restriction on the Political Activity of Aliens]

Nothing in Articles 10, 11 and 14 shall be regarded as preventing the High Contracting Parties from imposing restrictions on the political activity of aliens.

Article 17 [Prohibition of Abuse of Convention Rights]

Nothing in this Convention may be interpreted as implying for any State, group or person any right to engage in any activity or perform any act aimed at the destruction of any of the rights and freedoms set forth herein or at their limitation to a greater extent than is provided for in the Convention.

Article 18 [Permitted Restrictions of Rights may not be Misused]

The restrictions permitted under this Convention to the said rights and freedoms shall not be applied for any purpose other than those for which they have been prescribed.

Section II

Article 19 [Setting up of Commission and Court]

To ensure the observance of the engagements undertaken by the High Contracting Parties in the present Convention, there shall be set up:

(1) A European Commission of Human Rights hereinafter referred to as "the Commission";

(2) A European Court of Human Rights, hereinafter referred to as "the Court".

Section III

Article 20 [Composition of Commission]

The Commission shall consist of a number of members equal to that of the High Contracting Parties. No two members of the Commission may be nationals of the same State.

Article 21 [Election of Commission Members]

(1) The members of the Commission shall be elected by the Committee of Ministers by an absolute majority of votes, from a list of names drawn up by the Bureau of the Consultative Assembly; each group of the Representatives of the High Contracting Parties in the Consultative Assembly shall put forward three candidates, of whom two at least shall be its nationals.

(2) As far as applicable, the same procedure shall be followed to complete the Commission in the event of other States subsequently becoming Parties to this Convention, and in filling casual vacancies.

Article 22 [Terms of Office of Members]

(1) The members of the Commission shall be elected for a period of six years. They may be re-elected. However, of the members elected at the first election, the terms of seven members shall expire at the end of three years.

(2) The members whose terms are to expire at the end of the initial period of three years shall be chosen by lot by the Secretary-General of the Council of Europe immediately after the first election has been completed.

(3) A member of the Commission elected to replace a member whose term of office has not expired shall hold office for the remainder of his predecessor's term.

(4) The members of the Commission shall hold office until replaced. After having been replaced, they shall continue to deal with such cases as they already have under consideration.

Article 23 [Free Mandate of Members of Commission]

The members of the Commission shall sit on the Commission in their individual capacity.

Article 24 [Inter-state Complaints]

Any High Contracting Party may refer to the Commission, through the Secretary-General of the Council of Europe, any alleged breach of the provisions of the Convention by another High Contracting Party.

Article 25 [Individual Complaints]

(1) The Commission may receive petitions addressed to the Secretary-General of the Council of Europe from any person, non-governmental organisation or group of individuals claiming to be the victim of a violation by one of the High Contracting Parties of the rights set forth in this Convention, provided that the High Contracting Party against which the complaint has been lodged has declared that it recognises the competence of the Commission to receive such petitions. Those of the High Contracting Parties who have made such a declaration undertake not to hinder in any way the effective exercise of this right.

(2) Such declarations may be made for a specific period.

(3) The declarations shall be deposited with the Secretary-General of the Council of Europe who shall transmit copies thereof to the High Contracting Parties and publish them.

(4) The Commission shall only exercise the powers provided for in this Article when at least six High Contracting Parties are bound by declarations made in accordance with the preceding paragraphs.

Article 26 [Admissibility of Complaints]

The Commission may only deal with the matter after all the domestic remedies have been exhausted, according to the generally recognized rules of international law, and within a period of six months from the date on which the final decision was taken.

Article 27 [Further Admissibility Requirements]

(1) The Commission shall not deal with any petition submitted under Article 25 which

(a) is anonymous, or

(b) is substantially the same as a matter which has already been examined by the Commission or has already been submitted to another procedure of international investigation or settlement and if it contains no relevant new information.

(2) The Commission shall consider inadmissible any petition submitted under Article 25 which it considers incompatible with the provisions of the present Convention, manifestly ill-founded, or an abuse of the right of petition.

(3) The Commission shall reject any petition referred to it which it considers inadmissible under Article 26.

Article 28 [ESTABLISHING FACTS]

In the event of the Commission accepting a petition referred to it:

(a) it shall, with a view to ascertaining the facts, undertake together with the representatives of the parties an examination of the petition and, if need be, an investigation, for the effective conduct of which the States concerned shall furnish all necessary facilities, after an exchange of views with the Commission;

(b) it shall place itself at the disposal of the parties concerned with a view to securing a friendly settlement of the matter on the basis of respect for Human Rights as defined in this Convention.

Article 29 [SUB-COMMISSION]

(1) The Commission shall perform the functions set out in Article 28 by means of a Sub-Commission consisting of seven members of the Commission.

(2) Each of the parties concerned may appoint as members of this Sub-Commission a person of its choice.

(3) The remaining members shall be chosen by lot in accordance with arrangements prescribed in the Rules of Procedure of the Commission.

Article 30 [FRIENDLY SETTLEMENT]

If the Sub-Commission succeeds in effecting a friendly settlement in accordance with Article 28, it shall draw up a Report which shall be sent to the States concerned, to the Committee of Ministers and to the Secretary-General of the Council of Europe for publication. This Report shall be confined to a brief statement of the facts and of the solution reached.

Article 31 [COMMISSION'S REPORT]

(1) If a solution is not reached, the Commission shall draw up a Report on the facts and state its opinion as to whether the facts found disclose a breach by the State concerned of its obligations under the Convention. The opinions of all the members of the Commission on this point may be stated in the Report.

(2) The Report shall be transmitted to the Committee of Ministers. It shall also be transmitted to the States concerned, who shall not be at liberty to publish it.

(3) In transmitting the Report to the Committee of Ministers the Commission may make such proposals as it thinks fit.

Article 32 [DECISION BY COMMITTEE OF MINISTERS]

(1) If the question is not referred to the Court in accordance with Article 48 of this Convention within a period of three months from the date of the transmission of the

Report to the Committee of Ministers, the Committee of Ministers shall decide by a majority of two-thirds of the members entitled to sit on the Committee whether there has been a violation of the Convention.

(2) In the affirmative case the Committee of Ministers shall prescribe a period during which the High Contracting Party concerned must take the measures required by the decision of the Committee of Ministers.

(3) If the High Contracting Party concerned has not taken satisfactory measures within the prescribed period, the Committee of Ministers shall decide by the majority provided for in paragraph (1) above what effect shall be given to its original decision and shall publish the Report.

(4) The High Contracting Parties undertake to regard as binding on them any decision which the Committee of Ministers may take in application of the preceding paragraphs.

Article 33 [MEETING IN CAMERA]

The Commission shall meet in camera.

Article 34 [DECISIONS]

The Commission shall take its decisions by a majority of the Members present and voting; the Sub-Commission shall take its decisions by a majority of its members.

Article 35 [FREQUENCY OF MEETINGS]

The Commission shall meet as the circumstances require. The meetings shall be convened by the Secretary-General of the Council of Europe.

Article 36

The Commission shall draw up its own rules of procedure.

Article 37

The secretariat of the Commission shall be provided by the Secretary-General of the Council of Europe.

SECTION IV

Article 38 [COMPOSITION OF THE EUROPEAN COURT OF HUMAN RIGHTS]

The European Court of Human Rights shall consist of a number of judges equal to that of the Members of the Council of Europe. No two judges may be nationals of the same State.

Article 39 [ELECTION OF MEMBERS OF THE COURT]

(1) The members of the Court shall be elected by the Consultative Assembly by a majority of the votes cast from a list of persons nominated by the Members of the Council of Europe; each Member shall nominate three candidates, of whom two at least shall be its nationals.

(2) As far as applicable, the same procedure shall be followed to complete the Court in the event of the admission of new Members of the Council of Europe, and in filling casual vacancies.

(3) The candidates shall be of high moral character and must either possess the qualifications required for appointment to high judicial office or be jurisconsults of recognised competence.

Article 40 [Term of Office of Members of the Court]

(1) The members of the Court shall be elected for a period of nine years. They may be re-elected. However, of the members elected at the first election the terms of four members shall expire at the end of three years, and the terms of four more members shall expire at the end of six years.

(2) The members whose terms are to expire at the end of the initial periods of three and six years shall be chosen by lot by the Secretary-General immediately after the first election has been completed.

(3) A member of the Court elected to replace a member whose term of office has not expired shall hold office for the remainder of his predecessor's term.

(4) The members of the Court shall hold office until replaced. After having been replaced, they shall continue to deal with such cases as they already have under consideration.

Article 41 [President of the Court]

The Court shall elect its President and Vice-President for a period of three years. They may be re-elected.

Article 42 [Remuneration]

The members of the Court shall receive for each day of duty a compensation to be determined by the Committee of Ministers.

Article 43 [Composition of Court]

For the consideration of each case brought before it the Court shall consist of a Chamber composed of seven judges. There shall sit as an *ex officio* member of the Chamber the judge who is a national of any State party concerned, or, if there is none, a person of its choice who shall sit in the capacity of judge; the names of the other judges shall be chosen by lot by the President before the opening of the case.

Article 44 [Locus standi]

Only the High Contracting Parties and the Commission shall have the right to bring a case before the Court.

Article 45 [Jurisdiction]

The jurisdiction of the Court shall extend to all cases concerning the interpretation and application of the present Convention which the High Contracting Parties or the Commission shall refer to it in accordance with Article 48.

Article 46 [Compulsory Jurisdiction]

(1) Any of the High Contracting Parties may at any time declare that it recognises as compulsory *ipso facto* and without special agreement the jurisdiction of the Court in all matters concerning the interpretation and application of the present Convention.

(2) The declarations referred to above may be made unconditionally or on condition of reciprocity on the part of several or certain other High Contracting Parties or for a specified period.

(3) These declarations shall be deposited with the Secretary-General of the Council of Europe who shall transmit copies thereof to the High Contracting Parties.

Article 47 [FINDING BY COMMISION]

The Court may only deal with a case after the Commission has acknowledged the failure of efforts for a friendly settlement and within the period of three months provided for in Article 32.

Article 48 [WHO MAY BRING CASES]

The following may bring a case before the Court, provided that the High Contracting Party concerned, if there is only one, or the High Contracting Parties concerned, if there is more than one, are subject to the compulsory jurisdiction of the Court or, failing that, with the consent of the High Contracting Party concerned, if there is only one, or of the High Contracting Parties concerned if there is more than one:

(a) The Commission;

(b) a High Contracting Party whose national is alleged to be a victim;

(c) a High Contracting Party which referred the case to the Commission;

(d) a High Contracting Party against which the complaint has been lodged.

Article 49 [JURISDICTION DISPUTE]

In the event of dispute as to whether the Court has jurisdiction, the matter shall be settled by the decision of the Court.

Article 50 [COMPENSATION BY THE COURT]

If the Court finds that a decision or a measure taken by a legal authority or any other authority of a High Contracting Party is completely or partially in conflict with the obligations arising from the present Convention, and if the internal law of the said Party allows only partial reparation to be made for the consequences of this decision or measure, the decision of the Court shall, if necessary, afford just satisfaction to the injured party.

Article 51 [REASONS]

(1) Reasons shall be given for the judgment of the Court.

(2) If the judgment does not represent in whole or in part the unanimous opinion of the judges, any judge shall be entitled to deliver a separate opinion.

Article 52 [JUDGMENT FINAL]

The judgment of the Court shall be final.

Article 53 [PARTY COMPLIANCE WITH JUDGMENT]

The High Contracting Parties undertake to abide by the decision of the Court in any case to which they are parties.

Article 54 [Committee Supervises Execution]

The judgment of the Court shall be transmitted to the Committee of Ministers which shall supervise its execution.

Article 55

The Court shall draw up its own rules and shall determine its own procedure.

Article 56

(1) The first election of the members of the Court shall take place after the declaration by the High Contracting Party mentioned in Article 46 have reached a total of eight.

(2) No case can be brought before the Court before this election.

Section V

Article 57 [Implementation in Internal Law]

On receipt of a request from the Secretary-General of the Council of Europe any High Contracting Party shall furnish an explanation of the manner in which its internal law ensures the effective implementation of any of the provisions of this Convention.

Article 58 [Expenses]

The expenses of the Commission and the Court shall be borne by the Council of Europe.

Article 59 [Immunity]

The members of the Commission and of the Court shall be entitled, during the discharge of their functions, to the privileges and immunities provided for in Article 40 of the Statute of the Council of Europe and in the agreements made thereunder.

Article 60

Nothing in this Convention shall be construed as limiting or derogating from any of the human rights and fundamental freedoms which may be ensured under the laws of any High Contracting Party or under any other agreement to which it is a Party.

Article 61

Nothing in this Convention shall prejudice the powers conferred on the Committee of Ministers by the Statute of the Council of Europe.

Article 62

The High Contracting Parties agree that, except by special agreement, they will not avail themselves of treaties, conventions or declarations in force between them for the purpose of submitting, by way of petition, a dispute arising out of the interpretation or application of this Convention to a means of settlement other than those provided for in this Convention.

Article 63 [Application Extension]

(1) Any State may at the time of its ratification or at any time thereafter declare by notification addressed to the Secretary-General of the Council of Europe that the present

Convention shall extend to all or any of the territories for whose international relations it is responsible.

(2) The Convention shall extend to the territory or territories named in the notification as from the thirtieth day after the receipt of this notification by the Secretary-General of the Council of Europe.

(3) The provisions of this Convention shall be applied in such territories with due regard, however, to local requirements.

(4) Any State which has made a declaration in accordance with paragraph 1 of this Article may at any time thereafter declare on behalf of one or more of the territories to which the declaration relates that it accepts the competence of the Commission to receive petitions from individuals, non-governmental organisations or groups of individuals in accordance with Article 25 of the present Convention.

Article 64 [RESERVATIONS]

(1) Any State may, when signing this Convention or when depositing its instrument of ratification, make a reservation in respect of any particular provision of the Convention to the extent that any law then in force in its territory is not in conformity with the provision. Reservations of a general character shall not be permitted under this Article.

(2) Any reservation made under this Article shall contain a brief statement of the law concerned.

Article 65 [DENUNCIATION]

(1) A High Contracting Party may denounce the present Convention only after the expiry of five years from the date on which it became a Party to it and after six months' notice contained in a notification addressed to the Secretary-General of the Council of Europe, who shall inform the other High Contracting Parties.

(2) Such a denunciation shall not have the effect of releasing the High Contracting Party concerned from its obligations under this Convention in respect of any act which, being capable of constituting a violation of such obligations, may have been performed by it before the date at which the denunciation became effective.

(3) Any High Contracting Party which shall cease to be a Member of the Council of Europe shall cease to be a Party to this Convention under the same conditions.

(4) The Convention may be denounced in accordance with the provisions of the preceding paragraphs in respect of any territory to which it has been declared to extend under the terms of Article 63.

Article 66 [SIGNATURE AND RATIFICATION]

(1) This Convention shall be open to the signature of the Members of the Council of Europe. It shall be ratified. Ratifications shall be deposited with the Secretary-General of the Council of Europe.

(2) The present Convention shall come into force after the deposit of ten instruments of ratification.

(3) As regards any signatory ratifying subsequently, the Convention shall come into force at the date of the deposit of its instrument of ratification.

(4) The Secretary-General of the Council of Europe shall notify all the Members of the Council of Europe of the entry into force of the Convention, the names of the High Contracting Parties who have ratified it, and the deposit of all instruments of ratification which may be effected subsequently.

38.   American Convention on Human Rights
(1144 UNTS 123; 9 ILM 673 (1970))

Part 1. State obligations and rights protected

CHAPTER I   General Obligations

Article 1.   Obligation to Respect Rights

1. The States Parties to this Convention undertake to respect the rights and freedoms recognized herein and to ensure to all persons subject to their jurisdiction the free and full exercise of those rights and freedoms, without any discrimination for reasons of race, color, sex, language, religion, political or other opinion, national or social origin, economic status, birth, or any other social condition.

2. For the purposes of this Convention, ''person'' means every human being.

Article 2.   Domestic Legal Effects

Where the exercise of any of the rights or freedoms referred to in Article 1 is not already ensured by legislative or other provisions, the States Parties undertake to adopt, in accordance with their constitutional processes and the provisions of this Convention, such legislative or other measures as may be necessary to give effect to those rights or freedoms.

CHAPTER II   Civil and Political Rights

Article 3.   Right to Juridical Personality

Every person has the right to recognition as a person before the law.

Article 4.   Right to Life

1. Every person has the right to have his life respected. This right shall be protected by law, and, in general, from the moment of conception. No one shall be arbitrarily deprived of his life.

2. In countries that have not abolished the death penalty, it may be imposed only for the most serious crimes and pursuant to a final judgment rendered by a competent court and in accordance with a law establishing such punishment, enacted prior to the commission of the crime. The application of such punishment shall not be extended to crimes to which it does not presently apply.

3. The death penalty shall not be re-established in states that have abolished it.

4. In no case shall capital punishment be inflicted for political offences or related common crimes.

5. Capital punishment shall not be imposed upon persons who, at the time the crime was committed, were under 18 years of age or over 70 years of age; nor shall it be applied to pregnant women.

6. Every person condemned to death shall have the right to apply for amnesty, pardon, or commutation of sentence, which may be granted in all cases. Capital punishment shall not be imposed while such a petition is pending decision by the competent authority.

Article 5.   Right to Humane Treatment

1. Every person has the right to have his physical, mental, and moral integrity respected.

2. No one shall be subjected to torture or to cruel, inhuman, or degrading punishment or treatment. All persons deprived of their liberty shall be treated with respect for the inherent dignity of the human person.

3. Punishment shall not be extended to any person other than the criminal.

4. Accused persons shall, save in exceptional circumstances, be segregated from convicted persons, and shall be subject to separate treatment appropriate to their status as unconvicted persons.

5. Minors while subject to criminal proceedings shall be separated from adults and brought before specialized tribunals, as speedily as possible, so that they may be treated in accordance with their status as minors.

6. Punishments consisting of deprivation of liberty shall have as an essential aim the reform and social readaptation of the prisoners.

Article 6.   Freedom from Slavery

1. No one shall be subject to slavery or to involuntary servitude, which are prohibited in all their forms, as are the slave trade and traffic in women.

2. No one shall be required to perform forced or compulsory labor. This provision shall not be interpreted to mean that, in those countries in which the penalty established for certain crimes is deprivation of liberty at forced labor, the carrying out of such a sentence imposed by a competent court is prohibited. Forced labor shall not adversely affect the dignity or the physical or intellectual capacity of the prisoner.

3. For the purposes of this article the following do not constitute forced or compulsory labor:

(a) work or service normally required of a person imprisoned in execution of a sentence or formal decision passed by the competent judicial authority. Such work or service shall be carried out under the supervision and control of public authorities, and any persons performing such work or service shall not be placed at the disposal of any private party, company, or juridical person;

(b) military service and, in countries in which conscientious objectors are recognized, national service that the law may provide for in lieu of military service;

(c) service exacted in time of danger or calamity that threatens the existence or the well-being of the community; or

(d) work or service that forms part of normal civic obligations.

Article 7.   Right to Personal Liberty

1. Every person has the right to personal liberty and security.

2. No one shall be deprived of his physical liberty except for the reasons and under the conditions established beforehand by the constitution of the State Party concerned or by a law established pursuant thereto.

3. No one shall be subject to arbitrary arrest or imprisonment.

4. Anyone who is detained shall be informed of the reasons for his detention and shall be promptly notified of the charge or charges against him.

5. Any person detained shall be brought promptly before a judge or other officer authorized by law to exercise judicial power and shall be entitled to trial within a reasonable time or to be released without prejudice to the continuation of the proceedings. His release may be subject to guarantees to assure his appearance for trial.

6.   Anyone who is deprived of his liberty shall be entitled to recourse to a competent court, in order that the court may decide without delay on the lawfulness of his arrest or detention and order his release if the arrest or detention is unlawful. In States Parties whose laws provide that anyone who believes himself to be threatened with deprivation of his liberty is entitled to recourse to a competent court in order that it may decide on the lawfulness of such threat, this remedy may not be restricted or abolished. The interested party or another person in his behalf is entitled to seek these remedies.

7. No one shall be detained for debt. This principle shall not limit the orders of a competent judicial authority issued for nonfulfillment of duties of support.

Article 8.   Right to a Fair Trial

1. Every person has the right to a hearing with due guarantees and within a reasonable time, by a competent, independent, and impartial tribunal, previously established by law, in the substantiation of any accusation of a criminal nature made against him or for the determination of his rights and obligations of a civil, labor, fiscal, or any other nature.

2. Every person accused of a criminal offense has the right to be presumed innocent so long as his guilt has not been proven according to law. During the proceedings, every person is entitled, with full equality, to the following minimum guarantees:

(a)   the right of the accused to be assisted without charge by a translator or interpreter, if he does not understand or does not speak the language of the tribunal or court;

(b)   prior notification in detail to the accused of the charges against him;

(c)   adequate time and means for the preparation of his defense;

(d)   the right of the accused to defend himself personally or to be assisted by legal counsel of his own choosing, and to communicate freely and privately with his counsel;

(e)   the inalienable right to be assisted by counsel provided by the state, paid or not as the domestic law provides, if the accused does not defend himself personally or engage his own counsel within the time period established by law;

(f)   the right of the defense to examine witnesses present in the court and to obtain the appearance, as witnesses, of experts or other persons who may throw light on the facts;

(g)   the right not to be compelled to be a witness against himself or to pleady guilty; and

(h)   the right to appeal the judgment to a higher court.

3. A confession of guilt by the accused shall be valid only if it is made without coercion of any kind.

4. An accused person acquitted by a non-appealable judgment shall not be subjected to a new trial for the same cause.

5. Criminal proceedings shall be public, except insofar as may be necessary to protect the interests of justice.

Article 9.   Freedom from Ex Post Facto Laws

No one shall be convicted of any act or omission that did not constitute a criminal offense, under the applicable law, at the time it was committed. A heavier penalty shall not be imposed than the one that was applicable at the time the criminal offense was committed. If subsequent to the commission of the offense the law provides for the imposition of a lighter punishment, the guilty person shall benefit therefrom.

Article 10. *Right to Compensation*

Every person has the right to be compensated in accordance with the law in the event he has been sentenced by a final judgment through a miscarriage of justice.

Article 11. *Right to Privacy*

1. Everyone has the right to have his honor respected and his dignity recognized.

2. No one may be the object of arbitrary or abusive interference with his private life, his family, his home, or his correspondence, or of unlawful attacks on his honor or reputation.

3. Every one has the right to the protection of the law against such interference or attacks.

Article 12. *Freedom of Conscience and Religion*

1. Everyone has the right to freedom of conscience and of religion. This right includes freedom to maintain or to change one's religion or beliefs, and freedom to profess or disseminate one's religion or beliefs either individually or together with others, in public or in private.

2. No one shall be subject to restrictions that might impair his freedom to maintain or to change his religion or beliefs.

3. Freedom to manifest one's religion and beliefs may be subject only to the limitations prescribed by law that are necessary to protect public safety, order, health, or morals, or the rights or freedoms of others.

4. Parents or guardians, as the case may be, have the right to provide for the religious and moral education of their children or wards that is in accord with their own convictions.

Article 13. *Freedom of Thought and Expression*

1. Everyone shall have the right to freedom of thought and expression. This right shall include freedom to seek, receive, and impart information and ideas of all kinds, regardless of frontiers, either orally, in writing, in print, in the form of art, or through any other medium of his choice.

2. The exercise of the right provided for in the foregoing paragraph shall not be subject to prior censorship but shall be subject to subsequent imposition of liability, which shall be expressly established by law to the extent necessary in order to ensure:

   (a) respect for the rights or reputations of others; or

   (b) the protection of national security, public order, or public health or morals.

3. The right of expression may not be restricted by indirect methods or means, such as the abuse of government or private controls over newsprint, radio broadcasting frequencies, or equipment used in the dissemination of information, or by any other means tending to impede the communication and circulation of ideas and opinions.

4. Notwithstanding the provisions of paragraph 2 above, public entertainments may be subject by law to prior censorship for the sole purpose of regulating access to them for the moral protection of childhood and adolescence.

5. Any propaganda for war and any advocacy of national, racial, or religious hatred that constitute incitements to lawless violence or to any other similar illegal action against any person or group of persons on any grounds including those of race, colour, religion, language, or national origin shall be considered as offenses punishable by law.

Article 14.   Right of Reply

1. Anyone injured by inaccurate of offensive statements or ideas disseminated to the public in general by a legally regulated medium of communication has the right to reply or make a correction using the same communications outlet, under such conditions as the law may establish.

2. The correction or reply shall not in any case remit other legal liabilities that may have been incurred.

3. For the effective protection of honor and reputation, every publisher, and every newspaper, motion picture, radio, and television company, shall have a person responsible, who is not protected by immunities or special privileges.

Article 15.   Right of Assembly

The right of peaceful assembly, without arms, is recognized. No restrictions may be placed on the exercise of this right other than those imposed in conformity with the law and necessary in a democratic society in the interest of national security, public safety, or public order, or to protect public health or morals or the rights or freedoms of others.

Article 16.   Freedom of Association

1. Everyone has the right to associate freely for ideological, religious, political, economic, labor, social, cultural, sports, or other purposes.

2. The exercise of this right shall be subject only to such restrictions established by law as may be necessary in a democratic society, in the interest of national security, public safety, or public order, or to protect public health or morals or the rights and freedoms of others.

3. The provisions of this article do not bar the imposition of legal restrictions, including even deprivation of the exercise of the right of association, on members of the armed forces and the police.

Article 17.   Rights of the Family

1. The family is the natural and fundamental group unit of society and is entitled to protection by society and the state.

2. The right of men and women of marriageable age to marry and to raise a family shall be recognized, if they meet the conditions required by domestic laws, insofar as such conditions do not affect the principle of nondiscrimination established in this Convention.

3. No marriage shall be entered into without the free and full consent of the intending spouses.

4. The States Parties shall take appropriate steps to ensure the equality of rights and the adequate balancing of responsibilities of the spouses as to marriage, during marriage, and in the event of its dissolution. In case of dissolution, provision shall be made for the necessary protection of any children solely on the basis of their own best interests.

5. The law shall recognize equal rights for children born out of wedlock and those born in wedlock.

Article 18. Right to a Name

Every person has the right to a given name and to the surnames of his parents or that of one of them. The law shall regulate the manner in which this right shall be ensured for all, by the use of assumed names if necessary.

Article 19. Rights of the Child

Every minor child has the right to the measures of protection required by his condition as a minor on the part of his family, society, and the state.

Article 20. Right to Nationality

1. Every person has the right to a nationality.

2. Every person has the right to the nationality of the state in whose territory he was born if he does not have the right to any other nationality.

3. No one shall be arbitrarily deprived of his nationality or of the right to change it.

Article 21. Right to Property

1. Everyone has the right to the use and enjoyment of his property. The law may subordinate such use and enjoyment to the interest of society.

2. No one shall be deprived of his property except upon payment of just compensation, for reasons of public utility or social interest, and in the cases and according to the forms established by law.

3. Usury and any other form of exploitation of man by man shall be prohibited by law.

Article 22. Freedom of Movement and Residence

1. Every person lawfully in the territory of a State Party has the right to move about in it and to reside in it subject to the provisions of the law.

2. Every person has the right to leave any country freely, including his own.

3. The exercise of the foregoing rights may be restricted only pursuant to a law to the extent necessary in a democratic society to prevent crime or to protect national security, public safety, public order, public morals, public health, or the rights or freedoms of others.

4. The exercise of the rights recognized in paragraph 1 may also be restricted by law in designated zones for reasons of public interest.

5. No one can be expelled from the territory of the state of which he is a national or be deprived of the right to enter it.

6. An alien lawfully in the territory of a State Party to this Convention may be expelled from it only pursuant to a decision reached in accordance with law.

7. Every person has the right to seek and be granted asylum in a foreign territory, in accordance with the legislation of the state and international conventions, in the event he is being pursued for political offenses or related common crimes.

8. In no case may an alien be deported or returned to a country, regardless of whether or not it is his country of origin, if in that country his right to life or personal freedom

is in danger of being violated because of his race, nationality, religion, social status, or political opinions.

9. The collective expulsion of aliens is prohibited.

Article 23. *Right to Participate in Government*

1. Every citizen shall enjoy the following rights and opportunities:

(a) to take part in the conduct of public affairs, directly or through freely chosen representatives;

(b) to vote and to be elected in genuine periodic elections, which shall be by universal and equal suffrage and by secret ballot that guarantees the free expression of the will of the voters; and

(c) to have access, under general conditions of equality, to the public service of his country.

2. The law may regulate the exercise of the rights and opportunities referred to in the preceding paragraph only on the basis of age, nationality, residence, language, education, civil and mental capacity, or sentencing by a competent court in criminal proceedings.

Article 24. *Right to Equal Protection*

All persons are equal before the law. Consequently, they are entitled, without discrimination, to equal protection of the law.

Article 25 *Right to Judicial Protection*

1. Everyone has the right to simple and prompt recourse, or any other effective recourse, to a competent court or tribunal for protection against acts that violate his fundamental rights recognized by the constitution or laws of the state concerned or by this Convention, even though such violation may have been committed by persons acting in the course of their official duties.

2. The States Parties undertake:

(a) to ensure that any person claiming such remedy shall have his rights determined by the competent authority provided for by the legal system of the state;

(b) to develop the possibilities of judicial remedy; and

(c) to ensure that the competent authorities shall enforce such remedies when granted.

CHAPTER III **Economic, Social, and Cultural Rights**

Article 26. *Progressive Development*

The States Parties undertake to adopt measures, both internally and through international cooperation, especially those of an economic and technical nature, with a view to achieving progressively, by legislation or other appropriate means, the full realization of the rights implicit in the economic, social, educational, scientific, and cultural standards set forth in the Charter of the Organization of American States as amended by the Protocol of Buenos Aires.

CHAPTER IV **Suspension of Guarantees, Interpretation, and Application**

Article 27. Suspension of Guarantees

1. In time of war, public danger, or other emergency that threatens the independence or security of a State Party, it may take measures derogating from its obligations under the present Convention to the extent and for the period of time strictly required by the exigencies of the situation, provided that such measures are not inconsistent with its other obligations under international law and do not involve discrimination on the ground of race, colour, sex, language, religion, or social origin.

2. The foregoing provision does not authorize any suspension of the following articles: Article 3 (Right to Juridical Personality), Article 4 (Right to Life), Article 5 (Right to Humane Treatment), Article 6 (Freedom from Slavery), Article 9 (Freedom from Ex Post Facto Laws), Article 12 (Freedom of Conscience and Religion), Article 17 (Rights of the Family), Article 18 (Right to a Name), Article 19 (Rights of the Child), Article 20 (Right to Nationality), and Article 23 (Right to Participate in Government), or of the judicial guarantees essential for the protection of such rights.

3. Any State Party availing itself of the right of suspension shall immediately inform the other States Parties, through the Secretary General of the Organization of American States, of the provisions the application of which it has suspended, the reasons that gave rise to the suspension, and the date set for the termination of such suspension.

Article 28. Federal Clause

1. Where a State Party is constituted as a federal state, the national government of such State Party shall implement all the provisions of the Convention over whose subject matter it exercises legislative and judicial jurisdiction.

2. With respect to the provisions over whose subject matter the constituent units of the federal state have jurisdiction, the national government shall immediately take suitable measures, in accordance with its constitution and its laws, to the end that the competent authorities of the constituent units may adopt appropriate provisions for the fulfilment of this Convention.

3. Whenever two or more States Parties agree to form a federation or other type of association they shall take care that the resulting federal or other compact contains the provisions necessary for continuing and rendering effective the standards of this Convention in the new state that is organized.

Article 29. Restrictions Regarding Interpretation

No provision of this Convention shall be interpreted as:

(a) permitting any State Party, group, or person to suppress the enjoyment or exercise of the rights and freedoms recognized in this Convention or to restrict them to a greater extent than is provided for herein;

(b) restricting the enjoyment or exercise of any right or freedom recognized by virtue of the laws of any State Party or by virtue of another convention to which one of the said states is a party;

(c) precluding other rights or guarantees that are inherent in the human personality or derived from representative democracy as a form of government; or

(d) excluding or limiting the effect that the American Declaration of the Rights and Duties of Man and other international acts of the same nature may have.

Article 30. Scope of Restrictions

The restrictions that, pursuant to this Convention, may be placed on the enjoyment or exercise of the rights or freedoms recognized herein may not be applied except in accordance with laws enacted for reasons of general interest and in accordance with the purpose for which such restrictions have been established.

Article 31. Recognition of Other Rights

Other rights and freedoms recognized in accordance with the procedures established in Articles 76 and 77 may be included in the system of protection of this Convention.

CHAPTER V Personal Responsibilities

Article 32. Relationship between Duties and Rights

1. Every person has responsibilities to his family, his community, and mankind.

2. The rights of each person are limited by the rights of others, by the security of all, and by the just demands of the general welfare, in a democratic society.

Part II. Means of protection

CHAPTER VI Competent Organs

Article 33

The following organs shall have competence with respect to matters relating to the fulfillment of the commitments made by the States Parties to this Convention:

(a) the Inter-American Commission on Human Rights, referred to as "the Commission"; and

(b) the Inter-American Court of Human Rights, referred to as "The Court."

CHAPTER VII Inter-American Commission on Human Rights

Section 1. Organization

Article 34

The Inter-American Commission on Human Rights shall be composed of seven members, who shall be persons of high moral character and recognized competence in the field of human rights.

Article 35

The Commission shall represent all the member countries of the Organization of American States.

Article 36

1. The members of the Commission shall be elected in a personal capacity by the General Assembly of the Organization from a list of candidates proposed by the governments of the member states.

2. Each of those governments may propose up to three candidates, who may be nationals of the states proposing them or of any other member states of the Organization

of American States. When a slate of three is proposed, at least one of the candidates shall be a national of a state other than the one proposing the slate.

Article 37

1. The members of the Commission shall be elected for a term of four years and may be reelected only once, but the terms of three of the members chosen in the first election shall expire at the end of two years. Immediately following that election the General Assembly shall determine the names of those three members by lot.

2. No two nationals of the same state may be members of the Commission.

Article 38

Vacancies that may occur on the Commission for reasons other than the normal expiration of a term shall be filled by the Permanent Council of the Organization in accordance with the provisions of the Statute of the Commission.

Article 39

The Commission shall prepare its Statute, which it shall submit to the General Assembly for approval. It shall establish its own Regulations.

Article 40

Secretariat services for the Commission shall be furnished by the appropriate specialized unit of the General Secretariat of the Organization. This unit shall be provided with the resources required to accomplish the tasks assigned to it by the Commission.

SECTION 2. FUNCTIONS

Article 41

The main functions of the Commission shall be to promote respect for and defense of human rights. In the exercise of its mandate, it shall have the following functions and powers:

(a) to develop an awareness of human rights among the peoples of America;

(b) to make recommendations to the governments of the member states, when it considers such action advisable, for the adoption of progressive measures in favour of human rights within the framework of their domestic law and constitutional provisions as well as appropriate measures to further the observance of those rights;

(c) to prepare such studies or reports as it considers advisable in the performance of its duties;

(d) to request the governments of the member states to supply it with information on the measures adopted by them in matters of human rights;

(e) to respond, through the General Secretariat of the Organization of American States, to inquiries made by the member states on matters related to human rights and, within the limits of its possibilities, to provide those states with the advisory services they request;

(f) to take action on petitions and other communications pursuant to its authority, under the provisions of Articles 44 through 51 of this Convention; and *(g)* to submit an annual report to the General Assembly of the Organization of American States.

Article 42

The States Parties shall transmit to the Commission a copy of each of the reports and studies that they submit annually to the Executive Committees of the Inter-American Economic and Social Council and the Inter-American Council for Education, Science, and Culture, in their respective fields, so that the Commission may watch over the promotion of the rights implicit in the economic, social, educational, scientific, and cultural standards set forth in the Charter of the Organization of American States as amended by the Protocol of Buenos Aires.

Article 43

The States Parties undertake to provide the Commission with such information as it may request of them as to the manner in which their domestic law ensures the effective application of any provisions of this Convention.

SECTION 3.   COMPETENCE

Article 44

Any person or group of persons, or any nongovernmental entity legally recognized in one of more member states of the Organization, may lodge petitions with the Commission containing denunciations or complaints of violation of this Convention by a State Party.

Article 45

1. Any State Party may, when it deposits its instrument of ratification of or adherence to this Convention, or at any later time, declare that it recognizes the competence of the Commission to receive and examine communications in which a State Party alleges that another State Party has committed a violation of a human right set forth in this Convention.

2. Communications presented by virtue of this article may be admitted and examined only if they are presented by a State Party that has made a declaration recognizing the aforementioned competence of the Commission. The Commission shall not admit any communication against a State Party that has not made such a declaration.

3. A declaration concerning recognition of competence may be made to be valid for an indefinite time, for a specified period, or for a specific case.

4. Declarations shall be deposited with the General Secretariat of the Organization of American States, which shall transmit copies thereof to the member states of that Organization.

Article 46

1. Admission by the Commission of a petition or communication lodged in accordance with Articles 44 or 45 shall be subject to the following requirements:
   (a) that the remedies under domestic law have been pursued and exhausted, in accordance with generally recognized principles of international law;
   (b) that the petition or communication is lodged within a period of six months from the date on which the party alleging violation of his rights was notified of the final judgment;

(c) that the subject of the petition or communication is not pending before another international procedure for settlement; and

(d) that, in the case of Article 44, the petition contains the name, nationality, profession, domicile, and signature of the person or persons or of the legal representative of the entity lodging the petition.

2. The provisions of paragraphs 1*(a)* and 1*(b)* of this article shall not be applicable when:

(a) the domestic legislation of the state concerned does not afford due process of law for the protection of the right or rights that have allegedly been violated;

(b) the party alleging violation of his rights has been denied access to the remedies under domestic law or has been prevented from exhausting them; or

(c) there has been unwarranted delay in rendering a final judgment under the aforementioned remedies.

Article 47

The Commission shall consider inadmissible any petition or communication submitted under Articles 44 or 45 if:

(a) any of the requirements indicated in Article 46 has not been met;

(b) the petition or communication does not state facts that tend to establish a violation of the rights guaranteed by this Convention;

(c) the statements of the petitioner or of the state indicate that the petition or communication is manifestly groundless or obviously out of order; or

(d) the petition or communication is substantially the same as one previously studied by the Commission or by another international organization.

Section 4. Procedure

Article 48

1. When the Commission receives a petition or communication alleging violation of any of the rights protected by this Convention, it shall proceed as follows:

(a) If it considers the petition or communication admissible, it shall request information from the government of the state indicated as being responsible for the alleged violations and shall furnish that government a transcript of the pertinent portion of the petition or communication. This information shall be submitted within a reasonable period to be determined by the Commission in accordance with the circumstances of each case.

(b) After the information has been received, or after the period established has elapsed and the information has not been received, the Commission shall ascertain whether the grounds for the petition or communication still exist. If they do not, the Commission shall order the record to be closed.

(c) The Commission may also declare the petition or communication inadmissible or out of order on the basis of information or evidence subsequently received.

(d) If the record has not been closed, the Commission shall, with the knowledge of the parties, examine the matter set forth in the petition or communication in order to verify the facts. If necessary and advisable, the Commission shall carry out an investigation, for the effective conduct of which it shall request, and the states concerned shall furnish to it, all necessary facilities.

(e) The Commission may request the states concerned to furnish any pertinent information, and, if so requested, shall hear oral statements or receive written statements from the parties concerned.

(f) The Commission shall place itself at the disposal of the parties concerned with a view to reaching a friendly settlement of the matter on the basis of respect for the human rights recognized in this Convention.

2. However, in serious and urgent cases, only the presentation of a petition or communication that fulfills all the formal requirements of admissibility shall be necessary in order for the Commission to conduct an investigation with the prior consent of the state in whose territory a violation has allegedly been committed.

Article 49

If a friendly settlement has been reached in accordance with paragraph 1*(f)* of Article 48, the Commission shall draw up a report, which shall be transmitted to the petitioner and to the States Parties to this Convention, and shall then be communicated to the Secretary-General of the Organization of American States for publication. This report shall contain a brief statement of the facts and of the solution reached. If any party in the case so requests, the fullest possible information shall be provided to it.

Article 50

1. If a settlement is not reached, the Commission shall, within the time limit established by its Statute, draw up a report setting forth the facts and stating its conclusions. If the report, in whole or in part, does not represent the unanimous agreement of the members of the Commission, any member may attach to it a separate opinion. The written and oral statements made by the parties in accordance with paragraph 1*(e)* of Article 48 shall also be attached to the report.

2. The report shall be transmitted to the states concerned, which shall not be at liberty to publish it.

3. In transmitting the report, the Committee may make such proposals and recommendations as it sees fit.

Article 51

1. If, within a period of three months from the date of the transmittal of the report of the Commission to the states concerned, the matter has not either been settled or submitted by the Commission or by the state concerned to the Court and its jurisdiction accepted, the Commission may, by the vote of an absolute majority of its members, set forth its opinion and conclusions concerning the question submitted for its consideration.

2. Where appropriate, the Commission shall make pertinent recommendations and shall prescribe a period within which the state is to take the measures that are incumbent upon it to remedy the situation examined.

3. When the prescribed period has expired, the Commission shall decide by the vote of an absolute majority of its members whether the state has taken adequate measures and whether to publish its report.

CHAPTER VIII Inter-American Court of Human Rights

SECTION 1. ORGANIZATION

Article 52

1. The Court shall consist of seven judges, nationals of the member states of the Organization, elected in an individual capacity from among jurists of the highest moral authority and of recognized competence in the field of human rights, who possess the qualifications required for the exercise of the highest judicial functions in conformity with the law of the state of which they are nationals or of the state that proposes them as candidates.

2. No two judges may be nationals of the same state.

Article 53

1. The judges of the Court shall be elected by secret ballot by an absolute majority vote of the States Parties to the Convention in the General Assembly of the Organization, from a panel of candidates proposed by those states.

2. Each of the States Parties may propose up to three candidates, nationals of the state that proposes them or of any other member state of the Organization of American States. When a slate of three is proposed, at least one of the candidates shall be a national of a state other than the one proposing the slate.

Article 54

1. The judges of the Court shall be elected for a term of six years and may be reelected only once. The term of three of the judges chosen in the first election shall expire at the end of three years. Immediately after the election, the names of the three judges shall be determined by lot in the General Assembly.

2. A judge elected to replace a judge whose term has not expired shall complete the term of the latter.

3. The judges shall continue in office until the expiration of their term. However, they shall continue to serve with regard to cases that they have begun to hear and that are still pending, for which purposes they shall not be replaced by the newly elected judges.

Article 55

1. If a judge is a national of any of the States Parties to a case submitted to the Court, he shall retain his right to hear that case.

2. If one of the judges called upon to hear a case should be a national of one of the States Parties to the case, any other State Party in the case may appoint a person of its choice to serve on the Court as an *ad hoc* judge.

3. If among the judges called upon the hear a case none is a national of any of the States Parties to the case, each of the latter may appoint an *ad hoc* judge.

4. An *ad hoc* judge shall possess the qualifications indicated in Article 52. If several States Parties to the Convention should have the same interest in a case, they shall be considered as a single party for purposes of the above provisions. In case of doubt, the Court shall decide.

Article 56

Five judges shall constitute a quorum for the transaction of business by the Court.

Article 57

The Commission shall appear in all cases before the Court.

Article 58

1. The Court shall have its seat at the place determined by the States Parties to the Convention in the General Assembly of the Organization; however, it may convene in the territory of any member state of the Organization of American States when a majority of the Court consider it desirable, and with the prior consent of the state concerned.

The seat of the Court may be changed by the States Parties to the Convention in the General Assembly, by a two-thirds vote.

2. The Court shall appoint its own Secretary.

3. The Secretary shall have his office at the place where the Court has its seat and shall attend the meetings that the Court may hold away from its seat.

Article 59

The Court shall establish its secretariat, which shall function under the direction of the Secretary of the Court, in accordance with the administrative standards of the General Secretariat of the Organization in all respects not incompatible with the independence of the Court. The staff of the Court's secretariat shall be appointed by the Secretary General of the Organization in consultation with the Secretary of the Court.

Article 60

The Court shall draw up its statute, which it shall submit to the General Assembly for approval. It shall adopt its own Rules of Procedure.

SECTION 2.   JURISDICTION AND FUNCTIONS

Article 61

1. Only the States Parties and the Commission shall have the right to submit a case to the Court.

2. In order for the Court to hear a case, it is necessary that the procedures set forth in Articles 48 to 50 shall have been completed.

Article 62

1. A State Party may, upon depositing its instrument of ratification or adherence to this Convention, or at any subsequent time, declare that it recognizes as binding, *ipso facto*, and not requiring special agreement, the jurisdiction of the Court on all matters relating to the interpretation or application of this Convention.

2. Such declaration may be made unconditionally, on the condition of reciprocity, for a specified period, or for specific cases. It shall be presented to the Secretary General of the Organization, who shall transmit copies thereof to the other member states of the Organization and to the Secretary of the Court.

3. The jurisdiction of the Court shall comprise all cases concerning the interpretation and application of the provisions of this Convention that are submitted to it, provided that the States Parties to the case recognize or have recognized such jurisdiction, whether by special declaration pursuant to the preceding paragraphs, or by a special agreement.

Article 63

1. If the Court finds that there has been a violation of a right or freedom protected by this Convention, the Court shall rule that the injured party be ensured the enjoyment of his right or freedom that was violated. It shall also rule, if appropriate, that the consequences of the measure or situation that constituted the breach of such right or freedom be remedied and that fair compensation be paid to the injured party.

2. In cases of extreme gravity and urgency, and when necessary to avoid irreparable damage to persons, the Court shall adopt such provisional measures as it deems pertinent in matters it has under consideration. With respect to a case not yet submitted to the Court, it may act at the request of the Commission.

Article 64

1. The member states of the Organization may consult the Court regarding the interpretation of this Convention or of other treaties concerning the protection of human rights in the American States. Within their spheres of competence, the organs listed in Chapter X of the Charter of the Organization of American States, as amended by the Protocol of Buenos Aires, may in like manner consult the Court.

2. The Court, at the request of a member state of the Organization, may provide that state with opinions regarding the compatibility of any of its domestic laws with the aforesaid international instruments.

Article 65

To each regular session of the General Assembly of the Organization of American States the Court shall submit, for the Assembly's consideration, a report on its work during the previous years. It shall specify, in particular, the cases in which a state has not complied with its judgments, making any pertinent recommendations.

SECTION 3. PROCEDURE

Article 66

1. Reasons shall be given for the judgment of the Court.

2. If the judgment does not represent in whole or in part the unanimous opinion of the judges, any judge shall be entitled to have his dissenting or separate opinion attached to the judgment.

Article 67

The judgment of the Court shall be final and not subject to appeal. In case of disagreement as to the meaning or scope of the judgment, the Court shall interpret it at the request of any of the parties, provided the request is made within ninety days from the date of notification of the judgment.

Article 68

1. The States Parties to the Convention undertake to comply with the judgment of the Court in any case to which they are parties.

2. That part of a judgment that stipulates compensatory damages may be executed in the country concerned in accordance with domestic procedure governing the execution of judgments against the state.

Article 69

The parties to the case shall be notified of the judgment of the Court and it shall be transmitted to the States Parties to the Convention.

CHAPTER IX Common Provisions

Article 70

1. The judges of the Court and the members of the Commission shall enjoy, from the moment of their election and throughout their term of office, the immunities extended to diplomatic agents in accordance with international law. During the exercise of their official function they shall, in addition, enjoy the diplomatic privileges necessary for the performance of their duties.

2. At no time shall the judges of the Court or the members of the Commission be held liable for any decisions or opinions issued in the exercise of their functions.

Article 71

The position of judge of the Court or member of the Commission is incompatible with any other activity that might affect the independence or impartiality of such judge or member, as determined in the respective statutes.

Article 72

The judges of the Court and the members of the Commission shall receive emoluments and travel allowances in the form and under the conditions set forth in their statutes, with due regard for the importance and independence of their office. Such emoluments and travel allowances shall be determined in the budget of the Organization of American States, which shall also include the expenses of the Court and its secretariat. To this end, the Court shall draw up its own budget and submit it for approval to the General Assembly through the General Secretariat. The latter may not introduce any changes in it.

Article 73

The General Assembly may, only at the request of the Commission or the Court, as the case may be, determine sanctions to be applied against members of the Commission or judges of the Court when there are justifiable grounds for such action as set forth in the respective statutes. A vote of two-thirds majority of the member states of the Organization shall be required for a decision in the case of members of the Commission and, in the case of judges of the Court, a two-thirds majority vote of the States Parties to the Convention shall also be required.

Part III. General and transitory provisions

CHAPTER X Signature, Ratification, Reservations, Amendments, Protocols, and Denunciation

Article 74

1. This Convention shall be open for signature and ratification by or adherence of any member state of the Organization of American States.

2. Ratification of or adherence to this Convention shall be made by the deposit of an instrument of ratification or adherence with the General Secretariat of the Organization of American States. As soon as eleven states have deposited their instruments of ratification or adherence, the Convention shall enter into force. With respect to any state that ratifies or adheres thereafter, the Convention shall enter into force on the date of the deposit of its instrument of ratification or adherence.

3. The Secretary General shall inform all member states of the Organization of the entry into force of the Convention.

Article 75

This Convention shall be subject to reservations only in conformity with the provisions of the Vienna Convention on the Law of Treaties signed on May 23, 1969.

Article 76

1. Proposals to amend this Convention may be submitted to the General Assembly for the action it deems appropriate by any State Party directly, and by the Commission or the Court through the Secretary General.

2. Amendments shall enter into force for the states ratifying them on the date when two thirds of the States Parties to this Convention have deposited their respective instruments of ratification. With respect to the other States Parties, amendments shall enter into force on the dates on which they deposit their respective instruments of ratification.

Article 77

1. In accordance with Article 31, any State Party and the Commission may submit proposed Protocols to this Convention for consideration by the States Parties at the General Assembly with a view to gradually including other rights and freedoms within its system of protection.

2. Each Protocol shall determine the manner of its entry into force and shall be applied only among the States Parties to it.

Article 78

1. The States Parties may denounce this Convention at the expiration of a five-year period starting from the date of its entry into force and by means of notice given one year in advance. Notice of the denunciation shall be addressed to the Secretary General of the Organization, who shall inform the other States Parties.

2. Such a denunciation shall not have the effect of releasing the State Party concerned from the obligations contained in this Convention with respect to any act that may constitute a violation of those obligations and that has been taken by that state prior to the effective date of denunciation.

CHAPTER X Transitory Provisions

SECTION 1.   INTER-AMERICAN COMMISSION ON HUMAN RIGHTS

Article 79

Upon the entry into force of this Convention, the Secretary General shall, in writing, request each member state of the Organization to present, within ninety days, its candidates for membership on the Inter-American Commission on Human Rights. The Secretary General shall prepare a list in alphabetical order of the candidates presented, and transmit it to the member states of the Organization at least thirty days prior to the next session of the General Assembly.

Article 80

The members of the Commission shall be elected by secret ballot of the General Assembly from the list of candidates referred to in Article 79. The candidates who obtain the largest number of votes and an absolute majority of the votes of the representatives of the member states shall be declared elected. Should it become necessary to have several ballots in order to elect all the members of the Commission, the candidates who receive the smallest amount of votes shall be eliminated successively, in the manner determined by the General Assembly.

Section 2.   Inter-American Court of Human Rights

Article 81

Upon the entry into force of this Convention the Secretary General shall, in writing, request each State Party to present, within ninety days, its candidates for membership on the Inter-American Court of Human Rights. The Secretary General shall prepare a list in alphabetical order of the candidates presented and transmit it to the States Parties at least thirty days prior to the next session of the General Assembly.

Article 82

The judges of the Court shall be elected from the list of candidates referred to in Article 81, by secret ballot of the States Parties to the Convention in the General Assembly. The candidates who obtain the largest number of votes and an absolute majority of the votes of the representatives of the States Parties shall be declared elected. Should it become necessary to have several ballots in order to elect all the judges of the Court the candidates who receive the smallest number of votes shall be eliminated successively, in the manner determined by the States Parties.

STATEMENTS AND RESERVATIONS

STATEMENT OF CHILE

The Delegation of Chile signs this Convention, subject to its subsequent parliamentary approval and ratification, in accordance with the constitutional rules in force.

STATEMENT OF ECUADOR

The Delegation of Ecuador has the honour of signing the American Convention on Human Rights. It does not believe that it is necessary to make any specific reservation at this time, without prejudice to the general power set forth in the Convention itself that leaves the governments free to ratify it or not.

RESERVATION OF URUGUAY

Article 80.2 of the Constitution of Uruguay provides that citizenship is suspended for a person indicted according to law in a criminal prosecution that may result in a sentence of imprisonment in a penitentiary. This restriction of the exercise of the rights recognized in Article 23 of the Convention is not envisaged among the circumstances provided for in this respect by paragraph 2 of Article 23, for which reason the Delegation of Uruguay expresses a reservation on this matter.

IN WITNESS WHEREOF, the undersigned Plenipotentiaries, whose full powers were found in good and due form, sign this Convention, which shall be called ''PACT OF SAN JOSÉ, COSTA RICA'', (in the city of San José, Costa Rica, this twenty-second day of November, nineteen hundred and sixty-nine.)